FORENSIC ALCOHOL TEST EVIDENCE (FATE)

FORENSIC ALCOHOL TEST EVIDENCE (FATE)

A Handbook for Law Enforcement and Accident Investigation

By

JOHN BRICK, Ph.D., M.A.

Fellow (Psychopharmacology)
American Psychological Association

Executive Director
Intoxikon International
Yardley, Pennsylvania

CHARLES C THOMAS • PUBLISHER, LTD.
Springfield • Illinois • U.S.A.

Published and Distributed Throughout the World by

CHARLES C THOMAS • PUBLISHER, LTD.
2600 South First Street
Springfield, Illinois 62704

ISBN 978-0-398-09113-2 (paper)
ISBN 978-0-398-09114-9 (ebook)

With THOMAS BOOKS *careful attention is given to all details of manufacturing
and design. It is the Publisher's desire to present books that are satisfactory as to their
physical qualities and artistic possibilities and appropriate for their particular use.*
THOMAS BOOKS *will be true to those laws of quality that assure a good name
and good will.*

Printed in the United States of America
TO-C-1

Library of Congress Cataloging-in-Publication Data

Names: Brick, John, 1950- author.
Title: Forensic alcohol test evidence (FATE) : a handbook for law enforce-
    ment and accident investigation / by John Brick, Ph.D., M.A.
Description: Springfield, Illinois : Charles C Thomas, Publisher, Ltd.,
    [2017] | Includes bibliographical references and index.
Identifiers: LCCN 2016013916 (print) | LCCN 2016017167 (ebook) | ISBN
    9780398091132 (pbk.) | ISBN 9780398091149 (pdf)
Subjects: LCSH: Drunk driving--Investigation. | Drunkenness (Crime) |
    Alcohol--Physiological effect. | Alcoholism and crime. |
    Criminal   investigation.
Classification: LCC HV8079.D76 B75 2016 (print) | LCC HV8079.D76
    (ebook) | DDC 614/.13--dc23
LC record available at https://lccn.loc.gov/2016013916

FOREWORD

The legal world has needed a text such as this for a long time. Over-consumption of alcohol and the ensuing drunken behavior and its consequences have been around for centuries, if not millennia. Such over-consumption of alcohol exerts an enormous toll on individuals, families, marriages, society, and health. Even today, patients with physical and mental pain, discomfort, and frank diseases are seen by physicians, pharmacists, nurses, and social workers, who unknowingly are trying to overcome the physical and emotional consequences of drinking too much alcohol. Acute and long-term alcohol-using patients who are not well-handled by such health professionals often end up seeing lawyers and judges to sort out the social, physical, and legal consequences of drunken behavior leading to physical or mental impairment, traffic accidents, and criminal acts.

I have been a colleague of John Brick for almost 30 years, and in full disclosure, Dr. Brick and I have written several books together (and helped each other with others), except this one. Thus I know his writing well, I know his strengths and weaknesses, and therefore I am able to (and happy to) write this Foreword to his latest book. I promise to be as unbiased as I can.

I suggest that the reader begin reading this book by looking first at the chapter headings and subdivisions. If you do this, you will have difficulty finding a forensic topic regarding alcohol that isn't listed. In fact, it gets even better: I've noticed that the chapters and topics break down into four types of information, depending on what you are looking for: basic questions, classical topics, practical topics, and new topics. Let's see if I can make it simple for the reader and provide a quick overview of the panoply of information (the following list is illustrative, not meant to be exhaustive):

BASIC QUESTIONS

What is forensics?
What is alcohol?
What is forensic alcohol test evidence?
How do objective alcohol tests relate to intoxication?

How do neurons function?
Why do people combine drugs?
How much drinking will cause liver damage?
Who drinks?
What is a drink?
What is memory and how does it work?
Amnesia as a defense?

CLASSICAL TOPICS

types of alcohol
alcohol tolerance
collection of samples
chronic alcohol use
alcohol-induced liver injury
breath and blood alcohol testing
functional neuroanatomy

PRACTICAL TOPICS

types of research
years of life lost
misdiagnosis of intoxication
heavy drinking
alcohol intoxication and memory
translating [blood alcohol expression] into something understandable
alcohol proof and percentages
calculations of alcohol use and intoxication
standard field sobriety tests
alcohol and the law
the DWI and crash investigation, and arrest
alcohol-medication interactions

NEW TOPICS

alcohol and energy drinks
severe alcohol use disorder
calculation of breath alcohol detection threshold
alcohol and age and abstinence
emergence of laws related to alcohol intoxication
alcohol in everyday activities – water sports, aircraft, bicycling,
    thermal injuries, homicide and suicide, etc.

odor of alcohol beverages on the breath
alcohol and narcotic pain relievers
dram shop liability laws
biomarkers of alcohol use
alcohol and medical problems

Writing a book with this thoroughness and detail takes a great deal of talent, knowledge, and real-world experience. The only "missing" alcohol and law topics I would like to see Dr. Brick write about concern a) the treatment of alcohol use disorders in the criminal justice system, b) the importance of drug courts, c) the use of disulfiram (Antabuse) in the treatment of multiple DWI offenders, and d) new medications for people with severe alcohol use disorders. However, knowing John Brick as I do, he is probably working on those chapters for the next edition of FATE (although one may argue that these topics are far-removed from alcohol test evidence).

It feels to me that the word FATE in the title of this book should have some practical meaning. Is it fate that Dr. Brick and I are colleagues who both have an interest in forensic alcohol testing? Is it fate that positioned Dr. Brick to apply his unique combination of clinical and laboratory experience to forensic alcohol matters? Is it fate that this book is being published at the same time that drunk driving around the world is still a major problem, and that this book will help solve many of those problems? Or is it fate that brought you (the reader) to buy (or borrow) this book to deal with a major problem involving alcohol in your life (either professionally or personally)? Whichever question resonates with you, this book will certainly lead you to answers for questions that you may have had over the years or are dealing with now, because of the immense information contained herein.

FATE is good for beginners in the alcohol forensic field as well as those with previous experience. I recommend that the former read the book like a novel, beginning with the first chapter and reading it straight through. This way you will get an overview – if not the full details – of all the topics. For the latter, this book will make an excellent resource text – providing reminders of those topics that you may have forgotten, or finding the answer to a question about something new for the first time. In either case, I'll bet that both beginners and experienced scholars will return to this book many times. Its real value is in the details!

Carlton (Carl) K. Erickson, Ph.D.
Distinguished Professor of
Pharmacology and Toxicology
Director, Addiction Science
Research and Education Center
College of Pharmacy
Austin, Texas, July 2016

PREFACE

The motivation to write *Forensic Alcohol Test Evidence (FATE)* is an extension of my long-standing interest in learning and explaining how things work. As an undergraduate, my focus on the neurophysiology of the brain and behavior was a passion that grew, as did the opportunity to work with excellent mentors at Queens College of the City University of New York and at Rockefeller University, where I continued working after completing my undergraduate degree and before starting my graduate work in psychobiology at Binghamton University. My research at the Rutgers University Center of Alcohol Studies and the Rutgers Alcohol Behavior Research Lab allowed me to follow my scientific curiosity about the relationship between the brain, behavioral psychology, and alcohol. Coincidentally, this academic background in both laboratory research and clinical testing related to alcohol met the need of the legal community to have a resource to answer both analytical and biobehavioral questions about the role, if any, of alcohol in a crime or accident.

It is a privilege to apply my lifelong experience as an alcohol research scientist, teacher, and author on the biobehavioral effects of alcohol to matters of the law. Everyday medico-legal problems associated with the consequences of alcohol use disorders require answers, and it is for this reason, *FATE* was written. In *FATE*, many of the issues pertinent to a thorough forensic evaluation and trial testimony are discussed, but most importantly, my philosophy in forensic cases is to focus on consistent, unbiased, and comprehensive application of diverse scientific disciplines and research to questions of forensic interest. This philosophy requires evaluating behavioral, analytical, physiological, and pharmacological, and toxicological evidence in the puzzle; determining if the pieces go together; and reaching a conclusion to a reasonable degree of scientific certainty.

J.B.

ACKNOWLEDGMENTS

My thanks to Charles C Thomas Publisher and Michael Payne Thomas in particular, for such incredible patience and assistance during this journey and to fellow NJAAR board members David Benn and Jeff Grey for agreeing to co-author the chapter on Accident Reconstruction. Thanks to Drs. Mary Reuder and Carlton Erickson who have been consistently supportive and encouraging during my career and to my highly organized, meticulous and loyal secretary, Lisa Rickert, who endured what must have seemed like unending edits of the manuscript. My thanks to my daughters Kyla and Stephanie for brightening every day and inspiring me to always do my best. Finally, to my wife Laurie: for forty plus years, you have endured my thirst for knowledge, starting with our midnight lab runs to check the scintillation counter to my long work days and nights and everything in-between – thank you for your lifetime of love and support.

CONTENTS

FORENSIC ALCOHOL TEST EVIDENCE (FATE)

Chapter 1

WHAT IS FORENSIC ALCOHOL TEST EVIDENCE?

1.1 WHAT IS FORENSICS?

Forensics is the application of scientific knowledge and principles, from a number of disciplines, to a matter of law. Almost every field has a forensic application in criminal investigation and prosecution or civil litigation in which forensic examiners collect, analyze, or interpret evidence in order to render an opinion to assist in the interpretation of law or violations thereof.

Forensic alcohol test evidence focuses on the evaluation, interpretation and application of the effects of alcohol or an alcohol test result to some legal issue such as a crime, accident, or consequence of alcohol exposure. For example, was the person under the influence of alcohol, either as defined by a legal statute or as defined clinically? Was the methodology used to report intoxication reliable, and could the analytical results or behavioral observations be affected by some physiological condition? Was the cause of some event (e.g., an injury) due to intoxication or a mechanical failure (e.g., of a vehicle, structure, or machine)? The range of scientific disciplines that can be encompassed in this field of study is almost as large as the number of applications to which those fields of study can be applied. For example, forensic alcohol test evidence may include anatomy, biochemistry, biomechanics, chemistry, neuropharmacology, neurophysiology, physiology, psychology, and toxicology to answer questions about the role, if any, of alcohol in pedestrian, bicycle, boating, drowning or motor vehicle accident; fall-down injury; or overdose or in crimes ranging from first-degree murder to vehicular homicide to simple assault to medical consequences from chronic or acute high doses of alcohol that may cause organ damage or developmental changes.

1.2 WHY STUDY FORENSIC ASPECTS
OF ALCOHOL INTOXICATION?

Alcohol more than any other drug continues to be overrepresented in a wide range of injuries from accidents and crimes. In recent years, cocaine, other drugs such as cannabinoids, antianxiety medications (e.g., benzodiaze-pines), pain medications (e.g., oxycodone and other opioids), and inhalants (e.g., chlorinated hydrocarbons, toluene, and fluorocarbons) have been de-tected with increasing frequency. However, the fact remains that more people drink alcohol than consume any other psychoactive drug, and more is known about the causal role of alcohol intoxication in crimes and accidental injuries.

Historically, the study of the effects of alcohol has its earliest roots in the study of intoxicating poisons. In the most basic sense, alcohol is a poison, al-though that definition is often lost on the general public. The term intoxica-tion derived from the Greek *toxikon* and the Latin *toxikom* means poison. Hence, the derivation of the word intoxicate. Toxicology is the study of a wide range of poisons, including alcohols.

The poisonous effects of alcohol have been known at least since biblical times. The pernicious relationship between alcohol use in pregnancy and harm is expressed in The Book of Judges (13:7), which states "behold, thou shalt conceive and bear a son; and now drink no wine nor strong drink. . . ." It was not until the 1970s that the toxicological basis for this warning began to develop with the first reports of fetal alcohol syndrome (FAS). FAS (now also called fetal alcohol spectrum disorder FASD) results in anatomical (e.g., cra-niofacial dysmorphology, incomplete organ development) and psychological (e.g., developmental delay, impulse control, boundary and emotional attach-ment) problems. Alcohol abuse during pregnancy may result in criminal prosecution of the mother, who exposed her unborn child to a poison (child endangerment).

The physician-alchemist Paracelsus (1493–1541) is credited with some of the most basic concepts in toxicology and pharmacology that are directly rel-evant to the forensic psychopharmacology of alcohol and other drugs. Para-celsus believed that experimentation was essential in understanding the response to toxic agents (the "toxicon"). He further proposed that there is an important distinction between the therapeutic and the toxic effects of agents and that it is the dose of the toxic agents that often determines its helpful or harmful properties.

"All substances are poisons; there is none which is not a poison. The right dose differentiates a poison from a remedy." The views put forth by Paracel-sus are believed to have set the foundation for the dose–response relation, which is the basis of most studies in pharmacology and toxicology and many other services (Pachter, 1961, as cited by Gallo, 1996).

In the late eighteenth and early nineteenth century, American Surgeon General Dr. Benjamin Rush put forth the somewhat radical view that alcohol intoxication, or "inebriety," was an illness (Jellinek, 1960). This view, and many other social and historical events eventually led to a U.S. constitutional amendment that prohibited the manufacture, sale, or use of alcohol. Prohibition of alcohol did not work and eventually was repealed, but there was an interesting consequence: it generated studies on the neurotoxic effects of a variety of toxic agents in bootleg liquor that were probably used by some advocates as further evidence to support prohibition. One such toxin was the organophosphate, triorthocresyl phosphate (TOCP).

In the nineteenth century, TOCP was an additive to Ginger Beer, a high-alcohol patent medicine that circumvented prohibition laws. When ingested through bootleg liquor, TOCP causes a neurological syndrome commonly referred to as a "ginger-jake," a spastic gait that was also caused by drinking TOCP adulterated ginger beer. Today TOCP is a gasoline additive (Pachter, 1961).

Throughout history, people have been aware of the potential harmful effects of drugs like alcohol. It was not until the middle of the nineteenth century that scientific and public interest in alcohol really began to take off. In part, this interest was precipitated by two events: the development and widespread use of the motorized vehicles and the eventual development of quantitative methods of analysis for alcohol.

Certainly by the mid-1800s, concerns about safety and alcohol intoxication were already forcing changes in law and public policies. For example, the New York Central Railroad prohibited employees from drinking on the job as early as 1843. Apparently, the problem of intoxicated railroad employees was so great that in North America "Rule G" was adapted by the American Railway Association in 1899. Rule G prohibited drinking by railway crewmembers while on duty (cited by Borkenstein, 1984). By the turn of the last century, research using quantitative methods of analysis of alcohol and the effects of alcohol on the body was gaining momentum. It was not until the early 1900s, however, that there was enough data to correlate measured amounts of alcohol in the body with impaired behavior. E.M.P. Widmark, a Swedish physician, was probably the first person to develop a protocol to evaluate suspected drunk drivers. Some of Widmark's "diagnostic factors" are still used today by police and clinicians to assist in determining if someone is intoxicated and are discussed in Chapter 7.

In the United States, a U.S. Army physician, Dr. Herman Heise, was responsible for performing autopsies of soldiers who died in automobile crashes "after a night on the town." Heise observed that the majority of soldiers were "heavily loaded with alcohol" (as cited by Dubowski, 1985). After finishing his tour of duty in the Army, Heise returned to Uniontown, Pennsylvania, where he worked with Pennsylvania State Police to develop a drinking and driving protocol much like the one developed by Widmark in Sweden. Some elements of their early protocols are still used by police today.

For the most part, forensic alcohol test evidence will be collected at the request of law enforcement. The collection of the intoxication test evidence begins with the observations of motor vehicle operation or of alcohol containers in a vehicle that has been stopped or that has been involved in an accident and continues with the observations of individual witnesses or suspects. As will be discussed in subsequent chapters, the careful systematic collection of evidence is critical in the eventual interpretation of that evidence with regard to alcohol as a contributing factor to an accidental injury or crash or in the investigation of infractions of drinking and driving laws.

1.3 MERGER OF SCIENTIFIC DISCIPLINES

Forensic alcohol test evidence relies upon contributions that follow the merger of various disciplines to provide the most accurate and comprehensive evaluation of test evidence. For example, a chemist or toxicologist is often involved in quantifying the amount of alcohol in a sample of blood or other tissue. A law enforcement officer, or behavioral clinician, is often required to make observations and interpret behavior to determine if someone is intoxicated and impaired by alcohol. However, without additional specific training in physiology or biological sciences, chemists, toxicologists, psychologists, or others experts in one field may fail to recognize symptoms of impairment produced by factors unrelated to alcohol intoxication such as endocrine disorders, neurological disorders, or hepatic diseases. Similarly, an expert in medical physiology, for example, may not recognize a problem in the analytical measurement of alcohol before attempting to interpret other evidence. Consideration of many factors from different disciplines provides the most accurate reconstruction and interpretation of forensic alcohol evidence.

Since alcohol is overwhelming represented in fatal and serious bodily injuries secondary to motor vehicle crashes, both criminal investigations as well as civil litigation often require a reconstruction of the accident to determine the cause of a vehicle's leaving the roadway and crashing, for example. At the very least, accident reconstructionists, usually engineers or police with highly specified training in automotive mechanics and in the application of Newtonian physics, also need to know how alcohol affects perception and reaction time and other human factors that are required to reconstruct an accident. Let us take a closer look at how knowledge from specific disciplines can be merged to understand the effects of alcohol.

Anatomy, Histology, Pathology

Alcohol use can have both acute and chronic effects, depending on dose and duration of use. Although acute alcohol use and intoxication do not appear to permanently affect cell structure, chronic alcohol use can produce long-term changes in cells that form organs or glands. How does this relate to the forensic examiner's investigations? The chronic effects of alcohol may be of interest to the examiner seeking to determine any premorbid factors that would aid in the interpretation of both behavior and, in some cases, physiology. For example, it is well-known that heavy consumption of alcohol during pregnancy increases the risk for a constellation of behavioral and morphological symptoms (FASD). There is now evidence suggesting that the impulsive, sometimes uninhibited, behavior exhibited by children and adults with FASD may be due to specific structural changes in the brain areas, such as the corpus callosum, a bundle of fibers that connects the left and right hemispheres of the brain.

Corpus callosotomy, a radical surgical procedure in which the corpus callosum is cut, has been used to treat severe cases of epilepsy; this procedure decreases seizure severity but also may result in uninhibited, spontaneous, and often inappropriate behaviors. Patients diagnosed with FASD have, in some cases, a profound thinning of the corpus callosum and also often have uninhibited, spontaneous, and often inappropriate behavior (along with a number of other cognitive and medical disorders). In a case in which alcohol intoxication was established in a person with FASD, was the behavior due to intoxication, changes in brain structure due to FASD, or both?

Chronic heavy alcohol abuse can also produce structure changes in the central and peripheral nervous system. For example, alcohol can damage the cerebellum resulting in permanent ataxia. Since the cerebellum is an important brain structure in smoothing out motor movement commands from the cortex, chronic alcohol abuse can affect the peripheral nervous system (peripheral neuropathies), which also affects gait. Therefore, consideration must be given to determine if the impaired motor movement detected in a person who consumed alcohol is due to intoxication or nervous system damage due to chronic heavy alcohol abuse?

Microscopic examination of liver samples taken at autopsy and properly stained may reveal stenosis (fatty infiltration) or cirrhosis (cell death), offering a clue regarding the decedent's previous history of alcohol use or justifying the need for pharmacokinetic assumptions outside any "average" (e.g., rate of alcohol elimination).

Chemistry

Analytical chemistry plays a significant role in forensic alcohol analyses by providing the foundation for the identification and quantification of alcohol in body fluids and tissues. Beginning with the pioneering work of Nicloux (circa 1896) in France, Widmark (1922, 1932) in Sweden, and Borkenstein (circa 1950s) in the United States, and continuing through the modern era, analytical chemistry has been particularly helpful in quantifying breath and blood alcohol and allowing scientists to correlate these findings with behavior, risk, injuries, and other areas of interest to the general well-being and safety of the public.

Hospital enzyme tests, police breath testing, and laboratory gas chromatography are all based on different chemical principles and are used daily in the measurement of alcohol to assist in diagnosis and treatment of clinical observations.

Physiology

Principles in biology and physiology are important in accounting for differences in absorption, distribution, elimination, and pharmacokinetic analyses of alcohol. For example, liver damage from disease may affect behavior as well as alcohol metabolism and a diabetic in medical distress may appear intoxicated and have an alcohol-like odor on his or her breath due to the release of ketones (ketoacidosis). Differences in the respective water content of blood, serum, or plasma may similarly affect alcohol concentrations in those samples.

Physics and Engineering

The use of basic principles in physics is invaluable in the reconstruction of many accidents. For example, when a vehicle crashes, it brings with it into that collision elements of speed, momentum, and energy. The use of Newtonian physics helps determine the speed, momentum, energy, and path of the vehicle, along with other factors that can reconstruct the point at and the manner by which a vehicle lost control. When human factors (including perception and reaction time) and mechanical factors (including stopping distances and time to stop) are combined with biobehavioral effects of alcohol, such as changes in attention, reaction time, and proprioception, the manner of the events that immediately preceded the crash can be better determined.

Psychology

Psychology is the study of behavior and the causes, diagnosis, treatment, and understanding of internal and external factors that ultimately affect and predict human behavior. There are many subspecialties within the field of psychology relevant to forensic aspects of alcohol studies. For example, clinical psychologists (and psychiatrists) engaged in the treatment of behavioral disorders are trained in the diagnosis of general mental illnesses and may also have specialized training in the diagnosis of alcohol intoxication, abuse, or dependence. Experimental psychologists have contributed to various areas of understanding with regard to the effects of alcohol through the design and execution of various psychophysical tests. In fact, the first psychology laboratory in the world founded by Wilhelm Wundt (1832–1920) in Leipzig, Germany (1879), was devoted to sensory processing and mental processing through the study of reaction time, which is a key component of motor vehicle operation and accident reconstruction. Reaction time is the time that passes between a stimulus and a response and is an important part of accident reconstruction. Biological or physiological psychologists have multidisciplinary training in pharmacology, neurochemistry, and other neurosciences as well as psychology. A biological psychologist may apply this training to study the biological basis for changes in the nervous system that result in various behaviors, including those produced by alcohol intoxication or the interaction of alcohol and other psychoactive drugs.

Pharmacology and Toxicology

General principles in pharmacology and toxicology also play an important role in forensic alcohol analyses. When applied to forensic alcohol test evidence, these principles allow for accurate estimates of blood alcohol concentrations and how much alcohol was consumed, determining the distribution and elimination of alcohol and bringing objectivity to the often variable evidence that comes from subjective reporting. In recent years, training in toxicology has included topics such as "performance toxicology," incorporating findings from other disciplines (e.g., psychology) to relate behavior to objective chemical or toxicological test results.

In the last few decades our understanding of the mechanisms through which the drug alcohol changes the brain to change behavior has come largely from neuroscience and neuropharmacological research. Thus, it is apparent that understanding and interpreting alcohol intoxication evidence involves education and training in a number of overlapping disciplines, not one specific field. When possible, practical clinical experience combined with laboratory training will be particularly useful in the forensic examination of alcohol intoxication evidence.

REFERENCES

Borkenstein, R. (1984). *Historical Perspective: North American Traditional and Experimental Response.* Presented at the North American Conference on Alcohol and Highway Safety. Johns Hopkins Medical Institutions, Baltimore, MD, June 12 & 14, 1984.

Dubowski, K. M. (1985). Absorption, distribution and elimination of alcohol: Highway safety aspects. *Journal of Studies on Alcohol Supplement, 10,* 98–108.

Jellinek, E. M. (1960). *The Disease Concept of Alcoholism.* New Haven, CT: Hill House Press, p.1.

Nicloux, M. (1896). Analysis of ethyl alcohol in solutions or of such alcohol diluted in proportions between 1:500 and 1:3,000, C.R.Soc., Biol. Paris tenth series, Book III, pgs. 841-843

Gallo, M. (1996). History and scope of toxicology. In C. D. Klaasen (Ed.), *Casarett and Doull's Toxicology: The Basic Science of Poisons.* New York, McGraw-Hill, pp. 4-5.

Widmark, E. M. P (1932 translated 1981). *Principles and Applications of Medicolegal Alcohol Determination.* Davis, CA: Biomedical Publications.

Widmark, E. M. P. (1922). A micromethod for determining ethyl alcohol in blood. *Biochemical Zeitschrift, 131,* 473–484.

Chapter 2

WHAT IS FORENSIC ALCOHOL EVIDENCE?

Alcohol, more than any other drug, is overly represented in fatal and non-fatal accidents and acts of violence. Accident investigators, as well as law enforcement officers, are likely to encounter alcohol as a factor in many investigations throughout their careers and to initiate the collection of alcohol evidence as part of their investigation. This chapter provides an introduction to different forms of alcohol, and different types of forensic evidence and a review of the nomenclature used in the quantification of alcohol evidence relevant to forensic examiners, law enforcement, and other investigators.

2.1 WHAT IS ALCOHOL?

Types of Alcohol

In Chapter 1, we referred to alcohol without defining it because this term is commonly used to refer to the alcohol in beverages. However, there are many different types of alcohol. The four most common alcohols likely to be encountered in a forensic evaluation are ethyl alcohol (ethanol), methyl alcohol (methanol), isopropyl alcohol (isopropanol), and ethylene glycol. Figure 2.1 illustrates the structure of four widely used alcohols.

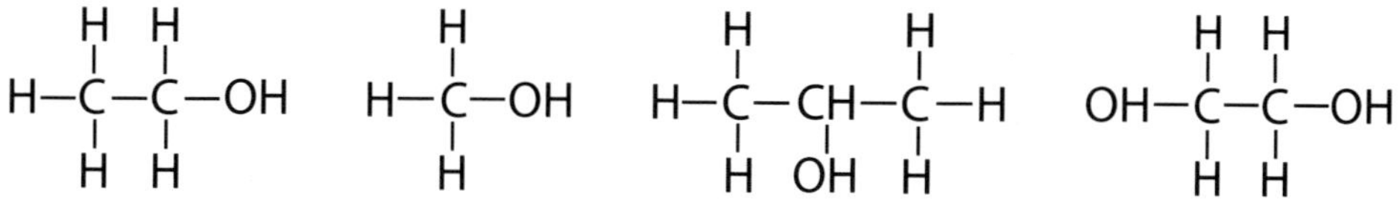

Ethanol Methanol Isopropanol Ethylene glycol

Figure 2.1: Structure of Common Alcohols.

Ethanol

Ethanol or ethyl alcohol is the most common form of alcohol and is the type of alcohol used in alcoholic beverages. Ethanol is sometimes referred to as grain alcohol because grains such as barley, corn, and so on are used in the fermentation process.

In this chapter, the term ethanol will be used to distinguish beverage alcohol from other alcohols discussed later. Elsewhere, the term alcohol will be used to denote ethanol and will be used interchangeably in this book. Because ethanol is the alcohol most often encountered in forensic evidence, the pharmacokinetics, pharmacodynamics, and biobehavioral effects of ethanol will be discussed separately in Chapters 3, 4, and 5 and only briefly in this chapter.

Ethanol is a clear, almost odorless chemical that is infinitely soluble in water. It is also a psychoactive drug. Compared to most other psychoactive drugs, it is a simple molecule with a molecular weight of 46 (by comparison Δ-9-THC, the primary psychoactive compound in marijuana, has a molecular weight of 314.4). Ethanol is made from fruits, flowers, and other plants that, combined with sugar and yeast, ferment to form ethanol. Ethanol is made up of one oxygen, two carbon, and six hydrogen molecules and has the chemical structure and formula CH_3-CH_2-OH. Ethanol is generally described as odorless but in high enough concentrations, even humans can subjectively distinguish it from water. Even so, in most instances, this is probably due to mild irritation of the nasal membrane rather than the detection of an aromatic compound. Although high-proof grain alcohols (e.g., Everclear) are sometimes used by younger drinkers to make high-potency alcoholic beverages, in most instances, the forensic examiner or investigator does not encounter individuals who have consumed absolute ethanol. More often, ethanol is part of a more complex formulation of beer, distilled spirits, or wine that is readily available to consume. Very low concentrations of ethanol (about 0.00001%) can also be formed endogenously (Lester, 1962) and measured in blood when no alcohol has been consumed.

Methanol

Methyl alcohol, or methanol, is another type of alcohol. Methanol is also called wood alcohol because it is produced from the destructive distillation of wood. Methanol is a colorless, volatile liquid and has the chemical formula CH^3-OH. Unlike ethanol, methanol has a distinctive odor, but it is often masked.

Methanol is frequently the primary compound commercially sold in products added to automobile gas tanks and radiators in cold weather to lower the freezing point of water and prevent fluids from freezing. It can be found in many common household products (Table 2.1). Methanol was used as part of the embalming process by ancient Egyptians. Some alcoholics unable to acquire ethanol will consume methanol because some of the effects are similar.

Table 2.1: Common Products Containing Methanol.

Products Containing Methanol	Approximate Methanol Concentration
Antifreeze	95%
Windshield washer fluids	35–95%
Sterno® (canned heat)	4%
Shellacs	varies
Paints and paint removers	varies
Gasoline additives	varies

Methanol is easily absorbed from the gastrointestinal tract, with peak levels occurring about 30 to 90 minutes after consumption (Becker, 1983). Absorption through the skin and lung is apparently greater than for ethanol, as suggested by an 8-year-old boy who died from a methanol-soaked pad placed on his chest (Kahn & Blum 1979a-b). Absorption of methanol through the skin also was reported to cause blindness in a painter after working in methanol-soaked clothing (Dutkiewicz, Konczalik & Karwacki, 1980).

In comparison to ethanol, methanol doses as low as 10 mL have been reported to cause retinal damage leading to blindness. Doses of 30 mL are considered a minimum lethal dose, but the consumption of as little as 15 mL of 40 percent methanol has been reported to be fatal. Toxicity can result from central nervous system (CNS) depression (similar to ethanol poisoning) or as a result of toxic metabolites.

Methanol is metabolized in the liver by the enzyme alcohol dehydrogenase (ADH), the same enzyme that oxidizes ethanol. Methanol's toxicity is the result of its metabolism to formaldehyde which is metabolized to formic acid. Formaldehyde, a potent cellular toxin, is believed to be the causative agent in methanol toxicity, but primate studies have demonstrated that formaldehyde is rapidly metabolized to formic acid, which can account for the metabolic acidosis that follows methanol ingestion (McMartin, Ambre & Tephly, 1980).

Because ethanol has about a ten to twenty times greater affinity for ADH than methanol has, ethanol will be preferentially oxidized over methanol.

The ability of ethanol to successfully compete with methanol for ADH prevents or at least minimizes the metabolism of methanol to more toxic metabolites (e.g., formic acid). The half-life of methanol is about 14 to 30 hours, depending upon the severity of toxicity (the more toxic, the longer the half-life), but is extended to about 30 to 35 hours when ethanol is administered (Lacouture & Lovejoy, 1981). This means that the metabolism of methanol to formaldehyde or formic acid will be significantly reduced by ethanol administration, allowing methanol to be excreted before significant and dangerous concentrations of formic acid are produced.

The antidote for methanol poisoning is to maintain ethanol levels between 100-150 mg/dL. Since ethanol increases the elimination half-life, it may be necessary to maintain patients in a state of ethanol intoxication for several days to completely inhibit toxic metabolite formation until methanol is cleared from the system. Ellenhorn and Barceloux (1988) recommend 10 percent ethanol in 5 percent dextrose in water (D_5W). When methanol concentrations are over 50 mg/dL, hemodialyses is recommended. With lower methanol levels, hemodialysis will decrease the length of time of ethanol coadministration.

Administration of ethanol enables methanol to be excreted with minimal formation of metabolic toxins. Unfortunately, for some alcoholics entering into a detoxification (detox) ward who have consumed methanol, a misdiagnosis of alcohol intoxication rather than methanol poisoning can be fatal. Workers in alcohol detox wards should always determine during intake if patients have any history of drinking anything other than beverage alcohol.

Clinical Signs and Symptoms of Methanol Poisoning

The symptoms of methanol intoxication affect the CNS (headache, dizziness, lethargy, and mental confusion) and visual system (light sensitivity and reports of "feeling of being in a snowfield"). Signs of methanol poisoning include dilated pupils (decreased pupillary reaction to light is relatively common), gastrointestinal problems (vomiting, nausea, abdominal pain), and renal system failure (Swartz et al., 1981). In comparison to ethanol, methanol produces only moderate euphoria.

Lab Findings

Acidosis, a change in the acidity of the blood and clinically defined by serum bicarbonate levels less than 18 mEq/L, is present in cases of severe methanol poisoning. The severity of acidosis is a better predictor of mortality than are methanol levels, and such clinical tests are often performed in a hospital whereas methanol testing may not be routinely performed. Formate levels of more than 20 mg/dL are associated with ocular damage and metabolic acidosis and strongly suggest testing and treatment for methanol poisoning (Ellenhorn & Barcelox, 1988).

Osmolar Gap

The osmolar gap is a diagnostic tool used to differentiate the causes of metabolic acidosis. The "gap" is the difference between serum osmolality measured by freezing point depression and the serum osmolality calculated from sodium (Na), glucose, and blood urea nitrogen (BUN). Methanol is one of many compounds that increase the osmolar gap, often and easily measured in hospital testing. The osmolar gap rises by about 0.34 mOsm for each milligram of methanol per deciliter (*see* Table 2.2). Methanol levels of more than 50 mg/dL (highly toxic) will increase the osmolar gap (Ellenhorn & Barceloux, 1988).

Table 2.2: Methanol, Osmolar Gap and Behavior.

Methanol Level	Source	Symptoms/Signs	Osmolar Gap
<.05 mg/dL	Endogenous	No effect	
>20 mg/dL	Exogenous	CNS symptoms	
>100 mg/dL	Exogenous	Ocular symptoms	>17 mOsm
>150 mg/dL	Exogenous	Fatal range	

Mean Corpuscular Volume

Mean corpuscular volume (MCV) is elevated in cases of severe methanol poisoning. However, this may be a misleading clinical test indicator because MCV is also increased as a result of chronic heavy ethanol consumption.

Isopropyl Alcohol

Isopropyl alcohol, or isopropanol (rubbing alcohol), is a common laboratory and industrial chemical frequently used as a disinfectant to cleanse the skin or disinfect objects. Isopropanol produces effects similar to ethanol and methanol and is the second most commonly ingested alcohol and a common cause of overdose. In some instances, ingestion is accidental, but like methanol there are numerous instances of alcoholics who voluntarily ingest isopropanol in lieu of ethanol. Isopropanol is absorbed readily from the gastrointestinal tract. About 80 percent of the dose is absorbed within 30 minutes. Total absorption occurs within 2 hours but significant amounts of isopropanol can be absorbed directly through the skin (e.g., during sponge baths). Exposure to airborne isopropanol produces measurable amounts of acetone but not isopropanol in blood. Isopropanol is also metabolized by alcohol dehydrogenase to acetone.

Many everyday products contain isopropanol and in varying concentrations (*see* Table 2.3). The CNS depressant effects of isopropanol are about twice that of ethanol but less toxic than methanol. About 2 to 3 ounces of a typical 70 percent preparation will produce central nervous system depression similar to ethanol intoxication. Higher doses produce coma, respiratory depression, and death. Acetone, a metabolite of isopropanol, may potentiate the duration of intoxication and produce mild acidosis because acetone is metabolized to acetic acid and formic acid. The lethal dose in adults is about 8 ounces (240 mL), and the average blood isopropanol concentration is 140 mg/dL (Baselt, 2014).

Table 2.3: Common Products Containing Isopropanol.

Product	Percent Isopropanol
Acne treatments	70
Antifreeze for motor vehicle	25–100
Automobile windshield deicers	20–60
Disinfectant cleaners	6–15
Dog/cat repellent	80
Gasket cement	40
Glass cleaners	0–25
Liquid detergents	0–12
Model cements	40–55
Racing motor fuel	0–70
Rubbing alcohol	70
Stain/Spot/Rust removers	10–30
Windshield washer solvent (various)	50–85

Modified from Lacouture, Watson, and Abrams (1983).

Clinical Signs and Symptoms of Isopropyl Alcohol Poisoning

CNS effects include dizziness, incoordination, headache, confusion, and ultimately stupor, coma, and death (Table 2.4). The euphoric effects common to ethanol are not present with isopropanol. Nystagmus and miotic pupils are also common. Cardiovascular system effects of isopropanol poisoning include hypotension from peripheral vasodilation. This is the most common and serious consequence of isopropanol toxicity and may explain the mild hypothermia that follows ingestion. Tachycardia has also been reported.

Table 2.4: Biobehavioral Effects of Isopropyl Alcohol.

Dizziness	Abdominal pain
Vomiting	Hypotension
Incoordination	Confusion
Stupor	Coma
Headache	Nystagmus
Miosis	Tachycardia

2.2 WHAT IS FORENSIC ALCOHOL TEST EVIDENCE?

Forensic evidence can be divided into two categories: subjective and objective. Each has advantages in determining alcohol intoxication, and whenever possible, both types of evidence should be evaluated. Agreement between subjective and objective evidence provides a clear picture of what the evidence means.

Subjective Alcohol Evidence

Subjective test evidence may come in different forms. Commonly, such evidence can be obtained from a self-report. That is, what someone says about themselves (e.g., "I feel too intoxicated to drive"), through some behavioral tests (*see* Chapter 7) as well as the overall appearance of the allegedly intoxicated person (AIP). In most instances, subjective evidence is not scientific evidence in that it is not quantified the way a blood or breath test is quantified. However, the way in which the AIP appears to lay witnesses may provide compelling evidence even though such observations are not measured, *per se*. For example, if a witness describes someone as "really drunk" or "falling down drunk", it immediately provides a graphic image that most people can see and identify with and that may be compared with objective scientific evidence obtained at a later date.

Interviewing Witnesses – General Observations

Other than the injured, or eyewitnesses, the first to arrive at the scene of a crime or an accident are police, other members of law enforcement, emergency medical technicians (EMTs) or paramedics. First responders are therefore able to collect subjective intoxication test evidence from their direct observations or by using an interview technique with eyewitnesses. In collecting alcohol evidence it is useful to follow up answers with additional questions. For example, if witnesses describe someone as "drunk, stoned, smashed, stupid, buzzed", follow up and ask what they mean. Ask what specific types of behavior led to the conclusion that the AIP was drunk for example. Such questions should be structured to assist the witness in recalling the event but should never be suggestive in nature. For example, the questions in Table 2.5 might be helpful in obtaining an accurate and detailed description. As a general interview rule, use open-ended questions and avoid questions that only provide yes/no answers except when specifically necessary (e.g., did you actually see the accident?).

Subjective Intoxication Evidence Related to Driving While Intoxicated Stops

For the law enforcement officer, a large percentage of cases involve intoxicated driving. Without explanation or additional information, the typical jurist may not understand field sobriety test results. On the other hand, because so many people have experience as drivers, they will readily appreciate accurate and detailed descriptions of impaired driving. The National Highway Traffic Safety Administration describes three phases of a typical driving while intoxicated (DWI) stop that allow the officer to collect relevant information. The observations from these phases assists in obtaining a complete picture of the events for legal purposes and in developing a picture to assist the jury to understand the basis of an opinion regarding the role, if any, of alcohol. The three phases are as follows: Phase I–Observation of the Suspect Operating the Vehicle, Phase II–First Face-to-Face Contact, Phase III–Administration of Screening Tests to Determine Impairment.

Table 2.5: Good and Bad Phraseology During an Interview.

Good Question	Comment	Example of a Poorly Worded Question
Do you remember seeing Mr. Smith today?	The question should not immediately suggest an answer.	You didn't see Mr. Smith today, did you?
Was that before or after lunch (dinner, some other event)? What time do you normally have lunch, etc.?	It is often easier to first recall an event in relation to another event, rather than to a time.	Do you remember what the exact time was when you saw him?
Could you tell if he had been drinking?	Witnesses, not questions, should infer conclusions.	Since he was in the bar you saw him drinking, right?
What, if anything, did you notice about his behavior?	Suggesting an answer can be disruptive to finding out what happened.	He wasn't drunk was he?
Would you agree that some people may sway, stagger, have slurred speech, or act differently when they are not intoxicated? Describe Mr. Smith's behavior when you saw him?	Question provides list of behaviors without suggesting one specific sign was present.	Did you see Mr. Smith fall down?
How much did you drink tonight?	Follow up to confirm (# drinks).	Did you have anything to drink tonight?

PHASE I—OBSERVATION OF THE SUSPECT OPERATING THE VEHICLE.

(a) driving too slowly
(b) excessive speed
(c) willingness to take risks (impaired judgment)
(d) wide turns
(e) inability to control vehicle lane position
(f) impaired attentional processing (e.g., failure to attend to traffic control device, other vehicles, pedestrians, hazards, failure to signal, etc.)

Once the officer has made sufficient observations of motor vehicle operation and has made the decision to initiate a DWI stop, other types of evidence can be collected, as part of Phase II.

PHASE II–FIRST FACE-TO-FACE CONTACT. First person-to-person contact refers to subjective evidence made as the officer makes direct observations of
the driver inside the car. Common observations at that point may include:

(a) abnormal speech
(b) wandering gaze
(c) mental confusion from simple question
(d) repetitive questions
(e) psychophysical impairment (e.g., fumbling)

Such roadside observations are discussed further in Chapter 7. Observations can also be made by clinicians (nurses, physicians, EMTs), witnesses (at
the scene), or others (including security camera data). Some face-to-face observations or behaviors are relevant to other issues of forensic interest, such as
administrative or legislative laws involving "visible intoxication" (*see* Chapter
6).

PHASE III–FIELD SOBRIETY TESTS (STANDARDIZED AND NON-STANDARDIZED
TESTS). Field sobriety tests are performance measures of balance, coordination, and psychomotor skills. Some tests reflect skills related to driving (e.g.,
divided attention) whereas others provide rough blood alcohol concentration (BAC) estimates (i.e., above or below the legal definition for DWI), all
of which assist the officer determining the course of the investigation and
are potential evidence-gathering tools. These forms of subjective evidence
are discussed in more detail in Chapter 7, as is the use and application of
standardized (also Chapters 4 and 7) and nonstandardized (Chapter 4) field
sobriety tests.

Objective Evidence

Objective test evidence is, for the most part, free from subjective interpretation. Usually, this form of evidence is quantified or measured.

Biobehavioral Tests

Some behavioral tests can be at least quasi-objective depending upon how
they are administered. For example, swaying can be quantified in a research
laboratory using an electromagnetic platform or sway harness in which movement can be precisely measured by movement-generated piezoelectric current (Niaura Nathan, Frankenstien, Shapiro & Brick, 1987). However,
observations in the field may not be metric based and do not include laboratory devices to measure swaying, for example, and therefore can be highly

subjective unless the investigator makes careful observations and notes. For example, simply reporting that the subject was swaying is far less informative than also estimating the amount of sway. Was the subject moving side to side or in circles? Was it a side-to-side, front-to-back, or circular movement? How much movement? Was it 1 inch, 6 inches, 12 inches, or more? Did the AIP use his or her arms for balance to correct the sway? Other tests, such as Standardized Field Sobriety Tests (SFSTs) are quasi-objective because they follow a specific protocol for administration and a numeric scoring of results.

Chemical Tests

The ultimate example of objective alcohol test evidence is the measured concentration of alcohol in the blood, other tissue, or elsewhere determined by standardized analytical testing of blood or breath samples. The results from field or laboratory tests are quantifiable based upon identifiable standards, not the officer's personal opinion. A blood or breath test can be used to support subjective intoxication test evidence. In forensic investigations regarding alcohol intoxication, there are several widely used approaches to measuring alcohol intoxication: gas chromatography-flame ionization, enzymatic oxidation (clinical analyzers), chemical oxidation-reduction (e.g., Breathalyzer®), infrared (IR) spectroscopy (e.g., Intoxilyzer®, Intoximeters), and fuel cell (preliminary breath tests).

Gas chromatography (GC) is an analytical method used to identify and measure unknown substances in fluid such as blood, vitreous humor, and homogenized tissue (e.g., brain). It is the gold standard for the identification and quantification of alcohol. Chromatography is a method physically separating components distributed between two phases: a stationary phase or bed and a fluid or moving phase that percolates through the stationary bed. This is a particularly useful analytical technique. In forensic analyses, GC is the gold standard because it is a direct quantitative measure of blood alcohol and can accurately differentiate different types of alcohol (e.g., ethanol, isopropanol, methanol) as these different alcohols pass through the stationary bed in the column of the instrument. The moving phase can be either liquid (liquid chromatography) or gas (GC). The latter is most commonly encountered in forensic alcohol analyses.

In GC, the mobile phase is a carrier gas that moves the sample through a column. In this method, all samples (standards with known amounts of alcohol and blood samples with unknown amounts of alcohol) are volatized by incubating the sample in a test tube. This causes alcohols and other volatiles to leave the liquid (e.g., blood) and enter the gas phase or "headspace" above the fluid. The headspace is then sampled with a syringe and injected into the GC column. Hence the term, headspace gas chromatography. Through a

process of absorption-desorption, the porous particles within the column separate the volatile contents within the mobile phase based on the molecular
configuration of what is in the sample.

As the carrier gas (usually helium or nitrogen) moves the sample through
the column and separates the analytes, detectors monitor their properties. An
electrochemical detector at the end of the column measures electrical energy
given off as each chemical in the sample is destroyed. The amount of electrical energy is translated to a graphic display and the results computed using an
integrator that measures the area under the curve (AUC) of each graph to determine the amount of alcohol in each sample (standards and blood sample).
Although there are different types of detectors used to continuously monitor
the effluent, the most common used by alcohol researchers and in forensic
analyses of alcohol by GC, is with a flame ionization detector (FID). The
greater the signal detected by the integrator, the greater the concentration of
alcohol in the sample. The quantification of alcohol is based on establishing a
series of known alcohol standards–injected into the column. The known
quantity in the standards typically includes a range of alcohol concentrations
(e.g., 10, 20, 50, 80, 100, 200, 300 mg/dL) and a blank (zero alcohol) sample.
Through a process of extrapolation, the electrical output from these standards
as they go through the FID is used to quantify the alcohol in the blood (or
other tissue) sample. The basic components of GC are illustrated in Figure
2.2. Other external or internal standards (e.g., methanol, isopropanol, acetaldehyde, acetone) may also be injected. Each of these will pass through the
column at a different time. The elution time (measured from the moment of
injection to the time the sample reaches the detector) is very consistent to
enable a precise identification of ethyl alcohol (alcohol) and avoiding any
concerns about contamination from cleaning the skin with rubbing alcohol
(isopropanol) prior to obtaining a blood sample.

Minor variation in the results obtained from GC analyses may exist. For
example, if the blood sample results are outside the range of the standards
used or if there is a greater than acceptable variance in duplication of standard or sample results, these may affect the results. However, such changes
are usually extremely small and will have no significant effect on the interpretation and application of the test results. GC is a highly accurate and reliable
analytical method when used appropriately.

Enzymatic Oxidation

In many hospitals, clinical chemistry results are derived from blood or, in
the case of alcohol testing, blood, or serum. Serum is the watery portion of
blood, and analyses of serum will almost always yield different results from a
blood or breath alcohol test. While some hospitals measure alcohol in blood,

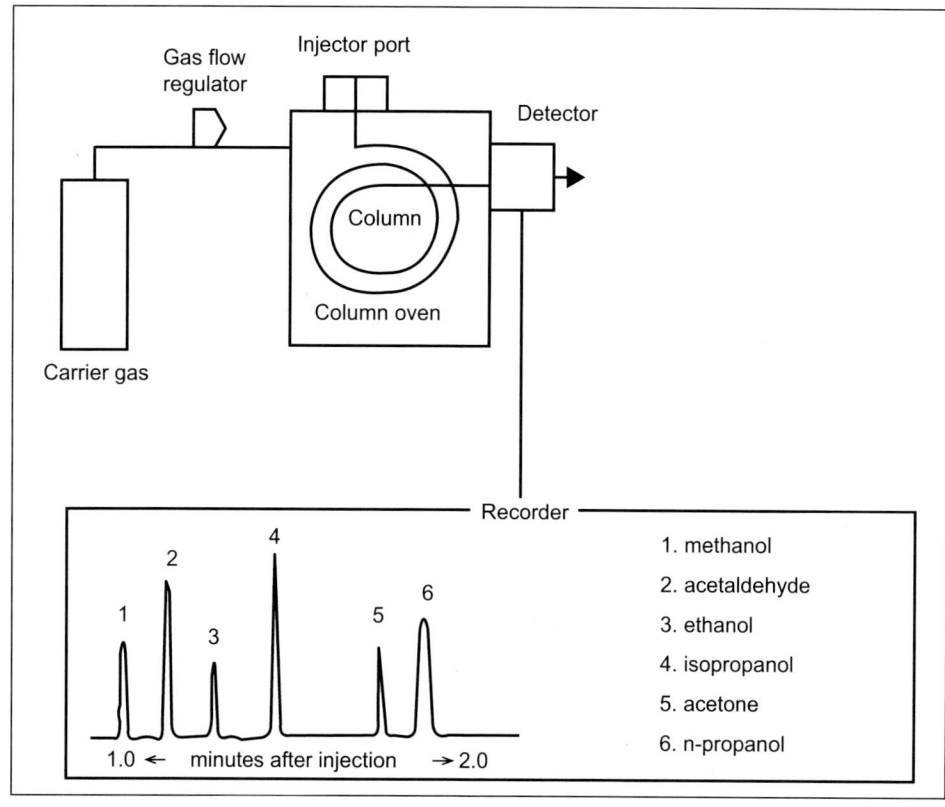

Figure 2.2: Schematic Components of a Gas Chromatographic Instrument.

most clinical labs measure alcohol in serum. The most common clinical method is referred to as the ADH method, the enzymatic oxidation of ADH. Older studies reported that the ADH method is susceptible to interference from isopropanol and methanol, the former being a common bacteriostat used to cleanse the skin prior to venupuncture (Vasiliade, Pollack & Robinson, 1978). However, cross-contamination from isopropyl alcohol is not significantly reactive (DuPont, 1985) or relatively small (about a 0% to 17% increase) even when up to 50 percent of the alcohol sample contains isopropanol (Baxter Diagnostics, Inc., 1993; Ektachem, 1995). The amount of isopropanol on the skin after a "wipe" that would enter a 10 mL collection tube would be infinitesimal.

The ADH method is based on the ability of the enzyme (ADH) to catalyze the oxidation of ethyl alcohol to acetaldehyde. This reaction results in the simultaneous reduction of nicotinamide adenine dinucleotide (NAD), a cofactor in this reaction. The absorbance of NADH at a specific wavelength (340 nanometers) is directly proportional to the concentration of alcohol as illustrated in Figure 2.3.

C2H5OH + NAD ——————— ADH——————→ CH3CHO + NADH + H⁺
(Non-absorbing at 340 nm)   (absorbs at 340 nm)

Figure 2.3: Oxidation of Ethanol by Co-enzyme NAD
and Absorbance of NADH

Hospital serum alcohol tests are potentially compromised if both lactate dehydrogenase (LDH) and lactate are present in the blood because LDH could catalyze the oxidation of lactate, which produces NADH (Nine, Moraca, Virji & Rao, 1995). Excess NADH could be misinterpreted as alcohol. In practice, the presence of both LDH and lactate in blood is theoretically possible because LDH is released as a consequence of trauma, damage to hepatocytes, and liver disease. In such cases, liver enzymes aspartate aminotransferase (ASAT) and alanine aminotransferase (ALAT) would be elevated, along with LDH. Lactate, a product of anaerobic glycolysis, is utilized in gluconeogenesis and may be elevated during hypovolemic shock, cardiac infarction, pulmonary edema or musculoskeletal trauma (Powers & Dean, 2009), or temporarily from Ringer's lactate. In death, LDH and lactate may be significantly elevated, and for this reason, postmortem serum alcohol measured by the ADH method should be avoided. In living subjects these changes are negligible (Powers & Dean, 2009) and hospital tests are valid.

If alcohol is measured in serum, the corresponding blood alcohol concentration will be proportionally lower than the reported serum alcohol because alcohol is distributed in the watery portion of the blood and because of the difference in water content between the same volume of blood and serum. Since a serum sample has proportionally more water than does the same volume of whole blood because the latter has blood components (cells, proteins, etc.), the concentration of alcohol will be higher in serum. The conversion of serum alcohol can be assumed based on an average or calculated based on the water content of the blood, as discussed in Chapter 11.

Breath Alcohol Testing

Early instruments and methods estimating the BAC from breath alcohol date back to the beginning of the last century but gained widespread application in law enforcement in the late 1950s with the development of easy to use and reliable instruments to measure breath alcohol concentrations (BrAC). Since the introduction of breath alcohol testing, many instruments and methods of analyses have been developed (Harger, 1974). Although many of the earlier instruments are of historical interest, in the last 60 years, breath alcohol testing has been popularized by four types of instruments, each using completely different methodologies:

1. GC (as discussed earlier) has been applied to both clinical (Brick, Nathan, Westerick, Frankenstein & Shapiro, 1986) and preclinical research (Pohorecky & Brick, 1982) but rarely by law enforcement or in the forensic field investigations because it is expensive, not easily moved, and requires extensive training; three analytical approaches to breath alcohol testing.
2. chemical oxidation and photometry (e.g., Breathalyzer), which dominated the field for more than 40 years and is still used in some locales.
3. IR (e.g. Intoxilyzer, Data Master®, BAC Verifier®), the most current methodology used by law enforcement when blood samples are not obtained.
4. electrochemical fuel cell devices for roadside preliminary breath testing (PBT).

All breath alcohol testing methodologies rely upon calculating the BAC from the BrAC. Although this is an indirect measure of blood alcohol, it is based on sound physiology. In the blood, alcohol crosses biological membranes until equilibrium with other water compartments is reached. The movement of alcohol across membranes, such as lung tissue, is a function of temperature and concentration. This relationship follows Henry's Law, which posits that the concentration of alcohol in gas or vapor at a steady temperature is a direct function of the alcohol concentration in the liquid phase (i.e., blood). In other words, the alcohol in blood crosses the alveolar membranes of the lung in proportion to the concentration in blood. The relationship between alcohol in blood and that which enters the lungs is affected by temperature and the relative water content of the blood. For example, the concentration of alcohol in breath can increase or decrease by about 6.8 percent for every 1 degree centigrade increase or decrease in body temperature. Similarly, low hematocrit values may produce higher alveolar air alcohol concentrations because of the higher water (and therefore corresponding alcohol) in blood (Dubowski, 1992).

Chemical Oxidation Photometric breath test instruments, such as the veritable Breathalyzer, estimate the BAC by passing a breath sample through a reagent solution of potassium dichromate contained inside a glass ampoule. Any alcohol in the breath sample is oxidized into acetic acid, causing a decrease in the optical density (color) of the ampoule solution. A monochromatic beam of light passing through the ampoule and a detector quantify the change in color intensity 90 seconds after the breath sample is introduced into the ampoule solution. The change in color from yellow to various shades of yellow-green is directly related to the concentration of alcohol in the breath sample. Although this methodology is accurate, it is susceptible to false positives because potassium dichromate may to some degree oxidize solvents and other alcohols. Nevertheless, such false positives are uncommon since breath does not usually contain other alcohols that are oxidized by potassium di-chromate or oxidized to any measurable degree at the same time as ethyl al-cohol or other interfering substances that might be oxidized, thereby producing false positives (Mason & Dubowski, 1975). This source of false pos-itives is unlikely because very few other substances found in exhaled air are oxidized at the same time as alcohol. One potential exception is that of dia-betic patients who have become ketoacidotic. In a glucose-deprived state of medical distress, ketones enter the circulation and pass through the capillaries surrounding the alveoli of the lungs. Ketones, which are oxidized by potas-sium dichromate, can create a false positive result. Although the actual contri-bution of ketones to a Breathalyzer reading is relatively low (usually less than 0.01%), the interpretation of such findings is made more complicated by the fact that such individuals will emit a slightly fruity, acetone-like odor on their breath and have clear signs of psychomotor impairment (Brick, 1993). The trend in law enforcement has been to move away from this workhorse instru-ment to other instruments based on IR spectrometry.

IR Spectrometry-based instruments are the latest in the evolution of breath alcohol analyzers and are commonly used by law enforcement, alco-hol research scientists, and clinicians (compliance testing). This method in-volves projecting an IR beam through a breath sample chamber and measuring the absorption of IR radiation at a specific wavelength correspond-ing to the vibration or harmonic motion of the excited molecules as they absorb IR radiation. When a specific combination of atoms related to ethyl alcohol (e.g., C-H or OH bonds) is detected at characteristic wavelengths, the presence of alcohol is confirmed and quantified. As the concentration of alco-hol in the sample increases, the transmittance of energy through the sample chamber decreases. Although other compounds, particularly those with aro-matic rings and carboxylic acids, can absorb IR energy at the same or wave-length as alcohol, the probability of these compounds in a breath sample are highly unlikely. However, IR instruments have the advantage of detecting and rejecting breath samples that contain potential interfering substances, in-cluding acetone or related compounds that might result from ketoacidosis in untreated diabetics. Also, IR instruments quantitatively measure breath sample volume and have slope detectors that continuously monitor BrAC as the breath sample is being provided. Any change in BrAC concentration during this period suggests residual mouth alcohol is present and the sample will be "rejected." These instruments may also include acetone detection (from ketoacidotic diabetics and alert the operator to a potential medical con-dition. Finally, unlike previous instruments, IR spectrometry instruments have a printout to document instrument operational status and test results.

Fuel Cell–Electrochemical Oxidation is a methodology applied to many fields, including aerospace engineering, where an electrical power is required but sources are limited. Fuel cells consist of two platinum electrodes separated by a porous electrolyte material. As alcohol in exhaled breath passes through the cell, it converts alcohol (a fuel) and acetic acid, protons, and electrons, (oxidant). The flow of electrons from the electrodes is proportional to the BAC. One distinct advantage of fuel cell-based breath alcohol testing devices is that they are very portable and can be used in the field and require very minimal training and very small volumes of breath to operate. However, most fuel cell-electrochemical oxidation devices are less accurate than other breath alcohol methods (e.g., chemical oxidation or IR absorption) and can react to methanol, n-propanol, isopropanol, and acetaldehyde and are usually not admissible evidence of intoxication. Rather, these devices are more helpful to law enforcement in the field to assist in determining if alcohol is present and therefore a potential factor in an investigation.

2.3 QUANTITATIVE EXPRESSION OF BLOOD ALCOHOL

Translating Results to Something Understandable

In most forensic investigations (e.g., involving DWI, serious bodily injury or fatal motor vehicle crashes), alcohol is measured in breath or tissue (e.g., blood) or in fatal cases, blood, brain, or other fluids. Some breath testing instruments give results as the concentration of alcohol in a volume of air (grams of alcohol per 210 L of breath) and will be discussed later in this chapter. However, most instruments report, and most legislators define legal intoxication based on a concentration of alcohol relative to a BAC.

What is a BAC? Scientists describe the concentration of solutions in terms of percent. A percentage is the amount of a particular chemical or substance in a fixed volume of fluid. Although the fluid can change (blood, serum, water), the volume unit does not. Percentages are always expressed as the weight in grams or milligrams of a chemical in 100 mL of liquid (expressed as w/v).

Metric System

Alcohol notations are expressed in metric terms. Whether we are talking about volume, weight, or distance, the metric system is based on units of ten (e.g., 10, 100, 1000) (*see* Table 2.6). Let us review some basic metric system notations and see why this is such a useful and easy system to use. For example, a 10 percent solution of salt means that there are 10 g of salt in every 100 mL of water.

Table 2.6: Common Metric Units.

Unit	Definition
Liter (L)	1000 cubic centimeters (1000 cc) = 1000 milliliters (1000 mL)
Deciliter (dL)	1/10 of a liter or 100 mL
Milliliter (mL)	1/1000 of a liter
Kilogram (kg)	1000 grams (1000 g)
Gram (g)	1/1000 of a kilogram
Milligram(mg)	1/1000 of a gram
Microgram (μg)	1/1000 of a milligram
Nanograms (ng)	1/1000 of a microgram

Problem 2.1

Calculate how much salt is in a standard 1 L bag of normal saline (salt) solution (hint, normal saline is 0.9%).

SOLUTION: We know that if 10 g of salt in 100 mL (1 dL) of water forms 10 percent saline, then 1 g in 100 mL forms 1 percent. Since we want 0.9 percent, we only need 0.9 g of salt per 100 mL. However, in our example we asked how much salt was needed to make a liter of saline. A liter is 1000 mL or 10 times the amount in 100 mL. Therefore, the answer is 0.9 g times 10 equals 9 g. You need 9 g of salt in a 1000 mL volumetric, add water to 1000 mL to make a 1 L solution of normal saline.

The same basic metric equivalents allow us to calculate alcohol concentrations in body fluids (Chapter 11).

How Do Objective Alcohol Tests Relate to Intoxication?

Currently, all states in the United States have 80 mg/dL (.08%) as the BAC that defines DWI or driving under the influence (DUI) of alcohol. This concentration of alcohol is just under one twelfth of 1 percent. Although this may seem like quite a small concentration to produce intoxication, it is extremely high in comparison to other psychoactive drugs. For example, blood LSD concentrations of 2 to 26 μg/L (0.0000002% to 0.0000026%) have been reported to produce profound mental and physical changes (e.g., hallucinations, hysteria, hyperactivity, vomiting, and coma).

Alcohol Proof and Percentages

Alcohol can be expressed in different nomenclatures. Commercially manufactured alcohol is experienced as "proof" or as percent of alcohol (volume/volume). Some common conversions are listed below and in Table 2.7.

0.08 g% (0.08 g of ethanol per 100 mL of blood or serum)
80 mg% (80 mg of ethanol per 100 mL of blood or serum)
80 mg/dL (milligrams per deciliter or tenth of a liter)
80 mM/L (millimoles per liter)
80 mg/210 mL (breath)

Table 2.7: Conversions: How to Translate mg/dL to Percent.

If alcohol reported as	To convert to	Conversion example
grams percent (g%) or %	mg/dL	$0.08\% \times 1000 = 80$ mg/dL
mg/dL	grams percent	80 mg/dL $\div 100 = .08\%$
mg/210 mL	grams percent	80 mg/dL $/100 = .08\%$
80 proof	Percent alcohol by volume	$80/2 = 40\%$(by volume)

REFERENCES

Baselt, R. C. (2014). *Disposition of Toxic Drugs and Chemicals in Man* (10th ed.). Seal Beach, CA: Biomedical Publications.

Becker, C. E. (1983). Methanol poisoning. *Journal of Emergency Medicine, 1,* 51–58

Brick, J. (1993). Diabetes, breath acetone and Breathalyzer accuracy: A case study. *Alcohol, Drugs and Driving, 9*(1), 27–28.

Brick, J., Nathan, P. E., Westrick, E., Frankenstein, W., and Shapiro, A. (1986). The effect of menstrual cycle of blood alcohol levels and behavior. *Journal of Studies on Alcohol, 47*(6), 472–477.

Dubowski, K. M. (1992). *The Technology of Breath-Alcohol Analysis.* DHHS Publication No. (ADM) 92-1728. Rockville, MD: U.S. Department of Health and Human Services. Public Health Service, Alcohol, Drug Abuse and Mental Health Administration, National Institute on Alcohol Abuse and Alcoholism.

DuPont®. (1985, February). *Test Methodology for the ACA Discrete Clinical Analyzer.* Wilmington, DE: Clinical and Instrument Systems Division.

Dutkiewicz, B., Konczalik, J., and Karwacki, W. (1980). Skin absorption of per os administration of methanol in men. *International Archives of Occupational and Environmental Health, 47,* 81–88.

Ektachem Clinical Chemistry Colorimetric Test, Publication No. MP2-110 May 1995; Baxter Diagnostics, Inc. Quantitative determination of alcohol in serum, July 1993.

Ellenhorn, M.J., and Barceloux, D.G. (1988). Alcohol and glycols. *In Medical Toxicology: Diagnosis and Treatment of Human Poisoning* (pp. 781–812). Rockville, MD: Elsevier.

Harger, R. (1974). Recently published analytical methods for determining alcohol in body materials–alcohol countermeasures (Literature Review). DOT HS-801 242 Final Report. Alexandria, VA: National Technical Information Service.

Kahn, A., and Blum, D. (1979a). Methanol poisoning. *Journal of Emergency Medicine, 1,* 51–68.

Kahn, A., and Blum, D. (1979b). Methyl alcohol poisoning in an 8 month old boy: An unusual route of intoxication. *Journal of Pediatrics, 94,* 841–843.

Lacouture, P., and Lovejoy F. H. (1981). *Methanol. Clinical Toxicology Review, 3,* 1–3.

Lacouture, P., Wason, S., Abrams, A., and Lovejoy, F. H. (1983). Acute isopropyl alcohol intoxication: Diagnosis and management. *American Journal of Medicine, 75,* 680–686.

Lester, D. (1962). The concentration of apparent endogenous ethanol. *Quarterly Journal of Studies on Alcohol, 23,* 17–25.

Mason, M., and Dubowski, K. (1975). Breath alcohol analysis: Uses, methods and some forensic problems. *Journal of Forensic Sciences, 21*(1), 9–41.

McMartin, K., Ambre, J., and Tephly, T. (1980). Methanol poisoning in human subjects: Role for formic acid accumulation in metabolic acidosis. *American Journal of Medicine, 68,* 414–418.

Niaura, R., Nathan, P., Frankenstein, W., Shapiro, A., and Brick, J. (1987). Gender differences in acute psychomotor, cognitive, and pharmacokinetic response to alcohol. *Addictive Behaviors, 12,* 345.

Nine, J., Moraca, M., Virji, M., and Rao, K. (1995). Serum-ethanol determination: Comparison of lactate and lactate dehydrogenase interference in three enzymatic assays. *Journal of Analytical Toxicology, 19*(3), 192–196.

Pohorecky, L., and Brick, J. (1982). Method for the measurement of breath ethanol and acetaldehyde: Correlation with blood and brain ethanol levels. Pharmacology, *Biochemistry and Behavior, 16,* 473–479.

Powers, R. H., and Dean, D. E. (2009). Evaluation of potential lactate/lactate dehydrogenase interference with an enzymatic alcohol analysis. *Journal of Analytical Toxicology, 33,* 561–563.

Swartz, R., Millman, R., Billi, J., Bondar, N., Migdal, S., Simonian, S., …, Cole, K. (1981). Epidemic methanol poisoning: Clinical and biochemical analysis of a recent episode. *Medicine, 60,* 373–382.

Vasiliades, J., Pollock, J., and Robinson, C. (1978). Pitfalls of the alcohol dehydrogenase procedure for the emergency assay of alcohol: A case study of isopropanol overdosage. *Clinical Chemistry, 24,* 383–385.

Chapter 3

PHARMACOLOGY OF ALCOHOL[1]

Pharmacology is an enormous field that includes the source and physical and chemical properties of drugs; their formulation and physiochemical effects; as well as the absorption, distribution, metabolism, elimination, therapeutic psychoactive, and toxic effects of drugs. Alcohol has a wide range of medical and behavioral consequences, but with few exceptions it has no effect in the brain or other organs or on behavior until it enters the circulation. The pharmacological effects of alcohol (and other drugs) encompass pharmacokinetics and pharmacodynamics. Pharmacokinetics is the journey of alcohol from the outside world to the brain and elsewhere; the psychoactive effects of alcohol fall under the more specific field of neuropharmacology (or psychopharmacology), directly related to the pharmacodynamics of drug action.

3.1 ALCOHOL PHARMACOKINETICS

Alcohol pharmacokinetics is the science of the absorption, distribution, and biotransformation, and ultimately the concentration of alcohol in the blood (or elsewhere). Pharmacokinetics is an important part of most forensic alcohol analyses and is a function of many factors, including (1) the amount, rate, and time course of alcohol consumption (2) the rate at which alcohol enters the circulatory system from the gastrointestinal tract (3) the diffusion and distribution of alcohol into the blood and fluid compartments, and (4) the rate at which alcohol is oxidized and eliminated.

Absorption Through the Gastrointestinal System

In most instances, alcohol is administered by mouth and is absorbed from the gastrointestinal tract into the circulation. When alcohol first enters the

---

1. Note: Some sections of this chapter were reproduced from Brick and Erickson (2013) with permission of the publisher.

31

mouth, it travels down the esophagus and into the stomach, a muscular sac that can hold about 1500 cc (approximately 50 ounces). The movement of alcohol from the stomach into the small intestine is regulated, in part, by the pyloric sphincter, a ring-shaped muscular valve at the base of the stomach leading to the small intestine. Under laboratory conditions in which the pylorus has been clamped closed (ligated) over the course of many hours, up to about half the alcohol in the stomach will eventually be absorbed through the stomach wall and into the surrounding tissues including the blood. However, under more natural drinking conditions, about 10 percent of the orally ingested alcohol is absorbed into the circulation by passing through the stomach lining and is either reabsorbed into the circulation or watery compartments within or between cells.

Under more practical (normal) drinking situations, the overwhelming majority of alcohol passes from the stomach into the upper intestine (the duodenum or small intestine), along with any digested food present in the stomach. Because alcohol is a weakly charged molecule and is highly water soluble, it passes easily through lipid membrane walls of the upper intestine (duodenum) and then through the walls of the tiny blood vessels, the capillary plexus, that surround the duodenum. At this point, alcohol has moved from the gastrointestinal system into the circulation. The surrounding network of capillaries eventually form the hepatic portal vein that transports alcohol to the liver. Alcohol continues its journey from the liver to the heart, where it is circulated throughout the body. From the heart, the next major organ system exposed to alcohol is the pulmonary system. Small amounts of alcohol, along with carbon dioxide, freely pass through the walls of the capillaries surrounding the alveoli (air sacs) in the lungs. The movement of alcohol through the pulmonary system is the basis for evidential and clinical breath alcohol testing. As the circulating alcohol returns to the heart from the lungs, it is pumped to the brain and other parts of the body (*see* Figure 3.1).

In addition to gastrointestinal administration, alcohol may enter the circulation through several other routes, including absorption through the skin or by injection (Pohorecky & Brick, 1990). Alcohol can also be inhaled as a vapor to directly enter the pulmonary blood. An expensive device that vaporizes alcoholic drinks was developed so alcohol could be inhaled through the pulmonary system. This is similar to experimental alcohol treatment in animals years ago wherein animals breathed and lived in an "alcohol" atmosphere. Although the safety and efficiency of some of these routes is questionable or not known, it is unclear why people would rather inhale alcohol than drink a cold beer or other drink (Erickson, 2007). Although intravenous alcohol injections and alcohol enemas by alcohol abusers have been self-reported, these routes of administration are rare, inefficient, and unpleasant for many people.

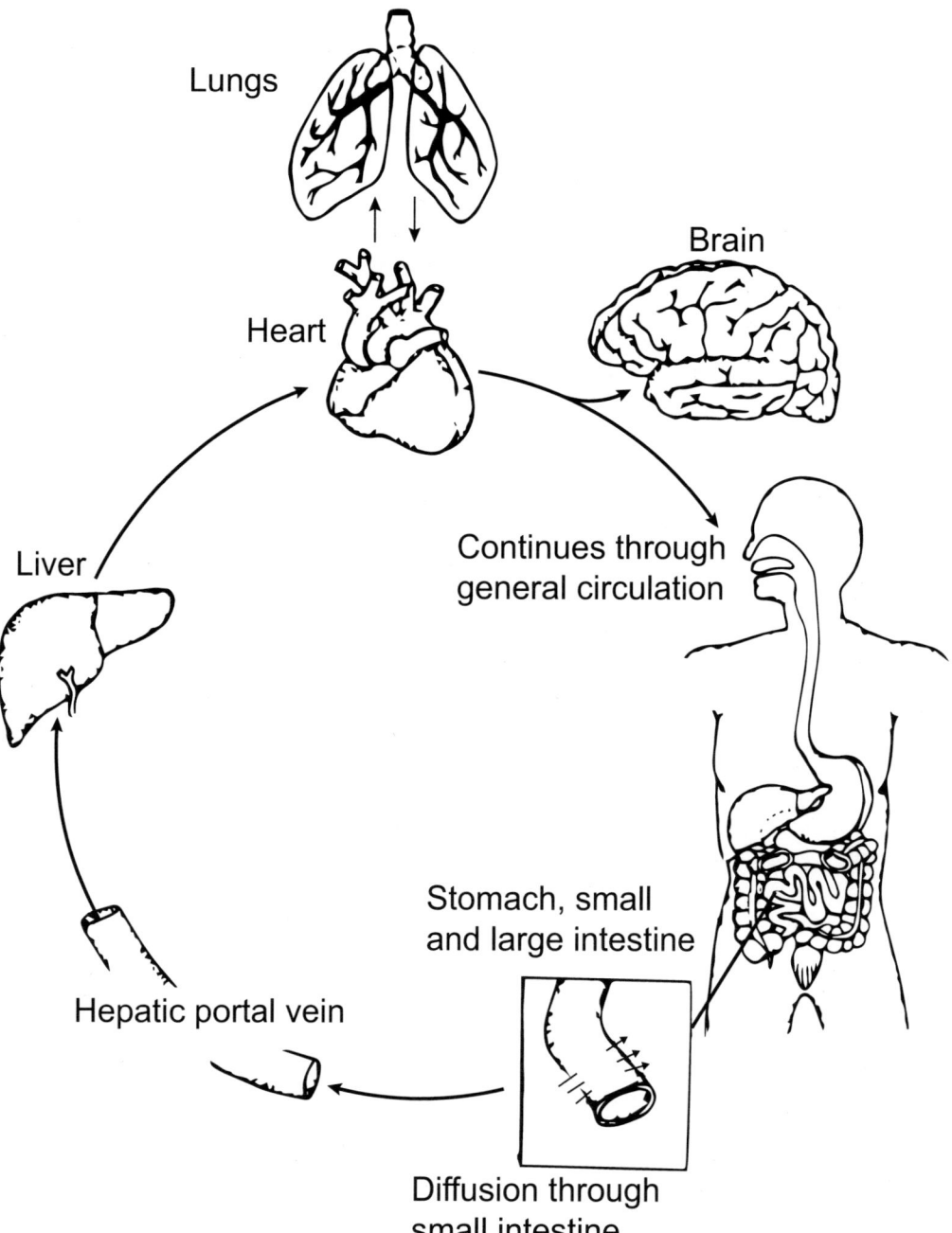

Lungs

Brain

Heart

Liver

Continues through
general circulation

Stomach, small
and large intestine

Hepatic portal vein

Diffusion through
small intestine

Figure 3.1: Absorption and Circulation of Alcohol in the Body.

Factors Affecting Absorption

Beverage Characteristics

Different beverage types may indirectly affect alcohol absorption characteristics. For example, beer is absorbed more slowly than whiskey or brandy probably because of relatively lower pure alcohol: fluid delivery system. Namely, whereas the amount of alcohol in a 12-ounce beer may be the same as that of a 1.5-ounce shot of liquor, the concentration of alcohol in a larger fluid volume is much less, which means there is more fluid to absorb. To a lesser extent but consistent with Fick's Law (the lower the concentration gradient, the slower the diffusion per unit area per unit time), some studies have found that in humans the absorption of alcohol is most rapid when administered in higher concentration solutions and less rapid when the concentration is below 10 percent. Other studies (Roine et al., 1991, 1993) showed the opposite effect if subjects drank after eating a fatty breakfast, suggesting that the absorption of alcohol is not predicted by Fick's law. These studies generally were conducted using relatively low alcohol doses and volumes different from most real world drinking situations.

Differences in carbohydrates, congeners (by-products of fermentation or additives), or carbonation have been reported to affect absorption, but these factors are minor in comparison to total volume of beverage and amount of alcohol delivered. These factors may account for some of the variability between expected and observed alcohol concentrations after controlled drinking studies, for example. For these reasons any attempt to estimate BAC by extrapolation (discussed in Chapter 11) should include a range of absorption rates to account for individual beverage (and other) characteristics. Recently it has been reported that alcoholic beverages are absorbed faster when combined with diet soda mixers (Stamates, Maloney & Marcziski, 2015). It is more likely that the sugar in regular soft drinks slows down the absorption of alcohol rather than a diet or other component speeding it up.

Once the alcohol passes out of the stomach and into the intestine, however, absorption into the circulation is rapid and not affected by the concentration of alcohol in either the stomach or the intestines. In other words, although genetic factors may also play some role, the stomach environment is the primary rate-limiting factor in alcohol's absorption.

When the rate of absorption exceeds the rate of elimination, BAC rises. Therefore, the rate of alcohol absorption directly affects the maximum BAC. The faster the rate of alcohol absorption, the greater the area under the BAC curve (*see* Figure 3.2) and the higher to maximum BAC. The increased bioavailability of alcohol from more rapid absorption is probably due to decreased first pass metabolism (*see* next section) and rates of absorption that

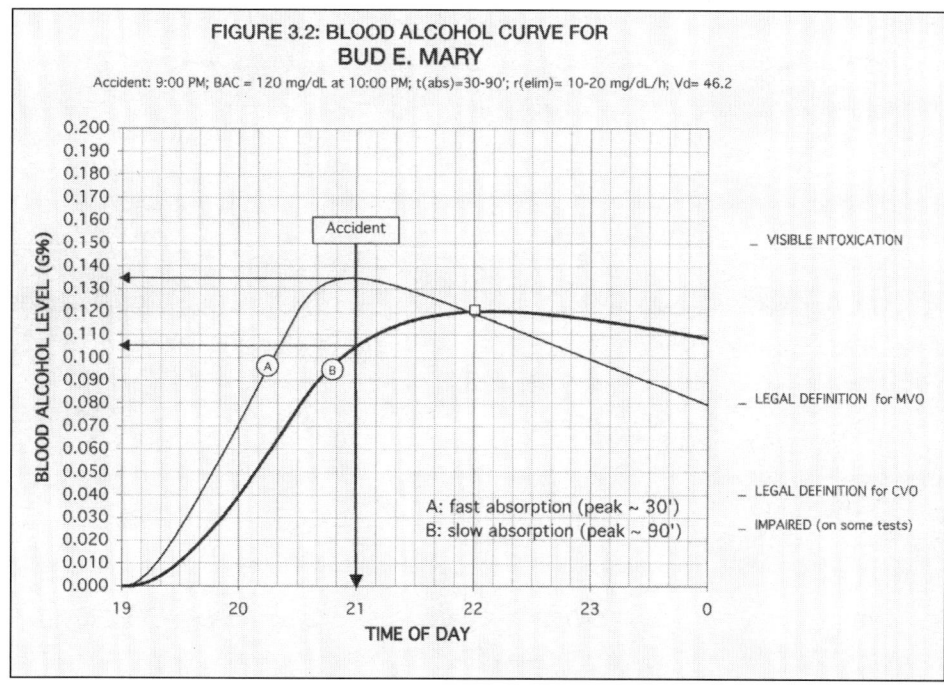

Figure 3.2: Factors Affecting Slow and Rapid Absorption and BAC.

allow significantly more alcohol to enter the circulation than can be metabolized with each pass through the liver. Similarly, decreasing the rate of absorption decreases the peak concentration and increases the time from the last drink to maximum concentration. Absorption is affected by many variables, but in the absence of pathology, the three most critical factors to consider in forensic analyses dependent on absorption are presence or absence of food, rate of drinking, and beverage characteristics (particularly volume).

Food

The absorption of alcohol from the gastrointestinal tract is significantly influenced by the presence of food in the stomach. It is common knowledge that alcohol is absorbed much more rapidly on an empty stomach than on a full one, but the degree to which alcohol absorption is delayed is not as widely appreciated. The presence of food in the stomach not only impairs absorption but also reduces gastric emptying time and consequently will result in lower BACs. Earlier studies indicated that food type might also affect absorption (e.g., proteins and carbohydrates in the stomach were more effective than fats were in delaying ethanol absorption) and that gastric emptying in general was influenced by osmotic pressure and chemical composition.

Directly introducing a fat emulsion into the ileum delayed the absorption of alcohol (McFarlane, Pooley, Welch, Rumsey & Read, 1986) for several hours, as might be expected but not likely to reflect real-world drinking and eating. Gastric emptying and the rate of alcohol absorption is influenced by many factors. Because the specific characteristics of these factors are rarely known and because alcohol easily passes through cells and the gastrointestinal system, in real-world drinking situations, pharmacokinetic predictions regarding alcohol levels based upon specific food types should be avoided. That does not mean food is not a factor. It is, in fact, one of the most significant factors regulating absorption of alcohol (Jones & Neri, 1991; Madsen, 1992; Rose, 1979; Ramchadnani, Kwo & Li, 2001; Wilkinson, Sedman, Sakmar, Kay & Wagner, 1977). Many studies, particularly those involving relatively low alcohol doses, have demonstrated that food reduces the maximum BAC achieved after drinking. For higher BACs likely to be encountered in forensic cases, this small difference is often obscured, in part because people who drink to very high blood alcohol concentrations probably do not also consume large meals. Detailed collection of subjective evidence regarding time and nature of a last meal is useful, as is postmortem gastric alcohol concentrations. The contribution of food (and other factors that affect absorption) can be accounted for more effectively by using a range of absorption times to maximum concentration rather than attempting to account for the effects of specific types of food (*see* later sections of this chapter as well as Chapter 11).

Volume

The volume of any beverage consumed directly affects gastric emptying because of the mechanisms by which stomach emptying is regulated. First, the receptive capacity of the intestine regulates outflow from the stomach based upon the volume and pressure within the intestine and by the pressure and volume of the contents in the stomach. In other words, alcohol does not flow unimpeded from the stomach to the intestines but is regulated by feedback mechanisms in which gastric emptying is a balance between the force and frequency of gastric peristalsis (the alternating contraction and relaxation of muscles in the gastrointestinal system) and the resistance of the pylorus (the muscular valve that regulates stomach emptying). The rate of gastric emptying is therefore directly related to the volume of fluid in the stomach. The distention of the stomach activates afferent vagus nerve impulses from gastric stretch receptors that increase gastric peristalsis and gastric emptying (Davenport, 1961). Working in concert with the stomach to control gastric emptying, the duodenum decreases gastric peristalsis and limits the volume of material that enters the intestine to allow for efficient processing of foodstuff, nutrients, and various fluids. This process is proportional so that as the volume of fluid in the stomach increases, so does the volume that passes into the intestines and quickly into the circulation. Large volumes of fluid ingested over a short period of time will result in a rapid increase in BAC. However, the large volumes will take longer to be fully absorbed from the gastrointestinal system to the blood.

Similarly, once drinking stops, the amount of alcohol remaining in the stomach decreases and the rate at which the BAC increases declines, eventually reaching a peak concentration. At that moment, the amount of alcohol being absorbed into the circulation is equal to the rate of metabolism and a plateau is reached. In actual tests, at plateau the BAC is, for all practical purposes, flat, even though minute changes in the BAC are present before and after the absolute peaks BAC.

Other Factors

Cigarette smoking, medications that delay gastric emptying (e.g., anticholinergics), and traumatic hemorrhaging have been reported to delay alcohol absorption, probably due to a shift from parasympathetic to sympathetic nervous system activity. However, in forensic applications, changes in gastric emptying after a traumatic event may not affect pharmacokinetic analyses of alcohol use and intoxication prior to injury. Nevertheless, forensic examiners should be aware of this phenomenon.

Similarly, higher (or lower) alcohol content beverages, carbonated drinks, low blood sugar, and drinking in the morning after fasting have been reported to increase the rate of alcohol absorption (Jones, 2008; Roberts & Robinson, 2007). Most of these studies involve relatively low BACs or unnatural drinking situations.

It is well known both in the scientific literature and among the general public that food can decrease the rate of alcohol absorption, maximum BAC, and subjective intoxication. It has been demonstrated that nonalcoholic mixers may alter breath alcohol concentration (BrAC). Rossheim and Thombs (2011) reported that breath alcohol BrAC was positively related to the number of diet soda drinks used as mixers for alcoholic drinks. Subjects with higher BrAC consumed more diet sodas. This was probable because higher calorie non-diet drinks delayed absorption more than did the low or no calorie diet drinks therefore allowing for first-pass metabolism.

More recently, Marczinski and Stamates (2013) replicated these findings but observed an 18- percent increase in BrAC with diet mixers, noting that other studies reported up to 56-percent increases at much lower BrACs.

At the higher BACs likely to be encountered in forensic applications, the contribution of these other factors is likely to be less and, for all practical and useful purposes, accounted for by bracketing any attempted pharmacokinetic analysis (Chapter 11).

Alcohol Absorption After Drinking Stops

There is an important distinction between alcohol absorption and maximum BAC that is often an important parameter in prospective or retrospective blood alcohol estimates over time. The maximum BAC almost always occurs well before absorption is complete. Complete absorption of every molecule of alcohol may take many hours after drinking stops, but in some instances (e.g., very low rate of drinking) the maximum BAC may occur within 15 or 20 minutes, or less, after the last drink. Single-dose studies of alcohol absorption show remarkable variability in time to maximum BAC. This variation is a function of many factors, including drinking density (amount of alcohol per hour). In controlled laboratory studies the between-subject variation for time to maximum BAC following the same dose is quite low (e.g., less than 15 minutes if the drinking rate is very low). There is a large amount of forensic literature on the many factors that affect alcohol absorption, demonstrating in some instances unusually large changes that clearly call into question the validity of a particular rate of alcohol absorption or time to maximum BAC.

In forensic applications in which BAC estimates are required, it is therefore critical to assume a range of times for alcohol absorption. The potential variability of individual differences in alcohol absorption is greatly reduced if an objective blood or other chemical test result is obtained as soon as possible and a range of alcohol absorption times is applied to any estimates of alcohol use or subsequent intoxication. Under most drinking scenarios, alcohol absorption exceeds elimination for about 30 to 90 minutes after the last drink. Figure 3.3 illustrates the variability in estimating BAC based on the number of drinks alone (a' and b'). Similar estimates that are anchored by a BAC at a specific time greatly reduce such estimates. Estimates of minimum and maximum BAC can be estimated with accuracy when a range of absorption and elimination rates is applied and when there is a known BAC.

Distribution

As alcohol is absorbed from the gastrointestinal system into the circulation, it begins to be distributed throughout the water compartments of the body. Therefore, individual anthropometrics are important in understanding and making pharmacokinetic estimates of alcohol use and intoxication because the larger the total body water content of the individual, the more dilute any amount of alcohol will become and vice-versa. Since blood is about 80 percent water, tissues with the greatest blood supply and capillaries receive alcohol more rapidly than tissues with fewer blood vessels do. Those target tissues will also have the highest alcohol content. For example, it may take

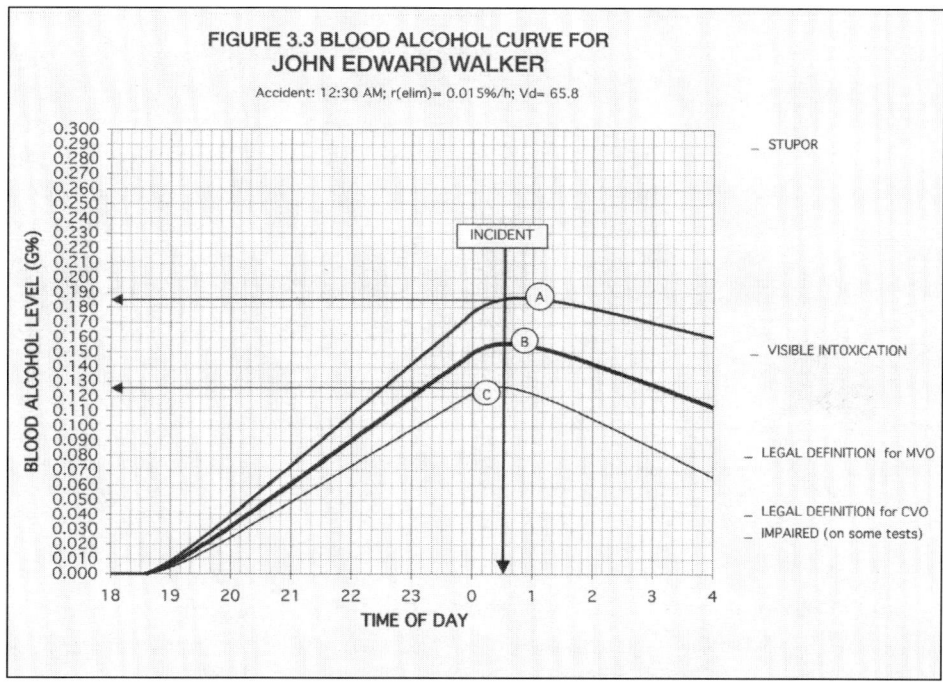

Figure 3.3: BAC Curves W/O BAC to Anchor.

many hours for alcohol to equilibrate in bone, which by relative weight contains little water, whereas brain, lung, kidney, and liver tissues equilibrate more rapidly because of their relatively high respective water contents. Since alcohol is infinitely water soluble, it is distributed differently throughout the body based on the water content of the organ or tissue. Once alcohol has been completely absorbed and equally distributed throughout the watery portions of the body it is at an equilibrium. The amount of water available for distribution is a function of many variables, including gender, age, height, and weight.

Factors Affecting Distribution

Gender Differences

Gender can affect the bioavailability of alcohol through gastric absorption, metabolism (discussed in the next section), or differences in the volume of distribution. Research on hormonal influence on BAC has been investigated (Brick, Nathan, Westrick, Frankenstein & Shapiro, 1986; Mumenthaler, Taylor & Yesavage, 2000; Sutker et al., 1987), but additional work is needed to reach a clear consensus. At this time there is insufficient evidence to use gender-based assumptions regarding alcohol elimination and BAC.

The volume of distribution is the amount of water available in a particular subject for alcohol to be distributed. Although much alcohol is distributed in the circulatory system, which is about 80 percent water, interstitial space in muscle, for example also contains water. Since muscle cells have more water than fat cells have and men, on average, have more muscle mass per pound of body weight than women have and, on average, women have more body fat per pound of body weight than men have, men generally have more total body water than women. Thus after a given dose of alcohol, a woman will have a higher BAC than a man has, even if they weigh the same. In total, the human body contains about 30 to 50 L of water (depending on body characteristics discussed in this chapter and in Chapter 5 and 11).

During the first third of the twentieth century, Swedish physiologist E. M. Widmark studied the interrelationship among the amount of alcohol consumed, body weight, elimination rate, and the BAC and recognized the gender difference in body water, which he called the Rho factor. Since the early work of Widmark (1932/1981), body water estimates have been modified to take into account more recent technological advances in the estimation of total body water (e.g., isotope dilution). Some forensic opinions still rely on Widmark's body water estimate, originally published at the beginning of the last century. However, the most accurate estimates of total body water incorporate age, weight, height, and gender. The various algorithms that derive total body water based upon known factors are recommended, rather than general averages, when making various forensic alcohol calculations (*see* Chapter 11).

Differences in beverage volume, volume of distribution (the size of the water compartments in the body), alcohol concentration, the presence or absence of food, and rate of elimination, coupled with drinking time and amount of alcohol consumed, determine the ultimate shape of the blood alcohol curve. Because of these many variables, blood alcohol estimates often required in forensic evaluations should be bracketed to include assumptions that illustrate a minimum and maximum range of results.

Metabolism and Elimination

The terms metabolism and elimination refer to different physiological processes but are used interchangeably in the alcohol literature. Ultimately, the oxidative metabolism and elimination of alcohol (also through urine, breath, and sweat) refer to changes in BAC over time based on a combination of factors.

First-Pass (Gastric) Metabolism

Some alcohol metabolism begins in the gastrointestinal tract through what is termed first-pass metabolism. This metabolism occurs prior to any alcohols reaching the liver. The mucosal lining of the stomach contains alcohol dehydrogenase ADH, the same enzyme that metabolizes alcohol in the liver. However, the contribution of gastric ADH to first-pass alcohol metabolism is controversial. Some researchers believed that gastric enzymes play a major role in first-pass metabolism (Lim et al., 1993); other investigators consider the liver to be the primary site of first-pass metabolism (Levitt & Levitt, 1998). Furthermore, some gender differences appear to exist in the overall extent of, and in the contribution of, gastric enzymes to first-pass metabolism. For example, the extent of first-pass metabolism is less in women than in men, and some studies have also found lower gastric GADH activity in women (Thomasson, 1995).

Although it is unclear as to what extent first-pass metabolism contributes to the overall elimination of alcohol, it is clear that such changes are mostly detectable after consumption of low alcohol doses or under conditions that cause delayed absorption, such as after a meal. Thus, under such conditions more alcohol can be metabolized in the stomach before transport to the liver. It has been suggested that only about 10 percent of ingested alcohol is eliminated by first-pass metabolism of low doses of alcohol (Weathermon & Crabb, 1999). Whereas, there is value in recognizing first-pass metabolism, in forensic evaluations there is little value in distinguishing among first-pass metabolism from GADH or from hepatic ADH or from other enzymes. Metabolism of alcohol proceeds regardless of the source and elimination continues within a range of known elimination rates.

Most of alcohol is oxidized in the liver by the enzyme ADH. There are several ADH variants (i.e., isozymes) that differ in their activity when studied in vitro, but in human subjects, the effect of different ADH isozymes on alcohol elimination is small (Thomasson, 1995, 2000).

The metabolism of alcohol by ADH produces acetaldehyde, a very toxic compound that is rapidly transformed by aldehyde dehydrogenase (ALDH) to acetyl coenzyme A, which is eventually broken down to carbon dioxide and water (*see* Figure 3.4).

There are two major types of ALDH. The ALDH1 requires relatively high acetaldehyde concentrations in the cell to become active. ALDH2 becomes active when extremely low acetaldehyde levels are present and may be more important in alcohol metabolism after moderate alcohol consumption. About 40 percent of Asians lack active ALDH2, so when they drink alcohol, acetaldehyde levels may become significantly elevated and cause an aversive reaction that includes bright facial flushing, nausea, and vomiting (Luu et al., 1995; Wall et al., 1997).

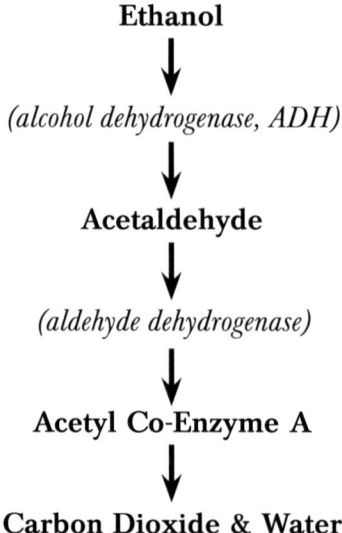

Figure 3.4: Oxidative Metabolism of Ethanol (Enzymes).

Briefly, the metabolism of organic compounds (e.g., alcohol) into usable forms of energy (such as adenosine, triphosphate) is used in the neogenesis of molecules to form new tissues and organs. In forensic applications, assumed or quantified rates of alcohol oxidative metabolism are important in determining how much alcohol has been consumed, for example. Elimination of alcohol from the body is a function of oxidative metabolism and the terms metabolism and elimination are often used interchangeably. Elimination is a relatively easy variable to measure in clinical, forensic and other applications.

Widmark was the first scientist to accurately describe the rate of alcohol elimination in humans and referred to this using the Greek letter beta (β). Widmark reported β to be about 15 mg/dL/h (.015%/h). As discussed in Chapter 11, Widmark's original measurements of alcohol elimination are still widely used and valuable in forensic calculations. Widmark's β is and remains a very good average of alcohol elimination, much like body temperature (also a good average for most people). Older studies post Widmark reported a very wide range of elimination rates, probably due to different experimental designs, poor subject screening, and other factors. More recent studies using better analytical techniques have confirmed Widmark's original measurement and except in some clinical populations, the rate of alcohol elimination is very centrally weighted at approximately 15 mg/dL/h. For example, in one study alcohol elimination in the postabsorptive state decreased at an average rate of 14.94 mg/dL/h. (Dubowski, 1985). Since the range of elimination from this data set was unusually large and the variance so small, these results indicate a distribution with a very central tendency and virtually identical to Widmark's original β. This average rate of 15 mg/dL/h has been observed in clinical research by many researchers including the author but it is not invariable (Brick & Carpenter, 1990).

Winek and Murphy (1984) reported alcohol elimination rates of 12 mg/dL/h ± 4 mg/dL/h in nondrinkers; 15 mg/dL ± 4 mg/dL/h in social drinkers, and 30 mg/dL/h ± 9 mg/dL in alcoholics. Clothier, Kelly & Read (1985) reported rates of alcohol elimination in fifteen patients admitted for alcohol dependency. From initial intake BACs of 250 mg/dL these alcohol-dependent patients eliminated alcohol at an average rate of 26.6 mg/dL/h ± 7 mg/dL (range of about 16 to 43 mg/dL/h). In such extreme cases, metabolic tolerance, alone or in combination with activity of both the cytochrome 2E1 isozyme (CYP2E1) and the ADH enzyme system, probably accounts for these exceptionally high rates of elimination. Also, studies of metabolism and elimination of patients going through alcohol withdrawal may not reflect metabolism and elimination during a drinking episode.

Most modern research indicates that the overwhelming majority of drinkers eliminate alcohol at rates of about 10 to 20 mg/dL/h. A small segment of more tolerant drinkers (faster metabolizers) may eliminate alcohol at rates of up to about 25 mg/dL/h, or even higher, in cases of exceptional metabolic tolerance, a hypermetabolic state due to thermal injury, or unusual genetic predisposition. Rates greater than 15 to 20 mg/dL/h should not routinely be assumed in forensic analyses unless there is evidence that the subject drinker is in a special clinical population in which such metabolic peculiarities might be present or if it is otherwise justified. Similarly, with the exception of subjects in special clinical populations (e.g., malnourished, advanced cirrhosis), elimination rates of less than 10 mg/dL/hr (slower metabolizers) are also rare and such rates applied in alcohol calculations used with great caution. Lieberman (1963) examined the rate of alcohol elimination in normal healthy patients and patients with alcoholic cirrhosis. Patients received about 2.5–3.5 ounces of 200-proof alcohol (equal to about 5–7 ounces of 100-proof liquor), and their rate of alcohol elimination was measured. Healthy subjects eliminated alcohol between 12 and 20 mg/dL/h (mean 15 mg/dL/h), patients with cirrhosis eliminated alcohol between 10 and 19 mg/dL/h), (mean 15 mg/dL/h); and patients with viral hepatitis (with jaundice) eliminated alcohol at 12 to 16 mg/dL/h (mean 14 mg/dL/h). Only the most severe form of cirrhosis (with jaundice) showed any significant differences in metabolism: 6 to 16 mg/dL/h (mean 10 mg/dL/h). Generally the rate of alcohol elimination is increased by chronic alcohol consumption and decreased by liver damage, but even in clinical populations these effects are relatively modest. Thus, although an average alcohol elimination rate of 15 mg/dL/h is a very good average, the need for applying a range of metabolic/elimination rates in forensic analyses is a standard that should be followed and is discussed in Chapter 11.

Hepatic Metabolism

Most of alcohol is oxidized by two families of enzymes found primarily in the liver ADH and the 2E1 isozyme (CYP2E1) system. Some research suggests that gender differences or stress may affect alcohol pharmacokinetics. However, the effects of various hormones on alcohol absorption and elimination have not been consistently reported so as to gain general acceptance in the field of alcohol studies or are usually detected only at relatively low BAC or under conditions of extreme stress, such as severe thermal injury or during withdrawal. An exposure-induced or a genetically atypical ADH enzyme system may increase the rate of alcohol elimination in some populations, whereas hepatic pathology or genetic variation may have the opposite effect.

Approximately 90 percent of all alcohol is metabolized by ADH. In addition to ADH, there is the alcohol-metabolizing enzyme cytochrome P450, also termed microsomal ethanol oxidizing system or MEOS (Lieber, 1994b). Cytochrome P450 consists of two enzymes: Cytochrome P450 reductase and the cytochrome 2E1 isozyme (CYP2E1). Both families of enzymes reside in the endoplasmic reticulum of the cells. The CYP2E1 variant can metabolize other compounds, including acetaldehyde and various medications, and therefore plays a role in the pharmacokinetic interaction between alcohol and other drugs (*see* Chapter 8). The CYP2E1 enzyme plays a limited role in the metabolism of alcohol in occasional drinkers; however, chronic heavy drinking increases CYP2E1 up to tenfold. In chronic heavy drinkers or after the consumption of large amounts of alcohol, most alcohol is metabolized by the CYP2EI enzyme rather than by ADH (Lieber, 1994a-b).

Alcohol can also be metabolized by other cytochrome enzymes, including CYP3A4 and CYP1A2 (Salmela et al., 1994). The CYP3A and CYP3A4 variants can increase from alcohol consumption.

Other Routes and Factors in Elimination

Small amounts of unchanged alcohol are also eliminated from the body through sweat, urine, and expired air. These can be measured in alcohol sweat patch tests, urinalysis, and breath testing. However, only breath alcohol measurement can be carried out in a forensically useful way.

External factors related to dieting also affect elimination. Lowenstein, Simore, Boulter, and Nathan (1970) reported that 10 percent fructose infusions coupled with 300 mL of bourbon (infused) lowered BAC by 43 percent. Mean BACs for alcohol/saline were 184 mg/dL, and for alcohol/fructose were 137 mg/dL. A similar fructose-reducing effect on BAC has been reported by others (e.g., Mascord, Smith, Starmer & Whitfield, 1991), but it has also been attributed to delayed absorption of alcohol (Jones, 1983; Perl & Starmer, 1983).

Zero and First-Order Kinetics

The preceding discussion of alcohol elimination implied that alcohol elimination proceeds at a fixed rate, with a practical range of 10 to 20 mg/dL/h for most drinkers and reflecting zero-order alcohol kinetics. Zero-order Michaelis-Menten Pharmacokinetics refers to alcohol elimination that occurs at the same rate for as long as alcohol is present, regardless of the concentration in blood. As the BAC increases, the enzymes regulating alcohol oxidation are quickly saturated and the rate of elimination remains constant.

In contrast, there is also evidence that the rate of elimination is not a constant but follows first-order kinetics in which the elimination rate changes as a function of BAC. For example, at very low BACs, generally below approximately 30 mg/dL/h, the elimination of alcohol from the blood appears to follow first-order kinetics, where the rate of elimination is lower. This results in a BAC profile that resembles a hockey stick and is sometimes referred to as a hockey stick effect because of the shape of the BAC curve. Unlike at higher BACs, the rate of alcohol elimination at very low BACs is not linear which makes pharmacokinetic analyses complex. Elimination may also increase at very high BACs, further complicating pharmacokinetic analyses and reinforcing the need for methodology that includes a wide range of scientific assumptions about alcohol pharmacokinetics.

Although individual differences in metabolism exist (Jones, 2010) and should be considered in any forensic analysis, the practical consequences of elimination rates below 10 mg/dL/h or above 20 mg/dL/h are not always of clinical or forensic significance. Table 3.1 illustrates the effect of different rates of alcohol elimination on estimates of alcohol consumption.

Summary

The application of the scientific principles of pharmacokinetics to forensic cases involves consideration of factors that affect rates of alcohol absorption, distribution, metabolism, and elimination. In laboratory studies with clinically screened subjects and controlled drinking and eating and other accounted for experimental variables, pharmacokinetic estimates based on averages of absorption and elimination may be sufficient. However, in forensic practice such laboratory controls are not present and the active rates are not known. It is therefore highly recommended that a range of alcohol

Table 3.1: Effect Elimination Rates on Total Drink Estimates.

r(elim) = g%/h	C1 $\beta = .008$	C2 $\beta = .010$	C3 $\beta = .015$	C4 $\beta = .020$	C5 $\beta = .030$	C6 $\beta = 0$
Regular beer (4.5% v/v),oz	110	120	146	172	225	68
Regular beer (5.0% v/v), oz	99	108	132	155	202	61
Light beer (4.0% v/v), oz	123	135	165	194	253	76
Wine/champagne (12% v/v), oz	41	45	55	65	84	25
60–Proof spirits, oz	16	18	22	26	34	10
80–Proof spirits, oz	12	14	16	19	25	8
100–Proof spirits, oz	10	11	13	16	20	6
Standard drink equivalent, no.	8.2	9.0	11.0	12.9	16.9	5.1

These figures are based on 35-year-old, 171-lb, 70-in male, drinking for 5 hours and a measured BAC of 130 mg/dL 10 hours after the start of drinking.

absorption and elimination rates be applied in forensic analyses. The use of ranges in alcohol pharmacokinetic calculations is discussed in Chapter 11.

3.2 ALCOHOL PHARMACODYNAMICS
SITE OF ALCOHOL ACTION

Up until now, we have focused on how alcohol gets from the outside world into the body, how it is distributed in different water components, and the different routes of metabolism. Increases or decreases in bioavailability of alcohol due to changes in pharmacokinetics affect the BAC, the amount of alcohol reaching the brain, and therefore human behavior and for all practical purposes changes in behavior are directly related to the pharmacodynamic specific effects of alcohol in specific areas of the brain. In the last three decades, neuroscience research, which encompasses neuropharmacology, neurophysiology, and neuroanatomy, has provided enormous insight into the mechanisms by which alcohol alters brain chemistry to change behavior. As a drug, alcohol's effects are directly related to neurophysiological changes within specific cells in the brain. The structural hierarchy starts with the brain, continues with the organization of the nervous system, and ends with individual brain cells.

The adult human brain weighs about 1400 g or about 3 pounds and is composed of about 100 to 200 billion specialized brain cells. Casual inspection of the brain reveals a wealth of distinct anatomical features, including the imposing cerebral cortex, a large convoluted structure that forms the front and uppermost portion of the brain, the cerebellum, and the spinal cord. What is not obvious is that the effects of alcohol are on the nervous system and not just the brain. The nervous system is comprised of two parts: the CNS and the peripheral nervous system (PNS). These parts are anatomically separate but highly interactive.

Organization of the Nervous System

The CNS consists of the brain and the spinal cord. The brain is responsible for processing sensory, motor, and cognitive information and sends commands or efferent signals down the spinal cord to muscles, organs, and glands. The CNS is also the conduit for sensorimotor information going from sensory organs to the brain, where these afferent signals are processed to allow the conscious experience of our environment, for example. Many of the acute effects of alcohol intoxication involve changes in the CNS. For example, alcohol can impair judgment and perception, affect risk-taking and purposeful behavior, and disrupt signals from the brain to muscles, organs, and glands.

Everything outside the brain and spinal cord is part of the PNS. The PNS consists of two branches: the somatic and the autonomic nervous systems. The somatic nervous system interacts with the outside environment and controls mostly voluntary movement (e.g., skeletal muscles that are under conscious control), carrying afferent sensory information from auditory, visual, tactile, stretch, proprioceptive, and other receptors located in various organs and muscles. The PNS sends this sensory information to the brain and sends efferent command signals from the CNS to muscles, for example. Alcohol interferes with the conduction of such information along nerves to the brain or from the brain to activate and control muscles. The autonomic nervous system controls involuntary smooth muscles, cardiac muscles, and glands and regulates and maintains homeostasis (steady state of temperature, oxygen, fluids, food/energy supplies, etc.) of the internal environment.

The autonomic nervous system is further divided into two branches: the sympathetic and parasympathetic systems. Most of the time, the sympathetic and parasympathetic nervous systems work in opposite directions. For example, during states of stress, the sympathetic nervous system arouses the body, causes pupil dilation and peripheral blood vessel constriction, shuts down digestion, increases heart rate, and prepares the body to fight or to take flight. The parasympathetic nervous system has the opposite effect. High levels of alcohol intoxication directly affect the autonomic nervous system and may affect circulation, heart rate, pupil dilation, and sensory information (e.g., perception of temperature, touch, or pain). Some sensory information (e.g., vision, hearing, smell) is communicating directly to the brain through one of twelve cranial nerves, which are also part of the PNS. Alcohol exerts its effect through both the CNS and the PNS. The basic functional components of the nervous system are illustrated in Figure 3.5

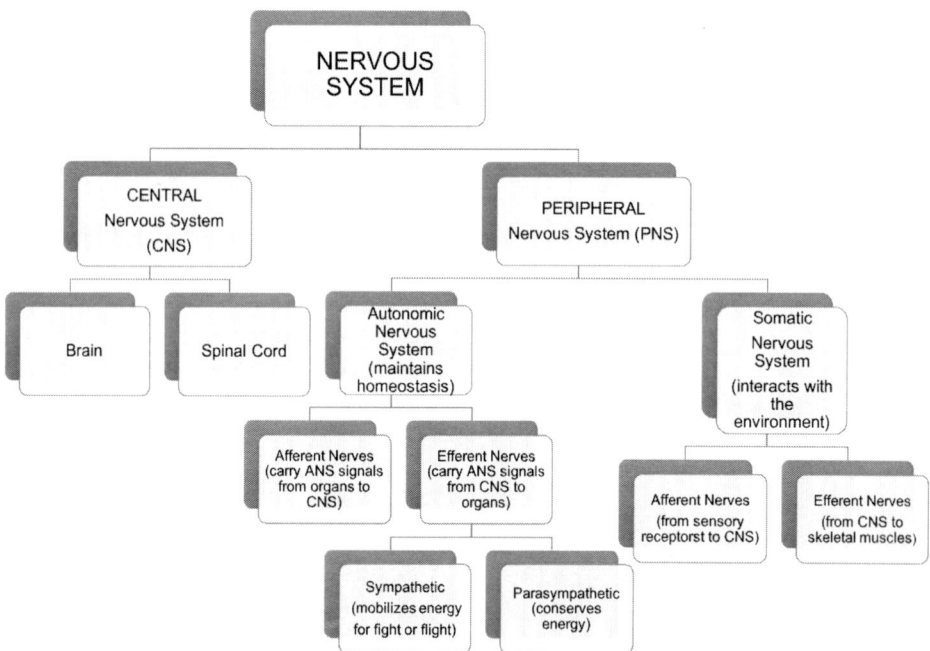

Figure 3.5: Organization of the Nervous System. (From Brick and Erickson, 2009.)

Functional Neuroanatomy

Alcohol affects a multitude of cognitive (thinking) and motor (movement-controlling) functions by altering the normal activity of specialized cells within the cortex, cerebellum, midbrain, and other brain structures. These areas are responsible for all human behaviors, including recognition, and responding to stimulation in our environment, learning, and memory.

The largest brain structure is the cerebral cortex. The cortex has left and right hemispheres that are interconnected by a band of fibers, the corpus callosum, that allows neurochemical information to pass from one side of the brain to the other. Damage to the corpus callosum occurs in many children exposed to high blood alcohol levels during fetal development and may result in behavioral and motor abnormalities, including impulsive, uninhibited behaviors not unlike those that are present during drug intoxication.

The six cellular layers that make up the cerebral cortex form a mosaic of anatomically different sensory (input) and motor (output) cells that perform a number of sensory, motor, and cognitive functions. Sensory signals from muscle and sensory organs from one side of the body go to the opposite side of the cortex. Similarly, sensori-motor afferent signals from the left side of the brain go to the right side of the body, and so on. Surrounding the primary sensory and motor areas are the association areas. Additional association areas are found in the frontal lobes of the cortex, but here there are few, if any, sensory or motor-related cells. Finally, some areas of the cortex are specifically tuned for particular functions (e.g., speech, spatial relationship detection) and are asymmetrically represented (i.e., they occur on one side of the brain but not the other). The functional anatomy of the cortex is depicted in Figure 3.6.

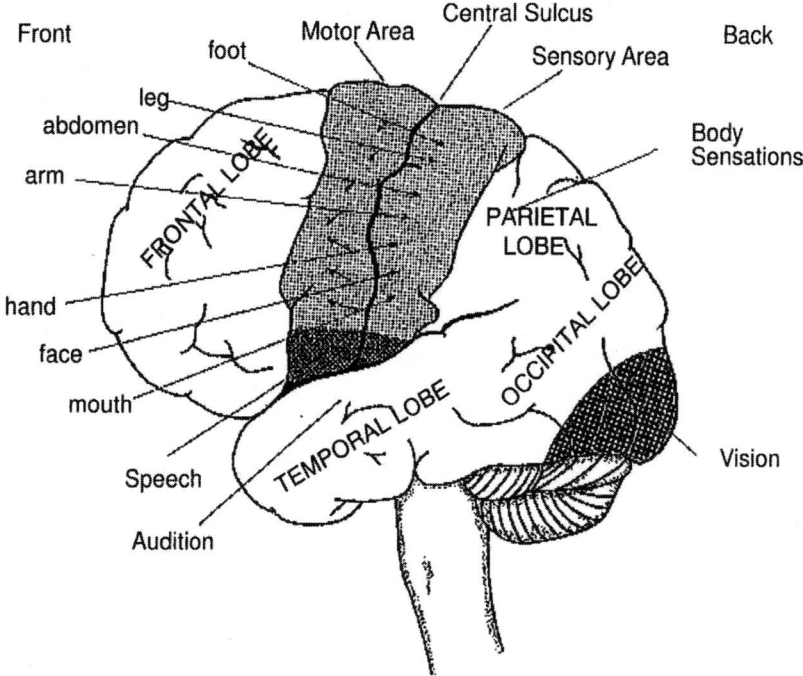

Figure 3.6: Functional Anatomy of the Cortex.

Subcortical Structures

Below the cortex (subcortical) are numerous structures, including the thalamus, hypothalamus, septum, and other groups of cells that form the limbic system. Some of these structures are illustrated in Figures 3.7 and 3.8. The limbic system, sometimes called the reptilian brain, is a collection of evolutionarily old structures involved in emotion. Radical changes in emotion often follow mechanical damage to the limbic system, and these brain areas are probably involved in the emotional lability associated with alcohol intoxication.

Cerebellum

The cerebellum is another prominent structure of the brain (*see* Figures 3.7 and 3.8). It has a multilayered appearance and a number of deeper nuclei. The cerebellum is richly innervated (connected by nerves) with sensory cells and acts as an anatomical way station, modulating information sent from the cortex down the spinal cord and from the spinal cord back to the cortex. The cerebellum is responsible for coordinating the timing and smoothing out of various muscle movements. Acute alcohol intoxication causes changes in nerve impulses routed through the cerebellum and causes ataxia and other motor impairments. Chronic alcohol abuse can result in permanent cerebellar damage and ataxia, even when no alcohol is present.

Brainstem (Midbrain, Pons, Medulla)

The brainstem connects the brain with the spinal cord. The upper part of the brainstem contains the midbrain, pons, and medulla. The midbrain is the most dorsal area of the brainstem. The midbrain is positioned above the pons, receives visual information, regulates eye movement, and processes auditory information. It also regulates muscle movement.

The pons contains a number of important nuclei, including (1) the reticular formation (also called reticular activating system, RAS), which plays an important role in the sleep/waking cycle and motor control; (2) the locus coeruleus, which supplies most of the brain's norepinephrine, a neurochemical transmitter and; (3) the raphe nuclei, another complex of nuclei that supply the neurotransmitter serotonin to many brain regions involved in sleep, pain, aggression, and other behaviors associated with alcohol intoxication. In addition, the pons contains a number of crossing fibers of the descending (efferent) motor system, most notably the pyramidal decussation (*see* Figure 3.7). It is here that neurons cross from one side of the brain to the opposite side of the body.

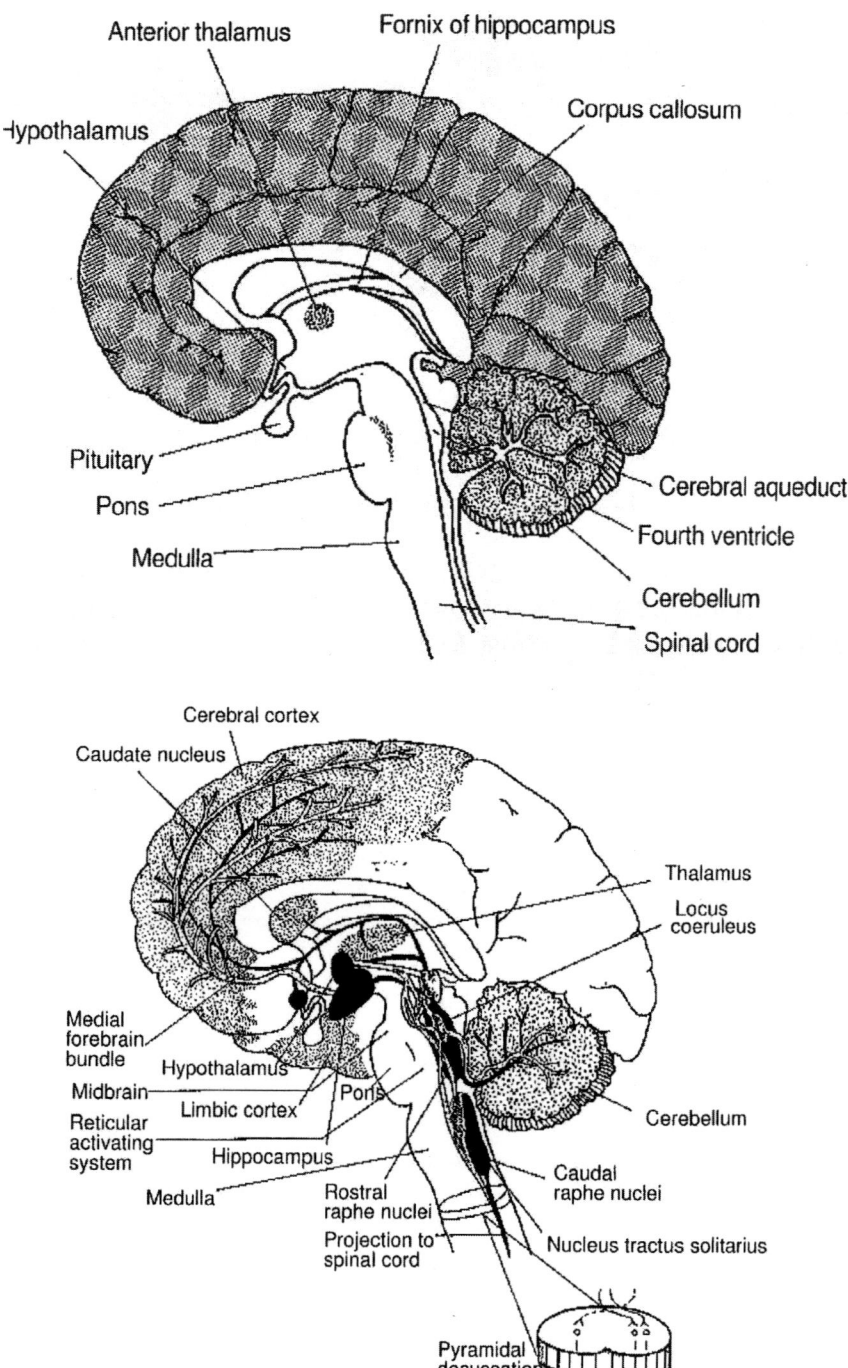

Figure 3.7: Sagittal View of the Brain Illustrating Subcortical Structures and Neural Pathways.

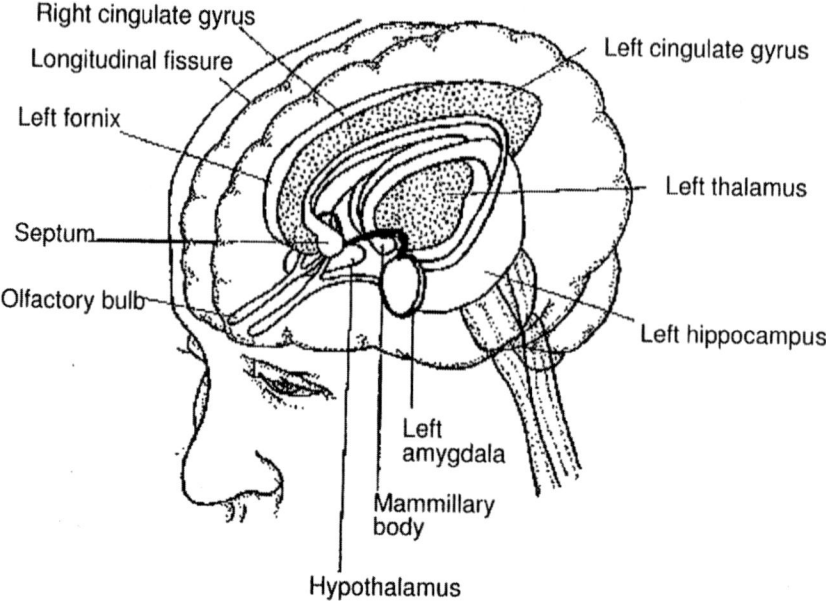

Figure 3.8: Anatomy of Subcortical Limbic System Structures.

Medulla

The medulla is positioned at the top of the spinal cord (Figure 3.7). A prominent feature of the medulla is the decussation (crossing over from one hemisphere to the other) of the corticospinal tracts of the motor cortex before their descent through the lateral corticospinal tract. Damage to one side of the brain may result in sensorimotor impairment on the opposite side of the body (because of the decussation of nerves). Portions of the medulla also contain specialized cells that control, among other things, the vomit reflex. Vomiting from alcohol intoxication is not due to an upset stomach but to the activation of receptors in the medulla. When high or rapidly changing BACs are detected by these receptors, a vomit reflex is activated as an attempt to rid the body of any yet unabsorbed alcohol.

Thalamus

The thalamus is a central subcortical structure that receives all sensory inputs, except olfactory signals, with projections to the sensory area of the cortex. There are seven major anatomical nuclei that make up the thalamus, each with subdivisions. Thus, the thalamus is essentially a relay station where some integrative analysis does occur, but it primarily serves to pass information to higher brain centers. The thalamus also receives projections from the motor cortex and the sensory (e.g., pain) pathways from the spinal cord with the exception of olfactory tract (smell) neurons. All sensory pathways go through the thalamus. The structural appearance of the thalamus suggests its role as a sensory and motor relay station.

Hypothalamus

The hypothalamus is just below the thalamus, hence its name (hypo: beneath, under). The hypothalamus also receives sensory input of many forms as well as input from all divisions of the brain. Because of its anatomical location, many fiber tracts from lower brain centers travel through the hypothalamus without making connections there. Electrical stimulation or destruction of different hypothalamic nuclei alters (among other functions) body weight, fluid intake, temperature regulation, and sexual and aggressive behavior. The hypothalamus communicates with the pituitary gland to regulate hormones as needed and to maintain homeostasis (keeping body functions in their normal limits). Some endocrine and biobehavioral effects of alcohol are due to the effects of alcohol on the hypothalamus. For example, stress-induced changes in the hypothalamic hypophyseal-adrenocortical axis can alter alcohol metabolism by increasing the activity of liver ADH. Such changes in metabolism are only associated with severe stress. The effect of endogenous gonadotropic hormones on alcohol pharmacokinetics and behavior remains controversial (Pohorecky & Brick, 1990; Brick, Nathan, Westrick, Frankenstein & Shapiro, 1986).

Limbic System

The limbic system (Figure 3.8) is involved in memory, emotion, and alcohol-drug effects. It consists of a number of interconnected brain structures and includes the amygdala, hippocampus, hypothalamus, septum, nucleus accumbens, cingulate gyrus, and parts of the cortex. These structures are anatomically interconnected, but whether they function as a unit or not is a topic of considerable debate.

Basal Ganglia

The basal ganglia are important in motor functioning and a key component of the extrapyramidal motor system (a major system coordinating movement). The basal ganglia consist of three major nuclei: the caudate nucleus, the putamen, and the globus pallidus. These nuclei are rich in dopamine, serotonin, and acetylcholine and are involved in the initiation of movement. Alcohol affects all of these neurochemicals and may contribute to the motor impairment characteristic of intoxication.

Pituitary (Master Gland)

The pituitary is an endocrine gland and not part of the nervous system. It receives direct neural inputs as well as vascular (blood vessel) secretions from the hypothalamus. The pituitary releases numerous hormones into the circulation in response to direct nervous system input from the hypothalamus. Hormone release from glands (e.g., adrenal gland) may also be a result of the influence of hormone releasing "factors" from the hypothalamus. The pituitary also responds to circulating levels of hormones in the blood to regulate and maintain physiology and is effected by alcohol (Pohorecky and Brick, 1990).

Ventricles

Between the brain tissue and the skull is a protective envelope of cerebrospinal fluid (CSF). The CSF also travels through the brain in a communicating network of cavities called ventricles. CSF is the circulatory fluid of the nervous system, supplying the neurons and glia (cells that support and nourish neurons) with the necessary nutrients and ions, and serves as a sink for the waste products of these cells. Measurements of drugs, neurotransmitters, or their metabolites are sometimes made in the CSF as an indirect measure of what occurs to the chemistry and function of the brain. Chronic alcohol abuse may lead to ventricular enlargement.

Cranial Nerves

Bundles of nerves transmit information from the outside world through cranial nerves and senses to the brain and within specialized cells in the brain and are responsible for many tasks (Table 3.2). Cranial nerves can be directly or indirectly affected by alcohol intoxication.

Brain Cells

The two major types of cells in the brain are neurons and glia. Neurons within the brain respond to internal changes in their environment as well as to external events, including changes produced by alcohol. In the normally functioning brain, it is the changes in *functional activity* of neurons that produces all behavior, including intoxication and alcohol use disorders.

Table 3.2: Cranial Nerve Function.

	Nerve	General Function
1	Olfactory	Smell
2	Optic	All eye muscles, including iris, vision
3	Oculomotor	Muscles to the eyes, sympathetic fibers to pupillary sphincter
4	Trochlear	Movement to the eyes outward and down
5	Trigeminal	Sensory motor to face, teeth, tongue, jaw muscles
6	Abducens	Nerves to lateral rectus muscle to rotate eyeball outward
7	Facial	Muscles of the face, including parts of tongue, innervates salivary glands, taste in parts of tongue
8	Acoustic	Hearing; vestibular division helps to maintain equilibrium
9	Glossopharyngeal	Sensory part of tongue, muscles of the pharyngeal
10	Vagus	*Motor*–nerve to heart, respiratory system, gastrointestinal system *Sensory*–to heart, larynx, gastrointestinal tract, external parts of the ear
11	Accessory	Sternomastoid and trapezius muscles of the neck
12	Hypoglossal	Muscles of the tongue

Glia help guide neuron connections during brain development, communicate with other cells, and modulate neuron activity as well as part of a local circuit that acts as part of a transporter mechanism that recycles neurotransmitters. For a neuron to transmit its chemical message to another neuron, a series of events involving changes in electrical activity within the cell must take place. This process is key to our current understanding of the mechanisms why all behaviors occur and by which alcohol produces intoxication.

3.3 BASIC NEUROPHYSIOLOGY:
HOW DO NEURONS FUNCTION?

All neurons maintain an electrical charge called a *resting membrane potential,* which is negative (–70 millivolts) in comparison to the charge outside the cell. This is the normal inactive state of brain cells during which there is a negative charge directly related to the distribution of charged ions and other substances within the neuron and in the surrounding environment outside the cell. Whether the brain is involved in sending a motor command to walk (motor skill) or in recalling information (memory task), at the most elementary level, it involves the process of sending a chemical message from one cell to another. This process, called *neurotransmission,* starts with a change in the permeability of the cell membrane to various types (species) of ions, such as sodium (Na^+), potassium (K^+), or chloride (Cl^-). The change in permeability of the cell and movement of ions of positive or negative charges directly alters the resting potential of the neuron and thus brain functioning. Although all discussions of neurotransmission cover the effects on a single neuron (or glia cell), for a neuron to become more or less permeable to ions is the result of many—up to 10,000—inputs from other neurons to ultimately affect the functional activity of that neuron, and changes in a single neuron do not affect behavior. It is the summation of a cascade of events that produces brain changes.

Ion-Gated and Non-Ion-Gated Neurotransmission

Most neurons that are involved in the pharmacological effects of alcohol are ion-gated, meaning activation of receptors on those neurons open or close membrane channels to allow ions to enter the neuron. Ions are molecules that are dissociated into different charged species, either positive or negative. In the brain, the membranes that make up neurons and specialized biological "pumps" separate the ions, keeping some ions outside of the neuron and preventing other ions from escaping from within the neuron. The distribution of variously charged ions and proteins between the inside and the outside of the neuron results in a resting electrical potential across the nerve membrane. Positively charged ions such as Na^+ and other ionic species are kept out of the cell. This results in a negative charge within the neuron. Biological membrane pumps help maintain this balance of a negative resting potential.

Certain physiological events alter the permeability of the membrane that maintains the resting potential, allowing oppositely charged particles to be attracted and similarly charged ions to be repelled. When the permeability of the membrane changes and Na^+ rushes into the neuron, positively charged, potassium (K^+) inside the neuron is forced out. If enough ions are exchanged, the inside resting potential of the cell becomes positively charged, causing a massive exchange of ions called an action potential. The action potential is a change in ion movement that travels down the length of the axon to the axon terminal, making the neuron more and more positively charged. When the action potential reaches the axon terminal of the neuron, it causes storage sacs called vesicles in the cell to move to the edge of the cell membrane and release chemicals stored in the vesicles. This type of neurotransmission is called ion-gated because the process of neurotransmission is directly related to the changes in the charged ions.

Some neurons have protein-linked signaling in which specific molecules function as a "second messenger" to initiate, amplify, and carry on signal transduction within the cell. This non–ion-gated neurotransmission in which a second messenger (the neurotransmitter) binds to a receptor to activate a "G-protein" that signals another change in the postsynaptic neuron. The change is related to a protein, adenyl cyclase, located inside the neuron, and not to ions. Adenyl cyclase in turn transforms chemicals in the cell to second messengers that add phosphate ions to proteins in the cell. This phosphorylation of proteins decreases the interaction between neurotransmitters and their receptors. Some examples of second messengers are cyclic nucleotides, such as cyclic adenosine monophosphate, inositol 1, 4,5-trisphosphate and diacylglycerol, and calcium ions. These and other second messengers may be linked to inhibitory or excitatory second messenger subtypes.

Neurons, glia, and nuclei communicate information about changes in their internal or external environments through the release of neurotransmitter. Neurotransmitters are manufactured and stored within the neuron and released as a consequence of the action potential. To date, more than sixty neurotransmitters have been identified. Some of the best-studied neurotransmitters, as well as some of the biobehavioral functions they relate to, are listed in Table 3.3.

Once released from the axon terminal of the neuron, neurotransmitters enter into a small physical space, the synapse that separates the presynaptic neuron from the postsynaptic neuron. The neurotransmitter then comes in contact with receptors (binding sites) in the next neuron, located across the synapse from the axon terminal of the "first" (presynaptic) neuron. Depending upon the type of receptor that it binds to, and the type of neurotransmitter, the neurotransmitter substance will then increase or decrease the probability of an action potential in the affected neuron. In some neurons, increases in ion flux that follow excitatory postsynaptic potentials (EPSPs) increase the probability of an action potential. This state is caused by excitatory neurotransmitters, such as glutamate, an important neurotransmitter modulating some of the effects of alcohol. Inhibitory postsynaptic potentials (IPSPs) that decrease ion flux in the postsynaptic neuron have the opposite effect. Inhibitory neurotransmitters, such as γ-aminobutyric acid (GABA), another

Table 3.3: Neurotransmitters and Identified Functions.

Neurotransmitter	Identified Function	Affected by Alcohol?
Acetylcholine (+)	Motor systems, learning, active nicotine dependence	Yes
Aspartate (+)	Alcohol intoxication, stimulates N-methyl-D-aspartate (NMDA, a type of glutamate receptor)	Yes
Dopamine (±)	Motor systems, pleasure/reward, mental illness, craving for alcohol	Yes
Endocannabinoids (–)	Receptor for tetrahydrocannabinol the active ingredient in marijuana, mood, pain control	?
Endorphins (–) (ß-endorphin, enkephalins, and dynorphins)	Released during stress, pain, learning, eating; affected by opioid drugs	Yes
Epinephrine (+)	Sympathetic arousal	Yes
γ-aminobutyric acid (GABA) (–)	Relaxation/anxiety, alcohol intoxication–metabolism, mood inhibiting transmitter	Yes
Glutamate (+)	Alcohol intoxication, other drugs as well, excitatory transmitter, stimulates NMDA receptors	Yes
Norepinephrine (+)	Arousal, stress, mental illness, learning, sleep	Yes
Opioid peptides (–)	Pain regulation, learning, eating, "addiction," relaxation, mood, pain control	Yes
Serotonin (–)	Sleep, dreaming, mental illness	Yes
Substance P (–)	Pain perception, stress, mood disorders	Yes

Key: (-) Inhibitory neurotransmitter, (+) Excitatory neurotransmitter

important neurotransmitter in the neuropharmacology of alcohol intoxication, decrease the probability of an action potential. Neurons have the ability to recognize and pass on signals from neurotransmitters. If a neuron fires continually at a certain rate, it can be excited or inhibited by changes in its environment (e.g., from toxins). If a neuron is normally at rest, changes will be excitatory. Alcohol (and other drugs) interferes with signal transmission mediated by a number of neurotransmitters (Table 3.3).

When the neurotransmitter returns to the synapse, (a) It may be metabolized by enzymes, (b) It may contact other receptors, (c) Neurotransporters may transport it back into the neuron from which it came (previously termed reuptake). Inside the neuron, the neurotransmitter may be subject to enzymatic degradation or it may be repackaged into storage vesicles for future release. There are some exceptions to this. For example, the neurotransmitter glutamate is transported from the synapse to glial cells, where is it restored for future synthesis back to glutamate, as needed.

3.4 NEUROPHARMACOLOGY OF ALCOHOL INTOXICATION

With the previous basic review, we can appreciate that alcohol affects virtually every organ system in the body and alters the activity of most major neurochemicals. This explains, in part, the wide range of biobehavioral effects produced by its ingestion. Although there are many scientific models of alcohol's effects on several different neurotransmitters in the brain, the current research focuses on the effects of alcohol on four neurotransmitter receptors. Although alcohol does not act at a specific receptor in the classic lock-and-key analogy that applies to some other drugs, such as opiates, the effects of alcohol at specific receptor sites explain many of the biobehavioral effects of alcohol intoxication and related alcohol use disorders.

The sites most relevant to understanding the effects of alcohol are the (1) *N*-methyl-D-aspartate (NMDA) glutamate receptor, (2) a (non-NMDA) glutamate receptor, (3) the GABA receptor, and (4) the nicotine (nicotinic) receptor.

Glutamate (also called glutamic acid) is a nonessential amino acid, meaning that it can be synthesized from other molecules in the body. Glutamate is a basic building block for proteins and an important excitatory neurotransmitter found in high concentrations throughout the brain. Glutamate exerts its effects on neurons through several types of receptors that, when activated, allow positively charged ions into the cell, causing depolarization and an action potential, as previously discussed (IPSP). Deactivation of glutamate receptor activation is accomplished by specific carrier proteins that transport glutamate back into the presynaptic neuron, where it is stored in synaptic vesicles, or transported into surrounding glial cells, where it is converted to glutamine to act as a precursor for future needed glutamate, and repackaged into synaptic vesicles.

There are two broad families of glutamate receptors: ionotropic and metabotropic. Ionotropic receptors are gated and when activated allow ions to enter the postsynaptic neuron; metabotropic receptors gate ions indirectly through second messengers. The three major ionotropic receptors are α-amino-3-hydroxy-5-methyl-4-isoxyazole-propionic acid (AMPA), kainate, and NMDA. Although the mechanisms vary, when activated by glutamate binding, all three receptors allow positively charged ions (Na_+, $Ca2_+$) to enter the postsynaptic neuron, causing depolarization. If sufficient numbers of receptors are activated, an action potential is initiated. Low concentrations of alcohol can inhibit the excitatory activity of the NMDA receptor. This inhibition of the NMDA receptor may contribute to changes in cellular development and abnormalities such as fetal alcohol syndrome, alcohol-related learning disabilities and cognitive deficits, and components of alcohol withdrawal. Although this is a complex field of study, there is evidence that alcohol-induced inhibition of NMDA receptors plays a role in many of the pharmacological and toxicological consequences of acute and chronic alcohol use. Studies of operate discrimination (e.g., reward taste tests) suggest that the inhibition of NMDA receptors may contribute to some of the behavioral effects of alcohol.

GABA

GABA is a major inhibitory neurotransmitter found throughout the brain that interacts with the receptor site that also recognizes anxiolytic and sedative benzodiazepines, anesthetic barbiturates, and endogenous neurosteroids related directly or indirectly to GABA ion-gated receptors. However, unlike glutamate, activation of GABA allows negative ions (e.g., Cl–) to enter the cell, causing hyperpolarization and inhibition. Activation of the GABA receptor produces behavior similar to that from alcohol, including anxiolytic and depressant properties, learning impairments, cross-tolerance and cross-dependence with alcohol (Crews, 2008; Hobbs, Rall & Verdoorn, 1996). There are several variants of the GABA receptor, including $GABA_A$. Alcohol also interacts with the $GABA_A$ receptor. Converging evidence from a variety of sources indicates that much like other anxiolytics, such as benzodiazepines, alcohol significantly alters GABA neurotransmission. GABA may mediate many of the acute behavioral effects, such as alcohol-induced motor incoordination, anxiolysis, and sedation. GABA also plays an important role in the development of alcohol tolerance and susceptibility to alcohol dependence (Mihic & Harris, 1997; Grobin, Matthews, Devaud & Marrow, 1998).

One interesting example is alcohol's effect on the GABA-linked changes in chloride ions. $GABA_A$ activation causes an influx of negatively charged chloride ions (Cl–) into neurons. Alcohol potentiates $GABA_A$ receptor activity at low BACs, but this effect is antagonized by imidazobenzodiazepine (RO 15-4513), an inverse antagonist. This experimental drug also blocked many of the behavioral effects of alcohol intoxication at low doses. Since other benzodiazepine receptor antagonists tested also blocked the anti-alcohol action of RO 15-4513, it is suggested that at least some of the effects of alcohol were mediated through this specific GABA receptor complex, much like but not exactly the same as benzodiazepines (Paul, 2006). What makes this effect so intriguing is that although altering the GABA receptor complex blocks alcohol-induced behavioral impairment, there is no change in BAC. In other words, the subject is still pharmacologically intoxicated (at high levels), but there is no impairment on behavioral tests that are normally sensitive to alcohol intoxication. Taken together, these findings suggest that there is a specific alcohol binding site on GABA A receptors that is shared by the alcohol antagonist Ro15-4513 however, electrophysiological studies show that this effect is not universal and occurs only in some brain areas.

REFERENCES

Brick, J., and Erickson, C. K. (2009). *Drugs, the Brain and Behavior: The Pharmacology of Drug Use Disorders.* New York, NY: Routledge Press.

Brick, J., Nathan, P. E., Westrick, E., Frankenstein, W., and Shapiro, A. (1986). The effect of menstrual cycle on blood alcohol levels and behavior. *Journal of Studies on Alcohol, 47,* 472–477.

Carpenter, T., and Lee, R. (1937). The effect of glucose on the metabolism of ethyl alcohol in man. *Journal of Pharmacology and Experimental Therapeutics, 60*(3), 264–285.

Clothier, J., Kelly, J., and Reed, K. (1985). Varying rates of alcohol metabolism in relation to detoxification and medication. *Alcohol, 2,* 443–445.

Crews, F. (2008). Effects of alcohol abuse on brain neurochemistry. In J. Brick (Ed.), *Handbook of the Medical Consequences of Alcohol and Drug Abuse* (pp. 123–176). New York, NY: Haworth Press.

Davenport, H. W. (1961). *Physiology of the Digestive Tract* (3rd ed.). Chicago, IL: Year Book Medical Publishing.

Dubowski, K. (1985). Absorption, distribution and elimination of alcohol: Highway safety aspects. *Journal on Studies of Alcohol Supplement, 10,* 98–108.

Erickson, C. K. (2007). *The Science of Addiction: From Neurobiology to Treatment.* New York, NY: W. W. Norton Company.

Grobin, A.C., Matthews, D.B., Devaud, L.L., and Morrow, A.L. (1998). The role of GABA(A) receptors in the acute and chronic effects of ethanol. *Psychopharmacology (Berlin), 139*(1-2), 2–19.

Hobbs, W., Rall, T., and Verdoorn, T. (1996). *Drugs Acting on the Central Nervous System* In J. G. Hardman, L. E. Limbard, P. B. Molinoff, R. W. Ruddon, and A. G. Gilman (Eds.), *Goodman & Gilman's The Pharmacological Basis of Therapeutics* (9th ed., pp. 361–396). New York, NY: McGraw-Hill.

Jones, A. W. (1983). Effects of fructose, glucose and mixed sugars on ethanol detoxification and blood glucose response in rats. *Medical Biology, 61*(6), 319-323.

Jones, A. W. (2008). Biochemical and physiological research on the disposition and fate of ethanol in the body. In J.C. Garriot (Ed.), *Garriot's Medicolegal Aspects of Alcohol* (5th ed., pp. 47–128). Tucson, AZ: Lawyers and Judges Publishing Company.

Jones, A. W. (2010). Evidence-based survey of the elimination rates of ethanol from blood with applications in forensic casework. *Forensic Sciences International, 200*(1-3), 1–20.

Jones, A. W., and Neri, A. (1991). Evaluation of blood-ethanol profiles after consumption of alcohol together with a large meal. *Canadian Society of Forensic Science Journal, 24*, 165–173.

Levitt, M. D., and Levitt, D. G. (1998). Use of a two-compartment model to assess the pharmacokinetics of human ethanol metabolism. *Alcoholism, Clinical and Experimental Research, 22*, 1680–1688.

Lieber, C. S. (1994a). Mechanisms of ethanol-drug-nutrition interactions. *Journal of Toxicology. Clinical Toxicology, 32*, 631–681.

Lieber, C. S. (1994b). Alcohol and the liver: 1994 update. *Gastroenterology, 106*, 1085–1105.

Lieberman, F. L. (1963). The effect of liver disease on the rate of ethanol metabolism in man. *Gastroenterology, 44*, 261–266.

Lim, R. T. Jr., Gentry, R. T., Ito, D., Yokoyama, H., Baraona, E., and Lieber, C. S. (1993). First-pass metabolism of ethanol is predominantly gastric. *Alcoholism, Clinical and Experimental Research, 17*, 1337–1344.

Lowenstein, L., Simore, R., Boulter, P., and Nathan, P. (1970). Effect of fructose on alcohol concentrations in the blood of man. *JAMA, 213*, 1899–1901.

Luu, S. U., Wang, M. F., Lin, D. L., Kao, M. H., Chen, M. L., Chiang, CH., …, Yin, S. J. (1995). Ethanol and acetaldehyde metabolism in Chinese with different aldehyde dehydrogenase-2 genotypes. *Proceedings of the National Science Council, Republic of China, Part B, Life Sciences, 19*(3), 129–136.

Madsen, J. L. (1992). Effects of gender, age, and body mass index on gastrointestinal transit times. *Digestive Diseases and Science, 37*(10), 1548–1553.

Marczinski, C. A., and Stamates, A. L. (2013). Artificial sweeteners versus regular mixers increase breath alcohol concentrations in male and female social drinkers. *Alcoholism, Clinical and Experimental Research, 37*(4), 696–702.

Mascord, D., Smith, J., Starmer, G.A., and Whitfield, J. B. (1991). The effect of fructose on alcohol metabolism and on the [lactate]/[pyruvate] ratio in man. *Alcohol and Alcoholism, 26*(1), 53–59.

McFarlane, A., Pooley, L., Welch, I. M., Rumsey, R. D., and Read, N.W. (1986). How does dietary lipid lower blood alcohol concentrations? *Gut, 27*, 15–18.

Mihic, S. J., and Harris, R. A. (1997). GABA and the GABAA receptor. *Alcohol Health & Research World, 21*(2), 127–131.

Mumenthaler, M. S., Taylor, J. L., and Yesavage, J. A. (2000). Ethanol pharmacokinetics in white women: Nonlinear model fitting versus zero-order elimination analyses. *Alcoholism, Clinical and Experimental Research, 24*(9), 1353–1362.

Paul, S. M. (2006). Alcohol-sensitive GABA receptors and alcohol antagonists. *Proceedings of the National Academy of Sciences of the United States of America, 103*(22), 8307–8308.

Perl, J., and Starmer G. (1983). Lowered blood ethanol concentrations after a sugar-based drink. *The Medical Journal of Australia, 1*(13): 600

Pohorecky, L., and Brick, J. (1990). The pharmacology of alcohol. In D. Balfour (Ed.), *Encyclopedia of Therapeutics* (pp. 189–582). New York, NY: Pergamon Press.

Ramchadnani, V. A., Kwo, P. Y., and Li, T. K. (2001). Effect of food and food composition on alcohol elimination rates in healthy men and women. *Journal of Clinical Pharmacology, 41*, 1345–1350.

Roberts, C., and Robinson, S. P. (2007). Alcohol concentration and carbonation of drinks: The effect on blood alcohol levels. *Journal of Forensic and Legal Medicine, 14*(7), 398–405.

Roine, R. P., Gentry, R. T., Lim, R. T. Jr., Baraona, E., and Lieber, C. S. (1991). Effect of concentration of ingested ethanol on blood alcohol levels. *Alcoholism, Clinical and Experimental Research, 15*, 734–738.

Roine, R. P., Gentry, R. T., Lim, R. T., Helkkonen, E., Salaspuro, M., and Lieber, C. S. (1993). Comparison of blood alcohol concentrations after beer and whiskey. *Alcoholism, Clinical and Experimental Research, 17*, 709–711.

Rose, E. F. (1979). Factors influencing gastric emptying. *Journal of Forensic Science, 24*, 200–206.

Rossheim, M. E., and Thombs, D. L. (2011). Artificial sweeteners, caffeine, and alcohol intoxication in bar patrons. *Alcoholism, Clinical and Experimental Research, 35*(10), 1891–1896.

Salmela, K. S., Salaspuro, M., Gentry, R. T., Methuen, T., Höök Nikanne, J., Kosunen, T. U., and Roine, R. P. (1994). Helicobacter infection and gastric ethanol metabolism. *Alcoholism, Clinical and Experimental Research, 18*(6), 1294–1299.

Stamates, A. L., Maloney, S. F., and Marczinski, C. A. (2015). Effects of artificial sweeteners on breath alcohol concentrations in male and female social drinkers. *Drug and Alcohol Dependence, 157*, 197–199.

Sutker, P. B., Goist, K. C. Jr., and King, A. R. (1987). Acute alcohol intoxication in women: Relationship to dose and menstrual cycle phase. *Alcoholism, Clinical and Experimental Research, 11*, 74–79.

Thomasson, H. (1995). Gender differences in alcohol metabolism. Physiological responses to ethanol. *Recent Developments in Alcoholism, 12*, 163–179.

Thomasson, H. (2000). Alcohol elimination: Faster in women? *Alcoholism, Clinical and Experimental Research, 24*(4), 419–420.

Wall, T. L., Peterson, C. M., Peterson, K. P., Johnson, M. L., Thomasson, H. R., Cole, M., and Ehlers, C. L. (1997). Alcohol metabolism in Asian-American men with genetic polymorphisms of aldehyde dehydrogenase. *Annals of Internal Medicine, 127*, 376–379.

Weathermon, R., and Crabb, D. W. (1999). *Alcohol and medication interactions. Alcohol Research & Health, 23*(1), 40–54.

Widmark, E. (1981). *Principles and Application of Medicolegal Alcohol Determination* (R.C. Baselt, trans.). Davis, CA: Biomedical Publications. (Original work published 1932).

Wilkinson, P. K., Sedman, A.J., Sakmar, E., Kay, D. R., and Wagner, J.G. (1977). Pharmacokinetics of ethanol after oral administration in the fasting state. *Journal of Pharmacokinetics and Biopharmaceuticals, 5*, 207–224.

Winek, C. L., and Murphy, K. L. (1984). The rate and kinetic order of ethanol elimination. *Forensic Science International, 25*(3), 159–166.

Chapter 4

LABORATORY AND CLINICAL-BASED
TESTS OF IMPAIRMENT

4.1 TYPES OF RESEARCH

There are basically two broad types of investigation on the biobehavioral effects of alcohol: research conducted in the laboratory and research conducted *in situ* or in simulated or actual real-world environments. Laboratory studies provide a scientific construct or model to explain events in the real world. For example, studies of perception, memory, reaction time, and sensory processing in the laboratory may explain why alcohol intoxication is overly represented in motor vehicle crashes, violent crimes and other well-observed relationships gleaned from large-scale data collection (epidemiological) studies. In addition to developing models of complex real-world behavior, laboratory studies have the distinct advantage of allowing researchers to create a controlled experimental design in which variables can be manipulated (independent variables), and some quantitative measurement (dependent variables) clearly identified or operationally defined. When independent variables (e.g., different doses of alcohol) can be identified as a causative factor in an experimental outcome, quantitative results from such research may have valuable and practical application to real-world situations. For example, if it can be demonstrated that alcohol produces a dose-dependent increase in reaction time or decrease in attention starting at a particular BAC, a logical conclusion might be that such impairment would explain any observed increase in motor vehicle crashes also starting at about the same BAC.

On the other hand, pure laboratory-based research has potential disadvantages because it may require subjects to respond to stimuli in an unnatural setting, which may affect behavior or measure behavior that is not related to real-world situations or responses. Also, some laboratory tests can be so complex that pretest training sessions are required or are overly sensitive to variables beyond the administration of alcohol. Such effects may yield statistically significant effects that have little clinical or practical value when applied to the real world.

Finally, although reviews of many hundreds of laboratory studies on a variety of tasks indicate that alcohol impairs sensory, motor, and psychomotor systems, some results are inconsistent. In most cases, these inconsistencies are not due to a failure to reproduce findings, although that does happen, but more often because different experimental designs make comparisons among studies difficult. Questions about human physiology and behavior are complex and require complex and often different approaches to answer the same question. Therefore, it is logical that different approaches might yield different results.

Regardless of the research approach, our knowledge of the biobehavioral effects of alcohol advances and is based on the scientific method. In the process, we (1) make observations leading to the formulation of a question, (2) develop a hypothesis, (3) conduct systematic observations and tests to determine if the hypothesis should be accepted or rejected, and (4) ask more questions and develop a conclusion based on evidence that allows us to test our hypothesis to allow accurate and reliable predictions.

In the case of alcohol studies, this knowledge is accumulated based on a combination of empirical laboratory testing and epidemiological fieldwork. Together these results bring us closer to understanding the effects of alcohol. In this chapter we will focus on research that has a reasonably direct application to the safe operation of a motor vehicle, as well as other activities, including cycling, water sports and pedestrian activity. Each of these activities requires specialized psychomotor skills and sensory abilities logically suspected and now known to be affected by alcohol.

Early Origins of Testing

Research on the biobehavioral effects of alcohol began to gain momentum in the early 1900s as society became motorized and brought with it a new type of injury, namely, those caused by intoxicated motorists. As both public and scientific interest in drunk driving increased, the need for identifying intoxication increased. Then, as now, simply describing someone as drunk was highly subjective and not reliable, as subjective criteria for being drunk were not standardized. In the early 1900s, Swedish scientist E.M.P. Widmark developed a list of "factors" to enable physicians who worked with police (police surgeons) to identify impaired drivers in a systematic manner. This early lab-based research is reflected in many police drinking and driving or alcohol-influence reports that still incorporate many of Widmark's original signs or factors of intoxication. Some of the factors identified by Widmark include pulse, reaction of pupils to light, signs of ataxia (insecure turning), Romberg test, finger-to-nose test, picking up small objects, speech, orientation, and mental power.

Although some of Widmark's factors were measurable (e.g., mental power, pupil size) or adapted from basic neurology (e.g., Romberg test, finger-to-nose, speech, orientation), others were quite subjective in nature (e.g., general appearance, ability to pick up objects). As interest and a need for more objective evidence-based measures of impairment related to driving increased, so did laboratory research in this area. This gave rise to the first widely used empirically based tests of impairment. Eventually, various psychophysical tests became routinely administered by police, later to be augmented through the use of research-based, standardized field sobriety tests (SFSTs), discussed at the end of this chapter.

4.2 SENSORY PSYCHOMOTOR EFFECTS OF ALCOHOL

Psychophysical tests and observations, such as those developed by Widmark, were helpful but a more detailed and specific examination of factors directly related to driving was needed. Laboratory-based examination of the visual and sensory responses, learning, memory, perception, judgment, expectation, and related effects of alcohol provided the answer. These data were eventually used by legislators to pass laws and by law enforcement in the investigation and enforcement of those laws prohibiting intoxicated driving. Driving and related activities (e.g., pedestrian activity, bicycling) require multiple levels of psychological and physiological processing. Many sensory and psychomotor systems are involved in tasks such as walking or riding a bicycle that expose subjects to potentially physically distracting stimuli such as rain, snow (tactile, temperature sensory mechanisms), and sounds from other vehicles (auditory system). These stimuli may be less distracting to the driver within the enclosed interior of a car or truck, for example. However, motor vehicle operation and other related behavioral activities are heavily dependent on the visual system. It has been stated that 90 percent of roadway information available to a driver is visual in nature (Sivak, 1996) and, although not documented, is believed to be a reasonable estimate (Dewer, Olson & Alexander, 2002). As a result of this logical assumption, there is abundant evidence from decades of research that the processing of visual sensory information is affected by alcohol.

To respond in any way to any event, in our world requires awareness of the event, and it matters not whether the subject is sober or intoxicated. The prerequisites for any situation include detection, perception, decision making and response. Together these elements make up what we call Total Detection Perception Reaction (ΣDPR).

Detection

In order to respond to any event, it must first be detected. Detection is defined as the threshold or period between presentation of a stimulus and seeing it. Seeing or detecting an object does not necessarily mean identifying it. Detection begins when energy (e.g., light, sound, vibration, odorants, heat) impacts on a sensory receptor designed to respond to that energy. If there is sufficient depolarization of these receptors, sensory information is transmitted to the nervous system, as described in Chapter 3. Some sensorimotor responses are reflexive in nature and involve parts of the nervous system but not the brain. However, in most forensic applications the sensory information travels via the cranial nerves or spinal cord to the brain. Light striking chromatic (cone) or achromatic (rod) receptors located in the retina of the eye, sound waves affecting receptors in the cochlea of the inner ear, or pressure temperature or pain receptors in the skin send signals upstream to the brain, where they are processed. If information is not detected at the sensory level, there will be no response because as far as the subject is concerned, the event (whatever it was) did not happen. This is an important condition in accidental injuries and in forensic alcohol cases. Moreover, if subjects are too intoxicated to be looking where they are driving, walking, or sitting, they may never detect a hazard and therefore never process and respond to it.

Laboratory research has focused on components of visual processing intuitively reasoned to be of importance in detecting hazards or other roadway issues that are primarily visual in nature. These include studies of the following:

- Visual Accommodation: The contraction and extension of the lens of the eyes to focus objects on the retina. For example, the ability to rapidly refocus between objects that are close (e.g., dashboard instruments) and distant objects (roadway) requires visual accommodation.
- Contrast Sensitivity: The ability to discriminate objects of similar brightness relative to their background would also seem to be important. For example, detecting a pedestrian in dark clothing or a dark vehicle at night or under conditions of low lighting requires contrast sensitivity.
- Stimulus Detection Thresholds: The effects of alcohol on vision, including the ability to detect low-intensity targets is of obvious importance in driving, particularly since most fatal alcohol-related motor vehicle accidents occur at night.
- Distance Vision: The distance required to detect an object.
- Evoked Potentials: The electrical response of the brain to visual or auditory signals (*see* Chapter 3 for a discussion of action potentials).

- Adaptation: The ability of the visual system to adjust to changes in light sensitivity that might be experienced when entering or exiting a tunnel, for example. Also, the majority of driver and pedestrian accidents occur at night under conditions of lower illumination. Although potentially important, many of these studies yielded equivocal results and in some instances the effect of alcohol was variable or not due to sensory impairment, as believed.
- Glare Sensitivity or Recovery: This is a measure of change in response or recovery encountering glare that might be relevant for driver looking at or exposed to oncoming headlights, for example.

Earlier researchers sometimes refer to these as studies of perception, but we believe they are more accurately described as studies of detection, a necessary first step in the process. These findings are of obvious relevance to driving, but results are sometimes inconsistent or the interpretation more complex than it appears. There are many studies demonstrating that alcohol deleteriously affects vision in some subjects and at some BACs (Moskowitz & Robinson, 1988; Moskowitz & Fiorentino, 2000), but some effects of alcohol are not as universal as commonly believed. For example, delay in glare recovery due to alcohol is commonly referred to as a factor in the lay literature and elsewhere. In one of the early classic studies, it was reported that 40 percent of the intoxicated subjects tested showed impaired recovery from glare. Not as widely reported in the popular literature, however, is the fact that a similar percentage of subjects showed improvement from glare recovery. Only 24 percent of the fifty subjects showed any change even though the BAC ranged from 58 to 218 mg/dL (Newman & Fletcher, 1940).

Adams and Brown (1975) reported that even extremely low BACs (10 mg/dL) impaired glare recovery. However, this effect has not always been replicated even at much higher BACs. Other studies show similar inconsistent results (Mortimer, 1963; Verriest & Laplasse, 1965). Wallgren and Barry (1970) found that low alcohol doses producing BACs of up to 65 mg/dL had no effect on dark adaptation or brightness sensitivity, and in some cases, alcohol has been shown to improve brightness sensitivity. Sekuler and MacArthur (1977) found no effect of alcohol (up to 100 mg/dL) on glare recovery, but they did find that alcohol affected target acquisition. In other words, in this, and possibly previous studies, the effect of alcohol may not have been on glare recovery but on the ability to acquire the brightness comparison target (used to measure recovery time).

Whether glare recovery is a detection failure, sensitivity change, or misidentified divided attention failure, it continues to be a reported effect of alcohol intoxication (Gupta, Lata & Kaur, 2012). Most studies on the effects of alcohol on basic visual detection, static visual acuity, contrast sensitivity, and ocular motor control appear at BACs above about 70 mg/dL (Moskowitz & Fiorentino, 2000; Starmer, 1989). Assuming that an object is detected either in the lab or on the roadway, the next step is to process and interpret the object and decide upon a response.

4.3 PERCEPTION AND INFORMATION PROCESSING

Although the effects of alcohol on detection are most apparent at higher BACs, what follows detection includes several different forms of perception, information processing, and attention that are sensitive to impairment at relatively low BACs. Research in this area often separates these as different tasks or fails to differentiate them because of methodological limitations. Collectively, and for the purposes of forensic analyses, they all share some common elements: each requires detection and the allocation of mental resources and processing of information. Research on the effects of alcohol on driving-related skills focuses on these dependent variables because they are believed to reflect skills necessary for safe motor vehicle operation and related activities. For our purpose, which is the application of research to everyday forensic evaluations, perception and information processing are not differentiated.

Perception, sometimes termed recognition, refers to cognitive processing that follows the detection of sensory information. Cognitive processing is a psychological term that typically includes components of learning, memory, and association. For example, once an object has been detected, that information is transmitted from sensory reception via cranial nerves to the brain, where cognitive processing identifies the information to determine, is it important? Has it been seen before? Is it perceived as moving closer or further away? Is it perceived as an immediate hazard or does it create a situation with the potential to increase risk or cause an accident or some other untoward event unless there is a response?

Consider the everyday task of driving an automobile. The driving environment is complex and contains many visual elements. Among these are other vehicles, signs, lane markings, traffic control devices, potholes, hazardous debris, animals, and pedestrians in or near the roadway. Other senses may be involved, such as detecting and processing a siren, horn, engine noise (auditory), or the vibration (tactile and auditory) from rumble strips, and so on. A sober person detects and processes environmental information and determines its relevance. For example, drivers may detect but not actively look for or process passing exit signs if they know their exit is far from the current location. Other roadway information, such as an oncoming vehicle, pedestrian, traffic control device, and roadway (or walkway) hazards will have a higher relative weighting that requires further cognitive processing. For example, a vehicle cutting in and out of lanes at high speed without signaling attracts and requires driver attention and processing to include mental computations of vehicle trajectory, speed, distance, and time, coupled with previous experience or expectations. Based on the totality of this processing, a response may be required. In contrast, a vehicle moving at the same rate as other vehicles and maintaining lane position is less likely to attract attention or be perceived as a hazard. Similarly, a pedestrian crossing a roadway must observe and identify oncoming vehicles and traffic control devices and make mental computations to determine if there is enough time to cross the roadway. Is the pedestrian (or driver) close enough to continue through an intersection when the light changes from green to yellow, or should he or she stop?

Decades of research on the effects of alcohol on widely varying tasks have demonstrated impairment starting at relatively low BACs for (mostly) visual and perceptual tasks involving reaction time (30 mg/dL); pursuit tracking (20–30 mg/dL); concentrated attention (60 mg/dL); divided attention (20–30 mg/dL); information processing (20–40 mg/dL); visual functions (30 mg/dL); perception (20–40 mg/dL); and driver-related tests such as steering, braking, and distance judgment (30 mg/dL) and has been widely reported (Moskowitz & Robinson, 1988). Although not all research has demonstrated impairment at such low BACs. For example, MacArthur and Sekuler (1982) reported that at a BAC of 60 mg/dL alcohol caused a 10 to 15 percent reduction in the perception of objects moving at very slow speeds, but perception of rapidly moving objects was not affected by alcohol. It is clear that with increasing BACs in multiple domains of behavior are further impaired and consistently reported (Moskowitz, 2008; Moskowitz and Fiorentino, 2000; Starmer, 1989).

Time estimates, visual searching, pattern recognition and traffic hazard perception studies require varying degrees of mental workload and different sensitivities to alcohol.

Attention

Concentrated Attention

If a driver does not pay attention to the roadway, the risk of an accident is obviously increased. It can be stated that all laboratory tests of detection and perception require attention, but research in this area has focused on two specific types of attention: concentrated attention and divided attention. Laboratory studies of concentrated attention examine vigilance, and the subject is asked to detect and process low levels of information over long periods. Generally, older studies on vigilance garnered little interest because the results were equivocal (Moskowitz & Robinson, 1988). Koelega (1995) noted that many reviews of the effect of alcohol on attention included relatively few studies on vigilance, noting further that studies purporting to measure vigilance were actually measuring a mixture of detection tasks and selected attention. Therefore, the effects of alcohol on attention probably include a combination of types of attention and different levels of processing that are task specific.

Dougherty, Marsh, Moeller, Chokshi, and Rosen (2000) noted that reviews of studies on vigilance included multiple measures over time spans that ranged from about 8 minutes to 8 hours, which coupled with different methodologies and variables, may have contributed to the reported inconsistencies in this literature. Dougherty's own research indicated few changes in concentrated attention across three phases of the blood alcohol curve (ascending, peak, and descending) in the low-dose condition (39 mg/dL peak BAC) but significant changes in the high-dose condition (91 mg/dL peak BAC). Most recent studies reported impairment in concentrated attention when BACs were 30 mg/dL or higher (Moskowitz, 2008), but there is no clear consensus of scientific opinion on the effects of alcohol on simple vigilance. Also, vigilance as operationally defined in some studies may not reflect the type of attention required during motor vehicle operation.

Of particular note is the fact that driving is a task requiring, if not sustained attention, ongoing attention, which may not be measured with some tests. The ongoing demand that the brain attend to or process an endless stream of environmental data suggests more research on the effect of time on task to certain performance measures is needed. Initially, performance may not be so impaired as to be of clinical or real-world influence but may deteriorate over time. Case in point: rarely do intoxicated drivers crash in the parking lots of bars or restaurants but more often crash some distance away. In addition to possible time on task effects, blood alcohol levels will continue to rise for some period after drinking ends. This may result in increasing intoxication after leaving the bar and while driving. This is a large and complex area of research as evidenced by many exhaustive reviews on the effects of alcohol on attention and information processing (Carpenter, 1962; Dinges and Kribbs, 1990; Koelega, 1995; Moskowitz, 1973; Moskowitz & Fiorentino 2000; Moskowitz & Robinson, 1988; Perrine, 1973).

Divided Attention

In real-world driving, however, in addition to psychomotor tasks (e.g., eye-arm-hand-leg-foot coordination) and possibly concentrated attention, a more relevant cognitive task is divided attention. Divided attention requires the driver to attend to multiple events in the roadway or elsewhere at the same time. For example, a driver must maintain lane position, and attend to traffic control devices and other vehicles. The ability to divide attention is a requirement of safe motor vehicle operation that applies to many other behaviors, including bicycling, pedestrian action, and water sports activities, for example. Although humans are limited to attending to single events at a time, we have the ability to divide our attention rapidly between events. When intoxicated, however, drivers limit their attention rather than divide it. It is well-known that divided-attention tasks are highly sensitive to intoxication (Landauer & Howat, 1983; Moskowitz & Robinson, 1988; Roehrs, Claiborue, Knox & Roth, 1994) and correlated with field crash data, suggesting a close relationship between alcohol and impaired attention (Johnson, 1982; Voas, Tippetts & Fell, 2000).

In a review of eighteen studies using fifty-two tests of divided attention, impairment in simultaneously required tasks (such as tracking a central target and performing a peripheral visual search task) was sensitive to decreased performance of BACs of 10 mg/dL (Moskowitz & Fiorentino, 2000) and as low as 5 mg/dL in some studies (*see* Roehrs, Claiborue, Knox & Roth, 1994) under some conditions. Divided attention failures are one of the most reliable reported effects of alcohol intoxication. However, not all studies show impairment in divided attention at such very low BACs. Verster and colleagues (2009) examined divided attention after different doses of alcohol for a controlled task also potentially related to real-world driving (lane-keeping tracking task with a steering wheel) while performing a secondary usual task, (responding to digits that also appeared on a computer screen). In this divided attention test, novice drivers (less than 5 years of licensed driving) showed impairment at all BACs above 50 mg/dL relative to placebo controls on this dual task. However, BACs of 20 mg/dL impaired performance on the single task condition, which is inconsistent with the theory of limited capacity and would predict that if attention is divided among multiple tasks, performance would be worse.

Caird, Willness, Steel, and Scialfa (2008) completed a meta-analysis of sixty-eight research articles measuring driving performance while using a cell phone and sixteen epidemiological studies on cell phone use and motor vehicle crashes. With regard to alcohol use during cell phone driving tasks, reaction time (RT) was the most common variable used to evaluate driving behavior and is an important variable in accident reconstruction (*see* later sections of this chapter and Chapter 12). In their analysis, RT included brake RT, choice, and simple RT in response to various events (e.g., pedestrians) and to secondary events, such as detection of a visual stimulus. For all the studies, cell phone distraction increases response time by more than 200 milliseconds in laboratory studies, but it was noted that on-road driving behavior tends to be worse than are laboratory-based results.

Rakauskas, Ward, Bernat, Cadwallader, and DeWaard (2005) examined the effect of alcohol intoxication (BAC 80 mg/dL) on common tasks such as adjusting the radio and climate and other vehicle controls. Surprisingly, secondary-task distractions (such as adjusting the radio, etc.) resulted in greater impairment than did alcohol intoxication. This effect occurred in part because intoxicated drivers were more cautious when negotiating or entering complex traffic areas and tended to wait for gaps before pulling out into traffic. However, the same intoxicated drivers had twice the number of collisions as did sober drivers. Thus, although intoxicated drivers were more cautious (fewer pull-out events), they were still impaired and unable to navigate through traffic.

Strayer, Drews, and Crouch (2006) examined driving simulators to compare the performance of drivers using a cell phone who were intoxicated at 80 mg/dL. Overall, braking reactions were delayed, and they were involved in more traffic accidents than when they were not conversing on a cell phone. Intoxicated drivers were more aggressive in their driving, followed closer to vehicles immediately in front of them and applied more force while braking, leading to the conclusion that cell phone use produced impairment similar to intoxication.

Leung, Croft, Jackson, Howard and McKenzie (2012) reported a clear interaction among cell phone use, intoxication, and impairment. At BACs of 70 and 100 mg/dL, intoxicated drivers spent less time in the designated speed range, more time speeding and, in the BAC range of 40 to 100 mg/dL, longer time to brake. In the no-alcohol cell phone condition, subjects took longer to brake speaking hands-free and during high-demand hand-free conversation and during texting spent less time in the designated speed range and more time speeding. Less demanding, naturalistic conversation produced results similar to driving with a BAC of 40 mg/dL (the legal definition for commercial vehicle operators in the United States and a BAC that produces increased risk for all age and gender groups). More cognitively demanding and texting conditions were similar to driving with a BAC of 70 to 100 mg/dL.

Visual Field Searches

A significant component of divided attention is visual searching within the driver's or pedestrian's field of view. In sober drivers, the ability to scan the roadway environment while ignoring less important factors improves with experience. Less experienced drivers tend to look straight ahead of the vehicle with narrow scanning. Their attention is narrowed because their lack of experience requires all brainpower be focused on the roadway immediately in front of their field. Such drivers are also more easily distracted by events that would be ignored by a more experienced driver. With increased driving experience, wider sampling of the visual field increases, seamlessly collecting information from further down the roadway or from the side of the roadway (periphery). The driver has learned to divide his or her attention. Less-experienced drivers process less information, whereas more experienced drivers process more.

Driver attention and information processing fall within a useful field of view (UFOV). The UFOV is the total visual field available to the subject and can be greatly enhanced by moving the eyes or turning the head from side to side. The more experienced and sober driver can divide his or her attention to objects or situations within the UFOV, ignore unimportant information or distractions, and focus on processing relevant information from the roadway. The UFOV is reduced as a function of age, vehicle speed, roadway complexity (complex traffic patterns, signs, markings), weather (e.g., rain, fog, lightening), and alcohol intoxication.

Alcohol narrows distribution of eye movement concentrating within a smaller central visual field (Belt & Krenek, 1969), creating a form of alcohol myopia with fewer eye movements to the periphery (Buikhuisen & Jongman, 1972). Alcohol shifts the distribution of eye movement within the visual UFOV requiring more time to perceive what the eyes are looking at (Moskowitz, Ziedman & Sharma, 1976). Of particular importance is that the UFOV is reduced from about 150 degrees at 30 mph to half that amount at 60 mph. This is particularly problematic because intoxicated drivers often drive at higher speeds. Similarly, some intoxicated drivers may drive below the speed limit, apparently in an effort to compensate for their limited ability to divide attention by reducing the speed of information coming at them from the roadway. Even so, intoxicated drivers are more likely to limit their visual search to the center of the field (Belt & Krenek, 1969; Buikhuisen & Jongman, 1972), resulting in performance decrements in other required tasks (Chiles & Jennings, 1969), a narrower UFOV, and reduced peripheral vision when other subsidiary test challenges are present (Moskowitz & Sharma, 1974), or reduced spatial distribution such that subjects were unable to disengage attention from the center to attend to stimuli on the left and right of the field gaze. This is similar to studies demonstrating other forms of alcohol myopia or limited allocation of brain resources (i.e., brainpower) to attend to multiple events (Steele & Josephs, 1990).

Decision Making and Processing

Once a roadway condition has been detected and cognitively processed, it may require an action decision. Should you brake, turn to avoid a collision, stop and return to the sidewalk, or do nothing? The more complicated the environment, the more decision options there are to choose from and the longer it takes to respond.

Response-Reaction Time

The analysis of a collision requires that the accident reconstructionist take into account a large number of variables and/or scientific assumptions, including mass, acceleration, friction coefficients, speed, distance, and in many cases, RT. Even though RT is often a critical element in accident reconstruction, it is often considered a static, rather than a dynamic, variable that changes with the nature of the task. RT is the difference in time from the initiation of one event, a target stimulus for example, to another event, usually a behavioral response such as pressing a keypad, brake pedal, and so on. Simple RT is the time between the presentation of a stimulus and the response.

The earliest scientific studies of RT were conducted without any intent to apply such empirical research to the field of accident reconstruction. One of the first experiments on RT was conducted by Helmholtz, who in 1850 concluded that one factor that limits RT must be the speed and distance at which electrical impulses travel along nerves from the brain to the spinal cord and to muscles. Helmholtz devised a clever experiment in which subjects had to bite on a contact switch as soon as they received a mild electric shock to either the foot or the face. The difference in time to respond between the foot and the face was the estimated conduction velocity of the nerves transmitting information from sensory (pain) receptors through nerves to the brain. The conduction velocity of the action potential was determined by measuring the distance traveled (length of the nerve in meters) and dividing by the time (seconds) taken to complete the reflex arc, also called the latency.

$$\text{Conduction velocity} = \text{distance (m)/time (sec)}.$$

As might be predicted, it takes longer for the information to get from the foot to the brain than from the face to the brain because the distance traveled is longer. How much longer does it take? Based upon more recent RT-like studies, the conduction velocity of nerves is approximately 60 to 70 meters per second (mps), depending on the type of nerve, temperature, how the measurements are made, and other factors. Since the distance from the brain to the hand or foot is about 1 to 2 m, respectively, and assuming that impulses from the brain to the nerves connected to muscle travel at 60 to 70 mps, the difference in RT could theoretically be in the 17 to 33 milliseconds range, depending on whether the arm or foot is involved and the type of nerves involved in the response.

The effects of acute intoxication on nerve conduction velocity are somewhat equivocal (Gage, 1965; Perris, Miles & Anderson, 1966; Sutton & Kimm, 1970; Wang et al., 1993) and may be dependent on which muscle groups are measured as well as previous drinking history (D'Amour, Brissette, Lavoie & Butterworth, 2000). For example, chronic alcohol abuse can result in peripheral neuropathies that may slow down conduction velocity. Quantifying such physiological differences or assigning a RT to cases where peripheral nerve velocity is potentially a factor might be useful in cases where some highway situations could be affected by RT differences of milliseconds (i.e., steering rather than braking). However, the estimate of 17 to 33 milliseconds accounts only for the time needed for the signal from the brain to reach the muscle groups to initiate a response. It does not include detection, perception, and decision-making time, which is lengthened by alcohol intoxication, or the actual execution of muscular skeletal responses, which would take longer (larger motor responses complete the responses involving smaller motoric action). Baxter (1995) reviewed a number of recent RT studies used by accident reconstructionists. Some of these studies reported that simple RT to touch a horn, for example, might be as short as 250 milliseconds, whereas RT to apply the brake pedal after the situation is perceived is from 500 to 700 milliseconds for most people. There are simple RT studies.

The RT generally used by accident reconstructionists is in the range of about 1500 to 2500 milliseconds to account for perception RT (Dewer et al., 2002) or other factors such as nighttime driving. Although longer RTs are often applied for night time accident reconstruction calculations (*see* Chapter 12), any nighttime contribution is probably more related to conspicuity because the conduction velocity of nerves actuating actual RT in healthy (and intoxicated) drivers will not change significantly. However, peripheral neuropathies in alcoholics may result in longer conduction velocity (*see* Chapter 9) to lengthen RT. Such temporal values do not include the effects of alcohol intoxication or other mitigating variables such as distractions that occur in real-world driving situations. Such factors could add seconds to the total RT (ΣDPR).

After an event has been detected, and processed, and a decision to act has been made, a motor response follows. For nonmotorists, that response may involve muscle movements such as defensive (or offensive) arm movements, compensatory movements to maintain balance, continuation or discontinuation of behavior (e.g., not entering the roadway because of a recognized hazard such as a oncoming vehicle or other danger). There is no shortage of good, bad, or other responses to the near infinite range of environmental events encountered by motor and nonmotorized vehicle operations, pedestrians, and others. Part of the response is the length of time, or RT, from the detection of an event to the time of a psychomotor task (i.e., the response). RT is an important element in forensic accident reconstruction (Chapter 12).

Factors Affecting Overall Response Time

COMPLEXITY OF TARGET. The latency to respond increases with the number of signals among which the subject has to discriminate. Also, the more similar the stimuli are to each other, the longer it takes to discriminate and react. In other words, the more complex the information, the longer it takes the brain to process and the longer the ΣDPR. Additionally, the driver's RT increases as a function of decision complexity and content and so does the error rate. The reason that longer RTs correlate with greater chance of error is probably due to a combination of psychological and physical factors. For example, if you are driving and a complex roadway situation presents itself that requires a second or so to process, you have moved physically closer to the event (e.g., a vehicle traveling at 60 mph is traveling at 88 ft per second). At a RT of 1500 milliseconds, the driver has already gone 196 feet before any response occurs. At that point, the driver will have even less time and distance to respond appropriately, resulting in an overreaction (such as oversteering), no reaction, or a delayed reaction (vehicle continues to travel).

Many pre-1970 experiments on RT employed a measure of simple RT in which the test subject is instructed to wait for an expected stimulus event. When the stimulus is detected, the subjected is required to make a specified (limited) motor response, such as pressing a button in response to a light or sound. Most of these studies consistently failed to demonstrate an effect of low to moderate doses of alcohol intoxication on simple RT. However, early studies on the effects of alcohol on RT were often seriously flawed in their design or execution (Carpenter, 1962). Caution, as well as a sufficient understanding of balanced placebo designs and alcohol research methodology, must be used to interpret these studies. Moreover, driving on a roadway is far more complex than are variables within a laboratory test of simple RT. Real-world roadway events that occur are not known a priori. There is no expectancy that a specific event will occur, and the range of possible and required response varies with each situation.

Complex RT studies are more closely related to driving and include experimental designs requiring divided attention, increased information processing, and often random presentation of events. Studies that require multitasking, that is, performing several psychomotor tasks simultaneously, show impairment by alcohol intoxication. The increased sensitivity to alcohol when tasks are combined is demonstrated by various studies. For example, Connors and Maisto (1980) found that alcohol impaired tracking ability but not reaction time performance, where as Maylor, Rabbitt, James, and Kerr (1992) found that alcohol affected RT but not tracking. When an RT task was combined with a target circling test, alcohol impaired the performance on both measured tasks. The effect of alcohol on combined tasks fits well with the reduced processing resources hypothesis originally proposed by Craik (1977) and the more recently developed attention allocation model proposed by Steele and Josephs (1990). These authors found that alcohol reduces (impairs) attentional resources so that intoxicated subjects may perform a primary task to which greater attentional resources are devoted but at the expense of impairment on a secondary task. This research has very real work implications. This "alcohol myopia" may explain impaired social behavior and the narrowing or inability to respond to internal or external queues. Similarly, an intoxicated motorist may be able to maintain lane position (e.g., a primary task) but fail to detect changes in the roadway, traffic control devices, or other secondary events. Complex RT is for all practical purposes indistinguishable from choice RT that uses multiple stimuli and a range of response possibilities. This approach, which may include anything from pencil and paper tests to driving simulators and related instrumentation, is believed to be much more reflective of the effects of alcohol on real-world driving.

EXPECTANCY. Expectancy relates to the driver's readiness to respond to common situations in predictable and successful ways. Expectancy affects how drivers perceive and respond to information and can affect reaction time in two different ways. For example, it is well-known that driver RT to expected information is shorter than the RT to unexpected information. Depending upon the density of information (i.e., how much information there is to process within a specified period), relatively simple RT for expected events are about 750 to 1500 milliseconds. Unexpected events lengthen reaction time by about 10 to 20 percent or even seconds longer. In more complex tasks, reaction times of 2500 milliseconds or more may apply (American Association of State Highway and Transportation Officials, 1994).

Roadway situations that generally repeat themselves the same way and without problems most of the time become part of the driver's cognitive map (i.e., deer do not typically run out from between parked cars, drivers do not panic stop on open highways). The driver does not have an expectancy that these events will happen, and when they do, they complicate (slow down) cognitive processing and therefore delay the RT. Some events, such as a change in a traffic control device have a higher level of expectancy than, say, a deer running into the roadway in an urban area.

All drivers form some expectancies as a function of experience and training. In part, this allows the driver to prioritize the relative importance of roadway information so that, with practice, less attention is directed to extraneous stimuli. Therefore, the psychological perception that the return trip is shorter is well-founded because in a real sense it is: having seen the same visual information before, the driver attends less to such extraneous information on the return trip. It is not that the distance is less; it is that the information highway is less congested when you can ignore some aspects of the trip. A consequence of this behavior is that more attention can be directed toward the roadway. Similarly, but in a different context, expectancy can enable the more experienced driver to anticipate possible high-risk roadway conditions, be more vigilant, and have a faster responses. On the other hand, expectancy can, under some conditions cause complacency. Drivers may become bored with a monotonous ride over the same stretch of roadway, mile after mile, hour after hour, and not attend to emergent events. There is an expectation of no change. The ability to remain on task for long periods (vigilance or as previously discussed, concentrated attention) becomes a factor that may affect driving. Other factors such as fatigue may also contribute to this effect.

Expectancy is also a factor in human behavior, and perceived use of alcohol, can produce a placebo effect (Kirsch, 1999). There is much research on the placebo effect in studying the behavioral effects of alcohol, where a placebo is administered to measure behavioral effect of expecting to receive alcohol or as a control in determining the actual pharmacological effect of alcohol. Individual expectations about alcohol affect social, affective, cognitive, and motor behaviors (e.g., Goldman, Del Boca & Darkes, 1999), some of which have important forensic implications. For example, Hoyer, Semenec, and Buchler (2007) found that high or low doses of alcohol or placebo drinks (that looked like and appeared to be but were not alcoholic drinks) had a detrimental effect on the visual search pattern. The effect was greater with larger doses of alcohol, but the expectation of alcohol also had a negative effect on the search of targets in a visual field. Such an effect can further complicate reactions to events in the roadway, for example. Distraction (discussed later in this chapter) and predetection distraction (Chapter 12) intoxication can have significant consequences in responding to roadway or other events while under the influence of alcohol.

4.4 ALCOHOL INTOXICATION AND REACTION TIME

Most CNS depressants may affect RT, but alcohol is by far the most commonly found and most well-studied drug in serious and fatal motor vehicle accidents. Research on the effects of alcohol on RT has been interpreted in terms of information processing models previously discussed. The five basic stages or phases to the total perception RT relevant to crash reconstruction analyses involving alcohol can be summarized as follows:

1. **Pre-Detection Distraction (PDD):** The time between when the object is present in the field of view and when it is detected is PDD. For example, window-shopping or texting while driving is a PDD. The object may be present and the driver may have an unobstructed view of the

object but is distracted elsewhere. During that period of PDD, the object is, for all practical purposes, invisible.

2. **Detection:** The driver, for example, must detect some event. Detection is the period between being able to see an object and actually detecting it. Usually, this is visual detection, but it could involve other sensory modalities (e.g., audition, olfaction). Since driving primarily involves visual senses, further discussion will use vision as the exemplar sense. For detection to occur, the object must be within the UFOV.

3. **Stimulus Recognition/Identification:** This is when enough visual information has been collected during the detection phase that information is processed and the object is identified. This phase may include determining if the object is moving (dynamic) or stationary (static), and if it presents a hazard or threat.

4. **Decision Making:** In this phase, the driver must decide what to do (e.g., brake, make evasive maneuvers), if anything.

5. **Response Execution:** This is the final phase of the RT process. The driver, for example, may need to take evasive action. Signals from the motor cortex of the brain send impulses down the spinal cord to innervate muscles to enable braking, steering, and so on. Depending upon the complexity of the information, expectancy, age, and mental state for example, this process can take from about several hundred milliseconds (in simple laboratory tests) to 2500 milliseconds or more (in real world driving scenarios) depending upon what is being measured, where it is being measured, how it is being measured and in whom it is being measured.

At very low BACs (20–30 mg/dL) impairment in complex divided attention tasks and other skills necessary for safe driving have been reported (Moskowitz & Robinson, 1988). Divided attention affects each phase in the total RT for obvious reasons. As such, we believe that divided attention failure is one of the primary causes of impaired driving and serious and fatal crashes. Multiple studies have demonstrated that increasing task complexity (choice RT tests; task uncertainty) produces 10 to 15 percent increases in RT at BACs between about 50 to 100 mg/dL (Huntley, 1973; Linnoila, Saario & Maki, 1974). The most consistent finding has been that moderate doses of alcohol, close to the legal definition for intoxicated driving (80 mg/dL in the United States) produce impairment when divided attention tasks are incorporated into RT tests (Tzambazis & Stough, 2000).

Ayuthaya, Thasanasuwan, Sasithonrojanachai, Ra-ngabphai, and Kussalanan (2005) reported increases in RT tasks requiring responding to red, yellow and green circles on a computer monitor (representing traffic lights) and found that BACs of 80 mg/dL produced approximately 16 to 18 percent increases from baseline depending on subject age and gender. What was interesting in this study was that RT was measured at the target (peak) BAC of 80 mg/dL and then at 70, 60, 50, 40, and 30 mg/dL as the BACs declined. A clear dose response was observed (Table 4.1) that may be due to acute tolerance (*see* Chapter 10). However, these results may underestimate the effects of alcohol on RT if the testing were to have occurred as BACs were increasing during the 30 to 90 minutes after the last drink (*see* Chapter 3). Even so, the increased RTs were similar to those reported in other studies.

Table 4.1: Age, Gender, and BAC Related Changes in Reaction Time.

BAC (mg/dL)	Percent RT increase from baseline			
	Men	Women	Age 18–24	Age 51–69
80	17	18	18	16
70	13	15	14	15
60	13	12	13	12
50	11	11	15	8
40	12	8	11	8
30	5	3	6	5

Modified from Ayuthaya et al. (2005).

In cases in which alcohol intoxication is a potential component in a serious or fatal crash, analytical crash reconstruction involves many factors, including perception reaction time (which does not include PDD). In an effort to consolidate research on the effects of alcohol on RT, Maylor and colleagues (1989, 1992, 1993) reviewed studies comparing RT in sober and in intoxicated subjects. It became apparent that comparing studies with different dependent and independent variables did not allow for interpretable results, so she selected studies that were similar enough to allow a meta-analysis of data. Maylor and Rabbitt (1993) reanalyzed the research of Huntley (1972, 1973), who found that alcohol lengthened RT to a variety of complex cognitive tests of perception RT. These investigators performed a regression analysis that of the response and found that the reaction time of subjects under the influence of alcohol (84 mg/dL) could be predicted by the following equation:

$$RT^{alcohol} = 1.22\ RT^{no\ alcohol} - 91.49.$$

This regression analysis accounted for about 99 percent of the variance, meaning it was a "good fit" for predicting the effect of alcohol in comparison to subjects who were sober.

In a 1993 review of eight of Maylor's own studies of choice RT subjects were dosed to blood alcohol levels between about 67 and 99 mg/dL, depending on the study. A linear regression analysis of these data also revealed a good fit. However, these data resulted in the following least-squares straight line equation:

$$RT^{alcohol} = 1.12 \ RT^{no \ alcohol} - 17.85.$$

Of particular note is that RT in the no-alcohol groups ranged from 255 to 1355 milliseconds (0.26 to 1.36 seconds), with the shorter RTs for tasks involving single-target simple responses and the longer times for more complex multiple-choice targets. The no-alcohol average RT was 600 milliseconds (0.6 seconds). RTs in the alcohol-treated groups, were slightly longer and averaged 654 milliseconds (0.65 seconds) with a range of 273 to 1500 milliseconds. Studies of perception RT responses to driving tasks that are more applicable to forensic evaluations are significantly longer (typically from 1500 to 2500 milliseconds in sober subjects), suggesting more real-world tasks are far more complex than represented in some laboratories.

In both studies, alcohol improved performance in very short (149 milliseconds) duration tasks. This effect was probably due to a decrease in inhibitions from alcohol and increased impulsive behavior (Dougherty et al., 2000; Moan, Norstrom & Storvoll, 2013). Neither decreased inhibitions or increased impulsivity are likely to improve driving, and this observation is not relevant to driving performance because emergent highway events are not less than 149 milliseconds. Finally, although the meta-analysis of Maylor's data resulted in slightly shorter RT compared to the analysis of Huntley with BACs of 80 mg/dL, 50 percent of the combined BACs from Maylor's eight studies were less than 70 mg/dL.

These algorithms may be helpful when applied to time-distance formulas in accident reconstruction (*see* Chapter 12) but should be considered starting points and an appropriate and well-defined range should be applied. Also, the approximate 10 to 20 percent increase in perception RT is based on laboratory studies that do not include the range of real-world driving experiences, including PDD. Moreover, since the effects of alcohol are known to be greater with increasing task complexity (Robinson & Peebles, 1974; Connors & Maisto, 1980, Maylor & Rabbitt, 1993) and the effects of alcohol overall are dose dependent, it is highly probable that application of these algorithms will underestimate the delay in RT due to intoxication at higher BACs.

Although meta-analysis provides useful information to the accident reconstructionist in calculating the effects of alcohol into a RT analysis, the algorithms provided should be considered conservative because these represent RTs to stimuli that are, if not expected by the subject, at least known to him or her. This is in stark contrast to the enriched driving environment replete with a range of potential, unanticipated events, which has no real counterpart even in complex RT studies. Also, subjects in a laboratory may be motivated to do well on tests whereas everyday driving rarely has a monetary reward for good performance. Finally, the level of intoxication at the time of the accident can be significantly higher (or lower) than at the time of testing by police during an investigation. Other physiological and pharmacokinetic factors may further complicate the interpretation of alcohol test evidence when intoxication is a factor in a reconstruction analysis. For example, caffeine, one of the most widely used drugs in the world may decrease RT under some conditions and interact with alcohol in a complex dose-dependent manner to antagonize the effects of alcohol on RT (Burns & Moskowitz, 1990), whereas nicotine can decrease RT (Koelega, 1995). Prelaboratory testing protocols do not always screen for or report caffeine or nicotine use by subjects. Finally, the lengthened RTs predicted by these algorithms are conservative in comparison with some studies (e.g., Ayuthaya et al., 2005).

Responses to an emergent event are affected by a number of variables, including target characteristics, age and mental state, lighting and weather, for example (*see* Chapter 12). Although widely used RT values are helpful, caution should be used in interpreting such results. Depending upon real-world task complexity and other factors discussed, RTs in the 2500-millisecond range or higher are probably realistic in healthy subjects (*see* Chapter 12). However, factors such as alcohol intoxication and resulting narrowing of attention may add seconds to the total RT analysis. In other words, in these and related cases, the ΣDPR must include a measurement or estimate of when the target was within UFOV, not just the time to detect, identify, and respond. It is therefore recommended that any analytical accident reconstruction include a range of total ΣDPRs. This adjustment may explain why an alcohol impaired driver, for example, failed to respond to a given set of roadway conditions that would have provided most drivers with enough time to respond.

In summary, the effects of alcohol across a range of behaviors believed to be related to safe motor vehicle operation show considerable diversity of results. In part, this is because there is no single test battery used by all researchers. Some tests are insensitive to the effects of alcohol; others are more sensitive. Given the clear increase in risk for a fatal motor vehicle crash at BACs well below 80 mg/dL, it is more likely that studies with higher threshold effects for impairment at that BAC are simply insensitive. Moreover, the very nature of experimental design limits variables so their contribution to an outcome can be identified. In the real world, however, driving requires multitasking, including detection, sustained attention, divided attention within the UFOV, and resistance to distraction.

Finally, it is noted that in Moskowitz's last review of this voluminous literature–and limiting findings to studies involving driving simulators and roadway driving, simulated flight operation, divided attention and vigilance–73 percent of those studies demonstrated driving impairment at BACs of 39 mg/dL. In the studies reviewed, virtually all subjects tested exhibited impairment on some critical driving measure at BACs of 80 mg/dL. Although that is coincidentally the legal definition for intoxicated driving in the United States, it is worth noting that impairment and increased risk for a fatal crash occurs at much lower BACs. It would require an egregious disregard of scientific evidence to conclude that impaired driving started at 80 mg/dL or that driving was not impaired at BACs below 80 mg/dL.

4.5 CLINICAL DIAGNOSES OF INTOXICATION

Structured tests based in clinical laboratory research are often based on observations of specific behavior and are useful in forensic evaluations. Such tests allow the examiner to diagnose intoxication based on known biobehavioral effects of alcohol. Some tests are qualitative; others are semi-quantitative. For example, the *Diagnostic and Statistical Manual of Mental Disorders* (DSM) of the American Psychiatric Association lists several criteria for clinicians to assess intoxicated patients. Standardized and non-standardized field sobriety tests are regularly used by police to assist in the investigation of suspected intoxicated drivers. These tests also have specific criteria for determining alcohol intoxication.

DSM Criteria for Intoxication

The primary feature of intoxication is the presence of psychological changes such as inappropriate behavior, affective changes or what is termed significant maladaptive behavior that develop during or immediately after alcohol consumption. For example, clinicians using DSM are trained to look for specific signs. There are four specific requirements for a diagnosis of intoxication: (1) recent use of alcohol (from the odor of an alcoholic beverage on the breath, self-report by the patient, report from another individual, or chemical test evidence); (2) clinically significant maladaptive or psychological changes (impaired judgment, impaired social or occupational functioning, driving while intoxicated, inappropriate sexual behavior, inappropriate violent or aggressive behavior, or emotional lability) that occur while drinking or shortly thereafter; (3) presence of one or more of the following signs: slurred speech, incoordination, unsteady gait, nystagmus, impairment in attention or memory, and stupor or coma; and (4) the diagnostician must determine that any of the signs observed are not the result of a general medical condition or better explained by another mental disorder.

The DSM provides no guidance with regard to how to quantify incoordination, unsteady gait, or nystagmus, nor does it provide any benchmark for maladaptive behavior or cognitive impairment. Nevertheless, evidence of alcohol use coupled with psychological changes and one or more of the specifically identified signs are sufficient to diagnose intoxication in the absence of a medical or mental disorder. For example, an untreated diabetic may have an acetone-like odor on the breath and exhibit slurred speech and have other signs of psychomotor impairment (Brick, 1993). Although such patients may show behavioral signs of impairment similar to alcohol intoxication, they are not impaired or intoxicated by alcohol.

4.6 STANDARDIZED FIELD SOBRIETY TESTS

The evolution of our definitions of terms such as gross or obvious intoxication began in the context of the early Uniform Vehicle Code in which driving while intoxicated meant "operating a motor vehicle with signs of intoxication by alcohol (or other drugs) manifested by gross behavior and, frequently, by chemical testing for alcohol" (Keller, McCormick & Efron, 1982, p. 106). In the past several decades, epidemiological research has supported the legislative need to lower the definition for DWI. The work of early researchers led to greater awareness of the role of alcohol in motor vehicle crashes and increasingly reliable methods to quickly and accurately measure BACs. By 1939 the first legislation defining intoxicated driving based on BAC was passed in Indiana. The original statute considered a BAC of 150 mg/dL or more to be "*prima facie*" (evident without proof; obvious) evidence of guilt (Borkenstein, 1984). However, it became clear that impairment in the ability to drive occurred at BACs well below the 150 mg/dL set by early legislators and the legal definition for intoxicated driving was lowered from 150 mg/dL (at which concentration intoxication was obvious) to 100 mg/dL, which did not reliably reflect gross signs of impairment (i.e., visible or obvious intoxication). With that change, law enforcement needed field tests to detect intoxication at lower BACs.

Thus, while the dose-dependent relationship between increasing BACs and the risk for a serious or fatal motor vehicle crash was well-known, law enforcement required better tools to detect intoxicated drivers. As discussed, laboratory studies revealed that divided attention tasks are sensitive to the effects of alcohol in the lab and extended logically to actual driving tasks. Lab tests of divided attention are not practical for police in the field. Beginning in 1975, alcohol researchers were tasked with developing practical valid and reliable field sobriety tests for the National Highway Traffic Safety Administration (NHTSA) (2002, HS178 R1/02) that could be used by police in the field. The test battery included psychomotor tests that require attention to be divided between the performance of a motor task (e.g., walking and balancing) coupled with mental tasks such as following instructions, remembering to walk a specified number of steps or counting (Burns & Moskowitz, 1977). Three tests were subsequently adapted by the NHTSA in the form of two specific tests: the walk and turn test (WAT) and one leg stand (OLS) test. A third test was included by the researchers who found that a test of ocular motor control commonly used in neurology, horizontal gaze nystagmus (HGN) was particularly sensitive to alcohol. Wilkinson, Kime, and Purnell, (1974) found that when applied to intoxicated subjects, smooth ocular pursuit becomes interrupted and jerky at BACs as low as 40 mg/dL in some subjects. Based upon both preexisting scientific literature and the specific need of tests to identify intoxicated drivers, the HGN, WAT and OLS were chosen to form the SFST battery now used by police departments throughout the United States and elsewhere.

The following description of the SFST battery comes from the U.S. Department of Transportation (DOT) HS 806 512 1984, which originally described these tests as effective procedures for testing roadside drivers to determine if their BAC was above 100 mg/dL, the legal definition for intoxicated driving at the time of test development. Since the original study and in response to a national change in the definition for intoxicated driving (from 100 mg/dL to 80 mg/dL), these tests have been revised with expanded criteria, presumably sensitive to detect impairment at the lower BAC (Burns & Anderson, 1995). It is noted that NIITSA describes these as tests to determine if a driver's BAC is above the legal definition and not as a measure of divided attention failure. Since two of the three tests are clearly sensitive to divided attention failure and driving is a psychomotor task requiring divided attention, this distinction seems odd and is never adequately explained.

Horizontal Gaze Nystagmus Test

What is HGN? HGN is an involuntary repetitive regular oscillation (jerking) of the eyes in a lateral, vertical, or rotary direction. Besides oscillation, there are two other components, slow and rapid movement in the opposite directions.

Is HGN specific? This test is effective in screening for alcohol intoxication, but HGN is also used to detect brain tumors; vascular disorders; various neurological disorders, including dyslexia; vestibular disorders, including vertigo and its many associated conditions; deafness, tinnitus; extreme fatigue; emotion and hypotension (Berkow, 1987; Wilson et al., 1991) as well as the use of seizure medications (U.S. DOT, 1984). About 4 percent of the general population will show nystagmus (1 out of 25). Unlike the other SFSTs, this test is not affected by other physical disabilities (e.g., old leg injuries), age, or being overweight. HGN alone is accurate 77 percent of the time. In combination with other SFSTs (e.g., WAT), accuracy rate increases to 82 percent under the original SFST validation study.

With all tests, it is important to determine that there are no preexisting or emergent medical conditions that would compromise the validity of the test or place the subject at risk for lack of medical attention. Obvious disabilities preclude the administration of these or most behavioral tests. The administration of SFSTs is not affected by the use of contacts (although some subjects may wish to remove contacts if they are subject to displacement or as a general precaution). The HGN test does not require visual acuity so the use of either contacts or eyeglasses is not necessary to perform the test. Similarly, the WAT and OLS may not be valid for subjects over the age of 60 or for those who are more than 50 pounds overweight.

Most people will show some jerking if the eyes move far enough to the side but three characteristic responses occur in persons who are intoxicated:

1. The jerking of the eyes occurs much sooner. The more intoxicated the person becomes, the less lateral movement is required to detect eye jerking.
2. Although most people show nystagmus when the eye is in the extreme lateral position, the greater the intoxication, the more distinct the nystagmus will be in the extreme gaze position.
3. Intoxicated people cannot follow a slowly moving object smoothly.

General Testing Procedure

The administration of this test includes the following steps:

STEP 1: Stand in front of the subject and
Test 1: Determine if there is smooth tracking left to right
Test 2: Check for nystagmus at maximum deviation
Test 3: Check if the angle of onset of nystagmus is less than 45 degrees

The specific administration protocol for HGN is clearly described in various other publications, including those of the NHTSA. Assuming that the test is administered properly, HGN is scored as follows:

Horizontal Gaze Nystagmus Scoring

Two of the following signs in each eye:
1. Onset of nystagmus in right eye occurs before 45 degrees
2. Distinct nystagmus when (right) eye is moved as far right as possible
3. Right eye cannot follow moving object smoothly
4. Onset of nystagmus in left eye occurs before 45 degrees
5. Distinct nystagmus when (left) eye is moved as far left as possible
6. Left eye cannot follow moving object smoothly

A score of four suggests alcohol intoxication at or above 80 mg/dL.

Walk and Turn (WAT)

What is WAT? This is a divided attention test in which the subject is asked to stand in a heel-to-toe position on a marked line. While maintaining this position, the subject is given the instructions (instruction phase).

Is WAT specific? This test detects alcohol intoxication and impairment produced by some other drugs. Physical disabilities confound this test, and it may be inaccurate in subjects over 60 years old or more than 50 lb overweight. WAT alone is accurate 68 percent of the time. In combination with other SFSTs (e.g., HGN), the accuracy rate increases to more than 80 percent. Increased accuracy has been reported.

The specific administration protocol for WAT is clearly described in various other publications, including those of the NHTSA. Assuming that the test is administered properly, WAT is scored as follows:

Signs of Intoxication

This test has a specific scoring procedure. It is not a subjective pass/fail test. Look for and record any of following signs of impairment demonstrated during this test.

1. Cannot keep balance while listening to instructions
2. Starts before instructions are completed
3. Stops while walking to steady self
4. Does not touch heel-to-toe
5. Steps off line
6. Uses arms to balance
7. Loses balance while turning
8. Incorrect number of steps
9. Cannot do test

A score of two or more suggests intoxication.

One-Leg Stand

What is OLS? This is a divided attention test in which subjects assume a standing position with their heels together and their arms down at their sides. The subjects are then asked to stand with one leg raised 6 in off the ground while counting rapidly from 1001 to 1030.

Is OLS specific? This test detects alcohol intoxication and also impairment produced by some other drugs. Physical disabilities confound this test, and it may be inaccurate in subjects over 60 years old or more than 50 lb overweight. OLS alone is accurate 65 percent of the time. In combination with other SFSTs (e.g., HGN), the accuracy rate increases to 78 percent.

The specific administration protocol for OLS is clearly described in various other publications including those of the National Highway Traffic Safety Administration. Assuming that the test is administered properly, OLS is scored as follows:

Scoring: Two or more of the following suggest legal intoxication.

1. Sways while balancing
2. Uses arms for balance
3. Hopping
4. Puts foot down
5. Cannot do test

Conclusions

In summary, research on the effects of alcohol have demonstrated several important facts: (1) The effects of alcohol are generally dose dependent. The greater the BAC, the greater the effect. (2) Alcohol impairs both cognitive and motor skills believed to be critical for safe motor vehicle operation and other behaviors requiring multi-tasking or divided attention. (3) Activities (driving, etc.) that require the performance of more than one task are particularly sensitive to the effects of alcohol. (4) Forensic analyses regarding the effects of alcohol on driving that require an analytical reconstruction of a crash must consider the effect of alcohol intoxication, which affects variables such as scanning the roadway (if driving), detecting environmental stimuli, processing what is detected, making a decision based on that information and responding. (5) We recommend extending perception RT analyses to include awareness or acknowledgment that there may be time "off target" or a predetection time (PDD) to acquire the target before detection. Any such reconstruction should take into account Total Detection Perception Reaction ΣDPR; which accounts for individual differences and alcohol intoxication.

REFERENCES

Adams, A., and Brown, B. (1975). Alcohol prolongs time course of glare recovery. *Nature, 257,* 481–483.

American Association of State Highway and Transportation Officials. (1994). *A Policy on Geometric Design of Highways and Streets.* Washington, D.C.: author

American Psychiatric Association. (2013). *Diagnostic and Statistical Manual of Mental Disorders* (5th Ed., DSM-V). Washington D.C.: Author.

Ayuthaya, P., Thasanasuwan, A., Sasithonrojanachai, S., Ra-ngabphai, C., and Kussalanan, A. (2005). Effects of low blood alcohol level on reaction time. *Siriraj Medical Journal, 57*(6), 193–196.

Baxter, A. (1995). *An Examination of Driver Reaction Times.* Presented at the 1995 NJAAR, NATARI, NAPARS, MATAI Annual Meeting, Lancaster, PA, October 5–7.

Belt, B., and Krenek, R. (1969). *Driver Eye Movement as a Function of Low Alcohol Concentrations.* Columbus, OH: Driving Research Laboratory, Ohio State University.

Berkow, R. (1987). *The Merck Manual of Diagnosis and Therapy* (15th ed.). West Point, PA: Merck & Co.

Borkenstein, R.F. (1984). Historical perspective North American traditional and experimental response. *Journal of Studies on Alcohol, Supplement 10* (pp. 3–12). New Brunswick, NJ: Rutgers University.

Brick, J. (1993). Diabetes, breath acetone and Breathalyzer accuracy: A case study. *Alcohol, Drugs and Driving, 9*(1), 27–28.

Buikhuisen, W., and Jongman, R. (1972). Traffic perception under the influence of alcohol. *Quarterly Journal of Studies on Alcohol, 33,* 800–806.

Burns, M., and Anderson, E. W. (1995). *A Colorado Validation Study of the Standardized Field Sobriety Test (SFST) Battery.* Washington, D.C.: U.S. Department of Transportation, National Highway Traffic Safety Administration.

Burns, M., and Moskowitz, H. (1977). *Psychophysical Tests for DWI Arrest.* Report DOT-HS-5-01242. Washington, D.C.: U.S. Department of Transportation, National Highway Traffic Safety Administration.

Burns, M., and Moskowitz, H. (1990). Two experiments on alcohol-caffeine interaction. *Alcohol, Drugs & Driving, 5/6*(4), 303–315.

Caird, J. K., Willness, C. R., Steel, P., and Scialfa, C. (2008). A meta-analysis of the effects of cell phone on driver performance. *Accident: Analysis and Prevention, 40*(4), 1282–1293.

Carpenter, J. (1962). Effects of alcohol on some psychological processes: A critical review with special reference to automobile driving skill. *Quarterly Journal of Studies on Alcohol, 23,* 274–314.

Chiles, W. D., and Jennings, A. E. (1969). Effects of alcohol on complex performance. *Human Factors, 12*(6), 605–612.

Connors, G. J., and Maisto, S. A. (1980). Effects of alcohol, instructions and consumption rate and motor performance. *Journal of Studies on Alcohol, 41,* 509–517.

Craik, F. (1977). Similarities between the effects of aging and alcoholic intoxication on memory performance, construed within a 'levels of processing' framework. In I. M. Birnbaum and E. S. Parker (Eds.), *Alcohol and Human Memory.* Hillsdale, NJ: Erlbaum.

D'Amour, M. L., Brissette, S., Lavoie, J., and Butterworth, R. F. (2000). Reduced sensory and motor nerve conduction velocities in moderate drinkers. *Addiction Biology, 5*(1), 71–75.

Dewer, R., Olson, P., and Alexander, G. (2002). Perception and information processing. In R. E. Dewer and P. L. Olson, *Human Factors in Traffic Safety* (pp. 13–42). Tucson, AZ: Lawyers and Judges Publishing Company.

Dinges, D. F., and Kribbs, N. B. (1990). Comparison of the effects of alcohol and sleepiness on simple reaction time performance: Enhanced habituation as a common process. *Alcohol, Drugs and Driving, 5*(4), 329–339.

Dougherty, D., Marsh, D., Moeller, G., Chokshi, R., and Rosen, V. (2000). Effects of moderate and high doses of alcohol on attention, impulsivity, discriminability, and response bias in immediate and delayed memory task performance. Alcoholism, *Clinical and Experimental Research, 24(*11), 1702–1711.

Gage, P. (1965). The effect of methyl, ethyl and n-propyl alcohol on neuromuscular transmission in the rat. *Journal of Pharmacology and Experimental Therapy, 150*, 236–243.

Goldman, M. S., Del Boca, F. K., and Darkes, J. (1999) Alcohol expectancy theory: The application of cognitive neuroscience. In K. E. Leonard and H. T. Blane (Eds.), *Psychological Theories of Drinking and Alcoholism* (2nd ed., pp. 203–246). New York, NY: Guilford Press.

Gupta, N., Lata, H., and Kaur, A. (2012). Effect of glare on night time driving in alcoholic versus non-alcoholic professional drivers. *International Journal of Applied and Basic Medical Research, 2*(2), 128–131.

Helmholtz, H. (1850) Mittheilung für die Physikalische Gesellschaft betreffend Versuche in den sensiblen Nerven des Menschen. *Archive of the Berlin-Brandenburgische Akademie der Wissenschaften* (NL Helmholtz) 540, 1–4, p. 3. Cited by: Schmidgen, H. (2002) of frogs and men: the origins of psychophysiological time experiments, 1850-1865

Hoyer, W., Semenec, S., and Buchler, N. (2007). Acute alcohol intoxication impairs controlled search across the visual field. *Journal of Studies on Alcohol and Drugs, 68(*5), 748–758.

Huntley, M. (1972). Influences of alcohol and S-R uncertainty upon spatial localization time. *Psychopharmacologia (Berlin), 27*, 131–140.

Huntley, M. (1973). Effects of alcohol and fixation-task difficulty on choice reaction time on extrafoveal stimulation. *Quarterly Journal of Studies on Alcohol, 34*(1), 89–103.

Johnson, I. (1982). The role of alcohol in road crashes. *Ergonomics, 25*, 941–946.

Keller, M., McCormick, M., and Efron, V. (1982). *A Dictionary of Words About Alcohol* (2nd ed.). New Brunswick, NJ: Publications Division, Rutgers Center of Alcohol Studies.

Kirsch, I. (1999). *How Expectancies Shape Experience.* Washington, D.C.: American Psychological Association.

Koelega, H. (1995). Alcohol and vigilance performance: A review. *Psychopharmacology, 118*, 233–249.

Landauer, A., and Howat, P. (1983). Low and moderate alcohol doses, psychomotor performance and perceived drowsiness. *Ergonomics, 26,* 647–657.

Leung, S., Croft, R., Jackson, M., Howard, M., and McKenzie, R. (2012). A comparison of the effect of mobile phone use and alcohol consumption on driving simulation performance. *Traffic Injury Prevention, 13*(6), 566–574.

Linnoila, M., Saario, I., and Maki., M. (1974). Effect of treatment with diazepam or lithium and alcohol on psychomotor skills related to driving. *European Journal of Clinical Pharmacology, 7*(5), 337–342.

MacArthur, R., and Sekuler, R. (1982). Alcohol and motion perception. *Perception and Psychopysics, 31,* 502–505.

Maylor, E., and Rabbitt, P. (1993). Alcohol, reaction time and memory: A meta-analysis. *British Journal of Psychology, 84,* 301–317.

Maylor, E., Rabbitt, P., and Connolly, S. (1989). Rate of processing and judgment of response speed: Comparing the effects of alcohol and practice. *Perception and Psychophysics, 45,* 431.

Maylor, E., Rabbitt, P., James, G., and Kerr, S. (1992). Effects of alcohol, practice and task complexity on reaction, time distributions. *Quarterly Journal of Experimental Psychology, 44a,* 119–139.

Moan, I., Norstrom, T., and Storvoll, E. (2013). Alcohol use and drunk driving: The modifying effect of impulsivity. *Journal of Studies on Alcohol and Drugs, 74,* 114–119.

Mortimer, R. G. (1963). Effect of low blood-alcohol concentrations in simulated day and night driving. *Perceptual and motor skills, 17*(2), 399–408.

Moskowitz, H. (1973). Laboratory studies of the effects of alcohol on some variables related to driving. *Journal of Safety Research, 5*(3), 185–199.

Moskowitz, H. (2008) Alcohol effects and driving impairment. In J. C. Garriott (Ed.), Garriott's *Medicolegal Aspects of Alcohol* (5th ed., pp. 285–302). Tucson, AZ: Lawyers and Judges Publishing Company.

Moskowitz, H., and Fiorentino, D. (2000). *A Review of the Literature on the Effects of Low Doses of Alcohol on Driving-Related Skills.* Report DOT-HS-809-028. Washington, D.C.: U.S. Department of Transportation, National Highway Traffic Safety Administration.

Moskowitz, H., and Robinson, C. (1988). *Effects of Low Doses of Alcohol on Driving-Related Skills: A Review of the Evidence.* Report DOT-HS-807-2. Springfield, VA: U.S. Department of Commerce, National Technical Information Service.

Moskowitz, H., and Sharma, S. (1974). Effects of alcohol on peripheral vision as a function of attention. *Human Factors, 16,* 174–180.

Moskowitz, H., Zeidman, K., and Sharma, S. (1976). Visual search behavior while viewing driving scenes under the influence of alcohol and marijuana. *Human Factors, 8,* 417–432.

National Highway Traffic Safety Administration. (2002). *DWI Detection and Standardized Field Sobriety Testing.* Report HS-178-R1/02. Washington, D.C.: U.S. Department of Transportation.

Newman, H., and Fletcher, E. (1940). The effect of alcohol on vision. *American Journal of Studies on Alcohol, 10,* 398–403.

Perrine, M. (1973). Alcohol influences on driving-related behavior: A critical review of laboratory studies of neurophysiological, neuromuscular, and sensory activity. *Journal of Safety Research, 5,* 165–184.

Perris, O., Miles, D., and Anderson, W. (1966). The action of ethyl alcohol on peripheral nerves. *American Journal of Medical Sciences, 251,* 207–210.

Rakauskas, M., Ward, N., Bernat, E., Cadwallader, M., and DeWaard, D. (2005). *Driving Performance During Cell Phone Conversations and Common In-Vehicle Tasks While Sober and Drunk.* Report MN/RC–2005-41. Human FIRST Program. Minneapolis, MN: University of Minnesota.

Robinson, G. H., and Peebles, W. J. (1974). Interaction between alcohol, task difficulty, and compatibility in a choice-reaction task. *Perceptual and Motor Skills, 38,* 459–466.

Roehrs, T., Beare, D., Zorick, F., and Roth, T. (1994). Sleepiness and ethanol effects on simulated driving. *Alcoholism, Clinical & Experimental Research, 18,* 154–158.

Roehrs, T., Claiborue, D., Knox, M., and Roth, T. (1994). Residual sedating effects of ethanol. *Alcoholism, Clinical and Experimental Research, 18,* 831–834.

Sekuler, R., and MacArthur, R. (1977). Alcohol retards visual recovery from glare by hampering target acquisition. *Nature, 270,* 428–429.

Sivak, M. (1996). The information that drivers use: Is it indeed 90% visual. *Perception, 25,* 1081–1089.

Starmer, G. (1989). Effects of low to moderate doses of ethanol on human driving-related performance. In K. Crow and R. Batt (Eds.), *Human Metabolism of Alcohol* (Vol. 1, pp. 101–130). Boca Raton, FL: CRC Press.

Steele, C., and Josephs, R. (1990). Alcohol myopia. Its prized and dangerous effects. *American Psychologist, 45*(8), 921–933.

Strayer, D. L., Drews, F. A., and Crouch, D. J. (2006). A comparison of the cell phone driver and the drunk driver. *Human Factors, 48*(2), 381–391.

Sutton, D., and Kimm, J. (1970). Alcohol effects on human motor unit, reaction time. *Physiology & Behavior, 5,* 889–892.

Tzambazis, K., and Stough, C. (2000). Alcohol impairs speed of information processing and simple and choice reaction time and differentially impairs higher-order cognitive abilities. *Alcohol & Alcoholism, 35,* 197–201.

U.S. Department of Transportation, National Highway Traffic Safety Administration. (1984). *Improved Sobriety Testing.* Report DOT-HS-806-512. Washington, D.C.: U.S. Government Printing Office.

Verriest, G., and Laplasse, D. (1965). New data concerning the influence of ethyl alcohol on human visual thresholds. *Experimental Eye Research, 4,* 95–101.

Verster, J., Wester, A., Goorden, M., Van Wieringen, J., Olivier, B., and Volkerts, E. (2009). Novice driver's performance after different alcohol doses and placebo in the divided attention steering simulator (DASS). *Psychopharmacology, 204,* 127–133.

Voas, R. B., Tippetts, A. S., and Fell, J. (2000). The relationship of alcohol safety laws to drinking drivers in fatal crashes. Accident; *Analysis and Prevention, 32,* 483–492.

Wallgren, H., and Barry, H. III. (1970). *Actions of Alcohol.* New York, NY: Elsevier.

Wang, M., Nicholson, M., Mahong, B., Li, Y., Fitzhugh, E., and Shea, J. (1993). The effects of high and low BACs on the Hoffman reflex. *Journal of Neurological Sciences, 117*, 107–110.

Wilkinson, I., Kime, R., and Purnell, M. (1974). Alcohol and human eye movement. *Brain, 97*, 785–792.

Wilson, J., Braunwald, E., Isselbacher, K., Petersdorf, R., Martin, J., Fauci, A., and Root, K. (Eds). (1991). *Harrison's Principles of Internal Medicine* (12th ed., pp. 26–27). New York, NY: McGraw-Hill Book Co.

Chapter 5

DWI, HIGH-RISK BEHAVIORS, AND INJURIES

5.1 EMERGENCE OF LAWS RELATED TO ALCOHOL INTOXICATION

Accidents, public intoxication and related social problems with alcohol were well-known by the nineteenth century and earlier. Until then, most alcohol-related injuries were generally local, involving the intoxicated individual and not the general public. As motorized transportation increased, so did a new mode of injuries. By the beginning of the twentieth century, a combination of scientific research and societal changes led to the awareness of public health issues caused by intoxicated motor vehicle operators (automobile drivers, locomotive engineers, etc.). Although systematic epidemiological research focused mostly on automobile operators and "drunk driving," such research was sparse. Nevertheless, the relationships among drinking alcohol, intoxication, and motor vehicle crashes were apparently sufficiently robust to attract public attention and, eventually after many years and a growing body of research, led to legislation to reduce drunk driving.

In Sweden, the pioneering work by Widmark (1981) and in the United States by Heise and Halporn (1932) and Heise (1934) led to protocols for use in evaluating suspected drunk drivers. Until then, such evaluations (usually performed by clinicians or police) were neither systematic nor objective. A diagnosis of drunk driving, often introduced by expert testimony, usually included highly exaggerated behaviors such as staggering gait and incoherent speech. These early studies provided improved methods to observe and report signs of intoxication and eventually to quantify alcohol in blood. Such work led to a general understanding that the signs of alcohol intoxication were proportional to the concentration of alcohol in the body, and these adversely affected safe motor vehicle operation. The work of Heise and other luminaries of the time contributed substantially to a body of evidence on

95

drunk driving that helped expand the newly formed interests of the National Safety Council Committee on Tests for Intoxication.

In the United States, by 1939 the first legislation defining intoxicated driving based on BAC was passed in Indiana and was three tiered. A BAC of less than 50 mg/dL was considered presumptive evidence of no intoxication; a BAC between 50 and 150 mg/dL was considered to be supportive evidence of intoxicated driving; and a BAC of 150 mg/dL or more was considered to be *prima facie*, meaning guilt of intoxicated driving was obvious or evident without proof (Borkenstein, 1964). In the context of the early Uniform Vehicle Code, driving while intoxicated has been defined as "operating a motor vehicle with signs of intoxication by alcohol (or other drugs) manifested by gross behavior and, frequently, by chemical testing for alcohol" (Keller, McCormick & Efron, p. 106, 1982) and set a BAC at which there is no doubt of obvious intoxication (Heise, 1956) namely, 150 mg/dL. Heise (1934) had earlier noted that a BAC of 150 mg/dL is considered *prima facie* evidence of intoxication to establish the fact that a person was too intoxicated to drive. *Prima facie* evidence shifts the burden of proof to the defense counsel to rebut the charge.

What eventually followed was the development of state alcohol control codes that, in consultation with lawmakers and the American Medical Association (AMA), led to the approval of the Model Uniform Vehicle Code. This legislation extended the previous regulations that drivers with a BAC of 150 mg/dL were grossly intoxicated and should be presumed to be too intoxicated for the purposes of driving (Langenbucher & Nathan, 1983). Over the ensuing decades, research on alcohol-related roadway crashes highlighted the effects of alcohol at BACs below the legal definition of 150 mg/dL for intoxicated driving. By 1960, the data on drunk driving crashes were so compelling that the AMA recommended that a BAC of 100 mg/dL be accepted as prima facie evidence of intoxication. The recommendation made note that with regard to driving, some individuals are under the influence at BACs of 50 to 100 mg/dL. This was the first shift from commonly and easily recognized signs of gross intoxication that were believed to reflect impairment in the ability to drive. The significance of this change in other aspects of law and the prevention of alcohol related problems is discussed in Chapter 6 and by Brick and Erickson (2009).

During the second half of the twentieth century, most but not all states defined, for the purposes of motor vehicle operation, a BAC of 100 mg/dL to be evidence of impairment; that is, too intoxicated to drive safely. At the time, such legislation was consistent with data from the NHTSA. In the late 1970s, NHTSA reported that about 35 percent of the nearly 14,000 motor vehicle fatalities involved at least one driver or nonoccupant (e.g., a pedestrian) who was intoxicated at a BAC of 100 mg/dL or more (U.S. Department of Transportation, 1994).

By 1985, the time the next update was completed, it appeared that about 50 percent of drivers in fatal crashes had a BAC of at least 100 mg/dL. Based on several decades of research and utilizing the most current drunk driving data, prevention efforts gained further traction by 1994, when states were encouraged with the promise of federal highway traffic funding (or the threat of withholding such funding) to lower to 80 mg/dL the BAC that defines driving while intoxicated (Model Driving While Under the Influence of Alcohol and Other Drugs Act, 1993).

Now, all states in the United States have revised their impaired driving laws to follow federal recommendations to define a BAC of 80 mg/dL as a violation of the motor vehicle code. Interstate commercial operators have an even lower definition of intoxicated driving (40 mg/dL), which is more consistent with many European countries that use 50 mg/dL or less to define intoxicated driving for automobile operators. In the United States, persons under the age of 21 typically fall under a zero tolerance statute, in which intoxicated driving for an underage drinker is defined as a BAC of 10 or 20 mg/dL, depending upon the state. These prevention efforts, coupled with increased public awareness about drinking and driving, may explain the gradual decline in fatal car crashes involving intoxicated drivers (Centers for Disease Control, 2001; Dee, 2001; Hingson, Heeren & Winter, 1996, 2000; Perrine, 1988; Shults, et al. 2001; Voas, Taylor, Baker & Tippetts, 2000).

Even with continued legislative prevention efforts, in 2004, the people who died in alcohol-related traffic crashes constituted about 40 percent of the fatal number of traffic fatalities (Yi, Chen & Williams, 2006), and in 2013, 10,076 people were killed in alcohol-impaired driving crashes, accounting for nearly one third (31%) of all traffic-related deaths in the United States. Although it is not disputed that alcohol intoxication is directly related to motor vehicle fatalities, statistical interpretation of such results is sometimes misleading. Unlike the earlier epidemiological research, more recent studies included drivers with any measurable BAC above zero. In some cases, alcohol was detected but these drivers would not be considered drunk or impaired. Moreover, NHTSA frequently uses a statistical method of intupation in which it is assumed that a fatally injured driver was intoxicated based upon the driver's profile (age, gender) and the nature of the crash, even when no BAC data are available (U.S. Department of Transportation, 2002). Although this and similar frequently cited statistics probably overestimate the number of fatalities caused by alcohol intoxication, there is little doubt that alcohol intoxication is a significant causal factor in fatal crashes. Over the last decade, alcohol-related traffic fatalities have gradually decreased, as research in other activities has increased and includes the role of alcohol in water sports, aircraft operations, high-risk sexual activities, pedestrian fall, pedestrian knock downs (by motor vehicles), and bicycling and thermal injuries.

Liability Laws

In addition to laws to deter intoxicated driving, there are three types of laws that relate to the service of alcohol to obviously or visibly intoxicated persons: Administrative laws and codes (usually enforced by a state alcohol control board), dram shop laws (a civil remedy to injuries caused by the over service of alcohol), and third-party actions under traditional tort reform (such as social hosts or homeowners). These laws as they relate to behavioral observations of intoxication are discussed in Chapter 6.

5.2 NONHUMAN FACTORS THAT CONTRIBUTE TO CRASHES

Based on data collected through the Fatal Analysis Reporting System (FARS), there are a number of variables that contribute to fatal crashes, including vehicle characteristics, time and location, and highway and driver characteristics.

Vehicle Type

About 82 percent of fatal crashes and about 95 percent of crashes resulting in injuries involve passenger cars or light trucks (NHTSA, 2009) (Table 5.1). Of the 42,636 traffic fatalities in 2004, 16,694, or about 39 percent, were alcohol related. NHTSA defines as alcohol related those crashes in which someone involved (passenger, driver or a nonoccupant such as a pedestrian) has a measured BAC of more than 10 mg/dL. About 34 percent (14,409) involved someone, including nondrivers, with a BAC of more than 80 mg/dL.

Table 5.1: Crashes by Vehicle Type and Severity.

Vehicle Type	Number of Fatalities (percent)	Number of Injuries (percent)
Passenger car	25,507 (44)	1,990,000 (58)
Light truck	22,337 (38)	1,246,000 (37)
Large truck	4862 (8)	87,000 (3)
Bus	275 (1)	13,000 (0)
Unknown/Other	635 (1)	9000 (0)
Motorcycles	4100 (7)	70,000 (2)
Total	58414 (100)	3,415,000 (100)

Note: Sum totals may not equal subcategory totals because of rounding. Modified from NHTSA (2009).

Vehicle weight (related to vehicle type) may be another factor, although modern improvements in vehicle design (energy-absorbing designs, multiple airbags, auto tensioning restraint devices) most likely improve injury outcomes more than overall vehicle weight.

Location

The urban accident rate per vehicle mile traveled (VMT) is about 2.5 times higher than the rural accident rate. However, rural accidents are more likely to be fatal compared to urban accidents. The higher fatality rate per VMT in rural locations is probably related, in part, to a combination of factors, including road design and speed (NHTSA, 2012).

Time

Overall, about one third of all fatal crashes involve intoxicated drivers. However, during certain hours of the day, these crashes occur more frequently. For example, intoxicated drivers are involved in about 66 percent of motor vehicle fatalities between midnight and 3 AM. Other times of day with especially high percentages of alcohol impaired driving were 6 PM. to midnight, and 3 AM. to 6 AM. The numbers and percentages across fatal crashes, fatalities, and drivers involved are relatively consistent over time and between studies (NHTSA, 1999, 2011, 2012).

Most alcohol impaired driving fatalities occur in June and July and the fewest occur in January and February (NHTSA, 2009). Alcohol-related crashes are also more likely to occur at night. About 77 percent of fatal alcohol related crashes involving drivers or pedestrians occur between 6:00 PM and 6:00 AM and on Fridays (16%), Saturdays (24%) or Sundays (21%) in comparison to sober driver or pedestrian fatalities that occur more uniformly distributed throughout the week (Table 5.2).

Interestingly, a similar time of day effect is observed for other unintentional deaths as well as homicides. Rates of fatal injury events involving alcohol are lowest in the morning, slightly higher in the afternoon, and significantly higher during evening and late-night hours (Goodman et al., 1991; Smith et al., 1989). In particular, traumatic injury deaths between 9 PM and 3 AM are likely to involve alcohol. Within 24-hour time periods, alcohol-related unintentional deaths (accidents) and homicides exhibit the most pronounced time variations. Researchers found comparatively small day or time variations in alcohol involvement among those who died of natural causes (Goodman et al., 1986; Smith et al., 1989).

Table 5.2: Fatal Crashes by Day of Week and BAC in Drivers and Pedestrians.

	0 mg/dL (n = 22,683)	10–70 mg/dL (n = 2129)	80–140 mg/dL (n = 4204)	150+ mg/dL (n = 9292)
Monday	14	10	9	9
Tuesday	14	11	9	9
Wednesday	15	10	11	9
Thursday	14	12	12	11
Friday	16	17	16	15
Saturday	14	22	24	25
Sunday	13	18	20	21

Source: NHTSA (2003).

Highway Characteristics

Highway characteristics are among the strongest factors in predicting accidents. For example, about half of all accidents occur at intersections. Barriers, width of medians, access control, and other design characteristics all interact with accident rate, but in a complex way. For example, divided highways and wide medians reduce accidents, whereas barriers may increase the frequency of accidents but reduce their severity (Dewar, 2002; Joksch, 1985).

Stopping and exiting distances and signage locations are also important. Since alcohol increases driver simple RT (0.5–1.0 seconds) and complex RT (more than 2 seconds), doubling the sight distances would reduce the accident risk for alcohol-intoxicated drivers. Or put another way, intoxicated drivers may need warning signs at far greater distances than required of other drivers to react to emergent situations. However, increasing the sight distance too far is equally problematic because alcohol impairs some forms of memory and increases divided attention failure.

Speed Limit

Accident and fatality rates per vehicle miles traveled (VMT) seem to be negatively correlated with speed limit. That is, the lower the speed limit the greater the accident rate, possibly because posted speed limits reflect roadway driving conditions. Lower speed limits are used to limit speed in less favorable driving areas or conditions (Joksch, 1985), but higher speeds are associated with greater risk for crash fatalities because the injuries sustained when a vehicle rapidly decelerates (upon impact with another object) are greater. However, high-speed crashes are associated with more severe injuries and may create greater risk for the intoxicated driver because of the effect of alcohol on injury outcome (Chapter 9).

Traffic

The risk of accident per VMT increases with traffic volume. Volume also influences the types of accident; collisions between vehicles are more frequent with increasing volume and single car accidents are less common. The presence of pedestrians, bicyclists, and trucks (slowing down of trucks on upgrades) greatly increases the accident risk. Cars involved in motor vehicle accidents with trucks risk underride, which also greatly increases risk of injury and death. In general, occupants of passenger cars are exposed to greater risks when they collide with medium and large trucks compared to, with other cars (due to weight differential).

Lighting

Predictably, there is a higher incidence of accidents at night when natural illumination is low. Illuminating highways can reduce accidents at night by as much as 30 percent. Other factors that may influence lighting are weather (rain, snow, fog, blowing sand, etc.).

5.3 DRIVER CHARACTERISTICS IN CRASHES

Gender, Age, and Alcohol Use

Traffic deaths by age follow a U-shaped function. Older people and children are less likely to be killed in alcohol related crashes than are young and middle-aged adults (Table 5.3). Male drivers, passengers, and pedestrians are more likely than are females to be involved in alcohol related fatal-crashes.

Table 5.3: Percent of Intoxication-Related Traffic Deaths by Age.

Age	Percent of Traffic Deaths
<16	15
16–20	37
21–29	57
30–45	53
46–64	38
65+	15

Source: NHTSA (2003).

Race, Ethnicity and Other Factors

There is extensive evidence that the risk of traffic crashes varies across racial and ethnic groups, with some groups being at greater or lesser risk than others due to a number of factors, not all of which are fully understood. This research is in constant flux because of changes in definitions, racial or ethnic identity or other important variables.

Because of the growing concern in the motor vehicle traffic safety community over the high number of minority fatalities, a report was written to describe the differences among racial and ethnic groups in the frequency of occurrence of characteristics or behaviors associated with fatalities in motor vehicle traffic crashes. When measured against deaths from all causes, motor vehicle traffic crashes have accounted for disproportionately large percentages, particularly among Native Americans and Hispanics. Alcohol has played a major role in the deaths of both drivers and pedestrians. Additional factors contributing to higher numbers have been lack of valid licensing for drivers and lower usage of safety belts, child safety seats, and motorcycle helmets by all but Asian American/Pacific Islanders. Compared to all others, African American children were killed in disproportionately high numbers in both urban and rural settings (Hilton, 2006).

Alcohol abstention is high among Asians and low among whites (Substance Abuse and Mental Health Services Administration [SAMHSA], 2000, 2004a, 2005). Similarly, there is consensus that rates of binge drinking and heavy drinking tend to be high among Native Americans, followed closely by Hispanics and Whites, with Asians showing the lowest rates of binge drinking and heavy drinking. Some reports indicate black drinkers show relatively low rates of binge drinking and heavy drinking; other reports show rates comparable to (or higher than) those for whites or Hispanics (Juarez, Walters, Dougherty & Radi, 2006).

Pompham, Schmidt, and Israelstam (1984) noted that the estimated relative risk of accidental death was 2.5 to 8 times greater among males defined as heavy drinkers or alcohol dependent than among the general population. Estimates suggest that alcoholics are nearly five times more likely than others to die in motor vehicle crashes, sixteen times more likely to die in falls, and ten times more likely to become fire or burn victims (Eckardt et al., 1981).

Anda, Williamson, and Remington (1988) used data from a sample of 13,251 noninstitutionalized United States adults included in the *National Health and Nutrition Examination Survey Epidemiologic Follow-Up Study* to estimate relative risk of fatal injury. This study is noteworthy because baseline data on alcohol use were collected approximately 10 years before follow-up data on fatal injuries. After adjusting for gender, age, race, and education, the investigators found that the relative risk of death from injury was significantly

Table 5.4: Alcohol Impaired Driving Based on Driver Characteristics.

Age	Measure	Years	Gender	Race/Ethnicity Group				
				Afr. Am.	Asian	Hisp.	Nat. Am.	White
18+	Drink and drive in last 30 days	1993	Both	1.5%	–	1.9%	–	2.6%
		1995	Both	1.5%	–	2.3%	–	2.4%
		1997	Both	1.3%	–	2.3%	–	2.2%
18+	Drunk and stopped by police in last year	1995	Males	14.0%	–	21.0%	–	22.0%
			Females	3.0%	–	6.0%	–	7.0%
	Arrested for DWI in past year	1995	Males	1%	–	4.0%	–	1%
			Females	0%	–	0%	–	0%
	Passenger in a car when driver drank too much in past year	1995	Males	14%	–	15%	–	10%
			Females	13%	–	11%	–	10%
16-64	Drove within 2 hours of drinking within past year	1993–1997	Both	16%	13%	17%	21%	28%
	Drove within 2 hours of drinking in last 30 days	1993–1997	Both	8%	6%	9%	10%	18%
18+	Drove more than once after drinking too much alcohol in the past year	2001–2002	Males	3%	2%	3%	6%	5%
			Females	1%	1%	1%	2%	2%
	Drinking and driving in past year	2001–2002	Males	5%	4%	6%	9%	8%
			Females	2%	1%	1%	5%	3%
16+	Drove within 2 hours of drinking in the past year	1996	Both	13%	–	17%	–	25%
18+	Drove after drinking too much alcohol within the past year	2000	Males	17%	14%	17%	21%	22%
			Females	9%	7%	7%	15%	12%
16+	BAC ≥ 50 mg/dL	1973	Both	17%	–	22%	–	13%
		1986	Both	14%	–	13%	–	7%
		1996	Both	9%	–	15%	–	7%
	BAC ≥ 100 mg/dL	1973	Both	6%	–	3%	–	5%
		1986	Both	6%	–	4%	–	3%
		1996	Both	4%	–	8%	–	2%
16+	BAC > 0 mg/dL	1990-1994	Both	37%	28%	41%	63%	38%
	BAC ≤ 80mg/dL	1999-2004	Both	7%	3%	5%	4%	4%
	BAC ≥ 80mg/dL	1999-2004	Both	31%	23%	42%	54%	29%

Note: This table is based upon twelve studies summarized and described in greater detail in Romano, Voas, and Lacey (2010).

greater among those reporting five or more drinks per occasion than among those who reported drinking fewer than five drinks per occasion (Anda et al., 1988). Among individuals reporting nine or more drinks per occasion, the relative risk of fatal injury was more than three times greater than among those reporting fewer than five drinks per occasion. Self reporting quantity of consumption per drinking occasion was found to be a stronger predictor of fatal injury than was frequency of consumption.

Evidence also indicates that alcohol involvement in fatal injury events is associated with victims' gender and ethnicity. Males are disproportionately represented in most serious and fatal injury events. Moreover, the probability of alcohol involvement in fatal injury events is considerably higher for male victims (Goodman et al., 1991; Smith et al., 1989).

In summary, there are complex cultural and other differences that differentiate patterns of drinking and driving or other injuries in the United States (Romano, Voas & Lacey; *see* Table 5.4).

Seat Belt Use

Seat belts save lives when used properly. Not wearing a seat belt introduces the issue of comparative negligence, which has important legal implications. About 40 percent of alcohol-impaired drivers operate above the speed limit and more than 60 percent of intoxicated drivers do not use seat belts (Table 5.5). There are data indicating that intoxicated drivers are less likely to wear seat belts; there is also evidence that African Americans and Hispanics do not wear safety belts as often as whites do (e.g., Bolen, Rhodes, Powell-Griner, Bland & Holtzman, 2000; Voas, Fisher & Tippetts, 2002; Boyle & Vanderwolf, 2004). Therefore, members affiliated with these groups may be overrepresented in fatal crashes in general. When intoxication is added to the mix, some groups may be at an even greater risk because of crash risk (due to intoxication) and less seat belt use, resulting in greater injuries. This may be of significant forensic value because alcohol changes injury outcome (*see* Chapter 9).

Understanding the nature of cultural, racial and ethnic beliefs and attitudes toward drinking and driving may help researchers to develop better tools to prevent intoxicated driving or to assist law enforcement in their

Table 5.5: Alcohol-Impaired Drivers by Belt Use and Speeding.

	Unbelted	Belted	Total
Speeding	27%	13%	40%
Not Speeding	35%	25%	60%
Total	62%	38%	100%

Source: NHTSA (2009)

interactions with certain groups. There is so much variability and diversity within and among groups, however, that single preventive messages to prevent intoxicated driving have emerged, and the use of these emerging data is of limited value in forensic evaluations.

5.4 RELATIVE RISK

As would be predicted from a drug with well-known dose-dependent effects, analyses of relative risk have revealed that crash risk increases as driver BAC increases. Of public safety importance is the finding that the relative probability of a fatal crash increases in a dose-dependent manner and strikingly so at higher BACs, when individual drinking driver characteristics are considered.

Relative risk research is very important in studying fatal crash probabilities, developing legislative initiatives, and educating the public. Epidemiological studies attempt to isolate factors that are the most significant in causing accidents. The two primary approaches to studying relative risk are (1) the "case control" method, in which the incidence of alcohol in crashes is compared with the incidence of alcohol in drivers sharing the same road, location, and time but who are not involved in motor vehicle crashes, and (2) the "induced exposure" method, which contrasts intoxicated drivers deemed responsible for accidents with intoxicated drivers who were not responsible for the crash but were innocent victims. The latter method would appear to be a more accurate method for determining risk but is more complicated because it is not always easy to determine which driver caused the crash. Moreover, there may be a potential for bias for determining fault if one driver is perceived to be intoxicated and the other is sober. This bias is minimized and the relationship stronger when data are limited to single-vehicle crashes (Zador, 1991). Logistic regression analyses using a range of covariates including age and BAC and gender to estimate relative risk have also been employed (Zador, Krawcuk & Voas, 2000; Peck, Gebers, Voas & Romano, 2008). Even though all earlier studies demonstrated that the risk for a fatal crash increased exponentially, more recent studies estimate the risk to be even greater than previously believed (Zador, 1991; Zador et al., 2000). When age, gender, and BAC are considered, the risk is staggeringly high.

Popkin (1991) analyzed changes in arrest rates, alcohol-related crashes, and single-vehicle nighttime crash rates by age and sex. For most subgroups, DWI arrest rates decreased between 1976 and 1985. DWI arrest rates decreased sharply for males in the age categories investigated. However, decreases in DWI rates were less significant for females than for males. In fact, females ages 21 through 24 years were the only group to experience an increased DWI arrest rate (26%) during the study.

Table 5.6: Alcohol Intoxication, Behavioral and Relative Risk for a Fatal Vehicle Crash.

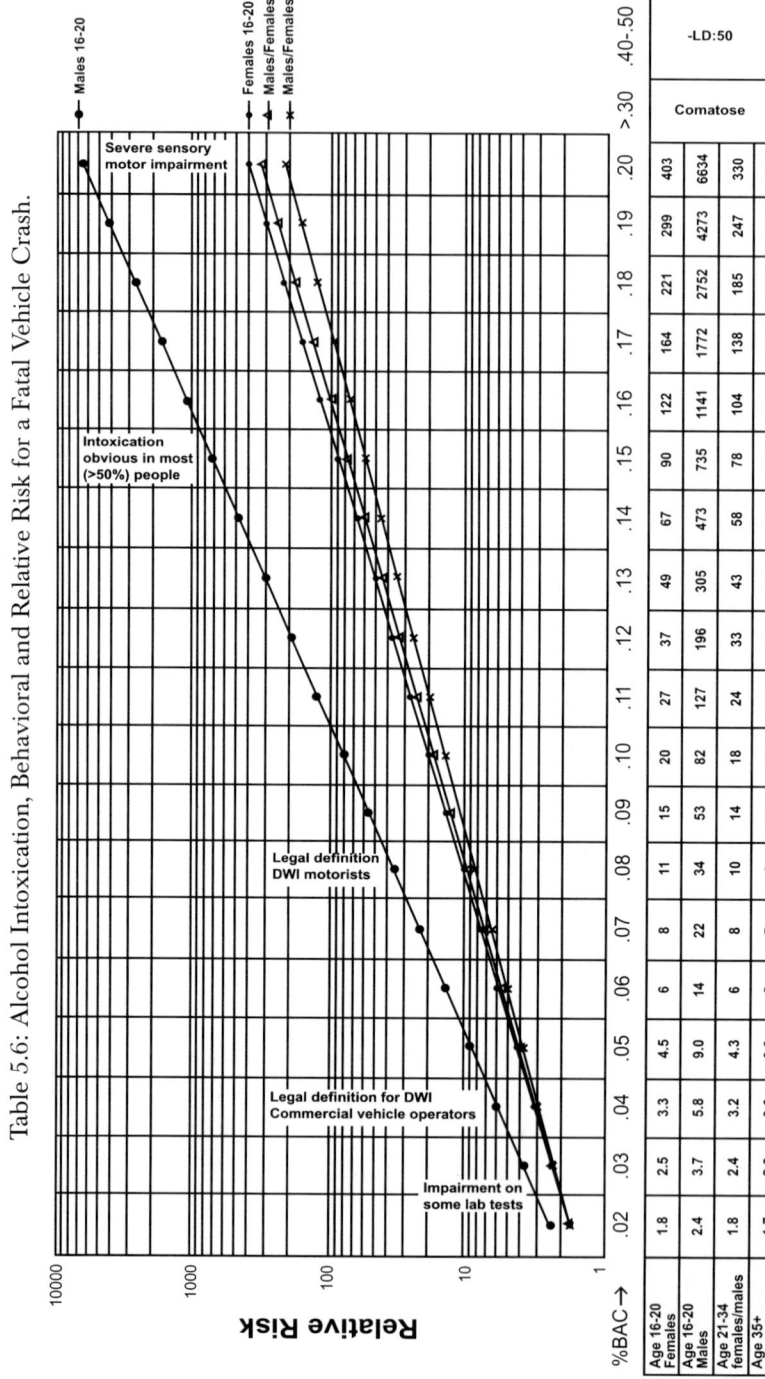

%BAC →	.02	.03	.04	.05	.06	.07	.08	.09	.10	.11	.12	.13	.14	.15	.16	.17	.18	.19	.20	>.30	.40-.50
Age 16-20 Females	1.8	2.5	3.3	4.5	6	8	11	15	20	27	37	49	67	90	122	164	221	299	403		
Age 16-20 Males	2.4	3.7	5.8	9.0	14	22	34	53	82	127	196	305	473	735	1141	1772	2752	4273	6634	Comatose	-LD:50
Age 21-34 females/males	1.8	2.4	3.2	4.3	6	8	10	14	18	24	33	43	58	78	104	138	185	247	330		
Age 35+ females/males	1.7	2.3	3.0	3.9	5	7	9	11	15	20	26	33	44	57	75	99	129	169	221		

Line graph shows relative risk (log) as a function of BAC, age and gender. Data derived from stepwise logistic regression coefficients for relative risk is presented in tabularized form below graph. Coefficients are rounded to nearest tenth or whole number. These coefficients apply to single vehicle fatalities. Note that for women age 16-20, a coefficient of 0.03 (range 0.044-0.014) was used (Zador et al., 2000, *J Stud Alc 61*(3)387-395. Copyright 2008, from *Handbook of the Medical Consequences of Alcohol and Drug Abuse* by *John Brick*. Reproduced by permission of Taylor and Francis Group, LLC, a division of Informa pic.

Striking gender differences were reported in the changing rate of alcohol-related crashes. Regardless of age, the rate of alcohol-related crashes among males declined between 1976 and 1985 (Popkin, 1991). Among females, the crash rate increased 74 percent for those age 18 through 20 years, 93 percent for those 21 through 24 years, and 45 percent for those 25 through 34 years. For females under age 18, the rate of alcohol related crashes decreased.

Zador (1991) noted that nearly 40 percent of drivers ages 16 to 19 who were involved in alcohol-related fatal traffic crashes had BACs under .10 percent. Alcohol may pose an especially serious risk for younger drivers because they have comparatively little experience with alcohol (and less tolerance) or driving.

Taking the apparent gender and age factors a step further, Zador (2000) used log-linear models to estimate the extent to which different BACs increased the relative risk of fatal crash by age and sex. Male drivers age 25 years or older with BACs equal to the criterion group were arbitrarily used as the reference category for calculating increased relative risk. Regardless of gender, alcohol increased relative crash risk most substantially among drivers ages 16 through 20 years.

This effect is even apparent at low to moderate BACs. Alcohol also appears to increase crash risk more for males than for females. Zador's (2000) analysis suggests that (1) alcohol increases fatal crash risk more for males than for females, (2) alcohol increases fatal crash risk more for younger drivers than for older ones, and (3) low to moderate BACs profoundly enhance crash risk among drivers aged 16 years through 20 years, (Table 5.6). This analysis also suggests that more attention should be given to the effects of low and moderate BACs and to gender and age differences when considering the effects of alcohol on behavior and safety.

Psychological Characteristics–Alcohol and Traffic Safety: A Complex Problem

A growing body of literature (Argeriou, McCarty & Blacker, 1985; Arstein-Kerslake & Peck, 1985; Donovan & Marlatt, 1982; Donovan, Queisser, Umlauf & Salzberg, 1986; McMillen, Smith & Wells-Parker, 1989; Perrine, 1990; Wells-Parker, Anderson, Pang & Timken, 1993; Wieczorek & Miller, 1992; Wilson, 1991) indicates that the impaired-driving population varies in terms of severity of alcohol problem, drinking patterns, driving-related attitudes, driving behaviors, involvement in deviant and criminal behavior, expectations about the effects of alcohol, and personality characteristics.

The literature suggests that these factors may mediate the relationship between alcohol and traffic safety. For example, in an experimental study using a balanced placebo design, drivers who initially scored high on measures of sensation seeking, hostility, aggressiveness, and psychopathic deviance and who believed that they had consumed alcohol subsequently displayed increased high-risk driving behaviors (McMillen et al., 1989). Drivers who initially scored low on these characteristics and believed that they had consumed alcohol subsequently displayed fewer high-risk driving behaviors.

McMillen and colleagues (1991) compared eight driver groups on personality measures (e.g., hostility, sensation seeking, psychopathic deviance, and mania) and behavior measures (e.g., number of drinks consumed per week, number of times per month of driving impaired, number of nontraffic arrests, number of crashes, and number of crashes after drinking). The researchers found that impaired drivers arrested after an accident or moving violation were significantly higher in hostility, psychopathic deviance, nontraffic arrests, frequency of impaired driving, crashes after drinking, and drinks consumed per week than were impaired drivers caught in roadblocks. The findings of this study suggest that impaired driving is part of a larger pattern of problematic characteristics and behaviors for some individuals.

Compared with men in the general driving population, male offenders convicted of driving under the influence of alcohol (DUI) are heavy drinkers with other psychosocial medicolegal problems. White and Gasperin (2007) note that about 40 to 70 percent of DWI first-time offenders have a prior alcohol or drug arrest history, more than 80 percent have drug or alcohol related-problems, and the overwhelming number of female (85 percent) and male (91 percent) DWI offenders meet lifetime diagnostic criteria for alcohol above a dependence. Largely, such violators are not "social drinkers" but hard-core drinkers who drive at least once a month with BACs in excess of 150 mg/dL.

In a study examining the extent and nature of criminal behavior among DUI offenders, Argeriou and associates (1985) reviewed the criminal records of 1406 randomly selected DUI offenders in Massachusetts. The records revealed a history of prior court arraignments in 76.5 percent of cases. Half of the individuals had been arraigned for criminal offenses other than or in addition to traffic and DUI offenses, and one-fourth had been arraigned previously for DUI. Among those with prior DUI arrests, 68 percent also had criminal arrests. A 3-year follow-up indicated that 63 percent of those rearrested for DUI had prior criminal arrests. These findings indicate (1) drinking then driving may be one of many illegal activities engaged in by DUI offenders and (2) intoxicated behavior increases risk to engage in and get arrested for criminal activity.

Alcohol and Injury Outcome

Epidemiological research on non–motor vehicle traumatic injury safety offers important baseline information on rates of alcohol involvement and strongly suggests that alcohol increases the risk of injury. Although it is commonly believed that alcohol may protect against injury once an accident occurs, research findings provide evidence to the contrary. Controlled animal studies indicate that alcohol exacerbates the injurious effects of trauma. Moreover, an analysis of data from more than 1 million drivers involved in motor vehicle crashes indicated that when effects of such injury-related variables as safety belt use, vehicle deformation, vehicle speed, driver age, and vehicle weight were accounted for drinking drivers were more likely than nondrinking drivers to suffer serious injury or death (Waller et al., 1986). The effects of alcohol on injury outcome are discussed further in Chapter 9.

5.5 YEARS AND POTENTIAL LIFE LOST

Traffic crashes are the leading cause of death among people under age 40 (National Center for Health Statistics, 1988). Fatal injuries resulting from alcohol-related traffic crashes represent a tremendous loss of human life. In 2001, alcohol-related traffic fatalities represented 442,943 years of potential life lost (YPLL) among males and 136,558 YPLL among females (Centers for Disease Control, 2004). Using sophisticated mathematical modeling procedures, Evans (1990) estimated that eliminating alcohol would reduce overall traffic fatalities by about 47 percent. Yet these estimates do not reflect the enormous human and economic costs that result from the nonfatal traffic injuries in which alcohol figures prominently (Stoduto et al., 1991; Vingilis, 1988).

5.6 SCOPE OF THE PROBLEM–
ALCOHOL IN EVERYDAY ACTIVITIES

Alcohol and accidental injury extend well beyond motor vehicle crashes to include other everyday activities. Impairment from alcohol is linked to an array of serious and fatal injuries, including spinal cord injuries (Branche, Sniezek, Sattin & Mirkin, 1991), traumatic brain injuries (Jones, 1989) and injuries incurred in general aviation crashes (Gibbons, 1988), drownings (Wintemute, Teret, Kraus & Wright, 1990), spousal violence (Miller, Downs & Gondoli, 1989), suicides (Conner, Beatrais & Conwell, 2003; Gomberg, 1989), and homicides (Welte & Abel, 1989). Studies based on medical examiner reports and records of emergency room patients present a panoramic perspective on alcohol-related injury.

Water Sports

The relationship between alcohol intoxication and many common recreational activities, such as swimming and boating, has been a subject of scientific interest for some time. From the well-known biobehavioral effects of alcohol it can be reasonably predicted that alcohol-impaired judgment, disorientation, hypothermia, impaired psychomotor skills, and a decrease in the ability to hold one's breath would be contributing factors in drowning accidents, but studies published prior to 1985 did not establish a causal relationship between these effects of alcohol intoxication and drowning deaths. Hoxie, Cardosi, Stearns, and Menger (1988) reported that 22 percent were intoxicated with BACs of 100 mg/dL or more at the time of death and nearly half (45%) of drowning victims had some alcohol in their system. About the same percentage of deaths associated with water sports involve alcohol (Cummings, Mueller & Quan, 2011; U.S. Coast Guard, 2010).

Estimates suggest that alcohol is associated with between 47 percent and 65 percent of adult drownings (Dietz & Baker, 1974; Patetta & Biddinger, 1988; Plueckhahn, 1982). Howland and Hingson (1987) proposed two reasons why research has not established alcohol's contribution to drownings more fully. First, studies have not included adequate control groups to estimate relative risk. This is true for most studies of alcohol involvement in non–motor vehicle injury events. Second, most studies have not established clear criteria for excluding cases in which the postmortem BAC might not accurately reflect BAC at immersion.

Wintemute, Teret, Kraus, and Wright (1990) analyzed coroners' reports for 442 drownings in Sacramento County, California, over a 10-year period. To ensure that their results reflected alcohol involvement in the event, Wintemute and colleagues analyzed only cases for which BACs had been determined within 24 hours of death and in which death had occurred within 6 hours of immersion (n = 234). Forty-one percent of the drowning victims tested alcohol positive, and 30 percent had BACs of 100 mg/dL or higher.

The rate of alcohol involvement in drownings appears to vary by gender, age, and activity type. Alcohol was less likely to be detected in teenage victims than in adults, and victims' BAC was positively associated with age (Wintemute et al., 1990). About 46 percent of victims ages 20 to 64 had BACs of 100 mg/dL or higher, and 38 percent of victims ages 46 to 64 had BACs at or above 200 mg/dL. Alcohol involvement was more likely among male (59 percent) than among female (40 percent) drowning victims. The highest rates of alcohol involvement (about 70%) were reported for drownings associated with land-based motor vehicles. Alcohol was also present in more than half the drownings associated with swimming, boating, or rafting. Lower rates of alcohol involvement were reported for drownings associated with other activities.

Alcohol consumption significantly increases risk for boating fatalities. In a review of the Boating Accident Report Files in Ohio from 1983 to 1986, Molberg, Hopkins, Paulson, and Gunn (1993) found that alcohol consumption was a factor in up to 21 percent of reported boating accidents. Because alcohol deleteriously impairs balance, motor function, and judgment, intoxicated passengers, as well as vessel operators, are probably at risk for injury (Hingson & Howland, 1993).

In another water sport activity, diving, alcohol intoxication contributes to and aggravates spinal cord injuries that frequently follow diving accidents. In this context, Perrine, Mundt, Winer (1994) examined the effects of alcohol on the ability to perform shallow-water entry dives under experimental conditions. The data revealed a progressive and significant impairment of specific aspects of diving performance at blood alcohol levels of 40 mg/dL and higher. Interestingly, this study also correlated diving performance with psychomotor performance using the same SFSTs used by many police to detect drunk drivers. Impaired diving correlated well with subjects who failed the validated scoring criteria for the detection of drivers with a blood alcohol level of more than 100 mg/dL (Perrine et al., 1994).

Alcohol may be an important factor in water-related spinal cord injuries. The Centers for Disease Control (1988) estimated that between 10,000 and 20,000 spinal cord injuries occur each year in the United States. About 10 percent of spinal cord injuries are diving related (National Committee for Injury Prevention and Control, 1989). Using a case-control design, Branche, and associates (1991) estimated that subjects who experienced diving-related spinal cord injuries were about four times more likely than were control subjects to have used alcohol. Although the investigators cited small sample size and difficulties in precisely matching controls to injury victims as important study limitations, their results suggest that alcohol may contribute to diving-related spinal cord injuries.

Alcohol intoxication at BACs of 40 mg/dL and higher produced a progressive and significant impairment of specific biomechanical components and overall performance of shallow water diving into a pool (Perrine et al., 1994). Impaired diving also correlated well with impairment on SFSTs used by police to detect drunk drivers. Finally, alcohol influences injury outcome (Brick, 2012), including spinal cord injuries that frequently follow diving accidents (Perrine et al., 1994).

Aircraft Operation

One of the more complex divided attention tasks is flying an aircraft. Pilots must attend to an array of instruments displaying information on speed, altitude, directional bearing, horizontal situation, vertical speed, engine status (e.g., oil pressure, fuel, temperature) while maneuvering with both the yoke (steering "wheel") and rudder pedals and making perceptual and cognitive decisions based on information that changes in all spatial dimensions as well as reporting course changes and attending to control tower messages. Although there have been relatively few cases of fatal airline crashes due to pilot intoxication, sufficient data are available to raise concern about this issue of airline safety. For example, it is known from research in other fields that alcohol impairs skills such as divided attention that are necessary for safe motor vehicle operation. It is also known that alcohol deleteriously influences the ability of pilots to evaluate their performance (Morrow, Leirer, Yesavage & Tinklenberg 1991). Moreover low levels of alcohol (25–40 mg/dL) impair performance of trained pilots in flight simulators (Billings, Demosthesen, White & O'Hara 1991; Ross, Yeazel & Chau 1992).

There is general agreement that even low BACs affect pilot safety by impairing a range of perceptual, cognitive, and psychomotor skills (Modell & Mountz, 1990). It is less well-known that pilot performance may be impaired long after the pilots eliminate detectable blood alcohol, although such impairments would not be detectable through standard blood or breath alcohol analysis. Ooserveld (1970) reported that flying-related increases in gravity force produce positional alcohol nystagmus (PAN), a disturbance in ocular motor control, up to 48 hours after drinking. Ryback and Dowd (1970) reported similar results 34 hours after drinking. After reviewing the literature on hangover effects, Gibbons (1988) hypothesized that disorientation PAN involving spatial disorientation may have contributed to many aviation crashes. It has also been suggested that alcohol can impair performance on flight simulators many hours after blood alcohol levels have returned to zero (Yesavage, Dolhert & Taylor, 1994). Takeoff heading, landing heading, instrument landing system localizer, and glide-slope deviation have been reported as impaired in pilots 8 hours after drinking (Taylor, O'Hara, Mumenthaler & Yesavage, 2000).

Although there have been some instances of airline pilots convicted of flying while under the influence of alcohol, alcohol has not been directly implicated in United States commercial airline crashes (Modell & Mountz, 1990) but appears to play a more visible role in general aviation crashes (Gibbons, 1988). Survey research indicates that pilots' drinking patterns closely parallel those found in the general population (Ross & Ross, 1988) but even so, compared with motor vehicle crashes, aviation crashes are quite rare. Copeland (1986) analyzed the medical examiner's files for noncommercial aircraft fatalities in Dade County, Florida, between 1977 and 1983. BACs were measured for forty nine of fifty seven cases; seventeen pilots (34.7% tested alcohol positive, and 4 pilots (8.1%) had BACs at or above 100 mg/dL. Harper and Albers (1964) detected positive BACs in more than 35 percent of pilots killed in aviation crashes. Modell and Mountz (1990) noted that typical estimates of alcohol involvement by pilots in fatal aviation crashes range from 10 percent to 30 percent.

Morrow, Leirer, and Yesavage (1990) examined the effects of alcohol and age on radio communication during simulated flight. They noted that radio communication–an essential element of aviation safety and a complex information-processing task that often competes with other flight-related tasks– could be particularly susceptible to divided attention failures. BACs as low as 40 mg/dL significantly impaired radio communication performance, and other studies have found that the effect is stronger among older pilots. Morrow and colleagues (1990) also found evidence of long-term hangover effects on pilots' radio communication performance, which was significantly impaired 8 hours after drinking to a BAC of 100 mg/dL.

Federal Aviation Administration (FAA) regulations deem it unlawful for any crewmember to have a BAC of 40 mg/dL (which is also the legal definition for DWI for commercial motor vehicle operators) or higher or to fly within 8 hours after consuming alcoholic beverages. In a survey of pilots, Ross and Ross (1990) found that only 37 percent of respondents knew FAA guidelines concerning the 40 mg/dL BAC limit. Respondents were asked to judge the amount of beer, wine, and liquor they could consume in 1 hour before reaching target BACs of 40 mg/dL and 100 mg/dL. Nearly half overestimated the amount of beer or wine they could consume before reaching 40 mg/dL. A small percentage overestimated the amount of liquor they could consume before reaching 100 mg/dL. Many pilots, especially heavy drinkers, underestimated the amount of time required for alcohol elimination. Such findings, coupled with experimental evidence about performance impairments at low BACs and potential long term performance deficits due to hangover effects, present a potentially troublesome picture.

Modell and Mountz (1990) recommended modifying FAA regulations to allow a maximum BAC of 10 mg/dL (allowing for errors in measuring devices). They also recommended extending the minimum required time interval between drinking and flying to at least 12 hours and adding a regulation to prohibit flying within 24 hours of consuming five or more standard drinks. Such a recommendation is in alignment with the maxim, "24 hours from bottle to throttle" espoused by many pilots.

Cook (1997) reviewed the specific domain-relevant functions impaired at different BACs and concluded that performance of flight tasks such as terrain separation, aircraft descent, and angular acceleration are impaired at BACs as low as 10 to 30 mg/dL. Piloting skills such as tracking radio signals, managing heavy workload conditions, vectoring airport traffic control, observing and avoiding air traffic, and performing linear acceleration were imposed at BACs below 50 mg/dL. In an experiment conducted in actual flights involving sixteen instrument-rated pilots (Billings et al., 1991), dose-dependent performance errors began when BACs reached 20 mg/dL and more than 50% of the pilots lost control of the aircraft.

Alcohol and High-Risk Sexual Behavior

Alcohol involvement is visible in cases of sexual abuse, misconduct, poor decision making, unprotected sex, and many other areas of human sexual behavior. Even so, ongoing work indicates that the relationship between alcohol (and other drug use) and behavior is more complex than was initially anticipated. Earleywine and Finn (1991) found that people who score high on general measures of sensation seeking were more likely to consume alcohol and to express behavioral disinhibition. Other sociological or psychological attributes may also help explain the relationship between alcohol use and sexual behavior, which is frequently a question in cases involving alleged sexual assault. From a broader public health perspective, the acquired immunodeficiency syndrome (AIDS) epidemic has increased public concern about factors that may contribute to high-risk behaviors leading to the spread of this disease. As Critchlow (1983) noted, alcohol is often used as an excuse for engaging in behavior that violates social norms. Impaired judgment and decreased behavioral inhibitions (Critchlow, 1986; Leigh, 1990c; Reinarman and Leigh, 1987) from intoxication may lead to enhanced sexual encounters and promiscuous behavior (Leigh, 1990). A better understanding of the relationship between alcohol use and sexual behavior could provide invaluable information for policymakers and program planners and for some forensic applications.

The emergence of AIDS among male homosexuals and intravenous drug users directed the focus of earlier research on these populations. Several studies found relatively strong associations between substance use (alcohol and recreational drugs) and high-risk sexual behavior among homosexual males (Stall et al., 1986, Valdiserri et al., 1988). In a longitudinal study of homosexually active men, McCusker and associates (1990) found that men who increased their alcohol use during the study period were about twice as likely as were those who reduced their alcohol consumption to maintain high-risk sexual practices.

The relationship between alcohol and other drug use and high-risk sexual behavior among heterosexuals is equivocal. Ericksen and Trocki (1992) reported that measures of problem drinking behavior were strongly predictive of self-reported sexually transmitted disease. They also reported that high-volume drinking was predictive of a high rate of change in sex partners, which in turn increases the risk of sexually transmitted disease. Temple and Leigh (1992) found that alcohol tended to be associated with encounters involving new sexual partners, but that alcohol use in the event was not predictive of risky sexual behavior. However, Hingson, Strunin, Berlin & Heeren (1990) reported that heavy drinkers (those consuming five or more drinks in a day) were about 2.8 times less likely to report regular condom use than nondrinkers.

Pedestrian Behavior

Fall Down Injuries

Unintentional injuries from falling down accounted for about 26,000 deaths in 2010, were the third leading cause of about 13,000 accidental deaths in the United States and were the leading cause of unintended injuries in 2011 (Centers for Disease Control and Prevention, 2013). It is estimated that about 21 to 77 percent of deaths from falls involve alcohol (Federal Emergency Managment Agency, 2003). Although walking and driving are different tasks, both activities require people to divide their attention among many different activities as well as attending and responding to environmental demands. For example, walking requires extensive psychomotor activity, the mechanics of which require the subject to lift the foot, flex the foot, step forward, rotate the hip, redistribute the weight to the load-bearing leg, maintain balance and forward momentum and repeat this sequence with the alternating leg while simultaneously making adjustments for changes in the walkway surface, and so on. Fall down injuries due to intoxication are directly related to the effects of alcohol on the ability to balance, to attend simultaneously to road or walkway hazards, and to make estimates of time and distance while simultaneously attending to a myriad of environmental factors (e.g., vehicles, changes in walkway characteristics).

The more complex the physical or cognitive complexities of the environment challenges, the more difficult it becomes to divide attention between tasks necessary for safe pedestrian activity. Moreover, the successful execution of some of these tasks (i.e., traveling from one location to another without incident) is more likely due to the narrowing of attention under less-challenging conditions and should not be misinterpreted as the absence of impairment. Negotiating stairs introduces an additional challenge to the vestibular system of the intoxicated pedestrian because the brain is receiving sensory information about movement in different spatial dimensions. At relatively high BACs alcohol has some analgesic effects, and the performance of these skills is further diminished by loss of sensation and the impaired proprioceptive feedback. Relative risk for fall-down injuries from falling down increases at BACs above 50 mg/dL (*see* Table 5.6).

Most studies suggest that alcohol increases the risk for injuries due to falls, but one study in particular included a control group that allowed researchers to analyze increases in relative risk for a fall due to alcohol intoxication. Honkanen and colleagues (1983) evaluated 313 emergency room patients, more than half of whom had blood alcohol levels greater than 200 mg/dL, and compared them with pedestrians whom were at the same location of the accident 1 week later at the same time of day. The comparison revealed the relative risk for a fall was three times greater for patients with blood alcohol levels between 50 and 100 mg/dL, ten times greater for patients with BAC between. 100 and 150 mg/dL, and 60 times greater for patients with BAC more than 160 mg/dL (Honkanen et al., 1983). More than two thirds of drivers, pedestrians, and bicyclists who are killed each year are intoxicated (NHTSA, 1994).

Pedestrians Versus Motor Vehicles

Pedestrians not only fall down but are often injured when they encounter motorized vehicles entering the roadway. Two behavioral categories in particular should be considered with regard to intoxicated pedestrians injured by vehicles: psychomotor impairment and risk taking. Blomberg, Preusser, Hale, and Ulmer (1979) found that intoxicated pedestrians made increased errors in decisions about where and how to cross roadways. Intoxicated pedestrians typically staggered into oncoming traffic even when the vehicle was in full view or stopped. About half the cases examined involved pedestrians with BACs greater than 50 mg/dL and the relative risk for injury increased slightly at BACs above 50 mg/dL and sharply above 100 mg/dL. Pedestrians showed increased risk taking by darting out at intersections or into the roadway from other locations and making selection errors as to where to cross or enter a roadway. Since blood samples from the nonfatally injured subjects were obtained within 2 hours or more after their injury, BACs may have been higher at the time of the injury and declining at the time of the test, thereby underestimating the BAC and risk at the time of the accident. Nevertheless, the authors concluded that increased risk taking would have been less likely were it not for alcohol use. Other well-known related factors, such as perception and attention are impaired by alcohol (Moskowitz, Burns & Williams, 1985) and the relationship between intoxication and increased risk taking and impulsivity, particularly among young males, has been known for some time (Cherpitel, 1993).

Until more data on pedestrian risk are available, an initial comparison with other types of accidents is appropriate to appreciate relative risk, because pedestrian activity and other behaviors (motor vehicle operation, etc.) rely significantly on vision, attentional processes, and other cognitive skills

(Moskowitz & Fiorentino, 2000; Sivak, 1996). Pedestrians are also exposed to other environmental (e.g., temperature, precipitation) distractions and must engage in more dynamic psychomotor activity than drivers do. Nevertheless, relative risk for a motor vehicle crash (which is well-studied) is just that, relative to motor vehicles but is useful for comparative purposes to demonstrate how alcohol intoxication relates to other well-known common activities.

The effects of alcohol on pedestrian risk taking and relative risk for an injury with a motor vehicle is less well-studied than other types of accidents. Until more data are available, an initial comparison with other types of accidents is appropriate to appreciate risk, because like other modes of injury (driving, cycling, diving, etc.) pedestrian behavior also relies significantly on vision, attentional processes and other cognitive skills (Moskowitz & Fiorentino, 2000; Sivak, 1996). Thus, such comparisons, while relative, are useful to demonstrate the wide-ranging impairment produced by alcohol and risk for injury. Pedestrians are also exposed to other environmental (e.g., temperature, precipitation) distractions and must engage in more dynamic psychomotor activity than drivers do.

Bicycling

Intoxication is a factor in non–motorized vehicle injuries as well. According to NHTSA, there are about 200 fatalities and 7000 injuries from alcohol related bicycle crashes each year. Bicyclists, like those engaging in other everyday activities affected by alcohol, must divide their attention and engage in psychomotor tasks including remembering to properly secure a helmet, mount the bicycle, push off (if from a stop), lift the leg, flex the foot, redistribute the weight to the opposite load-bearing leg, push down on the pedal (or pull up if toe clips are used). Then repeat this sequence while maintaining forward velocity, balancing, steering, braking, allowing for changes in the road surface and attending to traffic control devices, signs, road markings, traffic and making estimates of time, distance, speed, and risk. Bicyclists have the added distraction of being directly exposed to the elements.

Bicyclists who died at the scene were four times as likely as those who died at hospitals to be intoxicated at or above the legal definition for motorists, which may be due to the effects of alcohol on injury outcome (Chapter 9). Olkkonen, Lahdenranta, Slatis, and Honkanen (1993) used a case-control study method, to estimate the relative risk of an alcohol-related bicycle crash. The study involved 200 bicycle victims who were injured fatally in road traffic accidents during the years 1982 to 1988 and 700 cyclists who were used as unmatched controls for these cases. The study found that alcohol was involved in 25 percent of the collision accidents and in 63 percent of the single accidents involving cyclists ages 15 to 64 years and whose blood alcohol was measured. Only 4 percent of the controls were under the influence of alcohol. A relative risk was of the order of 3 overall and 58 for the collisions related to alcohol use. Li and colleagues (1996) reported that fatally injured bicyclists were about twice as likely to be intoxicated as cyclists treated for nonfatal injuries.

Thermal Injuries

Intoxication is also a contributing factor in injuries from fires and burns, which account for an estimated 5000 fatalities and about 1.4 million injuries a year, and is a leading cause of accidents and deaths in the United States (Baker, O'Neill & Karpf, 1992). In a review on the epidemiology and toxicological complications of burn cases involving alcohol and other drugs, Brick (2006) concluded that there is a clear relationship between alcohol or drug intoxication and the risk for thermal injury. For example, alcohol-intoxicated persons may be at increased risk for accidental injury because of impaired judgment or psychomotor coordination while engaging in normal fire-starting activities (e.g., cooking), but psychomotor impairment is only one part of the problem. Medical consequences of long-term alcohol abuse as well as acute neuropsychological status while intoxicated may impair various domains of cognitive functioning, decreasing the ability to anticipate problems, lower inhibitions and increase risky behaviors. Once a fire has started, mental confusion and failure to recognize risk or danger may lead to an inability to anticipate or respond to danger, particularly at high levels of intoxication. This evolving literature shows that the interaction between burn injuries and intoxication is often complex and includes many variables in addition to intoxication.

Howland and Hingson (1987) reviewed studies on alcohol and burn injuries published over the course of 40 years (1947–1986) and reported on the percentage of the victims who were intoxicated from alcohol. In the overwhelming majority of studies, it was concluded that alcohol exposure was more likely among those who died in fires ignited by cigarettes than from other causes. Although the evidence is not definitive, it strongly suggests that alcohol plays a role in the cause of fires and in subsequent burn injuries and is overly represented in burn victims. It is noteworthy that in a study of deaths due to fire, Hingson & Howland found that more than one third of the victims had blood alcohol levels greater than 100 mg/dL, which at the time of the study represented the blood alcohol level that defined intoxicated driving in most states. The authors concluded from these data that alcohol intoxication is a risk factor for fire deaths (Hingson & Howland, 1993). Later studies further revealed that alcohol was a factor in about 22 (Cherpitel, 1989, a,b) to 26 percent (Jones, Barber, Engrav & Heimbach, 1991) of burn injuries.

Overall, intoxicated patients have a significantly higher fatality rate in severe burn cases. These data are more thoroughly reviewed in the Ninth Special Report to the United States Congress on Alcohol and Health (National Institute on Alcohol Abuse and Achoholism, 1997).

Brezel and Kassenbrock (1988) examined drug and alcohol abusers, psychiatric patients, and those with neurological dysfunction to determine whether this group had more complications, more surgical procedures, and longer hospital stays than did burn patients without these disorders. However, alcohol abuse, defined as six or more cans of beer or the equivalent per day, was the most common form of impairment. Although impaired patients had more complications and required a longer period of hospitalization, alcohol intoxication was only one of several contributory factors. Psychiatric or neurological disabilities may have contributed to or interacted with intoxication so that longer hospital stays were required in these patients.

In a study of 1074 patients admitted to a medical center burn unit, McGill, Kowal-Vern, Kahn, and Gamelli (1995) found that the 40 percent who were positive for alcohol were more likely to have a greater proportion of bodily burns and a greater incidence of smoke inhalation than controls had. Chronic alcoholics also seem to have a higher fatality rate than do patients without a history of chronic alcohol abuse (Haum et al., 1995).

Interestingly, the authors found no significant differences between sober and acutely intoxicated alcoholics, suggesting that neurological or other long-lasting consequences of alcohol abuse and acute intoxication produce risk. The authors conclude that alcohol intake prior to burn injury is an independent risk factor in this population.

Homicide and Suicide

Alcohol is also overly represented in homicide and suicide. Goodman and associates (1991) examined death certificates for all intentional (n = 5776) and unintentional (n = 10,624) injury deaths in Oklahoma between 1978 and 1984. Unintentional injury deaths include all injuries (such as fatal traffic crashes) except suicide and homicide. Blood alcohol testing was performed on 83 percent of homicide victims and 56 percent of unintentional injury victims. Evidence of alcohol was found in approximately half of the homicide and unintentional injury victims tested. Also among those tested, nearly 24 percent of suicide victims, 34 percent of homicide victims, and 38 percent of unintentional injury victims had BACs of 100 mg/dL or greater. Only 20 percent of individuals who died of natural causes were alcohol positive. Goodman and colleagues (1991) note that because BAC testing for victims of suicide and unintentional injury deaths was selective, varying by the victim's age, by the time of day of the injury, and by the county in which the injury occurred, biases are present in the data. Accordingly, the researchers suggest that the results can be generalized to all injury deaths only with caution.

Smith and coworkers(1989) reported similar results in an analysis of more than 100,000 deaths investigated by North Carolina medical examiners from 1973 to 1983. BACs were determined for approximately 64 percent of the victims. Testing varied by victims' ages, gender, and manner of death. Homicide victims were tested most frequently (86%), followed by victims of suicide (78%) and unintentional injury death (68%). Positive BACs were detected in nearly 50 percent of unintentional injury deaths and approximately 35 percent of suicide deaths. Higher rates of alcohol involvement (63%) were observed among homicide victims. BACs exceeding 100 mg/dL were reported for approximately 40 percent of unintentional injury victims, 27 percent of suicide victims, and 52 percent of homicide victims. Only 8 percent of those who died of natural causes had BACs of 100 mg/dL or greater. The researchers noted that because alcohol and drug testing is performed routinely in North Carolina, regardless of the manner of death, this practice increases availability of BAC results and enables definition of the relationship between alcohol and all fatal injuries.

Conner and associates (2003) completed psychological autopsies of thirty eight completed suicides and sixty two medically serious suicide attempters in comparison with forty six controls. Among alcoholics, completed suicides were more often older men with mood disorders or with partner or relationship problems in comparison with community controls who attempted or completed suicide but were not alcoholics. Alcoholism is a risk factor for completed suicide (Harris & Barraclough, 1997) particularly when depression (Cheng, 1995), various mood disorders, partner relationships, and other life events are present (Conner et al., 2003).

Suicide ideation and attempts are common among depressed patients and alcoholics. Alcohol dependence and major depression are the most common dual diagnosis pathological disorders among those who commit suicide. Thus, it is of no surprise that about 21 percent of completed suicides are by alcoholics and that suicidal behavior and lifetime risk of suicide in U.S. alcoholics is about 2 to 4 percent. Many factors have been identified to predict suicide in alcoholics, including severity of alcoholism, aggression/impulsivity, negative affect, and hopelessness (Wallen and Lorman, 2008).

Traumatic Alcohol-Related Injury
in Specific Populations

Alcohol appears to be a prominent factor in traumatic injury deaths among Native Americans. In this population, however, alcohol involvement in a traumatic injury death varies little between men and women, in contrast to the sharp gender differences reported of other ethnic groups. Goodman and associates (1991) found that approximately 80 percent of unintentional injury deaths among Native Americans were alcohol related, regardless of gender. These investigators also reported that a high proportion of homicides and suicides among Native Americans involved alcohol. Yet it is important to note that rates of alcohol-involved deaths vary among tribes. Christian, Dufour, and Bertolucci (1989) observed a considerable disparity in alcohol-related deaths among eleven Oklahoma tribal groups.

Hispanic males are more likely to experience drinking problems than black or white males (Caetano, 1986). In addition, Hispanic males seem especially susceptible to alcohol-related traumatic injury death. For example, alcohol is involved in a greater proportion of homicide deaths among Hispanic men than among white or black men. Nearly 90 percent of male Hispanic homicide victims tested alcohol positive, and approximately 70 percent had BACs of 100 mg/dL or more (Goodman et al., 1991). Alcohol was detected in more than half of unintentional injuries and suicides for Hispanic males. Caetano (1989) found that Hispanic males exhibited drinking behaviors considerably different from those of Hispanic females. Such differences tend to characterize patterns of alcohol-related traumatic injury.

Goodman and colleagues (1991) reported similar gender-related patterns in alcohol involvement rates among black and white traumatic injury victims. In general, rates of alcohol-related trauma are greater among black and white males than among black, Hispanic, or white females. African-American and white males had lower rates of alcohol-related trauma than either male or female Native Americans or Hispanic males.

The risk of death from external causes (e.g., suicide, homicide, and accidental injuries) increases logarithmically among infrequent binge drinkers (Dawson, 2001, 2011), and there is no evidence of reduced risk of death among light or moderate drinkers. The group at highest risk of death from external causes are those who drink less than once a month but, when they did drink, consumed five or more drinks. Within this group, older subjects (defined as 65+ years) were at the highest risk, but younger drinkers (defined as 18–24 years of age) were also at high risk of death. Middle-aged drinkers (25–64 years of age) did not show the same increased mortality risk, which the author suggested was related to tolerance and experience. Although these data suggest that infrequent binge drinking, as defined, increases risk, as a function of age, possible tolerance, and age-related experience, the blood alcohol level that would result from five drinks would be relatively low, allowing the other variables to have a measurable impact.

Table 5.7: Relative Injury Risk: Effect of Mode, Age, Gender and BAC.

TYPE of INJURY	FATAL MOTOR VEHICLE				FATAL BOATING	FATAL or SERIOUS BICYCLE	PEDESTRIAN FALL-DOWN INJURY	BIOBEHAVIORAL EFFECTS OF ALCOHOL AND RELATED LEGAL DEFINITIONS OF INTOXICATION
BAC (%)	Age 16-20 ♀	Age 16-20 ♂	Age 21-34 ♀ and ♂	Age 35+ ♀ and ♂	ALL [including swimmers]	Effect of age/gender unknown	Effect of age/gender unknown	
	Relative Risk							
.02	1.8	2.4	1.8	1.7	1.7		-	.02% Zero Tolerance (<21)
.03	2.5	3.7	2.4	2.3	2.2			
.04	3.3	5.8	3.2	3.0	2.9	6x (.02-.08%)		.04% National DWI Commercial Operators
.05	4.5	9.0	4.3	3.9	3.7		3x (.05-.10%)	
.06	6	14	6	5	-			
.07	8	22	8	7	-			
.08	11	34	10	9	7.1			.08% National DWI Psychophysical Impairment (SFSTs)
.09	15	53	14	11	-			
.10	20	82	18	15	10.4			
.11	27	127	24	20	-	>20x (≥.08%)	10x (.10-.15%)	
.12	37	196	33	26	-			
.13	49	305	43	33	-			
.14	67	473	58	44	-			
.15	90	735	78	57	23.0			.15%
.16	122	1141	104	75	-			
.17	164	1772	138	99	-		>60x (>.16%)	Visible Intoxication (>50%)
.18	221	2752	185	129	-			
.19	299	4273	247	169	-			
.20	403	6634	330	221	39.4			Severe Sensory Motor Impairment
.22	735*	15995*	590*	380*	-			
.24	1339	38561	1054	652	-			
.26	2440	92967	1881	1119	-			Stupor
.28	4447	224134	3361	1920	-			
.30	8103	540365	6003	3264	-			Unconsciousness
>.40%	-	-	-	-	-			LD:50 (Est.)

Relative risk (RR) for a fatal single car crash derived from stepwise logistic regression coefficients rounded to nearest tenth or whole number. For women age 16-20, a coefficient of 0.03 (range 0.044-0.014) was used (Zador et al., 2000). Bicycle risk derived from Hokanen et al. (1983). Boating risk derived from Smith et al. (2001). Pedestrian risk derived from Li et al. (2001); Alcohol Intoxication: Risk and Mode of Injury. * Included only for comparative purposes. From: Brick.J. (2015) Also included are biobehavioral descriptors. From: Wiley Encyclopedia of Forensic Science. A. Jamieson and A. Moenssens (eds.), John Wiley: Chichester. doi:10.1002/9780470061589.fsa1131.

Summary

Alcohol is a nondiscriminating impairer that increases risk for injury through different modes and across age and gender, and although some populations are at greater risk than others, alcohol rarely decreases risk. The relative risks for injuries from water sports (swimming, boating), pedestrian, bicycling, falling down injuries, and motor vehicle crashes are summarized in Table 5.7. Relative risk is just that: relative. Although risk varies considerably among modes of injury, relative risk analyses yielding results greater than 2 or 3 are usually very significant. The important prevention message derived from decades of research is that consuming alcohol even relatively small increases risk for a wide range of injuries by people engaging in everyday activities.

REFERENCES

Anda, R., Williamson, D., and Remington, P. (1988). Alcohol and fatal injuries among U.S. adults. *Journal of the American Medical Association, 260*(17), 2529–2532.

Argeriou, M., McCarty, D., and Blacker, E. (1985). Criminality among individuals arraigned for drinking and driving in Massachusetts. *Journal of Studies on Alcohol, 46*(6), 525–530.

Arstein-Kerslake, G., and Peck, R. (1985). A typological analysis of California DUI offenders and DUI recidivism correlates. In *Proceedings of 34th International Congress on Alcoholism and Drug Dependence* (pp. A115–140), Calgary, Alberta, Canada, August 4–10.

Baker, S., O'Neill, B., and Karpf, R. (1992). *The Injury Fact Book* (2nd ed.). New York, NY: Oxford University Press.

Billings, C., Demosthesen, T., White, T., and O'Hara, D. (1991). Effects of alcohol on pilot performance in simulated flight. *Aviation, Space, and Environmental Medicine, 62*(3), 2323–2335.

Blomberg, R., Preusser, D., Hale, A., and Ulmer, R. (1979). *A Comparison of Alcohol Involvement in Pedestrians and Pedestrian Casualties.* Report DOT-HS-805-249. Washington, D.C.: National Highway Traffic Safety Administration.

Bolen, J. C., Rhodes, L., Powell-Griner, E. E., Bland, S. D., and Holtzman, D. (2000). State-specific prevalence of selected health behaviors, by race and ethnicity–Behavioral Risk Factor Surveillance System, 1997. *Morbidity and Mortality Weekly Report, Surveillance Summaries, 49*(S S02), 1–60.

Borkenstein, R. (1964). *The Role of the Drinking Driver in Traffic Accidents.* Bloomington, IN: Department of Police Administration.

Boyle, J. M., and Vanderwolf, P. (2004). *2003 Motor Vehicle Occupant Safety Survey.* (Vol. 2, Safety Belt Report). Report DOT-HS-809-789. Washington, D.C.: National Highway Traffic Safety Administration. Available from www.nhtsa.dot.gov/people/injury/research/2003MVOSS-SurveyVol2/pages/TRD.html

Branche, C., Sniezek, J., Sattin, R., and Mirkin, I. (1991). Water recreation-related spinal injuries: Risk factors in natural bodies of water. *Accident Analysis and Prevention, 23*(1), 13–17.

Brezel, B., and Kassenbrock, M. (1988). Burns in substance abusers and in neurologically and mentally impaired patients. *Journal of Burn Care and Rehabilitation, 9*(2), 169–191.

Brick, J. (2006). Interaction between toxicology and burn victim physiology. In A. D. Clark (Ed.), *Burns: The Medical and Forensic Model* (pp. 221–256). Tucson, AZ: Lawyers and Judges Publishing Company.

Brick, J. (2012). Alcohol: behavioral and medical effects. In A. Jamieson and A. Moenssens (Eds.), *Wiley Encyclopedia of Forensic Science.* Hoboken, NJ: John Wiley. DOI: 10.1002/978047006 1589.fsa630.pub2

Brick, J., and Erickson, C. (2009). Intoxication is not always visible: An unrecognized prevention challenge. *Alcoholism, Clinical and Experimental Research, 33*(9), 1489–1507.

Caetano, R. (1986). Patterns and problems of drinking among U.S. Hispanics. In *Report of the Secretary's Task Force on Black and Minority Health* (Vol. 7, pp. 143–186). Washington, D.C.: U.S. Government Printing Office.

Caetano, R. (1989). Drinking patterns and alcohol problems in a national sample of U.S. Hispanics. In *Alcohol Use and Abuse Among U.S. Minorities* (pp. 147–162). NIAAA Research Monograph No. 18. DHHS Pub. No. (ADM) 89-1435. Washington, D.C.: U.S. Government Printing Office.

Centers for Disease Control. (1988). Acute traumatic spinal cord injury surveillance–United States, 1987. MMWR. *Morbidity and Mortality Weekly Report, 34*, 285–286.

Centers for Disease Control. (2001). *Evidence of Effectiveness of 0.08% BAC (BAC) Laws: Findings from the Task Force on Community Preventive Services.* Atlanta, GA: author.

Centers for Disease Control. (2004). Alcohol-attributable deaths and years of potential life lost–United States, 2001. *MMWR. Morbidity and Mortality Weekly Report, 53*(37), 866–870.

Centers for Disease Control and Prevention. (2013). Available from www.cdc.gov. Retrieved on May 30, 2014.

Cheng, A. (1995). Mental illness and suicide: A case control study in East Taiwan. *Arch General Psychiatry, 52*, 594–603.

Cherpitel, C. (1989a). Breath analysis and self reports as measures of alcohol related emergency room admissions. *Journal of Studies on Alcohol, 50*(2), 155–161.

Cherpitel, C. (1989b). Prediction of alcohol-related casualties: A comparison of two emergency room populations. *Drug and Alcohol Dependence, 24*, 195–203.

Cherpitel, C. (1993). Alcohol, injury, and risk-taking behavior: Data from a national sample. *Alcoholism, Clinical and Experimental Research, 17*(4), 762–766.

Christian, C., Dufour, M., and Bertolucci, D. (1989). Differential alcohol-related mortality among American Indian tribes in Oklahoma. *Social Science and Medicine, 28*(3), 275–284.

Conner, K., Beatrais, A., and Conwell, Y. (2003). Risk factors for suicide and medically serious suicide attempts among alcoholics: Analysis of Canterbury Suicide Project. *Journal of Studies on Alcohol, 54*, 551–554.

Cook, C. (1997). Alcohol and aviation. *Addiction, 92*, 539–555.

Copeland, A. (1986). Accidental non-commercial aircraft fatalities. The 7-year Metro-Dade County experience from 1977–1983. *Forensic Science International, 31*(1), 13–20.

Critchlow, B. (1983). Blaming the booze: The attribution of responsibility for drunken behavior. *Personality and Social Psychology Bulletin, 9*(3), 451–473.

Critchlow, B. (1986). The powers of John Barleycorn: Beliefs about the effects of alcohol on social behavior. *American Psychologist, 41*, 751–764.

Cummings, P., Mueller, B.A., and Quan, L. (2011). Association between wearing a personal floatation device and death by drowning among recreational boaters: A matched cohort analysis of United States Coast Guard data. *Injury Prevention, 17*(3), 156–159.

Dee, T. (2001). Does setting limits save lives? The case of 0.08 BAC laws. *Journal of Policy Analysis and Management, 30*, 111–128.

Dewar, R. (2002). Roadway design. In R. Dewer and P. Olson (Eds.), *Human Factors in Traffic Safety* (pp. 381–420). Tucson, AZ: Lawyers and Judges Publishing Company.

Dietz, P., and Baker, S. (1974). Drowning: Epidemiology and prevention. *American Journal of Public Health, 64*(4), 303–312.

Donovan, D., and Marlatt, G. (1982). Personality subtypes among driving-while-intoxicated offenders: Relationship to drinking behavior and driving risk. *Journal of Consulting and Clinical Psychology, 50*, 241–249.

Donovan, D., Queisser, H., Umlauf, R., and Salzberg, P. (1986). Personality subtypes among driving-while-intoxicated offenders: Follow-up of subsequent driving records. *Journal of Consulting and Clinical Psychology, 4*(54), 563–565.

Earleywine, M., and Finn, P. (1991). Sensation-seeking explains the relation between behavioral disinhibition and alcohol consumption. *Addictive Behaviors, 16*(3/4), 123–128.

Eckardt, M., Harford, T., Kaelber, C., Parker, E., Rosenthal, L., Ryback, R., ..., Warren, K. (1981). Health hazards associated with alcohol consumption. *Journal of the American Medical Association, 246*(6), 648–666.

Ericksen, K., and Trocki, K. (1992). Behavioral risk factors for sexually transmitted diseases in American households. *Social Science & Medicine, 34*(8), 843–853.

Evans, L. (1990). The fraction of traffic fatalities attributable to alcohol. *Accident Analysis and Prevention, 22*(6), 587–602.

Federal Emergency Management Agency. (2003). Establishing a Relationship Between Alcohol and Casualties of Fire. *Topical Fire Research Series* (Vol. 3, July). Emmitsburg, MD: U.S. Fire Administration, National Fire Data Center.

Gibbons, H. (1988). Alcohol, aviation, and safety revisited: A historical review and a suggestion. *Aviation, Space, and Environmental Medicine, 59*(7), 657–660.

Gomberg, E. (1989). Suicide risk among women with alcohol problems. *American Journal of Public Health, 79*(10), 1363–1365.

Goodman, R., Mercy, J., Loya, F., Rosenberg, M., Smith, J., Allen, N., ..., Kolts, R. (1991). Alcohol use and interpersonal violence: Alcohol detected in homicide victims. *American Journal of Public Health, 76*(2), 144–149.

Harper, C., and Albers, W. (1964). Alcohol and general aviation accidents. *Aerospace Medicine, 35,* 462–464.

Harris, E., and Barraclough, B. (1997). Suicide as an outcome for mental disorders. A meta-analysis. *British Journal of Psychiatry, 170,* 205–228.

Haum, A., Perbix, W., Hack, H., Stark, G., Spilker, G., and Doehn, M. (1995). Alcohol and drug abuse in burn injuries. *Burns, 219*(3), 194–100.

Heise, H. (1934). Alcohol and automotive accidents. *Journal of the American Medical Association, 103,* 739–741.

Heise, H. (1956). Interpretation of tests for intoxication. *Journal of Forensic Science, 1,* 38–44

Heise, H., and Halporn, B. (1932). Medicolegal aspects of drunkenness. *Pennsylvania Medical Journal, 36,* 190–195.

Hilton, J. (2006). *Race and Ethnicity in Fatal Motor Vehicle Traffic Crashes 1999–2004.* Report DOT HS 809 956. Washington, D.C.: National Highway Traffic Safety Administration.

Hingson, R., Heeren, T., and Winter, M. (1996). Lowering state legal blood alcohol limits to 0.08%; the effect on fatal motor vehicle crashes. *American Journal of Public Health, 86,* 1297–1299.

Hingson, R., Heeren, T., and Winter, M. (2000). Effects of recent 0.08% legal blood alcohol limits on fatal crash involvement. *Injury Prevention, 6,* 109–114.

Hingson, R., and Howland, J. (1993). Alcohol and non-traffic unintended injuries. *Addiction, 88*(7), 877–883.

Hingson, R., Strunin, L., Berlin, B., and Heeren, T. (1990). Beliefs about AIDS, use of alcohol and drugs, and unprotected sex among Massachusetts adolescents. *American Journal of Public Health, 80*(3), 295–299.

Honkanen, R., Ertoma, L., Kuosmanen, P., Linnoina, M., Alah, A., and Visori, T. (1983). The role of alcohol in accident falls. *Journal of Studies on Alcohol, 44,* 231–245.

Howland, J., and Hingson, R. (1987). Alcohol as a risk factor for injuries or death due to fires and burns: Review of the literature. *Public Health Report, 102,* 475–483.

Hoxie, P., Cardosi, K., Stearns, M., and Mengert, P. (1988). *Alcohol in Fatal Recreational Boating Accidents.* Pub. No. DOT-CGD-0488. Washington, D.C.: U.S. Department of Transportation, U.S. Coast Guard.

Joksch, H. C. (1985). Review of the major risk factors. *Journal of Studies on Alcohol Supplement, s10,* 47–53.

Jones, G. (1989). Alcohol abuse and traumatic brain injury. *Alcohol Health and Research World, 13*(2), 105–109.

Jones, J., Barber, B., Engrav, L., and Heimbach, D. (1991). Alcohol use and burn injury. *Journal of Burn Care and Rehabilitation, 12*(2), 148–152.

Juarez, P., Walters, S., Daugherty, M., and Radi, C. (2006). A randomized trial of motivational interviewing and feedback with heavy drinking college students. *Journal of Drug Education, 36,* 233–246.

Keller, M., McCormick, M., and Efron, V. (1982). *A Dictionary of Words About Alcohol* (2nd ed.). New Brunswick, NJ: Publications Division, Rutgers Center of Alcohol Studies.

Langenbucher, J., and Nathan, P. (1983). Psychology, public policy and the evidence for alcohol intoxication. *American Psychologist, 38,* 1070–1077.

Leigh, B. (1990a). Relationship of sex-related alcohol expectancies to alcohol consumption and sexual behavior. *British Journal of Addiction, 85*(7), 919–928.

Leigh, B. (1990b). The relationship of substance use during sex to high-risk sexual behavior. *Journal of Sex Research, 27*(2), 199–213.

Leigh, B. (1990c). Alcohol and unsafe sex: An overview of research and theory. *Progressive Clinical Biology Research, 325:* 35–46

Li, G., Baker, S., Sterling, S., Smialek, J., Dischinger, P., and Soderstron, C. (1996). A comparative analysis of alcohol in fatal and non-fatal bicycling injuries. *Alcoholism, Clinical and Experimental Research, 20,* 1553–1559.

McCusker, J., Westenhouse, J., Stoddard, A., Zapka, J., Zorn, M., and Mayer, K. (1990). Use of drugs and alcohol by homosexually active men in relation to sexual practices. *Journal of Acquired Immune Deficiency Syndrome, 3*(7), 729–736.

McGill, V., Kowal-Vern, A., Kahn, S., and Gamelli, R. (1995). The impact of substance use on mortality and morbidity from thermal injury. *Journal of Trauma, 38*(6), 931–934.

McMillen, D., Pang, M., Wells-Parker, E., and Anderson, B. (1991). Behavior and personality traits among DUI arrestees, nonarrested impaired drivers and nonimpaired drivers. *International Journal of the Addictions, 26*(2), 227–235.

McMillen, D., Smith, S., and Wells-Parker, E. (1989). The effects of alcohol, expectancy, and sensation on driving risk taking. *Addictive Behaviors, 14*(4), 447–483.

Miller, B., Downs, W., and Gondoli, D. (1989). Spousal violence among alcoholic women as compared to a random household sample of women. *Journal of Studies on Alcohol, 50*(6), 533–540.

Model Driving While Under the Influence of Alcohol and Other Drugs Act. (1993). Crimes Code. President's Commission on Model State Drug Laws. The White House, Washington D.C.

Modell, J., and Mountz, J. (1990). Drinking and flying–the problem of alcohol use by pilots. *New England Journal of Medicine, 323*(7), 455–461.

Molberg, P., Hopkins, R., Paulson, J., and Gunn, R. (1993). Fatal incident risk factors in recreational boating in Ohio. *Public Health Report, 108*(3), 340–346.

Morrow, D., Leirer, V., and Yesavage, J. (1990). The influence of alcohol and aging on radio communication during flight. *Aviation, Space, and Environmental Medicine, 61*(1), 12–20.

Morrow, D., Leirer, V., Yesavage, J., and Tinklenberg, J. (1991). Alcohol, age, and piloting: Judgment, mood, and actual performance. *International Journal of the Addictions, 26*(6), 669–683.

Moskowitz, H., Burns, M., and Williams, A. (1985). Skills performance at low blood alcohol levels. *Journal of Studies on Alcohol, 46*(6), 482–485.

Moskowitz, H., and Fiorentino, D. (2000). *A Review of the Literature on the Effects of Low Doses of Alcohol on Driving Related Skills.* Report DOT-HS-809-028. Washington, D.C.: U.S. Department of Transportation, National Highway Traffic Safety Administration.

National Center for Health Statistics. (1988). *Vital Statistics of the United States 1985* (Vol. II, Mortality). Atlanta, GA: Centers for Disease Control and Prevention.

National Committee for Injury Prevention and Control. (1989). Recreational injuries. In Injury Prevention: Meeting the Challenge (pp. 163–176). *American Journal of Preventive Medicine.* New York, NY: Oxford University Press.

National Highway Traffic Safety Administration (NHTSA). (1994). *Traffic Safety Facts 1993: Alcohol.* Washington, D.C.: U.S. Department of Transportation, National Center for Statistics and Analysis.

National Highway Traffic Safety Administration (NHTSA). (2003). *2002 Annual Assessment of Motor Vehicle Crashes Based on the Fatality Analysis Reporting System, The National Accident Sampling System, and the General Estimates System.* Washington, D.C.: U.S. Department of Transportation, National Center for Statistics and Analysis.

National Highway Traffic Safety Administration (NHTSA). (2007). *Review of Technology to Prevent Alcohol-Impaired Crashes.* Report DOT-HS-810-827. Washington, D.C.: U.S. Department of Transportation.

National Highway Traffic Safety Administration (NHTSA). (2009). *Alcohol-Impaired Driving Fatalities Based on the Fatality Analysis Reporting System (FARS). Presented at the SAE Government/Industry Meeting on February 6, 2009.* Washington, D.C.: National Center for Statistics & Analysis.

National Highway Traffic Safety Administration (NHTSA). (2011). *Time of Day and Demographic Perspective of Fatal Alcohol-Impaired Driving Crashes.* Report DOT-HS-811-523. Washington, D.C.: U.S. Department of Transportation, National Highway Traffic Safety Administration.

National Highway Traffic Safety Administration (NHTSA). (2012). US Department of Transportation, *Traffic Safety Facts.* Report DOT-HS-811-637. Washington D.C: U.S.

National Institute on Alcohol Abuse and Alcoholism. (1997). *Ninth Special Report to the U.S. Congress on Alcohol and Health.* NIH Publication No. 97-4017. Bethesda, MD: author.

Olkkonen, S., Lahdenranta, U., Slatis, P., and Honkanen, R. (1993). Bicycle accidents often cause disability–an analysis of medical and social consequences of nonfatal bicycle accidents. *Scandinavian Journal of Social Medicine, 21*(2), 98–106.

Ooserveld, W. (1970). Effect of gravity on positional alcohol nystagmus (PAN). *Aerospace Medicine, 41*(5), 557–560.

Patetta, M., and Biddinger, P. (1988). Characteristics of drowning deaths in North Carolina. *Public Health Report, 103*(4), 406–411.

Peck, R., Gebers, M., Voas, R., and Romano, E. (2008). The relationship between blood alcohol concentration (BAC), age, and crash risk. *Journal of Safety Research, 39,* 311–319.

Perrine, M. (1990). Who are the drunk drivers? *Alcohol Health and Research World, 14*(1), 26–35.

Perrine, M. (1988). *Zero Tolerance and Other Options: Limits for Truck and Bus Drivers.* Washington, D.C.: Transportation Research Board, National Research Council.

Perrine, M., Mundt, J., and Winer, R. (1994). When alcohol and water don't mix: Diving under the influence. *Journal of Studies on Alcohol, 55,* 517–524.

Plueckhahn, V. (1982). Alcohol consumption and death by drowning in adults. *Journal of Studies on Alcohol, 43*(5), 445–452.

Pompham, R., Schmidt, W., and Israelstam, S. (1984). Heavy alcohol consumption and physical health problems: A review of the epidemiologic evidence. In R. G. Smart et al. (Eds.), *Research Advances in Alcohol and Drug Problems* (Vol. VIII, pp. 149–182). New York, NY: Plenum Press.

Popkin, C. (1991). Drinking and driving by young females. *Accident Analysis and Prevention, 23*(1), 37–44.

Reinarman, C., and Leigh, B. C. (1987). Culture, cognition and disinhibition: Notes on sexuality and alcohol in the age of AIDS (Acquired Immune Deficiency Syndrome). *Contemporary Drug Problems, 14*(3), 435–460.

Romano, E., Voas, R., and Lacey, J. (2010). *Alcohol and Highway Safety: Special Report on Race/Ethnicity and Impaired Driving.* Report DOT-HS-811-336 (Table 5). Washington, D.C.: National Highway Safety Traffic Administration.

Ross, L., and Ross, S. (1988). Pilots' attitude toward alcohol use and flying. *Aviation, Space, and Environmental Medicine, 59*(10), 912–919.

Ross, L., and Ross, S. (1990). Pilots' knowledge of blood alcohol levels and the 0.04 percent blood alcohol concentration rule. *Aviation, Space, and Environmental Medicine, 61*(5), 412–417.

Ross, L., Yeazel, L., and Chau, A. (1992). Pilot performance with blood alcohol concentrations below 0.04 percent. *Aviation, Space, and Environmental Medicine, 63*(11), 951–956.

Ryback, R., and Dowd, P. (1970). The after effects of various alcoholic beverages on positional nystagmus and coriolis acceleration. *Aerospace Medicine, 41,* 429–435.

Shults, R., Elder, R., Sleet, D., Nichols, J., Alao, M., Carande-Kulis, V., ..., Thompson, R. (2001). Task Force on Community Preventive Services: Reviews of evidence regarding interventions to reduce alcohol-impaired driving. *American Journal of Preventive Medicine, 21,* 66–88.

Sivak, M. (1996). The information that drivers use: Is it indeed 90% visual. *Perception, 25,* 1081–1089.

Smith, S., Goodman, R., Thacker, S., Burton, A., Parsons, J., and Hudson, P. (1989). Alcohol and fatal injuries: Temporal patterns. *American Journal of Preventive Medicine, 5*(5), 296–302.

Stall, R., McKusick, L., Wiley, J., Coates, T., and Ostrow, D. (1986). Alcohol and drug use during sexual activity and compliance with safe sex guidelines for AIDS: The AIDS Behavioral Research Project. *Health Education Quarterly, 13*(4), 359–371.

Stoduto, G., Vingilis, E., Kapur, B. M., Sheu, W. J., McLellan, B. A., and Liban, C. B. (1991). Alcohol and drugs in motor vehicle collision admissions to a regional trauma unit: Demographic, injury and crash characteristics. *Accident Analysis and Prevention, 25*(4), 411-20.

Substance Abuse and Mental Health Services Administration (SAMHSA). (2000). *National Household Survey on Drug Abuse: Main Findings 1999.* Rockville, MD: Author.

Substance Abuse and Mental Health Services Administration. (2004a). Driving under the influence (DUI) among young persons. In *National Survey on Drug Use and Health: The NSDUH Report*. Rockville, MD: Author.

Substance Abuse and Mental Health Services Administration. (2004b). *National Survey on Drug Use & Health* (formerly called the *National Household Survey on Drug Abuse* [NHSDA]). Rockville, MD: Author. Available from www.oas.samhsa .gov/24K/youthDUI/youthDUI.htm

Substance Abuse and Mental Health Services Administration. (2005). *Results from the 2004 National Survey on Drug Use and Mental Health: Detailed Tables (Prevalence Estimates, Standards, P Values and Sample Sizes)*. Rockville, MD: Author. Available from http://oas.samhsa.gov/2k5/DUI/DUI.pdf

Taylor, J. L., O'Hara, R., Mumenthaler, M. S., and Yesavage, J. A. (2000). Relationship of CogScreen-AE to flight simulator performance and pilot age. *Aviation, Space, and Environmental Medicine, 71*(4), 373–380.

Temple, M. T., and Leigh, B. C. (1992). Alcohol consumption and unsafe sexual behavior in discrete events. *The Journal of Sex Research, 29*(2), 207–219.

U.S. Coast Guard, U.S. Department of Homeland Security. (2010). *Recreational Boating Statistics–2010*. Commandant Publication P16754.24. Washington, D.C.: Author.

U.S. Department of Transportation, National Highway Traffic Safety Administration. (1994). *Traffic Safety Facts 1993: Alcohol*. Washington, D.C.: U.S. Department of Transportation, National Center for Statistics and Analysis.

U.S. Department of Transportation, National Highway Traffic Safety Administration. (2002). *Transitioning to Multiple Imputation–a New Method to Impute Missing Blood Alcohol Concentration (BAC) Values in FARS*. Report DOT-HS-809-403, Washington, D.C.: Author

Valdiserri, R., Lyter, D., Leviton, L., Callahan, C., Kingsley, L., and Rinaldo, C. (1988). Variables influencing condom use in a cohort of gay and bisexual men. *American Journal of Public Health, 78*(7), 801–805.

Vingilis, E. (1988). Blood alcohol concentrations among motor vehicle accident trauma admissions to a regional trauma unit. *Canadian Journal of Public Health, 79*(5), 392–393.

Voas, R., Fisher, D., and Tippetts, A. (2002). Children in fatal crashes: Driver blood alcohol concentration and demographics of child passengers and their drivers. *Addiction, 97,* 1439–1448.

Voas, R., Taylor, E., Baker, T., and Tippetts, A. (2000). *Effectiveness of the Illinois .08 Law*. Report DOT-HS-809-186. Washington, D.C.: National Highway Traffic Safety Administration.

Wallen, M. C., and Lorman, W. J. (2008). Special issues in patients with comorbid psychiatric and chemical dependency disorders. In J. Brick (Ed.), *Handbook of the Medical Consequences of Alcohol and Drug Abuse* (2nd ed., pp. 579–621). New York, NY: Haworth Press, Taylor & Francis Group.

Waller, P., Steward, J., Hansen, A., Stutts, J., Popkin, C., and Rodgman, E. (1986). The potentiating effects of alcohol on driver injury. *Journal of the American Medical Association, 256*(11), 1461–1466.

Wells-Parker, E., Anderson, B., Pang, M., and Timken, D. (1993). An examination of cluster-based classification schemes for DUI offenders. *Journal of Studies on Alcohol, 54*(2), 209–218.

Welte, J., and Abel, E. (1989). Homicide: Drinking by the victim. *Journal of Studies on Alcohol, 50*(3), 197–201.

White, W., and Gasperin, D. (2007). The "hard core drinking driver"–Identification, treatment and community management. *Alcohol Treatment Quarterly, 24*(3), 113–132.

Widmark, E. (1981). *Principles and Application of Medicolegal Alcohol Determination* (R. C. Baselt, trans.). Davis, CA: Biomedical Publications. (Original work published 1932).

Wieczorek, W., and Miller, B. (1992). Preliminary typology designed for treatment matching of driving-while-intoxicated offenders. *Journal of Consulting and Clinical Psychology, 60*(5), 757–765.

Wilson, R. (1991). Subtypes of DWIs and high-risk drivers: Implications for differential intervention. *Alcohol, Drugs and Driving, 7*(1), 1–12.

Wintemute, G., Teret, S., Kraus, J., and Wright, M. (1990). Alcohol and drowning: An analysis of contributing factors and a discussion of criteria for case selection. *Accident Analysis and Prevention, 22*(3), 291–296.

Yesavage, J., Dolhert, N., and Taylor, J. (1994). Flight simulator performance of younger and older aircraft pilots. Effects of age and alcohol. *Journal of the American Geriatric Society, 42*(6), 577–582.

Yi, H-Y., Chen, C. M., and Williams, G. D. (2006). *Trends in Alcohol-Related Fatal Traffic Crashes, United States, 1982–2004.* Surveillance Report #76. Bethesda, MD: National Institute on Alcohol Abuse and Alcoholism. Available at http://pubs.niaaa.nih.gov/publications/surveillance76/fars04.htm. Retrieved January 21, 2008.

Zador, P. (1991). Alcohol-related relative risk of fatal driver injuries in relation to driver and age and sex. *Journal of Studies on Alcohol, 52*(4), 302–310.

Zador, P., Krawchuk, S., and Voas, R. (2000). *Relative Risk of Fatal Crash Involvement by BAC, Age, and Gender.* Report DOT-HS-809-050. Springfield, VA: National Technical Information Service.

Chapter 6

ALCOHOL AND THE LAW:
DRUNK DRIVING, VISIBLE
INTOXICATION, AND AGGRESSION[1]

6.1 OVERVIEW

One of the challenges facing prevention specialists is that many factors contribute to intoxication, as well as to whether a person is too intoxicated to operate a vehicle, for example, or "visibly intoxicated" (meaning a series of perceptible acts and behaviors consistent with gross impairment) to the point that the service of alcohol should be discontinued. In some cases, visible intoxication is different from "obvious intoxication," a term used in some statutes and some older studies, to mean visibly intoxicated. Obvious intoxication relates to a combination of all the factors used to determine whether a person is or is likely to be alcohol impaired. However, intoxication is not always visible, even to trained observers.

Historically, most of the direct consequences of intoxication have been limited to individual drinkers who, if they lived long enough, would eventually incur significant medical consequences (Brick, 2008). In other words, the medical consequences of alcohol use often required many years of drinking to develop. However, the introduction of motor vehicles and the eventual proliferation of mechanized transportation dramatically changed society. No longer were the effects of alcohol overuse limited to the drinker but now included others (passengers, occupants of other vehicles, pedestrians). To meet the growing awareness and impact of intoxicated driving on society, legislators searched for ways to limit this problem. Although diverse approaches have been applied to prevent drunk driving (NIAAA, 2000; Hingson et al., 1996; Hingson et al., 1999; Holder et al., 2000), only three specifically relate to identifying signs of alcohol intoxication: DWI laws, dram shop and related

---

1. Note: Portions of this chapter were reproduced, in part, from Brick and Erickson (2009) with permission of the publisher.

host liability, and Alcohol Beverage Control board laws. A review of differences between DWI-related issues and visible intoxication (the focus of dram shop laws) is important to the forensic examiner investigating violation of these laws.

The use of alcohol (or other drugs) to alter consciousness and produce intoxication is not new. Alcohol is the most widely used and abused drug on earth and has been consumed for its intoxicating effects for thousands of years. One consequence of intoxication of social and forensic interest is impaired driving that often results in fatal or serious bodily injuries. Different prevention approaches to reduce drunk driving include laws defining and prohibiting intoxicated driving and legislation that limits alcohol service (e.g., dram shop or common negligence laws). A violation of the dram shop law occurs when someone is served alcohol while visibly intoxicated or, depending on the statute, the server should have known the person was intoxicated. In instances of comparative negligence, the question may be whether a passenger knew or should have known that the driver was visibly or obviously intoxicated before getting into the car. The lack of visible signs of impairment does not correlate with the inability to perform complex tasks such as driving which creates myriad problems for passengers, law enforcement, and bartenders, for example. Moskowitz (2008) suggested that the motion picture industry may have created the false impression that alcohol-impaired driving is associated with signs of gross motor impairment when, in fact, less obvious forms of impairment, such as decision and recognition errors (improper evasive action, excessive speed and divided attention or inattention) are the most often causal factors in accidents (Treat, 1980).

6.2 EVOLUTION OF LAWS TO PREVENT INTOXICATED DRIVING

Early Definitions of Intoxication

Insight into our current understanding of terms such as intoxicated and the current confusion by some as to how older terms are not applicable to current laws can be gained by examining the historical development of terms such as drunk, impaired, visible intoxication and obviously intoxicated and related descriptions of those who drink to excess. A combination of scientific research and societal changes was slowly leading to the awareness of public health issues caused by intoxicated motor vehicle operators in what became drunk driving. This eventually led to legislation to reduce drunk driving. As discussed in Chapter 5, drunk driving laws evolved, as did their definitions and related terms such as "under the influence of alcohol" and "alcohol-impaired" (Voas & Lacey, 1990).

In Sweden by Widmark (1932) and in the United States by Heise and Halporn (1932) and Heise (1934)—recommended written protocols in evaluating suspected drunk drivers. Previously, such evaluations (usually performed by clinicians or police) were neither systematic nor objective. In courts, expert testimony regarding suspected intoxicated drivers usually included highly exaggerated behaviors such as staggering gait and incoherent speech. As methods to measure alcohol in blood were developed, so was a general understanding that the signs of alcohol intoxication were proportional to the concentration of alcohol. These dose-dependent effects adversely affected safe motor vehicle operation.

The term *intoxication* and its various derivations is still strongly associated with impaired driving laws and the now well-known relationship between intoxication and accidental injury. However, early researchers, legislation, and prevention specialists did not have the benefit of decades of epidemiological data, driving-simulator, divided attention, and other laboratory test data to define intoxication. Therefore, intoxication was defined with a BAC at which it was obvious that driving was impaired and unsafe. Harger and Halpieu (1956) noted that in prior research on the relationship between BACs and behavior, "the definition of intoxication was practically synonymous with drunk" (p. 170), wherein common and easily recognized signs of intoxication were present. Heise (1934) had earlier noted that a BAC of 150 mg/dL is considered *prima facie* evidence of intoxication, meaning that there is sufficient evidence from the BAC alone to raise a presumption of fact or to establish the fact that a person was too intoxicated to drive. Thus, intoxication was formally associated with a BAC (of 150 mg/dL) and gross or obvious signs of intoxication.

Downward Shift in Definitions of Intoxication

What eventually followed was the development of state alcohol control codes that led to the approval of the Model Uniform Vehicle Code. This legislation extended the previous regulations that drivers with a BAC of 150 mg/dL were grossly intoxicated and should be presumed to be too intoxicated to drive safely (Langenbucher & Nathan, 1983). Over the ensuing decades, research on alcohol-related roadway crashes highlighted the effects of alcohol at BACs below 150 mg/dL. In other words, data were evolving that showed impairment of driving at BACs below which drivers presented gross, easily recognizable signs of intoxication (Harger & Halpieu, 1956).

Early researchers recognized that impaired driving occurred at BACs well below 150 mg/dL, when intoxication was easily detected and "obvious." However, in order to get legislation passed, they were apparently willing to begin with a legal definition of intoxication that was so high, and by which most persons would be obviously drunk, that a new law would be acceptable to most skeptics (Borkenstein, 1985). By 1960, the data on drunk driving crashes were so compelling that the AMA recommended that a BAC of 100 mg/dL be accepted as *prima facie* evidence of intoxication adding that with regard to driving, some individuals are under the influence at BACs of 50 to 100 mg/dL. This was the first shift from commonly and easily recognized signs of gross intoxication that were believed to reflect impairment in the ability to drive. Langenbucher and Nathan (1983) pointed out "this standard was subsequently adopted by most states as the statutory equivalent of the subjective terms of intoxicated, visibly intoxicated, and obviously intoxicated," although they did not provide a reference to any such statute (p. 1071). They also noted the vagueness of state alcohol and vehicle codes, which led legislators to objectively define intoxicated and visibly intoxicated without much distinction. In other words, older terms used to describe drunk driving (e.g., gross intoxication and easily recognized signs of intoxication) were still used even though new DWI laws defined intoxication on the basis of a chemical test.

Current Definitions of Intoxication: DWI Laws

During the second half of the twentieth century, most but not all of the United States defined, for the purposes of motor vehicle operation, a BAC of 100 mg/dL to be evidence of impairment—that is, too intoxicated to drive safely—after several decades of research and utilizing the most current drunk driving data. Prevention efforts gained further traction by 1994, when states were encouraged by NHTSA and other federal agencies to lower to 80 mg/dL the BAC that defines driving while intoxicated (Model Driving While Under the Influence of Alcohol and Other Drugs Act, 1993). Thus, the current definitions of DWI intoxication and "under the influence" are significantly different from the original use of these terms.

Now, all states in the United States have revised their impaired driving laws to follow federal recommendations to define a BAC of 80 mg/dL as a violation of the motor vehicle code. Commercial vehicle operators have a significantly lower legal standard for intoxication of 40 mg/dL, and for underage drivers the legal definition for intoxication is 10 to 20 mg/dL, depending on the state where persons under the age of 21 live, typically fall under a zero tolerance statute. These prevention efforts, coupled with increased public awareness about drinking and driving, may explain the gradual decline in fatal car crashes involving intoxicated drivers (Centers for Disease Control, 2001; Dee, 2001; Hingson et al., 1996, 2000; Perrine, 1988; Shults et al., 2001; Voas, Taylor, Baker & Tippetts, 2000).

6.3 PREVENTION EFFORTS CREATE
A DETECTION PROBLEM

In the past several decades, research has supported the need for more precise and lower legal definitions of driving while intoxicated, requiring ever-increasingly sophisticated testing to identify such drivers. Harkening back to an older mindset, when intoxicated driving was synonymous with the common meaning of drunk, some drunk driving defenses relied upon the lack of visible signs of impairment, even though the driver had a BAC in excess of the statute definition. Some states have passed legislation establishing case law in preventing such a defense (e.g., State v. Gheghan, 214 New Jersey Super. 383:A-2100-85-4 1986). Moreover, although behavioral signs of intoxication may be important in establishing probable cause in a DWI arrest, states with *per se* laws do not require any behavioral evidence of intoxication or direct motor vehicle operation to convict drivers of drunk driving, as long as the driver had a BAC that the legislature has defined as intoxicated driving (e.g., 80 mg/dL).

In more recent years, police have used an increasing arsenal of tools to detect and prosecute drunk drivers. Among these are portable breath alcohol tests that can be used at the scene, breath or blood samples collected and analyzed after a suspected drunk driver is apprehended, and SFSTs designed to detect impairment in psychomotor and ocular motor control related to low BACs (Burns & Anderson, 1995; Burns and Moskowitz, 1977;) and are discussed in detail in Chapter 4. Without special tests (e.g., chemical tests or SFSTs), the identification of alcohol intoxication at BACs producing impaired driving is not a simple matter to determine (Harger & Halpieu, 1956), even for skilled observers such as police (Brick & Carpenter, 2001; Langenbucher & Nathan, 1983; Pagano & Taylor, 1979; Vingilis, Adalf & Chung, 1982; Zusman & Huber, 1979). Thus, a significant obstacle to the further prevention of drunk driving exists, if intoxicated drivers are impaired and at an increased risk for fatal crashes, but signs are not detectable except through the use of special tests such as those used by police. Passengers, friends, social hosts, and others are at a disadvantage in their ability to make informed decisions regarding intoxication and impairment at low BACs, if intoxication is not readily apparent or obvious.

Low Dose Studies on Impaired Driving and Divided Attention Tasks

Since research on the effects of alcohol began nearly a century ago, an overwhelming number of studies have shown that alcohol impairs divided attention and other skills related to safe motor vehicle operation (Chapter 4). This impairment begins at BACs significantly lower than earlier investigators thought and is greater in younger drivers than in older drivers. One need only consider the consensus of scientists and physicians 60 years ago who believed that impaired driving statutes that used 150 mg/dL as the criterion for driving while intoxicated were reasonable and fair to appreciate how beneficial technological and epidemiological research has become to our understanding of driving impairment.

The literature on the effects of low BACs on motor vehicle operation, or on divided attention tasks believed to be critical to safe driving, is well-known and discussed in Chapter 4. Data from numerous studies demonstrate that divided attention deficits occur in the 20 to 30 mg/dL BAC range (NIAAA, 1990) with a 100% increase in the probability of being involved in an accident at 50 mg/dL or more (NIAAA, 1993; U.S. Department of Transportation, 1988). Twenty years ago, the National Safety Council Committee on Alcohol and Drugs recommended that the presumption that an individual is not impaired when the BAC is below 50 mg/dL be stricken from DWI legislation, because evidence shows that the performance of a substantial number of individuals is impaired at BACs below 50 mg/dL (Surgeon General's Workshop on Drunk Driving, 1988). Despite the increased risk for a fatal crash, even at very low BACs, most drivers with BACs in excess of the legal definition for intoxication may not be detained by police at a drunk driving checkpoint (Wells, Green, Foss, Ferguson & Williams, 1997), emphasizing further the distinction between impairment to drive and visible intoxication.

Legislation

In an effort to reduce the cost of services and fatal crashes of intoxicated drivers, legislative prevention efforts have shifted to include liability of bars, restaurants, and others. These efforts include administrative, dram shop, common negligence, and social host liability laws.

Administrative Liability Laws

In addition to impaired driving laws, there are three laws that relate to the service of alcohol to the obviously visibly intoxicated person: Alcohol Beverage Control (ABC) laws/codes, dram shop laws, and third-party actions under traditional tort reform. ABC board laws (or in some jurisdictions, administrative codes) provide municipalities authority to regulate the commerce of alcohol. The Twenty First Amendment to the U.S. Constitution gave each state the right to determine whether to allow alcoholic beverages, and if so, how to regulate them. Different states have slightly different names for the alcohol control board, the agency responsible for enforcing a wide range of rules and regulations, including determining a licensee's responsibilities toward intoxicated patrons. In New Jersey, for example, NJAC 13:2-23.1(b) "prohibits a licensee from selling, serving, or delivering any alcoholic beverage to a person who is actually or even appears to be drunk or intoxicated. The licensee may not allow such a person to consume any alcoholic beverage on the licensed premises… Such a person should never be served or allowed to continue to drink an alcoholic beverage while in such condition." Under NJSA 9:1:17B-1 it is illegal to purchase or consume alcoholic beverages for anyone who is actually or appears to be intoxicated. ABC violations result in fines or license revocation if an agent or investigator determines a bartender served alcohol to a visibly intoxicated patron. In some states (New Jersey for example), ABC agents do not need to actually see the bartender serve a visibly intoxicated patron but need only observe a visibly intoxicated patron at a bar or restaurant to issue a citation (Alcoholic Beverage Control Handbook for Retail Licensees, 2004).

Dram Shop Liability Laws

Another prevention approach is through dram shop legislation. A dram is an ancient apothecary term referring to a unit of volume because alcohol was originally served by volume. Hence, the contemporary equivalent of a dram shop is a bar or establishment that sells alcohol. Such laws are designed to prevent the service of alcohol to a "visibly intoxicated" person and impose liability on licensed establishments selling alcoholic beverages (dram shops) to anyone who appears intoxicated. Similar legislation also exists for social hosts who serve alcohol in their homes to guests. Under these laws, if a third party is injured as a result of the actions of an intoxicated person, the injured party may recover damages. The medicolegal question in dram shop and social host (*see* later) liability cases is, "Was someone served while visibly intoxicated?" If the intoxicated person is underage, the issue shifts from visible intoxication to whether or not intoxication was a significant contributing cause of an injurious event.

The issue of visible intoxication is not limited to dram shop cases and is relevant in cases of comparative negligence. For example, did a passenger knowingly enter a vehicle with an intoxicated driver? Similarly, in criminal negligence cases the question is, "Was an intoxicated person allowed to operate a vehicle?" which was the question in a landmark New Jersey case (State of New Jersey v. Kenneth Powell, Indictment – 01-0400170-I). In this case, a driver arrested for drunk driving was processed at police headquarters and picked up by his friend (Powell) who then returned the intoxicated driver to his vehicle. The drunk driver subsequently struck and killed a Navy Ensign on leave. This was the first case of its kind that hinged primarily on whether the arrested driver was visibly intoxicated and obviously too impaired to drive.

The BAC at which most persons appear to be visibly intoxicated is less well-publicized and in the case of dram shop laws is sometimes not well-defined. For example, in defining visible intoxication, the New Jersey statute states, "visibly intoxicated means a state of intoxication accompanied by a perceptible act or series of actions which present clear signs of intoxication" (NJSA 2A: 15-5-5). In most states the standard is intoxicated or visibly intoxicated or obviously intoxicated (National Alcoholic Beverage Control Association, 1984). The distinction between visibly intoxicated and obviously intoxicated is not always clear. One distinction is that visibly intoxicated persons display observable signs of impairment (e.g., slurred speech, difficulty walking, decreased inhibitions) whereas a person who is obviously intoxicated may or may not show such signs but because of the amount of alcohol consumed or the BAC, intoxication was or should have been obvious. For example, in Vermont, New Hampshire, and Rhode Island, it is unlawful to serve an apparently intoxicated person or someone whom it would be reasonable to expect would be under the influence as a result of the amount of alcohol served (Duffy, 2005; U.S. Department of Transportation, 1990). Other states have similar laws (U.S. Department of Transportation, 1990).

The interpretation or definition of what constitutes visible intoxication is often left to individual courts and can range from indirect evidence (e.g., number of drinks served or estimated or actual BAC) to direct eyewitness evidence (Maciszewski v. Flatley 705 A.2d 171, 173 [R.I. 1998], Fandozzi v. Kelly Hotel, Inc. supra 711 A.2d at 527). For example, the number of drinks or eyewitness accounts may establish the fact that the server contributed or did not prevent harm. Some agencies (State of Missouri Alcohol Responsibility Training, 2008) and training programs (e.g., Trainer Intervention Procedures for Servers—TIPS (2004); Techniques in Alcohol Management (2007)—TAM) include rapid or excess drinking as a sign of intoxication, presumably related to decreased inhibitions or impaired judgment.

Social Host Liability Laws

A different standard exists under some social host liability laws. For example, in New Jersey and elsewhere, it is unlawful for a host (e.g., a homeowner) to provide alcohol to a person who was "visibly intoxicated" (e.g., NJSA 2:15-5.6). However, in this statute, visible intoxication is in part defined by the BAC. The statute states that when the BAC is less than 100 mg/dL "there shall be an irrebuttable presumption that the person tested was not visibly intoxicated" (NJSA 2A: 15-5.6). Thus by current standards of intoxicated driving, lawmakers have concluded that merely being in violation of the impaired driving statute does not mean the driver was visibly intoxicated. The statute also states that at a BAC of at least 100 mg/dL and less than 150 mg/dL, "there shall be a rebuttable presumption that the person tested was not visibly intoxicated in the social host's presence" (NJSA 2A: 15-5.6). Such law leads to the logical inference that at BACs above 150 mg/dL, there is a rebuttable presumption of visible intoxication. This is strikingly similar to the early Uniform Vehicle Code (Brick & Erickson, 2009).

The concept of visible intoxication is important in the prevention of drunk driving and the enforcement of laws against the serving of alcohol to visibly intoxicated persons but also applies to persons who are neither police officers, bartenders, nor social hosts. For example, determining if someone is intoxicated is important to a potential passenger in a car operated by someone who has consumed alcohol. The popular phrase is "friends don't let friends drive drunk," but short of abstinence, what can prevention specialists do to assist untrained people to reliably recognize intoxication? Moreover, what signs constitute intoxication, in whom, and at what BACs?

Definition of Signs and Symptoms

The terms signs and symptoms are often used together or interchangeably. A sign is any abnormality that is seen during observation or is discoverable on specific examination. In the present context, signs might include observed performance on certain tests such as a gaze nystagmus test, a memory test, a psychophysical test, or a physiological measure but may also include visible changes such as slurred speech, decreased inhibitions, or grossly impaired cognitive or motor abilities. Technically, a symptom is a subjective indicator that the drinker perceives (e.g., dizziness, nausea) but that may not be visible to others. Sometimes, for expediency of language, the distinction between signs and symptoms is lost. For example, slurred speech is described as both a sign and a symptom in some of the studies cited in this review. We will use signs in this review for those observed abnormalities associated with alcohol intoxication.

Diagnosis of Intoxication

Clinical diagnoses of intoxication using the DSM involves specific behaviors (American Psychiatric Association, 2013). Some of the signs are detected by casual observation that include maladaptive behavioral or psychological changes, slurred speech, incoordination, and unsteady gait (*also see* Chapter 4). In one known instance, the State Supreme Court of Oregon (State v. Clark, 1979) took judicial notice of the following signs or symptoms of alcohol intoxication: odor of alcohol on the breath, flushed appearance, lack of muscular coordination, speech difficulties, disorderly or unusual conduct, mental disturbance, visual disorders, sleepiness, muscular tremors, dizziness, and nausea. Although collectively these signs and symptoms would be consistent with visible intoxication, some of the descriptions noted do not rise to a definition of visible intoxication. For example, (1) symptoms experienced by the subject but not obvious to an observer, (2) anyone drinking some amount of alcohol may have the odor of an alcoholic beverage (e.g., in the mouth), (3) dizziness may not rise to the level of impaired balance (which would be visible), and (4) some individuals (e.g., persons of Asian descent with atypical alcohol metabolism) may exhibit a flush reaction with a single drink.

Signs and symptoms of intoxication vary due to differences among people, but visible signs of intoxication can be reduced to three broad categories of behavior: (1) decreased inhibitions (doing or saying things that are inappropriate for the situation), (2) psychomotor impairment (e.g., slurred speech, slow, clumsy, incoordinated movements, stumbling), and (3) cognitive impairment (e.g., difficulty concentrating, remembering, or performing simple math tasks, such as counting change or following directions). Broader, more situation-specific criteria, such as the signs of obvious or visible intoxication listed in Table 6.1 may be more useful to lay persons such as social hosts, prospective passengers, parents, bartenders, and so on.

Early Studies of Intoxication

Alcohol is, for the most part, a CNS depressant that exhibits dose-dependent behavior. Although most of the effects of alcohol are related to decreased cognitive and psychomotor performance, biphasic effects (i.e., stimulation and depression) have been reported (Pohorecky, 1978). Early studies of the relationship between BAC and behavior often included a thousand or more subjects, a robustness that today is usually limited to epidemiological studies and rarely involving the analysis of acute intoxication in live subjects. Also, the technology available 50 or more years ago to measure alcohol in blood and experimental designs that included subjects with various degrees of experience with alcohol, require careful examination. For example, early studies typically did not report specific screening criteria for subjects. In some studies subjects were described as alcoholics, nondrinkers, or "not at all" drinkers. Chronic alcohol abuse or alcoholism and the very high BACs often reported in these studies suggest that many subjects were exceptionally tolerant to at least some of the effects of alcohol. Similarly, subjects in many of the older large-scale studies were being observed by police or physicians after a motor vehicle accident, arrest for drunk driving, or other potentially biasing circumstances. Nevertheless, the results from these large-scale studies are valuable in

Table 6.1: Major Categories and Common Signs of Alcohol Intoxication.*

Decreased Inhibitions	Psychomotor Impairment	Cognitive Impairment
1. Doing things that would normally not be done when sober 2. Saying things that would normally not be said when sober 3. Boisterous 4. Argumentative 5. Confrontational 6. Obnoxious 7. Annoying to others (e.g., strangers) 8. Hanging on to people or otherwise intruding on their personal space 9. Loud comments about other people in the vicinity 10. Animated or exaggerated actions 11. Rapid drinking 12. Acting silly or "cutesy" 13. Complaints about drink strength or service 14. Bravado	15. Slurred, mumbled or incoherent speech 16. Slow speech 17. Swaying while sitting, standing, or walking 18. Staggering, stumbling, holding onto objects for balance 19. Difficulty reaching for and picking up objects (money, food, drinks, etc.) 20. Inability to maintain eye contact (lack of focus or wandering gaze) 21. Head on bar or asleep 22. Falling off stools, chairs, etc. 23. Bumping into objects or people while walking 24. Leaning for support while standing or sitting 25. Exaggerated hand or arm gestures 26. Spilling food, drinks or dropping objects 27. Fell down or lost balance	28. Loss of concentration or train of thought, confused 29. Delayed response to questions 30. Illogical comments or answers to questions, non sequiturs 31. Impaired short or long-term memory 32. Lighting more than one cigarette at a time or not smoking a lit cigarette 33. Lighting the wrong end of a cigarette 34. Excessively quiet, sullen 35. Denial of impaired driving ability 36. Consumption of large amounts of alcohol or rapid drinking 37. Trouble counting money or with basic math 38. Difficulty following instructions or directions

*Not inclusive of every possible sign of intoxication. Adapted from Brick and Erickson (2009). (This list is not inclusive of all possible behaviors and there is an overlap between some categories, and some behaviors may be present in sober individuals.)

answering the questions of how signs of visible intoxication occur in relation to BAC and what signs are commonly present with relatively casual observation.

E. M. Widmark, a pioneer in alcohol research, was one of the first scientists to systematically examine the relationship between BAC and symptoms (signs) of intoxication. He developed a list of factors to enable physicians who were typically called upon by police to diagnose suspected intoxicated drivers. Excluding behaviors that would only be detected with the use of a test (e.g., Romberg balance), Widmark noted that difficulty picking up small objects, altered speech, general appearance, condition of clothing, and impaired mental powers were common and obvious (visible) signs that could be used to determine intoxication. In a study of 1942 subjects, Widmark (1981) found that 30 percent of those examined were influenced by alcohol when their BAC was 81 to 100 mg/dL and 40 percent were influenced by alcohol when their BACs were between 101-120 mg/dL as determined by the presence of various factors. Most, but not all, of the observed signs were of the nature that they could be detected without specialized tests and were within the behavioral repertoire likely to be recognized by persons who had or took the opportunity to make such observations. Widmark noted that as BACs increased, so did the percentage of subjects who appeared influenced by alcohol. It was not until BACs exceeded about 150 mg/dL that the percentage of subjects who appeared intoxicated significantly exceeded chance (i.e., more than 50%). Thus, Widmark found that about 68 percent of subjects were diagnosed as influenced by alcohol when BACs were 141 to 160 mg/dL (average of 150 mg/dL), and with the 160 to 180 mg/dL (average 170 mg/dL) BACs, about 79 percent of the subjects were diagnosed as influenced by alcohol. These percentages must be examined in the context in which they were made. For example, five of the seven factors (odor of alcohol on breath, speech, uncertainty picking up objects, swaying while turning while walking, and uncertainty while walking forward) can be observed by casual observation, but two of Widmark's factors included tests that required some specialized administration. Also, signs of intoxication do not occur as singular events in most drinkers, meaning that as BACs increased it is likely that both the number and the severity of signs also increased. The results of Widmark's classic study are presented in Table 6.2.

From these data, Widmark found that with the exception of the odor of alcohol on the breath and swaying during a balance (Romberg) test, no signs of intoxication were observed in any subjects when the BAC was below about 80 mg/dL. Also, reliable signs of visible intoxication do not occur until BACs are much higher. For example, at BACs in the 121 to 140 mg/dL range, fewer than half were identified as intoxicated, but at 141 to 160 mg/dL about 68 percent were identified as intoxicated, using multiple criteria. One would expect that less than 68 percent of the subjects were identified as intoxicated at BACs closer to 141 mg/dL, and more than 68 percent were identified as intoxicated at BACs closer to 160 mg/dL. Signs such as stammering speech, uncertainty picking up objects, swaying while turning when walking, and uncertain forward movement were present in 30, 40, 51, and 15 percent, respectively, in subjects with BACs of 141 to 160 mg/dL. Since it is statistically impossible that subjects presented only a single symptom (e.g., stammering speech) and none of the other three signs, it is more likely that two or more of

Table 6.2: Relationship Between BAC and Certain Behaviors.

Sign or Symptom Present	10–60 mg/dL	61–80 mg/dL	81–100 mg/dL	101–120 mg/dL	121–140 mg/dL	141–160 mg/dL	161–180 mg/dL	181–200 mg/dL	201–220 mg/dL	221–240 mg/dL	241–260 mg/dL
Diagnosis of "influenced"	0%	0%	30%	40%	46%	68%	79%	88%	93%	96%	97%
Alcohol odor on the breath	0%	33%	63%	81%	78%	82%	84%	91%	92%	93%	92%
Speech stammering	0%	0%	0%	9%	14%	30%	25%	35%	48%	50%	57%
Uncertainty picking up small objects	0%	0%	0%	21%	33%	40%	42%	45%	59%	69%	50%
Swaying while turning when walking	0%	0%	31%	30%	24%	51%	56%	62%	79%	73%	77%
Movement directly forward uncertain	0%	0%	6%	6%	4%	15%	25%	29%	36%	33%	36%
Swaying in Romberg's test	0%	17%	47%	50%	52%	60%	67%	71%	82%	83%	82%
Finger to finger	0%	0%	18%	15%	27%	42%	32%	52%	58%	68%	57%

Source: Widmark (1981).

these signs were observed in 45 to 91 percent of the subjects observed. Thus, for all practical purposes, Widmark's finding was that at BACs of about 150 mg/dL or more, the majority of subjects were diagnosed as influenced by alcohol.

Jetter (1938a) examined 1000 subjects who were patients preadmitted to hospital with a diagnosis of alcoholism and described elsewhere as chronic alcoholics. He reported the percentages of these patients who appeared visibly intoxicated. He specifically avoided "more delicate tests of incoordination, such as finger-to-nose test, or walk a straight line . . . because such tests are . . . of too sensitive a nature" (p. 484). To the contrary, a positive diagnosis of intoxication was made "only upon gross physical departure from normal" (p. 484). Jetter's "clinical criteria essential for the diagnosis of clinical intoxication" required that the subject have a gait abnormality or be unable to walk. Specifically, if gross swaying, reeling, or staggering were not present, the test was considered negative and an overall diagnosis of intoxication could not be made. By this operational definition, subjects who were diagnosed as intoxicated presented gait abnormalities. Of the subjects in this study, there were only four instances where gait abnormality was observed without a diagnosis of gross intoxication.

In addition to the mandatory requirement of gait abnormality, Jetter required that two of four other signs had to be present to diagnose gross intoxication: speech abnormality, flushed face, dilated pupils, or alcoholic odor on breath. For a diagnosis of speech abnormality, the subject was asked simple questions such as name, where he lived and so on. Only if definite slurred or incoherent speech was present could a diagnosis of intoxication be made. Therefore, the clinical signs of intoxication were those that were visible and that could be easily observed by casual observation. However, flushed face and the odor of alcohol on the breath are more related to the recent ingestion of alcohol than to impairment, *per se*. Jetter's results revealed that 47 percent of all subjects in the 150-mg/dL group had trouble walking or standing and had at least one other criterion (abnormal speech, dilated pupils, flushed face, odor of an alcoholic beverage). Because the effects of alcohol are dose dependent, one can expect greatest sensitivity to impairment at the highest BACs within and between ranges, and vice versa. In other words, at 125 mg/dL, the likelihood of visible intoxication in alcoholics was proportionally less than 47 percent, and at 175 mg/dL proportionally higher. At BACs in the 200 mg/dL (175–225 mg/dL) range, the percentage of subjects who appeared grossly intoxicated jumped to about 84 percent; at BAC >250 mg/dL, 90 percent; and by 400 mg/dL, 100 percent of the subjects appeared grossly intoxicated. These data showed that at BACs less than about 125 mg/dL, the overwhelming majority of alcoholics did not appear grossly intoxicated. It is not until BACs exceed about 150 to 175 mg/dL that most (more than half) of the subjects appear visibly intoxicated, presenting readily observable signs such as abnormal gait (i.e., gross swaying, reeling, or staggering) and at least two of the following signs: slurred speech, dilated pupils, flushed face, or the odor of an alcoholic beverage on the breath. These results are summarized in Table 6.3.

Table 6.3: Occurrence of Acute Clinical Intoxication in Alcoholics at Average BACS.

BAC Group	50 mg/dL	100 mg/dL	150 mg/dL	200 mg/dL	250 mg/dL	300 mg/dL	350 mg/dL	400 mg/dL	450 mg/dL	500 mg/dL	Total
BAC mg/dL Range	5–75	75–125	125–175	175–225	225–275	275–325	325–375	375–425	425–475	500	–
Number Ss	38	87	132	330	176	141	74	15	5	2	1000
Number intoxicated Ss	4	16	61	276	158	133	71	14	5	2	740
Percentage of Ss diagnosed as intoxicated	10.5%	18.4%	47%	83.6%	90%	95.1%	96%	93.3%	100%	100%	–

In a subsequent study, Jetter (1938b) applied the same criteria for a diagnosis of intoxication (impaired gait and at least two of the four other signs described earlier) to a different population of drinkers: nonalcoholics. The subjects in this study were described as occasional drinkers or nondrinkers. Aside from acute tolerance, which develops during a single episode in some drinkers, occasional drinkers or nondrinkers would have no residual tolerance to the effects of alcohol. As expected, acute signs of intoxication occurred at lower BACs than in the alcoholics mentioned previously. Although there were fewer subjects in Jetter's second study, it is valuable because today, ethical and federal guidelines for the protection of human subjects would preclude the administration of such large doses of alcohol to relatively naive or nondrinkers (Lawson, Nathan & Lipscomb, 1980). These results are summarized in Table 6.4, where more subjects in the 100 mg/dL, 150 mg/dL, and 200 mg/dL groups were rated as intoxicated in comparison to alcoholics, especially at the lower alcohol concentrations.

The results of Jetter's studies clearly demonstrate a tolerance to the effects of alcohol with regard to signs of visible intoxication and the difficulty in

Table 6.4: Number and Percentage Occurrence of Acute Clinical
Intoxication in Occasional or Non-Drinkers at Average BACS.

BAC Group	100 mg/dL	150 mg/dL	200 mg/dL	Total
BAC mg/dL	75–125	125–175	175–225	
Number Ss	8	7	5	20
Number intoxicated Ss	4	4	5	13
Percentage of Ss diagnosed as intoxicated	50	57	100	–

Source: Brick and Erickson (2009) and adapted from Jetter (1938b).

identifying intoxicated persons except at high BACs. Jetter is one of a small number of investigators who examined the effects of acute intoxication in subjects with varying degrees of drinking experience, later followed by Gold-berg (1943), one of the first researchers to systematically examine the effect of tolerance to alcohol on psychophysical tasks.

Jetter's research demonstrates that experience with alcohol affects signs of visible intoxication. Among occasional or nondrinkers (who would presumably have little or no tolerance to alcohol), about 50 percent showed signs of visible intoxication when BACs averaged 100 mg/dL (75–125 mg/dL range). A significant portion (57%) of nontolerant drinkers showed visible intoxication when BACs averaged 150 mg/dL (125–175 mg/dL) and all (100%) were visibly intoxicated when BACs averaged 200 mg/dL (175–225 mg/dL). Among alcoholics (who presumably had more tolerance to alcohol), signs of visible intoxication were present 47 percent of the time when BACs averaged 150 mg/dL (125–175 mg/dL) and 84 percent of the time when BACs averaged 200 mg/dL as previously discussed.

Since Jetter reported his data in ranges of BACs, it appears that among both naive and chronic drinkers, most of the time (more than 50%) at BACs above about 150 mg/dL, it was probable that visible intoxication was present, and the percentage of visibly intoxicated subjects increased dramatically at higher BACs. This conclusion is consistent with that of Heise (1956), who concluded that even in persons with "high tolerance to alcohol" there can be no doubt as to obvious intoxication at BACs above 150 mg/dL. He further noted that practically all people are "drunk" at BACs of about 200 mg/dL. Heise (1956) concludes; "Fifteen hundredths per cent or over is considered prima facie evidence of intoxication," noting that this high level (150 mg/dL) is "set so high that no injustice will be done even to the most intelligent person who can hide the obvious effects of alcohol temporarily, or the person who has a high tolerance to alcohol" (p. 41). These findings strongly influenced the recommendations of the AMA Committee on Medicolegal Problems, which concluded that at 150 mg/dL "every individual with this concentration would have lost to a measurable extent some of that clearness of intellect and control of himself that he would normally possess" (Turner, Heis & Meuhlberger, 1958).

The results of the studies by Widmark, Jetter, and Heise are consistent with the opinions of other authors of the time. In an exhaustive review of the literature, Harger and Halpieu (1956) noted that in prior research of the relationship among BACs, "the definition of intoxication was practically synonymous with drunk" (p. 170). The criteria for being drunk included signs of intoxication such as weaving gait and other signs of muscular incoordination, slurred speech, and marked loss of self-control. Referring to Widmark and other studies of intoxication, Harger and Halpieu noted that "while some of these authors have used the term 'under the influence' to describe diagnosed intoxication, an examination of the criteria for such diagnosis will show that they mean what we popularly call drunk" (1956, p. 170). Harger and Halpieu also pointed out that the term "under the influence of intoxicating liquor" is widely used and accepted in the courts of many states and "covers not only all the well-known and easily recognized conditions and degrees of intoxication, but any abnormal mental or physical condition which is the result of indulging in any degree in intoxicating liquors" (Harger & Halpieu, 1956, p. 182; *also* Heise, 1956, p. 39).

The diagnoses of intoxication applied in the studies reviewed by Harger and Halpieu often included a test of some sort. Therefore, some of the data summarized may underestimate the BAC at which frank intoxication or unmistakable signs of intoxication occur. Their conclusions with regard to driving are, by today's standards, more a reflection of how people appear physically and not the degree of impairment in the performance of driving-related tasks. In a summary of their work, Harger and Halpieu (1956) reached three conclusions: (1) very few people are drunk with a BAC below 50 mg/dL; (2) many people are drunk in the 50 to 150 mg/dL range, and (3) the BAC over which practically all people are drunk is around 200 mg/dL (p. 171).

In one of the largest single studies to date, Pentilla, Tenhu and Kataja, (1971) examined nearly 7000 cases of suspected drunk drivers who were examined by physicians specially trained in forensic alcohol intoxication identification. Although this study did not provide results relating specific BACs to casual behavior, it demonstrates the large number of drinking drivers who developed exceptional tolerance to some of the effects of alcohol. In this study, correlations between BAC (ranging from 0 to 360 mg/dL) and the physician's clinical evaluation ranged from approximately 0.38 to 0.67. Statistically, this means that the best physician was successful in identifying alcohol intoxication 44 percent of the time. As in previous reports (e.g., Jetter, 1938a;

Widmark, 1981), Pentilla and colleagues (1971) found the highest correlation between BAC and gait, which was accurate about 51 percent of the time. Using all of the measures of intoxication, which included psychophysical tests, the best physician was successful in identifying intoxicated drivers only 47 percent of the time. However, the clinical assessment of each case was performed within 2 hours of admission in about 65 percent of the cases and within 2 to 5 hours of admission in 12 percent of the cases. Thus, it is likely that some drivers were tested well into the elimination phase of alcohol intoxication and the results were affected to some degree by acute tolerance. Given the very high BACs in some subjects, some chronic heavy drinkers with exceptional tolerance were probably included in this study. Even so, of the 1842 subjects with BACs of more than 200 mg/dL, 89 percent received a score of drunkenness using specific testing criteria. These results are generally consistent with earlier studies, demonstrating that by 200 mg/dL intoxication is so high that almost all drinkers are visibly intoxicated.

As with studies reviewed eariler, the accuracy of raters improved with higher BACs. Zusman and Huber (1979) used skilled interviewers to identify drunk drivers and found that when BACs were 50 to 90 mg/dL, even interviewers with special training were only able to correctly identify drinkers 31 percent of the time. About 70 percent of drinkers not identified as intoxicated would be intoxicated by law for the purpose of operating a commercial vehicle (40 mg/dL) or other motorized vehicles when the driver is of legal age (80 mg/dL).

Conclusions from the Previous Studies. Overall, the results from the above studies lead to four conclusions:

1. Among nondrinkers, or drinkers with little or no tolerance, signs of visible intoxication are not reliably observed at BACs that currently define intoxicated driving (80 mg/dL). Visible signs are present in most subjects (i.e., >50%) at BACs of about 150 mg/dL or higher.
2. Among chronic drinkers or alcoholics with tolerance, at BACs of less than the 150 mg/dL range, most (i.e., >50%) will not appear visibly intoxicated.
3. At BACs of about 200 mg/dL (175–225 mg/dL), the overwhelming majority (more than 84%) of all drinkers, including chronic alcoholics, will be visibly intoxicated.
4. Visible intoxication is affected by tolerance. Some drinkers have exceptional tolerance (*see* later) to alcohol that masks visible signs of intoxication, even at BACs that would produce unconsciousness or death in some drinkers.

Recent Studies on Signs of Intoxication:
Observer Reliability Studies

Langenbucher and Nathan (1983) were among the first to observe that after the development of the Model Uniform Vehicle Code, legislators followed the recommendation by the AMA that a BAC of 100 mg/dL be accepted as *prima facie* evidence of intoxication. The legal standard (100 mg/dL at the time) to define intoxicated driving was subsequently adopted by most states as the statutory equivalent of the subjective terms intoxicated, visibly intoxicated, and obviously intoxicated. In three different experiments, these investigators examined the ability of different groups of observers to make accurate judgment calls regarding intoxication in subjects (targets) with different BACs. Observers consisted of social drinkers, bartenders, and police officers.

In the first study, observers were forty nine social drinkers (ages 18–25), half of whom were women and who were mostly moderate drinkers (Oates & McCay Drinking Inventory scores ranged from 8–30 with an average of 18). The male and female target (drinking) subjects (ages 21–29) were also diagnosed as moderate social drinkers (Oates & McCay, 1973). Targets consumed enough alcohol to reach one of three BACs: 0 (controls), 50 mg/dL, or 100 mg/dL. Each target was rated by four groups of observers for a total of sixteen group categorical ratings at various BACs. Observers rated each target as sober, moderately intoxicated, or very intoxicated (meaning intoxicated in violation of the impaired-driving statute). In the first study, targets were asked to walk into the room, sit down, and answer interview questions designed to elicit a range of verbal behavior. At the end of the interview, the target stood up and walked out. The observers correctly rated intoxication in the target drinkers about 25 percent of the time. Not one of the targets with BACs of 100 mg/dL or more was identified as intoxicated by law (100 mg/dL at the time of the study). BAC estimates of most moderately intoxicated and all four very intoxicated targets were grossly inaccurate. Underestimates of the BAC of both moderately and very intoxicated targets were most frequent. The authors conclude that contrary to some public opinion and one court ruling (NJ Division of Alcohol Beverage Control v. Zane, 1961), the determination of whether a person is sober or intoxicated is not a matter of common observation, at least not at low BACs.

In Langenbucher and Nathan's second experiment, (1983) the observers rated target subjects as they entered the lounge area of a large hotel complex (off-business hours). Observers were twelve full-time or part-time bartenders (ages 21-39) with 1 to 15 years of bartending experience. Targets were two men (19 and 28 years old) and two women (both 24 years old) who were moderate drinkers (Oates scores ranging from 13–24), resulting in twelve categorical ratings. In this study, targets were asked to descend a short flight of steps, cross the room, and sit on a barstool. Interviews lasted 2 to 3 minutes, then the targets walked out of the lounge area. Bartenders correctly rated a target in only one of four instances (this target was sober). The second sober target was rated as moderately intoxicated. The third target, who had a BAC of 45 mg/dL, was rated as sober by eight bartenders. The fourth target (BAC of 110 mg/dL) was rated as moderately intoxicated, as drunk by equal numbers of bartenders, and as sober by two bartenders. All bartenders agreed that they would continue to serve alcohol to the (sober) targets. One bartender said she would refuse service to the third target (BAC = 45 mg/dL) and nine of the twelve bartenders indicated that they would continue to sell drinks to the most intoxicated target (BAC = 110 mg/dL).

In the third experiment, the observers were thirty New Jersey law enforcement personnel (police) ages 23 to 50 with 1 to 29 years of full time employment as a police officer with varying experience in DWI arrests. Police were recruited to observe and rate intoxication of target subjects (same subjects as in the previous experiment) in a nighttime simulated roadside arrest (target's vehicle, marked police cruiser, headlights, rotating overhead lights, spotlights, radio transmissions, etc.). Police raters had 3 minutes to test the sobriety of the target in any way they chose. Typically, the police would ask the target to exit the vehicle and perform psychophysical tests, but the target had to return to his or her vehicle at the end of the 3-minute evaluation period. As in the previous experiments, the two legally intoxicated and one moderately intoxicated target subjects were consistently underestimated with regard to the BAC. This similarity is striking considering that the police had an opportunity to observe the targets perform various sobriety tests. Only five police officers were very accurate in their ratings and four of those five officers were members of a special tactical unit for the apprehension of drunk drivers. The fifth officer was a municipal officer with fifty alcohol related arrests during his 7 years on the force.

CONCLUSIONS FROM THE THREE EXPERIMENTS. This series of studies found that overall, social drinkers, bartenders, and most police officers correctly judged the target's level of intoxication only 25 percent of the time. Raters consistently underestimated BACs and at no time was a by law intoxicated target identified by a significant proportion of the observers. As such, the studies concluded that the then legal definition of intoxication (100 mg/dL) was not an appropriate standard for visible intoxication under dram shop laws.

Compton (1986) tested the ability of police officers to determine whether subjects had a BAC of 100 mg/dL or more. In this study, police were given different methods to make their determination, including (1) driving behavior, (2) driver appearance, (3) horizontal gaze nystagmus, (4) divided attention, (5) passive alcohol sensor device, and (6) stopping distance. Of these, driver observation is the most relevant to the question of visible intoxication and included characteristics such as the odor of alcoholic beverages, flushed appearance of the face, slurred speech, demeanor, and manual dexterity. Using an experimental DWI checkpoint, police used a typical procedure that included only quick observations and a brief conversation before they rated the subject's state of impairment. The information obtained during the brief observation and conversation led police raters to believe that 47 percent of the subjects were impaired even though they were sober (0 mg/dL BAC). However, at higher BACs (100–150 mg/dL), 87 percent of the drinking subjects were deemed impaired. Although there was obviously a strong tendency for police to believe that almost half the subjects were driving impaired when they were not intoxicated, the results also indicate that at higher BACs (nearer to 150 mg/dL) most subjects appeared to be intoxicated when police were able to use screening procedures and make observations of driving. Although law enforcement has many tools available in the apprehension of drunk drivers (compared to bartenders, social hosts, passengers, etc.), and potentially different motivations, the results of Compton's study are useful for showing that proper screening procedures enhance the accuracy of observing drivers and their level of impairment, at least defined in the study.

Wells, Green, Foss, Ferguson, and Williams (1997) based their study on previous research that concluded it is difficult for police to determine whether drivers are impaired at checkpoints. The survey team conducted interviews or obtained information from police on drivers at 156 sobriety checkpoints. Based on brief screenings, 111 drivers were detained by police because of suspected DWI, whereas 182 drivers were not suspected and allowed to pass through the checkpoint. Of the 111 drivers detained for SFSTs, 66 had BACs that exceeded 80 mg/dL (64 of whom were arrested) and 19 had BACs between 50 and 70 mg/dL. The remaining 26 had BACs below 50 mg/dL. The 182 drivers not detained were informed they were selected for a survey that was then conducted by the research team. Of these, 90 surveyed drivers had BACs at or above 80 mg/dL and 92 drivers had BACs between 50 and 79 mg/dL. These impaired drivers were missed by police. Wells and associates found that brief contact with drivers make it difficult to identify drinking drivers and a large percentage of false positives can be noted. Women were missed more often than were men (74% vs. 60%) and younger drivers (18–35) were missed more often than were older drivers (36+).

Rubenzer (2011) reached similar conclusions. He concluded that observers relying on "common-sense clues of intoxication" have limited ability to assess intoxication when the BAC is less than 100 mg/dL. Although he noted some signs of visible intoxication occur in some subjects some of the time, even at such low BACs, the ability to accurately and reliably identify intoxication is difficult even with the use of field sobriety tests utilized by law enforcement in DWI investigations.

Teplin and Lutz (1985) developed an Alcohol Symptom Checklist (ASC) that consisted of twenty-eight items obtained from randomly selected emergency room patients. They narrowed the list down to eleven signs, most of which could be easily observed by casual observation. They concluded that the most reliably detected signs of alcohol intoxication included impairment of fine motor control (e.g., fumbling with cigarettes, retrieving ID from a wallet or purse), impaired gross motor control (stumbling, accidentally brushing against objects, difficulty maintaining an upright posture, walking straight or balancing), slurred speech (difficulty enunciating words distinctly), change in speech volume (deviation from normal conversational volume appropriate to the situation), decreased alertness (increased response time to social or other environmental stimuli, including conversation), excessive perspiration (not due to temperature or nervousness), slow or shallow respiration, sleepiness, changes in rate of speaking (consistently slow, fast, or alternating), and bloodshot eyes. These investigators found that the presence of three to four of the signs noted previously were necessary to make an identification of intoxication, when BACs were greater than 50 mg/dL; however, four to five of the just cited signs were necessary to make an identification when the BACs were greater than 100 mg/dL. Unfortunately, the maximum BACs at which these signs occurred were not reported. The sensitivity of the ASC may also be due to the fact that raters had a significantly long period of time to make observations of the subjects while they were in the hospital. Therefore, these results may not be applicable to the observations within the purview of a bartender, social host, or passenger during a casual conversation. Also, the large number of cues that raters had to choose from may have increased the sensitivity of the instrument as well as the awareness of the raters. Longer periods of observation and a list of cues have potential prevention implications. As in most studies, some inference could have been drawn from raters because the subjects were being treated in a hospital. Nevertheless, the study suggests that those who might need this skill could be trained to identify signs of intoxication.

Maguire (1986) examined roadside survey data from the California Highway Patrol and analyzed it to determine to what extent BACs can be judged by observation. The sample of 934 cases included a 30-second interview by a patrol officer who was charged with determining whether the driver was sober, possibly under the influence, or definitely under the influence (BAC of >100 mg/dL). The interviewers correctly identified only about 21 percent of drivers with BACs over 100 mg/dL and failed to identify about 79 percent who were, by law, intoxicated. Unfortunately, BACs above 100 mg/dL were not separated into further groups. McGuire concluded that although sobriety checkpoints are effective in detecting 20 percent of drunk drivers, applying the same standard to restaurant proprietors and/or hosts of private parties "seems unfair." Applying these findings to today's legal definition of intoxication (80 mg/dL) would no doubt reveal an even smaller percentage of drivers who were intoxicated based upon both their BAC and casual observation during an interview.

Sullivan, Hauptman, and Bronstein (1987) attempted to use the ASC developed by Teplin and Lutz to assist in bartenders' identification of intoxication. The eleven symptom checklist included odor of alcohol on breath (AOB) detected during face-to-face discussions; impaired fine motor control (digit dexterity); gross motor control such as difficulty walking, sitting, standing, walking a straight line, or performing a finger to nose test; slurred speech; changes in speech volume; decreased alertness; excessive perspiration discernible; slow or shallow respiration; sleepiness or drowsiness out of the ordinary for the time of day; changes in speed of speech; and bloodshot eyes. Sullivan and coworkers found significantly lower ASC scores (i.e., 2.6) than Teplin and Lutz did (46) for alcohol concentrations of 100 mg/dL or more. In other words, Sullivan needed fewer signs of intoxication than were reported by Teplin and Lutz for subjects at the same BAC. Compared to other studies, the increased detection sensitivity is probably due to the inclusion of signs such as bloodshot eyes AOB and psychophysical testing, including walking a straight line and finger to nose tests.

Carroll, Rosenberg, and Funke (1988) examined the ability of mental health therapists with no alcohol experience and more experienced alcoholism counselors to recognize intoxication or estimate BACs in community mental health volunteers. Observers viewed videos of an intoxicated drinker engaged in simulated counseling interviews, which included conversations about school, relationships, employment, and opinions about faculty. Observers completed an observation rating form that categorized the target as sober (BAC = 0), moderately intoxicated (50 mg/dL), intoxicated (100 mg/dL), or very intoxicated (150 mg/dL). For the most part, experience working with alcohol-impaired clients did not enhance the counselor's ability to recognize intoxication compared to mental health therapists. Almost all subjects recognized that the target was at least moderately intoxicated when BACs reached 150 mg/dL, but experience working with alcohol-impaired patients did not improve rater accuracy. In fact, Carroll and associates found "the ability of alcohol and mental health counselors to judge intoxication in a clinical interview to be no better than that of the previously investigated social drinkers, bartenders, police officers, and roadside interviewers" employed in other studies (1988, p. 245).

Brick, Adler, Cocco, and Westrick (1992) examined the identification of intoxication from a different perspective. Instead of asking raters to make categorical ratings of BACs, these investigators asked raters whether target subjects had been drinking, whether it would be okay to serve them additional drinks, and whether they were okay to drive. Drinking subjects were mostly college-age men and women (ages 22–35), screened to ensure that all subjects were within the normal weight range for their age and height and had no medical or psychological history, including alcoholism, that would preclude their participation in the study. Neurological status, blood pressure, respiration, and temperature were all within normal limits. Females were tested to ensure they were not pregnant. All subjects regularly consumed alcohol, could drink 2 to 3 drinks per hour without illness or discomfort, and had on at least one recent occasion consumed enough alcohol to produce a BAC of 150 mg/dL without illness. Based upon the Oates Drinking Inventory and Michigan Alcoholism Screening Test and structured interviews, only moderate drinkers without evidence of prior drinking problems or other risks were accepted into the study. Subjects were dosed to accurately reach BACs of 80 to 90 mg/dL, 110 to 130 mg/dL or 150 to 160 mg/dL and asked to consume about three drinks per hour. Blood alcohol estimates were obtained using a Breathalyzer. Subjects were tested at two different BACs so that there were four target subjects in each of the three BAC ranges and twelve categorical ratings. Testing was performed in an experimental living room set up in a professional television studio.

Based on preintervention questioning, subjects engaged in a series of recorded 30 to 60 second social interactions with an interviewer. Sober raters then viewed the video and were asked to determine whether the target subjects (1) had been drinking (no implication of intoxication, but only if the subject had been consuming alcohol); (2) were okay to serve another drink (if the rater was serving alcohol to the target at a party or as a bartender, would they continue to serve the target); and (3) were okay to drive (that is, was the target able to safely operate a motor vehicle). Brick and colleagues (1992) found that target subjects with BACs of 150 mg/dL or more were correctly identified as drinking about 53 percent of the time and the subject with the highest BAC (160 mg/dL) was correctly identified as having been drinking by 88 percent of the raters. The identification of intoxication was also not reliably obtained until BACs were quite high (150 to 160 mg/dL). Continued service of alcohol to the targets was considered acceptable by 47 percent of the raters, and 41 percent of the raters judged the intoxicated drinkers to be unable to drive. However, the most intoxicated target (160 mg/dL) was deemed not able to drive by 100 percent of the raters. At the highest BACs, 82 percent of the raters believed subjects were too intoxicated to drive or were not sure if they could drive safely. Only 18 percent of the raters thought these subjects were "okay to drive." Although specific signs used to decide who was too intoxicated to drive were not part of the study, the fact that BACs of 150 mg/dL or more were needed before a substantial percentage of raters determined that it was not okay to drive is revealing.

The results of this study (Brick et al., 1992) are probably conservative because raters were deprived of one very important cue: the odor of alcohol on the breath. Although this cue is not a sign of impairment, it does convey knowledge that the subject had been drinking. From other studies, the detection of the odor of an alcohol beverage is an important cue in determining intoxication. More than twice as many raters in these studies thought it was not okay to drive for subjects in the 150 to 160 mg/dL range. If raters had more information (e.g., observed the targets drink alcohol or detected the odor of alcohol on the breath) the identification of intoxication and impaired driving ability decisions would have been more likely.

In a follow up study, Brick and Carpenter (2001) examined the ability of police to determine intoxication by casual observation. As in an earlier study, raters (primarily police lieutenants, captains, and chiefs) were asked to determine whether a target subject had been drinking, whether or not it was okay to serve the target another drink, and whether the target drinkers were okay to drive. In this study, a measure of raters' confidence in the accuracy of their decision was also obtained. Brick and Carpenter found that raters were "pretty sure" that targets in the 150 to 160 mg/dL range had been drinking but not sure whether or not serving another drink or driving a car was okay. When BACs were in the 150 to 160 mg/dL range, 67 percent of the police raters did not think it was okay for subjects to drive a car or were unsure if it was okay for them to drive. At a BAC of 160 mg/dL, 90 percent of the raters identified drinking and 83 percent of the raters responded that it was not okay to drive (Table 6.5). At lower and intermediate BACs drinking was not readily detected, the service of additional alcohol was considered okay, and targets were deemed able to drive a car. Again, observers were denied any information to suggest or confirm that the target subjects had been drinking alcohol (e.g., no observed drinking and no odor cues).

Brick and Carpenter (2001) concluded that if two thirds of the raters thought that the targets with BACs of 150 to 160 mg/dL were too intoxicated to drive or did not know if they were okay to drive, then common sense would indicate that they should not drive and that server intervention was appropriate. One important factor in interpreting these studies is that the drinking targets remained seated for short 30- to 60-second video interviews and the raters were deprived of observations of moving and standing. Therefore, it is reasonable to assume that if raters had more information, such as knowledge that the targets were drinking alcohol, their observations and conclusions regarding the targets' abilities to drive would be more accurate.

Table 6.5: Perceived Ability of Intoxicated
Subjects to Drive — Comparison of Studies.

		Ability to drive (%)		
	BAC (mg/dL)	Not okay	Not sure	Okay
Brick et al. (1992)	80–90	25	53	22
	150–160	41	53	22
Brick and Carpenter (2001)	150–160	36	31	33

Conclusions from Studies of Visible Intoxication

Most, if not all, of the studies suggest that BACs that would impair driving and be in violation of the drinking and driving statutes (80–100 mg/dL, depending on the state and year of the study) do not produce reliable signs of visible intoxication in most subjects (Brick & Carpenter, 2001; Brick et al., 1992; Carroll et al., 1988; Compton, 1986; Harger & Halpieu, 1956; Jetter, 1938a,b; Langenbucher & Nathan, 1983; Maguire, 1986; Pagano & Taylor, 1979; Wells et al., 1997; Widmark, 1981; Zusman and Huber, 1979). Visible intoxication was only reliably detected when BACs were very high, typically above 150 mg/dL (Brick & Carpenter, 2001; Brick et al., 1992; Carroll et al., 1988; Jetter, 1938a,b; Widmark, 1981). At the present time, all states use 80 mg/dL to define intoxicated driving. It is therefore concluded based on research conducted over the last 70 years that most people do not display reliable signs of visible intoxication or signs of clear impairment at BACs less than 150 mg/dL unless special tests are used. Similarly, the majority of all drinkers will appear visibly intoxicated at BACs of 150 mg/dL or more. As the BAC increases, the number and/or intensity of signs of impairment will also increase leaving little doubt that the subject is visibly or obviously intoxicated. As pointed, there are exceptions, namely a very small percentage of the drinking population for whom this standard may not apply because of exceptional tolerance. In such instances information, regarding previous drinking history, reliable observation from witnesses, or clinical test results should be examined.

Not all studies paint such a bleak picture for prevention specialists. Research by McKnight, Langston, Marques, and Tippetts (1997) suggests that with the use of instructional guidance, the identification of alcohol intoxication is possible at lower BACs. (These results are interesting but the criteria for classifying intoxication were described as arbitrary and may be overly sensitive.) In this study, McKnight and coworkers asked observers to rate small groups of intoxicated subjects in a social setting. Half of the observers were given instructional guidance on the relationship between signs of impairment and BAC. Drinkers were classified based on the BAC (<40 mg/dL, >40 mg/dL, and >80 mg/dL) and group size (small social group, large social group, public drinking establishment). BACs ranged from less than 40 mg/dL to 120 mg/dL, and there were about 25 to 35 drinking subjects in each group. Observers were somewhat successful in identifying subjects with BACs over 40 mg/dL as somewhat impaired (arbitrarily defined as some loss of ability; not illegal to be served or perform activities that involve potential risk) and less successful in identifying subjects with BACs of more than 80 mg/dL (arbitrarily defined as great loss of ability and risk of injury; illegal to be served alcohol or to perform activities that involve potential risk). About half to two thirds of drinkers with BACs of about 80 to 120 mg/dL were not identified as intoxicated, and there was significant overlap among groups. Guided instruction did increase the accuracy of identifying subjects at the lowest BAC, but not for those over 80 mg/dL.

Odor of Alcoholic Beverages on the Breath

The human olfactory system is capable of detecting the odor of various alcoholic beverages or components as these molecules diffuse through the lungs and are expired in the breath. However, traditionally, toxicologists and law enforcement are trained that alcohol is odorless and that what is detected on breath is the nonquantifiable odor of an alcoholic beverage. Although pure ethanol is virtually odorless, beverage alcohol once consumed and absorbed into the circulation is detectable by breath alcohol testing and by casual olfactory detection under some conditions. For example, one should be sure that what is detected is not residual alcohol in the buccal cavity. Most likely what is discovered during casual detection is a combination of olfactorants that correlate with the alcohol in blood. The threshold for alcohol detection can be estimated mathematically based on knowledge of physical chemistry and physiology. Theoretical calculations of odor detection place the minimum BAC for olfactory detection of ethanol at approximately 40 to 60 mg/dL, but empirical studies suggest the actual threshold is higher.

For example, an early study (Widmark, 1981) evaluated the ability of physicians to detect the odor of an alcoholic beverage in subjects who were arrested for allegedly driving while intoxicated. Widmark tested 562 subjects on a variety of tasks, and specifically tested whether raters, in this case 150 trained physicians, could detect the odor of alcoholic beverages. After waiting a sufficient amount of time for residual mouth alcohol to dissipate (about 15 minutes), the physicians sampled expired breath of the subjects, and a blood sample was obtained and subsequently analyzed. Of the 562 subjects tested, no one had a detectable odor of alcohol on the breath when the blood alcohol was less than 60 mg/dL. At BAC in the 61 to 80 mg/dL range, 33 percent of the subjects had detectable breath alcohol by human olfaction. At BACs of 81 mg/dL and higher, about half the subjects, or more, had an alcoholic odor of the breath (Table 6.6).

Table 6.6: Detection of Odor of Alcohol on Breath.

	<50% detection	>50% detection	>85% detection
Widmark (1981)	60–80 mg/dL	81 mg/dL	>181 mg/dL
Moskowitz et al. (1999)	<40 mg/dL for beer	40–80 mg/dL for beer	>97 mg/dL
	<40 to 80 mg/dL for wine	90 mg/dL for wine	–
	–	<40–80 mg/dL for vodka	–
	–	80 mg/dL for bourbon	100 mg/dL for bourbon

More recently, a study by Moskowitz, Burns, and Fuguson. (1999) examined the ability of police officers to detect beverage odor (beer, wine, vodka and bourbon), also under relatively ideal laboratory conditions. Beverage type had little influence on detection threshold, but bourbon or high BACs resulted in a greater percentage of positive responses. At BACs of less than 80 mg/dL, detection probability was less than chance and above 80 mg/dL, more likely than not. From these studies, it can be concluded that there is considerable variability in detection threshold.

As previously discussed, decades ago, when DWI characterizations were first written, the legal definition for intoxicated driving was set very high. Even then, it was known that the odor of an alcoholic beverage on the breath was detectable at blood alcohol levels well below the legal definition of 150 mg/dL. This concern continued for decades, even after the legal definition for DWI in most states was lowered. Today, it is still widely accepted that the relationship between the perceived strength of an alcoholic beverage on the breath and the actual blood alcohol concentration is relatively weak. However, there is a relationship between the olfactory detection threshold and minimum BACs. Assuming circumstances are such that an observer is positioned to detect the odor of an alcoholic beverage, such evidence may be useful in forensic evaluations.

Significance of the Available Studies Identifying Alcohol Use and Intoxication

The findings reviewed are relevant to a reduction in drunk-driving injuries and fatalities and improvement in the application of dram shop or social host liability laws and in the arrest of persons driving while intoxicated. As with all other dose-dependent drug effects, the BAC is related to a proportional increase in the degree of impairment as well as the percentage of drinkers who are impaired in the performance of complex tasks such as driving an automobile, many of who appear visibly intoxicated. However, not all intoxication is visible.

In Chapter 4 we learned that in the laboratory, and in some drinkers, divided attention failure can be demonstrated at very low BACs, often in the 20 to 30 mg/dL range. Underage drinkers are at particular risk and sensitive to the effects of very low BACs. In most drinkers, at slightly higher BACs (about 50 mg/dL) there is clear evidence that the relative risk for a fatal crash is significantly elevated, especially in young men (NIAAA, 1990; Surgeon General's Workshop on Drunk Driving, 1988; U.S. Department of Transportation, 1994; Zador, Krawchuk & Voas, 2000). At low BACs, behavioral changes such as increased talkativeness, relaxation, and tension reduction are often observed but would not be distinguishable from normal social behavior. At BACs above 50 to 80 mg/dL there is significant impairment in mental and cognitive ability and subsequent risk for motor vehicle fatalities that increases exponentially in virtually all drivers. However, impairment and intoxication at a BAC that constitutes *prima facie* evidence of drunk driving no longer reliably equates with gross, obvious, or visible intoxication as it once did when motor vehicle laws were first established. To the contrary, available studies suggest that BACs that would impair driving and be in violation of the impaired driving statute in the United States (80 mg/dL) do not produce reliable signs of visible intoxication in most subjects (Brick & Carpenter, 2001; Brick & Erickson, 2009; Brick et al., 1992; Carroll et al., 1988; Compton, 1986; Harger & Halpieu, 1956; Jetter, 1938a,b; Langenbucher & Nathan, 1983; Maguire, 1986; Pagano & Taylor, 1979; Wells et al., 1997; Widmark, 1981; Zusman & Huber, 1979). The odor of an alcoholic beverage on the breath, which occurs at BAC well below that required for visible intoxication is variable and not reliable to determine alcohol use for a large percentage of subjects. Identifying intoxicated drinkers before they drive is very difficult and presents a serious challenge in further reducing impaired driving fatalities. It also highlights the need for more sensitive methods of training to identify intoxication before gross abnormalities appear.

Perhaps most useful in the prevention of drunk driving is the realization that when intoxication is visible, the BAC is almost always well above the current definition for intoxicated driving in the United States. Based upon empirical research, most textbooks, reviews, and other publications during the last 70 years concur that at BACs of about 150 mg/dL, the majority (i.e., more than 50% of drinkers) will present one or more reliable signs of visible intoxication, even among alcoholics. As BACs increase, the probability of detecting intoxication also increases dramatically. Whereas most drinkers are probably visibly intoxicated at a BAC of 150 mg/dL, by 200 mg/dL virtually all drinkers (including alcohol abusers and alcoholics) will appear visibly intoxicated. Yet, there are those rare individuals who by virtue of their exceptional tolerance may not appear visibly intoxicated even at much higher BACs (*see* Chapter 10).

Prevention specialists including law enforcement face the often-unrecognized challenge of the need to increase awareness within their profession and the general public about the relationship between alcohol intoxication and behavior. To date, prevention efforts have focused on the harmful consequences of drinking and driving and the message "don't drink and drive." The message that people who drink should not drive is an important one, but as evidenced by a multitude of state and national statistics on drunk driving arrests, accidents and fatalities, it is not an effective message. Current strategies in the prevention of drunk driving must include an additional message involving the importance of proper identification of impaired driving.

Two conclusions having direct implications for police and other specialists are apparent as a result of this review (1) the lack of visible signs of alcohol intoxication is no guarantee that the drinking driver is not impaired; and (2) if signs of visible intoxication (i.e., trouble walking, speech impairment, impaired cognition or affect, or other signs of intoxication) are present, the person is probably (more likely than not) intoxicated well in excess of the legal definition for driving while intoxicated and is at significantly increased risk for a fatal crash or injury. Better training of alcohol beverage servers and social hosts, and broader public awareness of the relationship between BAC, visible intoxication, obvious intoxication, and risk for a motor vehicle crash should be part of future prevention strategies. Most importantly, drivers who drink but do not show signs of visible intoxication may have BACs that exceed the current legal definition for intoxicated driving and may be at high risk for injury to themselves and others. This problem is greatly enhanced in underage drinking drivers, who as a group are at higher risk for intoxication and fatal accidents than are older drinking drivers. Thus, extra vigilance is required of hosts and bar employees whose responsibility it is to prevent drunk driving and its consequences in those they serve. Although a portion of the responsibility for reducing drunk driving harm rests with the consumer, alcohol at higher levels clearly reduces inhibitions and impairs judgment so that a responsible drinker can become an irresponsible driver. The consequences of drunk driving are simply too costly for hosts and servers to abrogate their responsibility of over serving entirely to the consumer.

Conclusions

Based upon a review of relevant studies conducted over the last seven decades, we conclude that obvious intoxication as defined in some courts is not always the same as visible intoxication. Obvious intoxication may include factors such as the number of drinks served, whereas visible intoxication refers to specific signs. The signs of visible intoxication occur on a continuum, and higher BACs lead to a greater likelihood of identifying individuals who are alcohol impaired in cases involving the negative consequences of drinking and driving. Training individuals in the quantification of signs of intoxication enhances the accuracy of observation and may modify serving practices to limit over service, particularly if bartenders are supported by management, laws are enforced (NIAAA, 2000) and police are well-trained. Yet, it is clear that even well-trained individuals (e.g., trained counselors, bartenders, police officers) often have difficulty discriminating those who are sober from those who should not be driving. This is a problem in the prevention of drunk driving since the totality of the scientific research reviewed leads us to conclude that BACs of 150 mg/dL or more are most related to visible signs of intoxication, even in the most highly tolerant individuals. Factors involved with determining visible intoxication include biological differences among individuals (i.e., some people are less sensitive to the effects of alcohol than others are), acquired tolerance in experienced drinkers, BAC, and the environment in which the observations were made. Even so, above 150 mg/dL, one or more signs of visible intoxication will probably be present and identifiable by casual observation if persons who care make an effort to find such signs. At BACs of 200 mg/dL or above, almost all individuals, whether experienced or exceptionally tolerant, will show visible signs of intoxication.

The identification of alcohol and intoxication may be further complicated by gender differences in the description of people who are intoxicated. For example, Levitt, Sher, and Bartholow (2009) and Levitt, Schlauch, Bartholow, and Sher (2013) found that women were more likely to describe their own intoxication with moderate terms (e.g., tipsy, buzzed) even after the consumption of four to five drinks in 2 hours, whereas men were more likely to self-use heavy terms (e.g., wasted, trashed) to describe themselves (Levitt et al., 2009). Follow-up research on this interesting subject indicated that both men and women were more likely to apply moderate terms to describe intoxication to females even if they were heavily intoxicated whereas males were more consistently described using terms that reflected heavy intoxication. The fact that women apply euphemistic terms to describe intoxication is a misperception of intoxication in others that can lead to poor decision making, including increased risk taking (driving while impaired, unplanned sexual activity), and other serious alcohol-related problems (Levitt et al., 2013). Such terms may also obscure visible intoxication because of sociocultural or gender-bias rather than factual observations.

6.4 ALCOHOL, VIOLENCE, AND AGGRESSION

Assault in all its forms is against the law, and alcohol, more than any other drug, is found in victims and perpetrators of assaults and other crimes of violence that are the subject of forensic evaluations (Pernanen, 1991). Although there is abundant evidence that alcohol consumption facilitates aggressive behavior (Chermack and Giancola, 1997; Miczek et al., 1994), the causal relationship between intoxication and aggression has not always been so clear (Murdoch, Pihl & Ross, 1990), although qualitative and quantitative reviews have clearly demonstrated that intoxication can increase aggression (Ito, Miller & Pollock, 1996). Forensic evaluations often involve injuries from assaults between one or more intoxicated persons. Social scientists who study aggression and violence usually define these terms, but often they are used without distinction. In some instances the misuse of either term may introduce a pejorative stigma or bias with potential legal and courtroom implications.

Aggression is a behavior that usually arises in response to frustration, self-defense (self-assertive), or internal or external drives. It is manifested by destructive and hostile attacks to another person or the environment or in some cases it is self-directed. Aggression can be physical, verbal, or symbolic. Violence is an extreme form of aggression and includes acts such as assault, rape, and murder. The relationship between alcohol and aggression may be studied in the laboratory whereas violent behavior cannot be ethnically or legally studied in the laboratory. The study of violent behavior is typically limited to epidemiological data and their relationship between crimes and alcohol and statistically examined. The nexus between intoxication and aggression (or violence) is complex, situational, and subject dependent. Empirical research on the relationship between alcohol and aggression is based upon different models and experimental designs. However, research on alcohol and violence (as opposed to aggression) is not the subject of empirical laboratory research. Nevertheless, the terms aggression and violence are often used interchangeably in the alcohol literature.

The causes of aggression invariably relate to changes or differences in the brain. As a CNS depressant, alcohol produces a dose-dependent decrease in cognitive and motor functioning. With increasing BACs, the signs and symptoms of intoxication increase in number and intensity, many of these effects were discussed earlier. Of particular note are the deleterious effects of alcohol on cognitive faculties, including memory, attention, decision making, reasoning, problem solving, and learning abilities in general. These domains of impairment contribute to many social problems, including the well-known and documented association between alcohol use and aggression, particularly crimes of violence (Greenfield, 1998). Many correlational studies support the conclusion that members of clinical and nonclinical populations are more aggressive when intoxicated, as evidenced in part by the overrepresentation of alcohol use immediately prior to a violent crime (Collins & Schlenger, 1988; Evans, 1986). A number of models have been proposed to disentangle the complex web of correlated and causal factors that contribute to this psychosocial problem. Although the selected heuristic models described later are not exhaustive, there is at this time no single model to explain the relationship between alcohol and aggression and the apparent overlapping concepts between models reflecting the complex nature of human behavior.

Causal Pharmacological Model

The causal model suggests that alcohol use directly causes aggression or violence, presumably due to the pharmacological effects of alcohol on the limbic system or other brain areas involved in sympathetic nervous system arousal.

Traditional models of the alcohol-aggression relationship focus on the direct psychopharmacological effects of alcohol (and pharmacologically related drugs) on behavior. In the pharmacological model, the depressant effects of alcohol result in well-known biobehavioral changes including decreased inhibition, cognitive and perceptual distortion, poor judgment, increased risk taking, alcohol myopia, and related behaviors (Fagan, 1991). To the extent that impairment in these behavioral domains is critical in the ability to formulate and engage in directed behaviors, alcohol has a number of relevant effects.

The pharmacological effects of alcohol may also interfere with the ability to successfully execute or defend against an assault. This is a logical inference from the well-known impairment in psychomotor skills and CNS depression produced by intoxication and the high incidence of intoxicated victims in violent crimes. At very high BACs, the performance of these skills will be further impaired by analgesia and the impaired proprioceptive feedback.

If the effects of alcohol were simply related to a pharmacological action on aggression-regulating neurons, the effects of alcohol would be dose-dependent, as it is for other effects. Generally, this is not the case. However, Dougherty, Bjork, Bennett, and Moeller, (1999) found that aggression was related to the ascending or descending limb of the blood alcohol curve. Subjects received the equivalent of about 4 to 5 standard drinks but in three staggered servings to achieve a maximum BAC of about 100 mg/dL. Aggression was greatest after the second serving and while the BAC was increasing but continued to be elevated for several hours after drinking, suggesting that acute tolerance to the effects of alcohol on aggression did not eliminate aggression.

Attention-Cognitive Model

One specific example related to impairment in attention, previously discussed, is the effect of alcohol intoxication on narrowing cognitive awareness and processing. This results in a decrease in the ability to recognize social boundaries and high risk or dangerous social or environmental cues and to identify threatening situations. Intoxicated persons are often stimulus bound and likely to focus on immediate superficial cues at the expense of potentially more important cues indicating danger, risk, negativity, and so on. (Chermack & Giancola, 1997; Taylor & Leonard, 1983). When sober, most people exert self-control, think clearly, use good judgment, appreciate high risk or dangerous environments and boundary issues, and avoid verbal or physical behaviors that are likely to lead to altercation, and in many cases, have the good sense to change environments. Steele and Josephs (1990) refer to a narrowing of attention or alcoholic myopia following alcohol intoxication that may result in a range of behaviors. Moreover, intoxication decrease, the ability to think abstractly. For example, an intoxicated person may not accurately perceive social cues or has decreases in the number of cues that can be attended. Similarly, the intoxicated person may not correctly interpret the behavior of others, find such puzzling behavior provocative and make it more likely to respond aggressively (Pernanen, 1976; Taylor & Chermack, 1993).

Disinhibition Model

Decreased inhibitions are often associated with aggression and the acute effects of alcohol intoxication. Although this model is intuitive and consistent with what is frequently observed in social situations, wherein intoxicated persons do or say things that are misinterpreted and lead to altercations (similar to the attention-cognitive model), the association is probably more complexly related to anxiety. Anxiety is often a warning sign for potential danger, which would certainly define an aggression-eliciting situation. Psychologically, anxiety may suppress aggressive behavior because it elicits fear or potential injury. Ito and associates (1996) suggest an anxiolytic-disinhibition model in which alcohol decreases the arousal of anxiety, which then decreases the suppression of aggression. Therefore, alcohol increases aggression in situations in which stress would normally inhibit it. This is similar to self-focused attention models wherein personal standards of appropriate behavior are self-regulated when sober, inhibit impulsive behavior, and promote positive or acceptable social behavior. When self-focus is decreased so are the personal standards of behavior, which leads to increased aggression (Carver & Scheier, 1981, 1990).

Aggression Predicts Alcohol Use

This model suggests that people who are aggressive are more likely to live in a subculture and social milieu in which heavy drinking is encouraged and accepted than people who are not aggressive. Moreover, aggressive individuals who live in this subculture drink heavily to self-medicate (Khantzian, 1990) or as an excuse for their violent and aggressive behavior (Collins, 1988; Fagan, 1992). Dougherty and coworkers (1999) found that the increase in aggressive behavior in both men and women was greater in subjects who were more aggressive, even in the absence of alcohol. These researchers also noted that alcohol induced aggression is gender neutral.

Spurious Model

The spurious model suggests that intoxication and aggression related because they share common causes rather than a direct causal relationship. Related but more complex models suggest that alcohol intoxication does result in aggressive behavior but only in some individuals and only under some circumstances. Clearly, not everyone who drinks becomes violent, but some do. There is also evidence that early displays of aggression in teenagers lead to increased alcohol use, but alcohol use does not lead to increased aggression (White, Brick & Hansell, 1993), although the sample population of white, middle and working class adolescents in New Jersey may not generalize to other populations.

Triggering and Dispositional and Constitutional Models

Alcohol may serve as a triggering mechanism in persons with a preexisting tendency toward aggression or a propensity for violence. In this situation, alcohol is a secondary reinforcer acting as a violence cue or signal. Similarly, persons who drink are more likely to engage in aggressive or violent acts than are sober persons in the same situation. Therefore, alcohol use in any situation will lead to greater risk of eliciting aggression. Thus, alcohol acts as a vehicle or trigger for preexisting behavioral dispositions regardless of the situation (Pernanen, 1991). A number of laboratory studies support the notion that individuals predisposed to aggression are more likely to express it when intoxicated (Bailey & Taylor, 1991; George, Derman & Nochajski, 1989; Pihl, Smith & Farrell, 1984).

Alcohol and Personal Violence

Epidemiological studies of domestic and criminal violence often document high rates of alcohol involvement, and alcohol consumption is thought to impair moral judgment, reduce inhibition, and increase aggression. High rates of alcohol involvement among fight-related homicide (Goodman, Istre, Jordan, Herndon & Kelaghan, 1991) and assault victims (Cherpitel, 1989a) and the substantial proportion of perpetrators who are under the influence of alcohol (Pernanen, 1991; Roizen, 1982; Welte & Abel, 1989) are generally consistent with the hypothesis that alcohol increases aggression.

Welte and Abel (1989) reported that alcohol was most likely to be detected among homicide victims killed by stabbing, among those killed in bars and restaurants, among those killed on Saturday and Sunday nights, and among males killed by females. The prevalence of alcohol involvement was lower among victims killed as a result of other criminal activities. From these findings, Welte and Abel (1989) concluded that alcohol use was most likely to be detected in situations that emerged spontaneously from personal disputes.

The role of alcohol in violent episodes is not well-understood. Alcohol is not the sole cause of violent behavior—many violent episodes occur between sober people with no history of drug or alcohol abuse. Most drinkers, even heavy drinkers, never engage in violent behavior (Leonard & Jacob, 1988). As Pernanen (1991) stated, "really dangerous behavior among drinkers is rare. Harmless folly is much more prevalent. On the other hand . . . such behavior is even rarer in a totally sober state" (p. 212).

Personal violence, property offenders (Welte & Miller, 1987), and various forms of aggression are often associated with drinking by perpetrators. Rates of alcohol involvement and abuse are higher among perpetrators than among victims (Pernanen, 1991). Nevertheless, research also indicates that higher self-reported alcohol consumption was predictive of increased victimization, believed to be due to an impaired ability to accurately interpret assault cues (Koss & Dinero, 1989; Leonard & Jacob, 1988).

Drinking by offenders and victims is clearly associated with domestic and criminal violence, but too little is known about causal mechanisms through which alcohol may contribute to increased interpersonal violence and aggression. A clearer understanding will require the development of integrated models that simultaneously account for the interplay between the characteristics of the victim, the perpetrator-victim relationship, the environmental settings in which violence takes place, and the cultural definitions establishing alcohol expectancies and behavioral norms.

Summary

Although there is a large scientific and epidemiological literature relating alcohol and aggression, this inter-relationship is complex and in some cases includes the inhibitory, psychomotor stimulant, analgesic, and cognitive effects of alcohol related to the pharmacological actions of this drug as well as individual personality factors and psychological factors. Under some conditions, alcohol increases aggression but is a function of anthropometric, pharmacokinetic and pharmacodynamic factors, and the social context variables resulting in aggressive outcomes (Brick, 1993). Clearly, not everyone who drinks becomes aggressive or the victim of violence, but overall, it appears that alcohol acts as a moderating variable in aggression and violence that is expressed based on individual psychological, pharmacological, and situational factors. However, there is also a substantial body of research that childhood aggression may be a predictor of alcohol use disorders in adulthood (Zucker & Gomberg, 1986). Family history of aggression may also be a risk factor (Fuller et al., 2003).

Therefore, unlike the use of a *per se* law to define intoxication in the context of motor vehicle operation and the known relationship between intoxicated driving and accidental injuries, no simple metric exists that can be applied to violent and aggressive behavior observed after alcohol use. Alcohol is never the direct cause of violent or aggressive behavior in that it causes a specific action. However, alcohol intoxication is one of several variables that contribute to such events influenced by individual differences and the specific situation. Whether the intoxicated person is the assailant or the victim, the degree to which decreased inhibition, failure to recognize sound boundaries, risk, and failure to exercise good judgment will be situation specific.

REFERENCES

Alcoholic Beverage Control Handbook for Retail Licensees. (2004). State of New Jersey. Trenton, NJ: Department of Law & Public Safety, Division of Alcohol Beverage Control.

American Psychiatric Association. (2013). *Diagnostic and Statistical Manual of Mental Disorders* (5th ed., DSM-V). Washington, D.C.: Author.

Bailey, A., and Taylor, S. (1991). Effects of alcohol and aggressive disposition on human physical aggression. *Journal of Research in Personality, 25*(3), 334–342.

Borkenstein, R. F. (1985). Historical perspective North American traditional and experimental response. *Journal on Alcohol Studies*, Suppl. 10:3–12 New Brunswick, NJ: Rutgers University.

Brick, J. (1993). Symposium commentaries. *Journal of Studies on Alcohol, Supplement*, (11), 192–193.

Brick, J. (2008). *Handbook of the Medical Consequences of Alcohol and Drug Abuse* (2nd ed.). New York, NY: Haworth Press.

Brick, J. (2009). Alcohol intoxication, behavioral, and medical effects. In A. Jamieson and A. Moenssens (Eds.), *Wiley Encyclopedia of Forensic Science* (pp. 99–108). Chichester, UK: John Wiley & Sons Ltd.

Brick, J., Adler, J., Cocco, K., and Westrick, E. (1992). Alcohol intoxication: Pharmacokinetic prediction and behavioral analysis in humans. *Current Topics in Pharmacology*, *1*, 57–67.

Brick, J., and Carpenter, J. (2001). The identification of alcohol intoxication by police. *Alcoholism, Clinical and Experimental Research*, *25*, 850–885.

Brick, J., and Erickson, C. (2009). Intoxication is not always visible: An unrecognized prevention challenge. *Alcoholism, Clinical and Experimental Research*, *33*(9), 1489–1507.

Burns, M., and Anderson, E. W. (1995). *A Colorado Validation Study of the Standardized Field Sobriety Test (SFST) Battery*. Washington, D.C.: U.S. Department of Transportation, National Highway Traffic Safety Administration.

Burns, M., and Moskowitz, H. (1977). *Psychophysical Tests for DWI Arrest*. Report DOT-HS-5-01242. Washington, D.C.: U.S. Department of Transportation, National Highway Traffic Safety Administration.

Carroll, N., Rosenberg, H., and Funke, S. (1988). Recognition of intoxication by alcohol counselors. *Journal of Substance Abuse Treatment*, *5*, 239–246.

Carver, C., and Scheier, M. (1981). *Attention and Self-Regulation: A Control Theory Approach to Human Behavior*. New York, NY: Springer-Verlag.

Carver, C., and Scheier, M. (1990). Origins and functions of positive and negative affect: A control-process view. *Psychological Review*, *97*, 19–35.

Centers for Disease Control. (2001). *Evidence of Effectiveness of 0.08% Blood Alcohol Concentration (BAC) Laws: Findings from the Task Force on Community Preventive Services*. Atlanta, GA: Author.

Chermack, S., and Giancola, P. (1997). The relation between alcohol and aggression: An integrated biopsychosocial conceptualization. *Clinical Psychology Review*, *17*, 621–649.

Cherpitel, C. J. (1989). Breath analysis and self-reports as measures of alcohol-related emergency room admissions. *Journal of Studies on Alcohol*, *50*(2), 155–161.

Collins, J. J. (1988). Suggested explanatory frameworks to clarify the alcohol use/violence relationship. *Contemporary Drug Problems*, *15*, 107–121.

Collins, J. J., and Schlenger, W. E. (1988). Acute and chronic effects of alcohol use on violence. *Journal of Studies on Alcohol*, *49*(6), 516–521.

Compton, R. P. (1986). Pilot test of selected DWI screening procedures for use at sobriety checkpoints. *Journal of Traffic Safety Education*, *April*, 20.

Dee, T. S. (2001). Does setting limits save lives? The case of 0.08 BAC laws. *Journal of Policy Analysis and Management, 20*(1), 111–128.

Dougherty, D., Bjork, J., Bennett, R., and Moeller, F. (1999). The effects of a cumulative alcohol dosing procedure on laboratory aggression in women and men. *Journal of Studies on Alcohol, 60*, 322–329.

Duffy, D. (2005). *Dram Shop Acts.* OLR Research Report, 2005-R-0922. Available at http://www.cga.ct.gov/2005/rpt/2005-R-0922.htm

Evans, C. (1986). Alcohol and violence: Problems relating to methodology statistics and causation. In P. Brain (Ed.), *Alcohol and Aggression* (pp. 138–160). Dover, NH: Croom Helm.

Fagan, J. (1991). Intoxication and aggression. In M. Tonry and J. Q. Wilson (Eds.), *Drugs and Crime* (Vol. 13, *Crime and Justice*, pp. 241–320). Chicago, IL: University of Chicago Press.

Fagan, J. (1992). *Set and Setting Revisited: Influences of Alcohol and Illicit Drugs on the Social Context of Violent Events.* Paper presented at the Working Group on Alcohol-Related Violence, Workshop of Alcohol-Related Violence, May 1992. Washington, D.C.: National Institute on Alcohol Abuse and Alcoholism.

Fandozzi v. Kelly Hotel, Inc., Supreme Court of Pennsylvania, Supra 711 A.2d at 527.

Fuller, B., Chermack, S., Cruise, K., Kirsch, E., Fitzgerald, H., and Zucker, R. (2003). Predictors of aggression across three generations among sons of alcoholics: Relationship involving grandparental and parental alcoholism, child aggression, marital aggression and parenting practices. *Journal of Studies on Alcohol, 64*(4), 472–483.

George, W., Derman, J., and Nochajski, T. (1989). Expectancy set, reported expectancies and predispositional traits: Predicting interest in violence and erotica. *Journal of Studies on Alcohol, 50*, 541–551.

Goldberg, L. (1943). Quantitative studies on alcohol tolerance in man. The influence of ethyl alcohol on sensory, motor and psychological functions referred to blood alcohol in normal and habituated individuals. *Acta Physiologica Scandinavica, 5*, 1–128.

Goodman, R., Istre, G., Jordan, F., Herndon, J., and Kelaghan, J. (1991). Alcohol and fatal injuries in Oklahoma. *Journal of Studies on Alcohol, 52*(2), 156–161.

Greenfield, L. (1998). *Alcohol and Crime: An Analysis of National Data on the Prevalence of Alcohol Involvement in Crime* (NCJ 168632). Washington, D.C.: U.S. Department of Justice.

Harger, R., and Halpieu, H. (1956). The pharmacology of alcohol. In G.N. Thompson (Ed.), *Alcoholism* (pp. 103–222). Springfield, IL: Charles C Thomas.

Heise, H. (1934). Alcohol and automobile accidents. *Journal of the American Medical Association, 103*, 739–741.

Heise, H. (1956). Interpretation of tests for intoxication. *Journal of Forensic Science, 1*, 38–44.

Heise, H., and Halporn, B. (1932). Medicolegal aspects of drunkenness. *Pennsylvania Medical Journal, 36*, 190–195.

Hingson, R., Heeren, T., and Winter, M. (1996). Lowering state legal blood alcohol limits to 0.08%; the effect on fatal motor vehicle crashes. *American Journal of Public Health, 86*, 1297–1299.

Hingson, R., Heeren, T., and Winter, M. (1999). Preventing impaired driving. *Alcohol Research and Health, 23*(1), 31–39.

Hingson, R., Heeren, T., and Winter, M. (2000). Effects of recent 0.08% legal blood alcohol limits on fatal crash involvement. Injury Prevention, 6, 109–114.

Hingson, R., McGovern, T., Howland, T., Heeren, T., Winter, M., and Zakocs, R. (1996). Reducing alcohol-impaired driving in Massachusetts: The Saving Lives Program. *American Journal of Public Health, 86*(6), 791–797.

Holder, H., Gruenewald, P., Ponicki, W., Treno, A., Grube, J., Saltz, R., ..., Roeper, P. (2000). Effect of community-based interventions on high-risk drinking and alcohol-related injuries. *Journal of the American Medical Association, 284*, 2341–2347.

Ito, T. A., Miller, N., and Pollock, V. (1996). Alcohol and aggression: A meta-analysis on the moderating effects of inhibitory cues, triggering events and self-focused attention. *Psychological Bulletin, 120*, 60–82.

Jetter, W. (1938a). Studies in alcohol. I. Diagnosis of acute alcoholic intoxication by a correlation of clinical and chemical findings. *American Journal of Medical Science, 196*, 475–487.

Jetter, W. (1938b). Studies in alcohol. II. Experimental feeding of alcohol to non-alcoholic individuals. *American Journal of Medical Science, 196*, 487–493.

Khantzian, E. J. (1990). Self-regulation and self-medication factors in alcoholism and the addictions. Similarities and differences. *Recent Developments in Alcoholism, 8*, 255–271.

Koss, M. P., and Dinero, T. E. (1989). Discriminant analysis of risk factors for sexual victimization among a national sample of college women. *Journal of Consulting Clinical Psychology, 57*(2), 242–250.

Langenbucher, J., and Nathan, P. (1983). Psychology, public policy and the evidence for alcohol intoxication. *American Psychologist, 38*, 1070–1077.

Lawson, D., Nathan, P., and Lipscomb, T. (1980). Guidelines for the administration of alcohol to human subjects in behavioral research. *Journal of Studies on Alcohol, 41*, 871–881.

Leonard, K. E., and Jacob, T. (1988). Alcohol, alcoholism and family violence. In V. B. Van Hasselt, R. L. Morrison, A. S. Bellack, and M. Hersen (Eds.), *Handbook of Family Violence* (pp. 383–406). New York, NY: Springer-Verlag US.

Levitt, A., Schlauch, R., Bartholow, B., and Sher, K. (2013). Gender differences in natural language factor of subjective intoxication in college students: An experimental vignette study. *Alcoholism, Clinical and Experimental Research, 37*(12), 2145–2151.

Levitt, A., Sher, K., and Bartholow, B. (2009). The language of intoxication: Preliminary investigations. *Alcoholism, Clinical and Experimental Research, 33*, 448–454.

Maciszewski v. Flatley 705 A.2d 171, 173 (R.I. 1998).

Maguire, F. (1986). The accuracy of estimating the sobriety of drinking drivers. *Journal of Safety Research, 17*, 81–85.

McKnight, A., Langston, E., Marques, P., and Tippetts, A. (1997). Estimating BAC from observable signs. *Accident Analysis and Prevention, 29*, 247–255.

Miczek, K., DeBold, J., Haney, M., Tidey, J., Vivian, J., and Weerts, E. (1994). Alcohol, drugs of abuse, aggression and violence. In A. J. Reiss, J. A. Roth, and K. A. Miczek (Eds.), *Understanding and Prevention Violence* (Vol. 3. Social Influences, pp. 377–570). Washington, D.C.: National Academy Press.

Model Driving While Under the Influence of Alcohol and Other Drugs Act. (1993). President's Commission on Model State Drug Laws. Crimes Code (pp. F125–F156). Washington, D. C.: The White House.

Moskowitz, H. (2008). Alcohol effects and driving impairment. In J. C. Garriott (Ed.), *Garriott's Medicolegal Aspects of Alcohol* (5th ed., pp. 285–302). Tucson, AZ: Lawyers and Judges Publishing Company.

Moskowitz, H., Burns, M., and Ferguson, S. (1999). Police officers' detection of breath odors from alcohol ingestion. *Accident Analysis and Prevention, 31*(3), 175–180.

Murdoch, D., Pihl, R., and Ross, D. (1990). Alcohol and crimes and violence. Present issues. *International Journal of the Addictions, 25,* 1065–1088.

National Alcoholic Beverage Control Association. (1984). *A Compilation of Dram Shop Statutes and Judicial Rulings.* Alexandria, VA: Author. ISSN 0749-0860.

National Institute on Alcohol Abuse and Alcoholism (NIAAA), U.S. Department of Health and Human Services. (1990). Effects of Alcohol on Driving Performance. *Alcohol World, 14*(1).

National Institute on Alcohol Abuse and Alcoholism (NIAAA). (1993). *Eighth Special Report to the U.S. Congress on Alcohol and Health from the Secretary of Health and Human Services.* Rockville, MD: U.S. Department of Health and Human Services, Public Health Service, National Institutes of Health, National Institute on Alcohol Abuse and Alcoholism.

National Institute on Alcohol Abuse and Alcoholism (NIAAA). (2000). Reducing Alcohol-Impaired Driving. In *10th Special Report to the U.S. Congress on Alcohol and Health* (pp. 375–396). Rockville, MD: U.S. Department of Health and Human Services, Public Health Service, National Institutes of Health, National Institute on Alcohol Abuse and Alcoholism.

NJ Division of Alcohol Beverage Control v. Zane, 1961, 99 NJ Supra 196 (App Div 1961).

Oates, J. F. Jr., and McCay, R. T. (1973). *Laboratory Evaluation of Alcohol Safety Interlock Systems* (Vol 3, Instrument Performance at High BAL). Report DOT-TSC-NHTSA-73-3, III. Springfield, VA: National Technical Information Service.

Pagano, M., and Taylor, S. (1979). Police perceptions of alcohol intoxication. *Journal of Applied Social Psychology, 10,* 166–174.

Pentilla, A., Tenhu, M., and Kataja, M. (1971). *Clinical Examination for Intoxication in Cases of Suspected Drunken Driving. An Evaluation of the Finnish System on the Basis of 6839 Cases.* Reports from Talja 11:43, Helsinki, Finland. Statistical and Research Bureau of Talja: Iso Roobertinkatu 20 Helsinki.

Pernanen, K. (1976). Alcohol and crimes of violence. In B. Kissen and H. Begleiter (Eds.), *The Biology of Alcoholism* (Vol. 4, Social Aspects of Alcoholism, pp. 351–441). New York, NY: Plenum Press.

Pernanen, K. (1991). *Alcohol in Human Violence.* New York, NY: Guilford Press.

Perrine, M. (1988). *Zero Tolerance and Other Options: Limits for Truck and Bus Drivers.* Washington, D.C.: Transportation Research Board, National Research Council.

Pihl, R., Smith, M., and Farrell, B. (1984). Alcohol and aggression in men: A comparison of brewed and distilled beverages. *Journal of Studies on Alcohol, 45,* 278–282.

Pohorecky, L. A. (1978). Biphasic action of ethanol. *Biobehavioral Reviews, 1*(4), 231–240.

Roizen, J. (1982). Estimating alcohol involvement in serious events. In Alcohol and Health Monograph No.1: *Alcohol Consumption and Related Problems* (pp. 179–219), DHHS Pub. No. (ADM) 82-1190. Washington D.C.: U.S. Government Printing Office.

Rubenzer, S. (2011). Judging intoxication. *Behavioral Sciences and the Law, 29,* 116–137.

Shults, R., Elder, R., Sleet, D., Nichols, J., Alao, M., Carande-Kulis, V., ..., Thompson, R. (2001). Task Force on Community Preventive Services: Reviews of evidence regarding interventions to reduce alcohol-impaired driving. *American Journal of Preventive Medicine, 21,* 66–88.

State of Missouri Alcohol Responsibility Training. (2008). Missouri Department of Transportation's Highway Safety Division, State of Missouri Alcohol Responsibility Training (SMART). Available at VI. Man.Refs.doc. Retrieved January 16, 2008.

State of New Jersey v. Kenneth Powell, Indictment–01-04-00170.

State v. Clark, p.2d 123, Oregon, 1979.

State v. Gheghan, 214 New Jersey Supra 383: A-2100-85-4 1986.

Steele, C., and Josephs, R. (1990). Alcohol myopia. Its prized and dangerous effects. *American Psychologist, 45*(8), 921–933.

Sullivan, J., Hauptman, M., and Bronstein, A. (1987). Lack of observable intoxication in humans with high plasma alcoholic concentrations. *Journal of Forensic Science, 32,* 1660–1665.

Surgeon General's Workshop on Drunk Driving. (1988). *Proceedings,* Washington, D.C., December 14–16. Rockville, MD: U.S. Department of Health and Human Services, Public Health Services, Office of the Surgeon General.

Taylor, S., and Chermack, S. (1983). Alcohol, drugs and human physical aggression. *Journal of Studies on Alcohol* (Suppl.), *11,* 70–88.

Taylor, S., and Leonard, K. (1983). Alcohol and human physical aggression. In R. D. Geen and E. I. Donnerstein (Eds.), *Aggression: Theoretical and Empirical Reviews* (Vol. 2, Issues in Research, pp. 77–101). San Diego, CA: Academic Press.

Techniques in Alcohol Management. (2007). Server/Seller Participant Manual. East Lansing, MI: National Hospitality Institute.

Teplin, L., and Lutz, G. (1985). Measuring alcohol intoxication: The development, reliability and validity of an observational instrument. *Quarterly Journal on Alcohol Studies, 46,* 459–466.

Trainer Intervention Procedures. (2004). TIPS on Premise. Arlington, VA: Health Communications, Inc.

Treat, J. (1980). *Study of Precrash Factors Involved in Traffic Accidents.* (The HSRI Research Review, Vol. 10[4]/Vol. 11[1]). Ann Arbor, MI: University of Michigan Highway Safety Research Institute.

Turner, R., Heis, H., and Meuhlberger, C. (1958). Interpretation of tests for intoxication. *Journal of the American Medical Association, 168,* 1359–1362.

U.S. Department of Transportation, National Highway Traffic Safety Administration. (1988). *Effects of Low Doses of Alcohol on Driving-Related Skills: A Review of the Evidence.* Report DOT-HS-807-280. Washington, D.C.: Author.

U.S. Department of Transportation, National Highway Traffic Safety Administration. (1990). *Alcoholic Beverage Server Liability and the Reduction of Alcohol-Related Problems: Evaluation of Dram Shop Laws.* Report DOT-HS-807-629. Washington, D.C.: Author.

U.S. Department of Transportation, National Highway Traffic Safety Administration. (1994). *Traffic Safety Facts 1993: Alcohol.* Washington, D.C.: U.S. Department of Transportation, National Center for Statistics and Analysis.

Vingilis, E., Adalf, E., and Chung, L. (1982). Comparison of age and sex characteristics of police-suspected impaired drivers. *Accident Analysis and Prevention, 14,* 425–430.

Voas, R., and Lacey, J. (1990). Drunk driving enforcement, adjudication, and sanctions in the United States. In R. J. Wilson and R. E. Mann (Eds.), *Drinking and Driving: Advances in Research and Prevention* (pp. 116–158). New York, NY: Guilford Press.

Voas, R., Taylor, E., Baker, T., and Tippetts, A. (2000). *Effectiveness of the Illinois .08 Law.* Report DOT-HS-809-186. Washington, D.C.: National Highway Traffic Safety Administration.

Wells, J., Green, M., Foss, F., Ferguson, S., and Williams, A. (1997). Drinking drivers missed at sobriety checkpoints. *Journal of Studies on Alcohol, 58,* 513–517.

Welte, J. W., and Abel, E. L. (1989). Homicide: Drinking by the victim. *Journal of Studies on Alcohol, 50*(3), 197–201.

Welte, J. W., and Miller, B. (1987). Alcohol use by violent and property offenders. *Drug and Alcohol Dependence, 19*(4), 313–324.

White, H., Brick, J., and Hansell, S. (1993). A longitudinal investigation of alcohol use and aggression in adolescence. *Journal of Studies on Alcohol, Supplement* (11), 62–77.

Widmark, E. (1981). *Principles and Application of Medicolegal Alcohol Determination* (R.C. Baselt, trans.). Davis, CA: Biomedical Publications. (Original work published 1932).

Zador, P., Krawchuk, S., and Voas, R. (2000). Alcohol-related risk of driver fatalities and driver involvement in fatal crashes in relation to driver age and gender: An update using 1996 data. *Journal of Studies on Alcohol, 61,* 387–395.

Zucker, R., and Gomberg, E. (1986). Etiology of alcoholism reconsidered. The case for a biopsychosocial process. *American Psychologist, 41,* 483–493.

Zusman, M., and Huber, J. (1979). Multiple measures and the validity of response in research on drinking drivers. *Journal of Safety Research, 11,* 132–137.

Chapter 7

THE DWI INVESTIGATION AND ARREST

7.1 NEED FOR COMPREHENSIVE INVESTIGATIONS

Investigation of a possible DWI offense and the ultimate disposition of a police investigation relies on the officer's ability to accurately and effectively communicate what was observed. Observations in the DWI investigation begin with justification of probable cause, the collection of intoxication test evidence, and ultimately the interpretation of the totality of the investigation by the courts, expert testimony, and a jury. The investigation should be systematic and avoid common errors that may compromise a thorough investigation and appropriate outcome.

Early police investigations of DWI were related to subjective observations and some forms of testing as discussed in Chapter 6. As it became increasingly obvious that impairment and increased risk for a motor vehicle crash occurred at BACs well below the initial statute of definition of 150 mg/dL, the legal definitions for intoxicated driving decreased to 100 mg/dL, and then 80 mg/dL in the United States. Although the justification for the lower legal definition for intoxicating driving is both justified and useful, it created a prevention problem. Namely, signs of gross intoxication were not always apparent in drivers who were nevertheless impaired and at increased risk for fatal or serious bodily injury to themselves or others (*see* Chapter 6). In the last several decades, standardization of DWI investigations have become increasingly useful and contain elements to allow the investigating officer to reach an informed decision about the state of sobriety of drivers at BACs well below those necessary for gross impairment. Such investigation begins with observations of the vehicle, initial contact with the driver, and roadside and related testing.

7.2 ELEMENTS OF THE DWI REPORT

The DWI report contains information gathered from four phases of the investigation: (1) vehicle in motion, (2) personal contact, (3) prearrest screening, and (4) chemical test results. The report is a critical step in gathering information about an intoxicated driver. For the arresting officer, this information is necessary to determine if a driver is under the influence of alcohol and if so, sets the stage for a proper arrest and conviction. However, the data collected may go far beyond the motor vehicle violation. Serious or fatal crashes require a deeper examination of the intoxication test evidence and a higher standard in criminal cases or subsequent civil litigation in state or federal court than is necessary for a conviction of drunk driving in a lower court. All DWI investigations involving fatal or serious bodily injury should be treated as a criminal investigation and potential homicide.

7.3 VEHICLE IN MOTION

Unless the officer is called to the scene of a crash after the fact, the first opportunity to observe the potentially intoxicated driver is observing the operation of a vehicle. Observations of how the vehicle is being operated may suggest impairment due to any number of factors, such as being lost, illness, mechanical problems, weather or roadway conditions or intoxication. The NHTSA published a list of visual cues for the detection of intoxicated drivers (NHTSA, 2010). The list consisted of twenty four cues obtained from three field studies involving hundreds of officers and more than 12,000 enforcement stops. The list was sorted into four broad categories related to driving that are impaired by alcohol:

1. maintaining lane position (e.g., weaving across lane markings, straddling the lane line, swerving, wide turns, drifting, almost striking another vehicle or object)
2. speeding and braking (e.g., stopping too far, too short, or too jerky, accelerating or decelerating for no apparent reason, varying speed, driving 10+ mph under limit)
3. vigilance (e.g., driving in opposing lanes or the wrong way on one-way street, slow response to traffic control devices, slow or failure to respond to officer's signals, stopping in lane for no apparent reason, driving without headlights at night, failure to signal or signal inconsistent with action)
4. judgment (e.g., following too closely; improper or unsafe lane change; illegal or fast, jerky, sharp or otherwise improper turn; driving on other

than the roadway; stopping inappropriately in response to officer; inappropriate or unusual behavior, such as throwing objects or arguing and the appearance of being impaired).

Weaving plus any other cue was determined to be associated with DWI at least 65 percent of the time, whereas the combination of any two cues (other than weaving) was associated with DWI at least 50 percent of the time. These associated categories indicate those driving behaviors most often detected in intoxicated drivers. They are not categories required to be present for a possible drunk-driving stop.

Once the decision to stop the vehicle is made and the motor vehicle stop initiated, additional opportunities of driving may present themselves to the investigating officer. For example, did the driver respond promptly to overhead lights or other commands in a timely manner? Was the stop a controlled stop? Did the driver stop in a safe location or in an unexpected dangerous manner? Evidence of unusual or inappropriate behavior at this point may further assist in formulating a reasonable suspicion that a driver is impaired and also alerts the officer to the need for possible safety precautions.

Observations during the vehicle in motion phase should be clear and specific. Terms such as erratic driving or appears drunk convey some information but they are vague. Table 7.1 lists some common terms found in police reports along with more useful and specific descriptions of driving behavior.

7.4 PERSONAL CONTACT: PRE-ARREST SCREENING

After initiating a stop, a number of relevant observations can be made of the driver immediately upon the walk up to the motor vehicle. These observations may be visual (all aspects of what you observed), auditory (all aspects of what you heard), and olfactory (all aspects of what you could smell), in nature. For example, visual observations include slow fumbling hand movements, difficulty with motor vehicle controls, difficulty exiting the vehicle, swaying, unsteadiness, or balance problems, leaning on the vehicle or other object, unusual actions, and bloodshot or watery eyes. Auditory observations include detection of slow or slurred speech, admission of drinking, unusual and incorrect or inconsistent statements. Olfactory observations include an odor of an alcoholic beverage on the breath or from within the vehicle or cover-up odors (e.g., gum, mint, smoking a cigarette) or the odor of urine or feces (incontinence and lack of awareness of loss of bladder or bowel control may occur, particularly at high BACs).

These observations may be evidence of alcohol use (odor of an alcoholic beverage on the breath; bloodshot, watery eyes), cognitive impairment (e.g.,

Table 7.1: Common Terms Used in Police Reports Related to Driving Behavior.

Description of Vehicle in Motion	Examples of Better Description of Vehicle in Motion
Weaving	Weaving from side to side crossing into adjacent lanes, crossed center line twice, drove on shoulder of roadway. Completely, halfway, etc.
Straddling the lane line	Vehicle straddled the lane line with both left wheels at least 3 feet into the adjacent lane for a period of 5 seconds (use appropriate measure).
Made an illegal left turn	Operator made an illegal left turn (northbound) on Jefferson Street, which is a one way (southbound).
Vehicle stopped in an unusual fashion	After overhead lights were activated, operator slowly pulled onto the shoulder of the roadway and continued driving for several hundred feet. After activating overhead lights, operator abruptly swerved from center lane onto the right shoulder of the roadway without signaling.
Ignored light or sirens to stop	After following the vehicle for 30 seconds with lights activated, driver did not respond. Driver finally responded after activation siren.

mental confusion, unresponsive to commands) and psychomotor impairment (e.g., slurred speech, slow fumbling hand movements). Questions consistent with standard investigation coupled with other inquiries can be seen on Table 7.2. Such observations may be useful in determining the course of an investigation. For example, is the driver lost, nervous, injured, or intoxicated?

The observations and simple tests conducted while the driver is still in the vehicle may be useful in determining the direction of an investigation and helpful later in presenting a clear description of the driver's actions. If the initial impression is that the driver may be intoxicated, the next step is additional testing outside the vehicle.

7.5 OUTSIDE VEHICLE TESTS

Numerous tests can be applied during the initial personal contact with the driver. The results of these tests may help the officer decide how best to proceed (e.g., to ask or not to ask the driver to exit the vehicle for more specific tests). During the initial contact phase, if the officer has cause to believe that the driver has been drinking, the officer can ask the driver to perform any number of psychophysical tests at the scene or back at the police station. Such tests fall into two categories: nonstandardized and standardized testing.

Table 7.2: Standard Investigation Questions and Observations.

Questions	Behavior Clues
How are you tonight (today)? Do you know why you were stopped?	Is the driver responsive? (does he or she answer questions in a timely manner and maintain eye contact?) Is his speech normal? (slurred, slow, accent, etc.) Is his affect normal? (is he respectful, excited, dull, etc.) Can you detect the odor of an alcoholic beverage from within the vehicle or from the driver?
May I have your license and registration?	Is the driver able to produce the correct credentials? Are her hand movements normal? If not, is the person just nervous or do their motor skills seem impaired? (fumbling, dropping credentials, passing over credentials in their "search").
Where are you coming from? Where are you going?	Is the driver's memory intact? Is his route logical? Does he have the cognitive skills to recall previous and explain future intended travel route to his stated destination?
It appears to me that you may have been drinking but I may be wrong. So I am going to ask you to do a couple of simple tests. Would you recite the alphabet without singing it? Or Would you count backwards for me from 121 to 109? Okay I'd like you to rapidly touch your thumb to each of your fingers back and forth (demonstrate).	Was the recitation completed and correct? Was speech slurred or normal? Was finger movement smooth and without exaggerated slowness or clumsiness (some older persons may have more difficulty doing this test than others).

Nonstandardized Testing

Nonstandardized tests (NSTs) of intoxication include a wide range of "tests" often used by police to assist in their investigation. Generally, NSTs have no scientific validity and have evolved from modifications of existing tests or guesswork as to tests that may reflect intoxication. Although NSTs are not laboratory-based tests of impairment, they are commonly administered in the field as part of the DWI investigation with or without SFSTs discussed in

Chapter 4. Such tests do have value in assisting the investigating officer in determining how to proceed. These tests are generally done outside of the vehicle in a safe location. Based upon the officer's experience, NSTs provide guidance in deciding to do additional tests (e.g., SFSTs).

For example, police often ask suspects in a DWI investigation to perform a Romberg balance test. This test is borrowed from neurology and was originally designed as a test of sensory ataxia and disequilibrium and compares performance with eyes open versus performance with the eyes closed. The test was considered positive if performance was poor with eyes closed but adequate with eyes open. The original Romberg test was a measure of proprioception (self-perception of body movement and position), but various permutations of this test are still referred to as Romberg tests.

Swaying while standing (Bogen, 1928) or while standing with one foot in front of the other (Widmark, 1981, are other noted variations in performance with different concentrations of alcohol in urine or blood. Goldberg (1943) demonstrated the utility of the Romberg test to determine kinesthetic and vestibular status (balance). Goldberg found that at BACs of 100 mg/dL body sway increased 300 to 400 percent. However, body sway was measured in a laboratory using instruments and not by subjective observation. Other researchers found little or no correlation between BAC and performance in the Romberg test (Penner & Coldwell, 1958; Penttila et al., 1971).

Variations of the Romberg test continue to be widely used by law enforcement agencies. For example, one version requires the subject to stand heel-to-toe (not with the heels and balls of the feet touching as originally designed), keep arms at the side, look up at the ceiling (or sky), and count backwards by threes from 30 with eyes closed or estimating the passage of 30 seconds. This is a very difficult test to perform sober[1]. Other NSTs include global tests of orientation in which subjects are asked where they are, where they came from, and where they are going. Estimates of time passed are sometimes included in NSTs but again the basis of this test is questionable. One study reported alcohol impairment in time estimation tasks at less than 40 mg/dL, whereas another found no impairment at 80 mg/dL (Moskowitz & Fiorentino, 2000). Such tests continue to be used without any metric as to what the known range of estimates is in sober subjects.

Psychophysical tests such as a finger-to-nose test (also from neurology) or finger tapping test (rapidly touching each finger to the thumb), bending at the waist with arms hanging (to observe swaying and balance), hand pat (alternating clapping the hands with the palm and back of the hand while counting

---

1. This test was routinely administered to subjects at the Rutgers University Alcohol Behavior Research Laboratory and Center of Alcohol Studies prior to their discharge from controlled drinking studies. It was a final demonstration (reminder) of impairment and the need to go home, stay home for the night, and not drive.

one, two . . .), and other related NSTs are not scientific and are not validated to detect alcohol intoxication in any quantifiable or reliable way (Rubenzer, 2010). Nevertheless, these and other NSTs can also be useful. Based on the officer's experience in administering such quick and informal tests to individuals, he or she may form a preliminary suspicion that the subject driver is under the influence of alcohol.

Based upon the results of the nonstandardized tests and other observations, the officer may elect to stop or continue the investigation of a possible drunk driving. If the decision is made to continue with a possible drunk driver arrest, validated laboratory based SFSTs should be administered (Chapter 4).

Additional Information to be Collected

Usually, the subject matter expert (e.g., in accident reconstruction, toxicology) consulted by the prosecutor to present expert opinion in a criminal case is not involved in the arrest procedure or the processing of the subject. Yet, the subject matter expert may need critical information available only at the scene and collected in the course of the field officer's investigation. Consider the following common problem. An officer completes an investigation of a serious or fatal crash in which a surviving driver is believed to be intoxicated. Because of injuries, the subject driver is transported to the hospital. The officer asks that blood be drawn so it can be analyzed by the State Police or suitable forensic laboratory. The officer witnesses the drawing of the blood but does not report the time that the blood was drawn. This omission forces the alcohol toxicology expert to assume a range of temporal assumptions to calculate how much alcohol was consumed and the level of intoxication at the time of the crash (Chapter 11). Such information is not only helpful to the trier of fact in understanding what a BAC means but also useful in validating or challenging witness statements about drinking (e.g., how much they drank). The lack of such information (e.g., time of the blood draw) for one expert (e.g., alcohol toxicology expert) may also make it difficult for another expert, the accident reconstructionist, to factor RT into the analysis if the degree of alcohol intoxication and impairment at the time of a crash cannot be estimated because of missing data. The important evidence-collecting role of the investigating officer at the scene of a serious or fatal crash cannot be overemphasized.

The following basic questions should be asked of drivers suspected of driving under the influence of alcohol (*see* Table 7.3).

For the police officer making a motor vehicle stop, initial observations of the way the vehicle is operated constitute subjective test evidence. In fact, those observations usually form the basis of probable cause (a legal requirement necessary to initialize a motor vehicle stop). As in the case of

Table 7.3: Forensic Alcohol Investigation Form.

Name of the alleged intoxicated person (AIP):	
Age of AIP at time of incident:	
Weight of AIP at time of incident:	
Height of AIP at time of incident: (if unknown, give best estimate)	
Time of incident:	: AM/PM
Date of incident:	
Indicate the location, drinking period and type of alcohol consumed, if known:	
Name of first location:	
Time of first drink:	: AM/PM
Type and amount of alcohol consumed:	
Name of second location:	
Time of first drink:	: AM/PM
Type and amount of alcohol consumed:	
Name of third location:	
Time of first drink:	: AM/PM
Type and amount of alcohol consumed:	
Name of fourth location:	
Time of first drink:	: AM/PM
Type and amount of alcohol consumed:	
Time and nature of last known meal:	: AM/PM
What was the length of time, or distance from the last drink to the incident?	

observations made by lay witnesses, a detailed description of driving provides a useful visual image of the events. For police officers, these initial observations should be specific and detailed and avoid terms like erratic when describing motor vehicle operation. The term erratic, although popular, does not explain what was observed. Was the vehicle weaving, crossing from one lane to another, crossing the fog line, simply moving within the boundaries of its lane of travel? The following partial list of questions may be helpful in specifying the type of erratic driving that was observed by a witness.

- What observations did you make about the speed of the vehicle? For example, was it steady or did it increase and decrease for no apparent reason (e.g., speed up, slow down)?

- In relation to you, was the driver going faster or slower?
- How fast were you going?
- Was the speed appropriate for the roadway or within the posted speed limit?
- Were the lights on?
- Were the brake lights activated when there was no reason to stop or slow down?
- Was the vehicle traveling inside or outside its lane of travel? If so, how far into the adjacent lane (in car widths) did the suspect's vehicle move? How many wheels went over?
- How many times did any of the previous operations occur?
- Over what period of time did you make these observations?

Witness Evidence

Witnesses at the scene should be interviewed to determine their knowledge of the accident, alcohol use of parties involved, observations of driving, or observations of a driver after an accident. Credit card or other receipts may provide clues to where an individual was prior to the accident. Interviewing witnesses at a bar or restaurant can provide additional evidence that may be helpful in reconstructing an accident. Witness information is discussed further in Chapter 12.

7.6 OBTAINING BLOOD SAMPLES

Based upon the totality of evidence collected at the scene, including the subject's overall appearance, performance on standardized and/or nonstandardized tests, or the nature of the crash (fatal or serious bodily injury), blood samples should then be obtained. There is no urgency in collecting blood samples because the metabolism and elimination of alcohol is relatively slow, but samples should be obtained as soon as is reasonably possible.

Relevant Case Law

To obtain a blood sample, the intoxicated driver should be transported to a hospital or other facility where a sample can be drawn in a medically acceptable manner, although some agencies have a phlebotomist at the scene with evidence collection kits ready to draw blood. In some jurisdictions, a telephone warrant may be required to obtain a blood sample. For example, in Schmerber v. California (384 US 757, 1966) the U.S. Supreme Court ruled that searches of the body are protected by the Fourth Amendment and that police require a warrant to seize blood unless the seizure fell into a recognized "exceptional" rule. In this landmark case, police were engaged at the scene for 2 hours then went to the hospital to obtain blood samples from the defendant. No warrant was required because police were confronted with an emergency; there was no time to obtain a warrant and the police deemed the toxicological evidence to be evanescent. In other words, they wanted to collect it quickly because metabolism would decrease the BAC. In State of New Jersey v. Dyal (97 N.J. 229 [1984]) the court specifically stated that based on probable cause, police were permitted to obtain blood samples in DWI cases without a warrant or consent. However, in 2013, the U.S. Supreme Court concluded that the metabolism of alcohol did not constitute a *per se* exigency that justifies an exception to the Fourth Amendment and ruled that a warrant was necessary to obtain blood.

In some states, such as Pennsylvania, courts require that a blood sample must be taken within 2 hours of an arrest or show good cause why there was a delay in obtaining blood. The so-called 2-hour rule (75 Pa.C.S.A. § 3802) is based on the undocumented premise that if the BAC is above the statute definition of .08 percent within 2 hours of the arrest, it is assumed that the BAC was .08 percent at the time of the offense. Although this may be true most of the time, based on the rate of alcohol absorption for most (but not all) people post drinking, it is often argued that blood samples obtained after 2 hours are unreliable.[2] There is no scientific basis for such a defense unless the BAC at that time is so low that the rate of elimination is no longer linear (an assumption required of most pharmacokinetics calculation) (*see* Chapter 3).

Whether or not a search warrant is required, the investigating agency should have a standard protocol regarding the time the blood sample is obtained and the chain of custody for the sample after it is received by the officer. The suspect may be asked to sign a consent form to provide a blood sample. This form should be signed in the presence of an officer. A departmental request form for hospital staff to withdraw the specimen should also be completed. A standard commercially available blood sample collection kit should be part of any investigation although not absolutely critical if samples are collected and stored properly. The use of standard blood sample collection kits includes collection tubes that contain an anticoagulant and a chemical to minimize endogenous alcohol fermentation. Such kits also include a non–alcohol-based antiseptic swab (e.g., Betadine) to remove any question of contamination of the skin and sample site by using isopropyl alcohol. However, the method usually used by almost all forensic laboratories (e.g., police crime labs) is headspace gas chromatography, which easily distinguishes between different types of alcohol (e.g., rubbing alcohol from beverage alcohol).

---

2. http://news.yahoo.com/vehicular-homicide-defendant-blood-evidence-1-minute-150103704.html

The use of isopropyl (rubbing) alcohol to clean the skin has no effect on the measurement of ethyl alcohol by gas chromatography.

In some instances, an alcohol test result is obtained from medical record in which blood was tested for alcohol in the course diagnosis and treatment. Many clinical (hospital) tests measure alcohol in serum, not whole blood, using a different methodology than that used by forensic laboratories (*see* Chapter 2). Such tests results are not compromised if a nonalcohol swab is used to clean the skin. For example, isopropyl alcohol has virtually no cross-reactivity with most current hospital methodologies. The validity of a blood sample from a site cleaned with ethyl alcohol, the chances of which are extremely remote, would not be measurably comprised (Senior & Sloan, 1981).

REFERENCES

Bogen, E. (1928). Drunkenness: A quantitative study of acute alcohol intoxication: *Journal of the American Medical Association, 176*(2), 153–167.

Goldberg, L. (1943). Quantitative studies on alcohol tolerance in man. The influence of ethyl alcohol on sensory, motor and psychological functions referred to blood alcohol in normal and habituated individuals. *Acta Physiologica Scandinavica, 5,* 1–128.

Moskowitz, H., and Fiorentino, D. (2000). *A Review of the Literature on the Effects of Low Doses of Alcohol on Driving Related Skills.* Report DOT-HS-809-028. Washington, D.C.: U.S. Department of Transportation, National Highway Traffic Safety Administration.

National Highway Traffic Safety Administration (NHTSA). (2010). The Visual Detection of DWI Motorists. Report DOT HS 808 677. Washington, D.C.: U.S. Department of Transportation, National Highway Traffic Safety Administration.

Penner, D., and Coldwell, B. (1958). Car driving and alcohol intoxication: Medical observations on an experiment. *Canadian Medical Association Journal, 79,* 793–800.

Penttila, A., Tenhu, M., and Kataja, M. (1971). *Clinical Examination for Intoxication in Cases of Suspected Drunken Driving. An Evaluation of the Finnish System on the Basis of 6839 Cases.* Reports from Talja 11:43, Helsinki, Finland. Statistical and Research Bureau of Talja: Iso Roobertinkatu 20 Helsinki.

Rubenzer, S. (2011). Judging intoxication. *Behavioral Sciences and the Law, 29,* 116–137.

Schmerber v. California (384 U.S. 757 [1966])

Senior, J. and Sloan, B. (1981) Emergency measurement of stat, timed, serum ethanol levels for medical management. *Alcoholism: Clinical and Experimental Research 5* (1), 6-11.

State of New Jersey v. Dyal (97 N.J. 229 [1984])

Widmark, E. (1981). *Principles and Application of Medicolegal Alcohol Determination* (R.C. Baselt, trans.). Davis, CA: Biomedical Publications. (Original work published 1932).

Chapter 8

ALCOHOL–DRUG INTERACTIONS[1]

8.1 WHY DO PEOPLE COMBINE DRUGS?

The combination of alcohol with other drugs is often encountered during clinical evaluations of a multidrug abuser, in the course of treatment for alcohol dependence, in patients being treated for mental illnesses who continue to drink, and in forensic examinations. So why do people combine drugs? The answer is to change their mental state, a common denominator, likely to be encountered in forensic evaluations.

For example, even though alcohol is a depressant, under some conditions, alcohol increases locomotor activity, loquaciousness, and other behaviors leading to the perception that alcohol is also a stimulant, in part because of the decreased inhibitions associated with intoxication. Pharmacologically, alcohol acts much more like a CNS depressant or anxiolytic than a true stimulant. As discussed in Chapter 2, the pharmacology of alcohol is complex and its biobehavioral effects quite broad, probably because alcohol is capable of altering receptors, neurotransmission, cell membranes, ion transport, and most neurophysiological mechanisms critical to physiology and behavior. Because of this ubiquitous nature, alcohol has the ability to interact with the pharmacokinetics and pharmacodynamics of other drugs.

Changes in bioavailability and efficacy of drugs in the presence of alcohol or in patients with a history of alcohol dependence have important implications for diagnoses, treatment, and outcome and should be part of a complete forensic evaluation.

Use of medication and alcohol is common in our society. In an age when people live longer and are treated for multiple illnesses using multiple medications, the risk for drug–drug interactions is greater. However, the risk for harmful drug interactions is greater when those drugs are not prescribed and their use monitored, such as in the case of illicit drugs or when commonly

---

1. Note: Portions of this chapter were reproduced, in part, from Brick and Erickson (2009) with permission of the publisher.

used and available drugs such as alcohol are used in combination with other psychoactive medications (which now includes cannabis in some states). Most doctors trained in pharmacology, toxicology, and related sciences are keenly aware of the pernicious effects of many commonly used drugs and more so of the inherent dangers of combining drugs. Yet, multiple drug ingestion is relatively common in our society. The following four explanations may be helpful in understanding why this phenomenon is so pervasive.

1. *Increase the Subjective Drug Effects.* Combining alcohol with other drugs increases the intensity of the "high" or, when used clinically, increases the effectiveness of treatment.
2. *Decrease the Undesirable Side Effects of the Primary Drug.* Use of cocaine or other stimulants produces an unpleasant edgy feeling during the dysphoric crash. Alcohol is often used to reduce these symptoms.
3. *Short Supply of the Primary Drug.* Sometimes when the availability of the drug of choice is limited, another drug with similar properties (e.g., depressant) will be substituted. Heroin addicts, for example, often drink large amounts of alcohol or use other depressants to reduce or delay the opioid withdrawal syndrome when their drug of choice (heroin) is not available.
4. *Sensation Seeking.* When the desire to change consciousness exceeds any rational concern for safety, some individuals will often drink alcohol and take any combination of other drugs without any particular rationale other than to become intoxicated ("garbage heads").

The high percentage of drug use is remarkably common throughout the world, including the United States, where most high-school-age children have experimented with more than one psychoactive drug, including alcohol. Worldwide, the four most commonly used addictive substances are cocaine, cannabis, tobacco, and alcohol (*see* Table 8.1). Alcohol and other drugs are overrepresented in domestic disputes, motor vehicle crashes, violent altercations, and a range of accidental injuries. It is not uncommon to find alcohol and another psychoactive drug in a forensic case. It is therefore useful to understand alcohol-drug interactions in interpreting the pharmacokinetic and pharmacodynamic effects of other drugs and alcohol as well as the effects of alcohol and other drugs.

Alcohol-other drug interactions can produce changes in physiology and ultimately behavior through two broad but interrelated mechanisms: changes in pharmacokinetics and changes in pharmacodynamics. Pharmacokinetic mechanisms account for drug interactions when the presence of one drug affects the bioavailability of another drug. Pharmacodynamic interactions account for drug interactions when drugs interact at the receptor level.

Table 8.1: Percentage of Lifetime Drug Use in the Population by Country.

Country	Cocaine	Cannabis	Tobacco	Alcohol
Columbia	4.0	10.8	48.1	94.3
Mexico	4.0	7.8	60.2	85.9
USA	16.2	42.4	73.6	91.6
France	1.5	19.0	48.3	91.3
Germany	1.9	17.5	51.9	95.3
Italy	1.0	6.6	48.0	73.5
Netherlands	1.9	19.8	58.0	93.3
Ukraine	0.1	6.4	60.6	97.0
New Zealand	4.3	41.9	51.3	94.8

Modified from Degenhardt et al. (2008).

8.2 PHARMACOLOGY OF ALCOHOL–DRUG INTERACTIONS

Pharmacokinetic Interactions

The bioavailability of alcohol or another drug can be affected by changes in drug absorption, distribution, metabolism, and excretion. The greater the availability of a drug to interact with receptors or other cellular components, the greater the intoxication or other effect. There are four mechanisms by which alcohol can interact with other drugs to effect bioavailability (Figure 8.1).

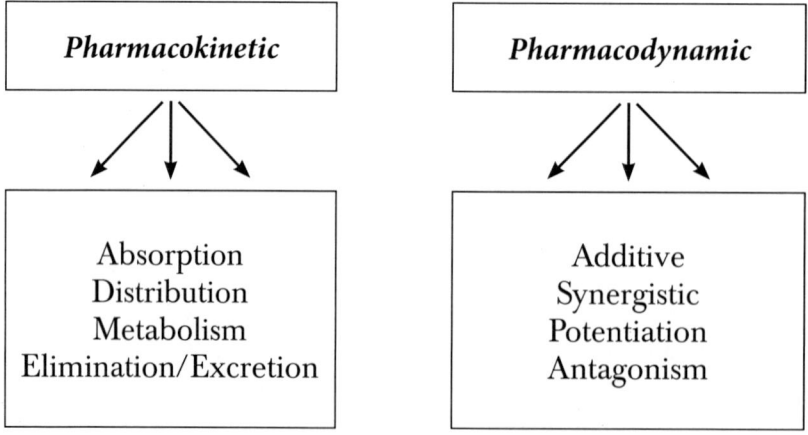

Figure 8.1: Pharmacological Basis of Drug Interactions.

Absorption

Alcohol is almost always consumed by drinking and absorption through the gastrointestinal system. Delays or acceleration in absorption can alter the amount of drug that enters the circulation. Alcohol increases the absorption rate of some sedatives such as benzodiazepine, so that more drug will enter the circulation than if the drug were taken without alcohol in the stomach.

Distribution

Once absorbed from the gastrointestinal tract into the circulation, alcohol is for all practical purposes distributed throughout the watery portions of the body. Therefore, changes in the volume of distribution may alter the effectiveness of that or some other drug also present. For example, alcohol increases the volume of distribution of cocaine, which may decrease the concentration of cocaine in the circulation.

Metabolism

Once alcohol or another drug has entered the body, it is subject to biotransformation. As previously discussed, one family of enzymes in the metabolism of alcohol is cytochrome P450 and its various isozymes located primarily in the endoplasmic reticulum of liver cells. Cytochrome P450 is involved in the oxidative metabolism of many other drugs besides alcohol. The P450 isozymes are identified based upon their amino acid sequence. The nomenclature is as follows: prefix CYP is followed by the family (Arabic number), the subfamily (upper case letter), followed by the individual isoenzyme (Arabic number). The major isoenzymes involved in drug metabolism are CYP3A4, CYP2D6, CYP1A2, CYP2E1, and the subfamily of CYP2C.

Since many drugs share enzyme systems (e.g., cytochrome P450, ADH, ALDH) in their biotransformation, when alcohol and another drug share the same metabolic pathway, the metabolism of one compound can alter that of another.

For example, beverage alcohol alters the metabolism of methanol by competing for the enzyme that transforms methanol to toxic metabolites. Since the metabolism directly affects bioavailability, changes in drug half-life (the time it takes for the concentration of a drug in circulation to decrease 50%) can have significant consequences on the efficacy and toxicity of one or more drugs.

Elimination and Excretion

Alcohol is eliminated from the body through the lungs, kidneys, and less important routes, such as sweat, saliva, or tears. With the exception of the pulmonary system, excretory organs eliminate alcohol based upon their electrical charge (e.g., polar compounds leave the body more easily than lipid- soluble drugs). Therefore, changes in the pH of the urine produced by a physiological condition such as respiratory or metabolic acidosis or alkalosis that might result from alcoholism may alter drug elimination. For example, there is maximum excretion of drugs that are weak acids (such as salicylate and phenobarbital) when the urine is alkaline. On the other hand, renal excretion of alkaline drugs (such as amphetamines and phencylidine) is enhanced when the urine is acidic. Thus, shifts in acid-base physiology may alter drug bioavailability (Ellenhorn & Barceloux, 1988).

Pharmacodynamic Interactions

Pharmacodynamic action of alcohol or other drugs is the basis for intoxication. It is the study of the physiological and biochemical mechanism of action in the brain, in the case of psychoactive drugs. Changes in the pharmacodynamics or functional activity of neurons that modulate cognitive and psychomotor effects, for example, will alter physiology and behavior. The four major types of pharmacodynamic drug interactions are shown in Figure 8.1.

Additive

An additive interaction is when two drugs combined are equal to the sum of the effect of each drug (e.g., $2 + 2 = 4$). For example, many CNS depressants have an additive effect with alcohol.

Synergistic

A synergistic interaction occurs when the combination of two drugs produces an effect greater than the effect of either drug combined (e.g., $2 + 2 = 6$). In other words, a synergistic interaction produces effects far greater than from the sum of either drug. For example, alcohol and carbon tetrachloride, a cleaning fluid, are both toxic to the liver. However, the combination of the two produces much more liver damage than would be predicted from the sum of their individual effects. Alcohol and barbiturates as well as alcohol and some opiates may produce a synergistic sedation.

Potentiation

Potentiated drug interactions are similar to synergistic effects but includes a nontoxic drug (e.g., $0 + 1 = 2$). For example, the histamine H2 antagonist cimetadine, which is not considered toxic, can potentiate the toxic effects of alcohol by increasing alcohol bioavailability.

Antagonism

Drug antagonism occurs when one drug blocks the effect of another drug (e.g., $2 + 2 = 1$ or $2 + 2 = 0$). Antagonists are very specific. For example, naloxone has a much higher affinity for opiate receptors than heroin has. Administering naloxone to someone who has overdosed on heroin will produce a rapid reversal of the respiratory depression produced by the heroin. Naloxone has also been used in alcohol overdose cases, with varying degrees of success. Dispositional antagonism occurs when the absorption, metabolism, distribution or excretion of one drug is affected by another drug. For example, alcohol increases the absorption rates of some non-psychoactive drugs.

8.3 ALCOHOL–MEDICATION INTERACTIONS

Alcohol is a legal, socially accepted drug used widely by much of the population. Because alcohol's effects on the body are ubiquitous, the potential to interact with other drugs and medications is present. Table 8.2 lists some of the major interactions, followed by a review of the interaction between alcohol and other drugs.

Alcohol and Amphetamines

Amphetamines and other CNS stimulants decrease fatigue and RT while causing an increase in arousal, body temperature, heart rate, blood pressure, and other changes. Although there is some evidence that stimulants may decrease some of the depressant effects of alcohol (e.g., sleepiness), the combination of a stimulant and a depressant is often erroneously assumed by laypersons to result in a neutralizing or balancing out of these two opposite effects. In general, drug combinations and interactions produce unpredictable effects, especially when the drugs have seemingly opposite biobehavioral consequences.

As expected, BAC of about 100 mg/dL decrease performance on driving simulator tasks designed to test attention, memory, recognition, decision making, and RT. Doses of dexamphetamine (0.09 or 0.18 mg/kg) improved

Table 8.2: Alcohol Interactions with Medications.

Medications Interacting With Alcohol	Effect	Severity of Interactions With Medications
aspirin (acetyl salicyclic acid)	stomach bleeding, ulcer	major
antihistamines	increased sedation	major
verapamil (Calan®, Isoptin®)	increased alcohol levels	major
disulfiram (Antabuse®)	increased acetaldehyde levels	major*
metronidazole (Flagyl®)	increased acetaldehyde levels	major*
cephalosporins (Cefobid®)	disulfiram-like reaction	moderate
opioid analgesics	enhanced CNS depression	major*
antidepressants	enhanced CNS depression	moderate
insulin	increased insulin lowering	moderate
antipsychotics	enhanced CNS depression	moderate
benzodiazepines	enhanced CNS depression	major*
nitroglycerin	reduced blood pressure	minor
warfarin	increased anticoagulant effects	moderate
chlorpropamide (Diabinese®)	disulfiram-like reaction	major
tolbutamide (Orinase®)	disulfiram-like reaction	moderate
erythromycin	increased blood alcohol levels	minor
cimetidine (Tagamet®)	increased blood alcohol levels	moderate
ranitidine (Zantac®)	increased blood alcohol levels	moderate

* Found in most people.
Note: The frequency and severity of these interactions vary greatly among individuals.

performance on some of these tasks, but overall, the combination of alcohol and dexamphetamine did not. The bioavailability of alcohol is also slightly increased by dexamphetamine (Perez-Reyes, White, McDonald & Hicks, 1992). Older studies using different testing methods found that amphetamine altered the effects of alcohol in a complex way (Kaplan, Forney, Richards & Hughes, 1966; Wilson, Taylor, Nash & Cameron, 1966). While the interaction between alcohol and amphetamines have been studied, the only clear conclusion is that the interaction is complex, task specific and that there is no simple antagonism between alcohol and amphetamines.

Alcohol and Cocaine

Epidemiological studies over the last 20 years have revealed that polydrug use is much more common than in the past or than previously believed. Combined cocaine and alcohol use is an example of the changing patient profile. Cocaine does reverse, to some degree, impairment from sleep deprivation, which might suggest it would reduce some of the depressant effects of alcohol. Interestingly, cocaine alone has no effect on cognitive or psychomotor performance (Hopper et al., 2004) at least in relatively low-dose laboratory studies.

In another study, the combinations of cocaine and alcohol produced a non-significant decrease in subjective feelings of drunkenness, and increase in cocaine induced euphoria and a significant improvement in alcohol-related changes in psychomotor performance along with a marked increase in heart rate. Subjects that were administered cocaine and alcohol interpreted the effects as "more pleasant" than compared to alcohol alone (Farre et al., 1993).

One novel consequence of cocaine and alcohol use is that a third compound called cocaethylene is formed (sometimes referred to as ethyl cocaine or cocaine ethyl-ester). Cocaethylene is not a natural alkaloid of the coca plant and is not found in pharmaceutical or street cocaine. In fact, cocaine is metabolized to its ethyl configuration only in the presence of ethanol.

The effects of cocaethylene are similar to but extend the euphorogenic and reinforcing effects of cocaine. In humans, the combination of alcohol and cocaine is greater than the effect of either drug alone and is associated with an enhanced subjective euphoria, increased heart rate, and increased plasma cocaine concentrations (McCance, Price, Kosten & Jatlow, 1993; McCance-Katz et al., 1993). Like cocaine, cocaethylene appears to block presynaptic dopamine transporters. This action increases the functional activity of dopamine by enhancing the availability of neurotransmitter to engage postsynaptic receptors but produces lower ratings of "high" and changes in heart rate than cocaine does, even though the concentrations of cocaethylene and cocaine were statistically indistinguishable (Perez-Reyes, Jeffcoat, Myers, Sihler & Cook, 1994).

In animals (pigs), preadministration of alcohol for 10 days decreases the plasma half-life of cocaine but increases its volume of distribution and clearance rate. Alcohol also seems to increase the plasma concentrations of cocaine's metabolite, benzoylecgonine (Kambam et al., 1994). It is not clear that a simple pharmacokinetic effect occurs in humans. Insufflation of cocaine before alcohol ingestion does not appear to alter blood alcohol levels or subjective ratings of alcohol intoxication. When alcohol is administered prior to cocaine insufflation, there is a significant increase in both cocaine plasma levels (possibly due to an inhibition of hepatic cocaine metabolism produced by alcohol) and an augmentation of cocaine's subjective and heart rate effects (Perez-Reyes, 1994; Perez-Reyes & Jeffcoat, 1992).

Cocaethylene is about 1.5 times more lethal than cocaine in animals. Although both drugs produce convulsions in mice, cocaethylene had a greater propensity to cause death. Moreover, the administration of alcohol and cocaine is associated with greater risk for cardiovascular toxicity (e.g., increased systolic and diastolic blood pressure and heart rate) than alcohol or cocaine alone. Some clinicians believe that cocaethylene is primarily responsible for deaths that occur among cocaine abusers (Bunn & Ginnini, 1992). To date, cocaethylene is the only known example of a third psychoactive drug being formed as a result of administering two other psychoactive drugs of abuse. Since cocaine-induced deaths have been observed with a wide range of post-mortem cocaine concentrations, often with presence of low blood alcohol levels, the possibility exists that cocaethylene may be partially responsible for these deaths. Additional research is clearly required in this area.

Alcohol and Energy Drinks

Energy drinks are nonalcoholic beverages marketed for their ability to increase energy and stamina, lose weight, and provide other stimulant-associated effects. These drinks contain high concentrations of caffeine but may contain other ingredients such as guarana, kola nut, and cocoa, which have stimulant actions including cardiac effects. However, caffeine is usually the primary psychoactive ingredient in these drinks. Millions of people use caffeine (from coffee or tea, for example) for its well-known stimulant properties. Caffeine and glucose (a common duo in energy drinks) can improve cognitive performance and subjective fatigue. However, caffeine intoxication is a clinical syndrome that includes a constellation of signs and symptoms including anxiety, irritability, insomnia, tremor, tachycardia, palpitations, gastrointestinal upset, and vomiting. A number of more serious but less common effects have been reported, including hypokalemia, hallucinations, cerebral edema, stroke, paralysis, blood disorders (rhabdomyolysis), muscular rigidity, seizure, and death. Nevertheless, the use of energy drinks is becoming increasingly more common among younger consumers (Oteri, Salvo, Caputi, & Calapi, 2007). By comparison with a typical cup of coffee that contains about 150 mg of caffeine, some energy drinks contain 80 mg (Red Bull®), 160 mg (Monster Energy®), or 505 mg (Wired X505®) of caffeine. When caffeine is combined with alcohol, the interaction is predictable, to a certain extent. Although some of the depressant effects of alcohol are reduced by the caffeine, this should not be misinterpreted to imply that alcohol intoxication is reduced. Drinkers are still intoxicated by alcohol and impaired without the invariable fatigue associated with alcohol use. Moreover, the combination of energy drinks with alcohol results in increased alcohol consumption (Oteri et al., 2007).

Alcohol and Methanol

Alcoholics may drink other forms of alcohol when ethanol is not available. One such alcohol, methanol, is highly toxic. The interaction between these alcohols is critical in averting methanol poisoning and possibly death. Methanol is metabolized by the enzyme ADH to formic acid, a highly toxic compound. Relatively small doses of methanol (several ounces) can be fatal, but methanol poisoning can be prevented by the administration of ethanol because ethanol is preferentially metabolized by ADH. Therefore, less methanol is transformed to formic acid. The decrease in methanol metabolism allows methanol to be excreted unchanged and before toxic metabolites are formed (*also see* Chapter 2).

Alcohol and Nonnarcotic Pain Relievers

Aspirin and other nonsteroidal antiinflammatory drugs (NSAIDs) are the most frequently employed drugs for relieving mild to moderate pain of varied origin (e.g., headache and musculoskeletal pain). Many of these drugs can cause gastric bleeding and inhibit blood from clotting; alcohol can exacerbate these effects by enhancing the ability of these medications to damage the gastric mucosa (Adams, 1995; Kaufman et al., 1999). Older persons who mix alcoholic beverages with large doses of aspirin to self medicate for pain are therefore at particularly high risk for episodes of gastric bleeding (Dufour, Archer & Gordis, 1992). NSAID, and alcohol may also cause liver damage.

Aspirin has been found to decrease the activity of gastric alcohol dehydrogenase, thus increasing the bioavailability of ingested alcohol, and heightening the effects of a given dose of alcohol (Roine, Gentry, Henandez-Munoz, Baraona & Lieber, 1990). However, the anxiolytic effects of alcohol have been found to be attenuated with the use of aspirin (LaBuda & Fuchs, 2000).

Alcohol and Antihistamines

Antihistamines (H_1-receptor antagonists) are the mainstay of symptomatic therapy for allergic disorders. Drugs such as diphenhydramine (Benadryl® and others) are available without prescription to treat allergic symptoms and insomnia. Others, such as hydroxyzine (Vistaril®, Atarax®) are used to treat anxiety and require a prescription. Many antihistamines cause drowsiness and alone can impair skills necessary for safe motor vehicle operation or other complex divided attention tasks. Alcohol can substantially enhance the sedating effects of these agents and may further impair the ability to drive or operate other types of machinery (Ridout, Shamsi, Meadows, Johnson & Hindmarch, 2003). Many common sedative antihistamines, such as chlorpheniramine and diphenhydramine, significantly impair psychomotor performance and significantly increases the deleterious effects of alcohol on RT; and coordination tests (Burns & Moskowitz, 1980; Franks, V. Hensley, W. Hemsley, Starmer & Teo, 1979). Newer antihistamines such as fexofenadine, loratadine, and cetirizine have been developed to minimize drowsiness and sedation while providing effective therapeutic value. However, these newer medications may still be associated with an increased risk of hypotension and injuries from falls among the elderly, particularly when combined with alcohol (Weathermon & Crabb, 1999). Since the relative risk for a injury from a fall is significantly elevated by alcohol alone (Chapter 5), and older patients or alcohol abusers may have osteopenia, the interaction of alcohol and antihistamines in this population is of significant interest.

The deleterious interaction between alcohol and most sedative antihistamines is well-documented. Antihistamines can produce significant drowsiness, which is worsened by the use of an additional depressant, alcohol. When an interaction occurs, it appears to be due to the combined or additive CNS depressant effects of both the alcohol and the antihistamine. The effects of many of the antihistamines combined with alcohol have not been formally studied, but it seems almost certain that combined use will result in increased drowsiness and increased driving risks (Roehrs, Zwyghuizen-Doorenbos & Roth, 1993). This has been further clarified by Zimatkin and Anichtchik (1999), who have found that histamine receptor antagonism can affect ethanol metabolism and changes the sensitivity to the hypnotic effects of alcohol.

Alcohol and Cimetidine, and Other H2 Receptor Antagonists

One of the medical consequences of alcohol abuse is gastrointestinal disease, including gastric ulcers. H_2-antagonists such as cimetidine, ranitidine, and nizatidine are often used to treat gastrointestinal diseases. Since these drugs inhibit gastric ADH, an increase in the bioavailability of alcohol might result. Several studies have demonstrated the effect of these H_2 receptor antagonists on first-pass alcohol metabolism (Roine et al., 1990a). In many studies, the effect was quite significant: increases of BACs of about 17 to 33 percent by cimetidine but not ranitidine (Caballeria, Baroana, Rodamilans & Leiber, 1989; Roine et al., 1990a). Although these investigators examined this effect through a series of detailed studies and demonstrated dose, drug type, gender, and drinking history to be important variables, the clinical significance of this interaction has been questioned by many other researchers (Levitt, 1993). Nevertheless, until fully resolved, patients treated with H_2 receptor antagonists should probably be advised to limit their drinking and be cognizant of any increased response to alcohol.

Alcohol and Cannabinoids

In recent years, substance use-related problems has increased dramatically for many drugs. Consistent with an overall trend, marijuana has been used by about 40 percent of the population and is the illegal drug most commonly detected in drivers involved in traffic accidents, second only to alcohol. As a result, the relationship among cannabis use and alcohol (the two most widely used psychoactive drugs overall) and motor vehicle crashes is of significant forensic interest. Reviews of the interaction cannabis and alcohol and either drug alone or together have sometimes provided mixed results.

In one of the earlier interactive studies on the effects of marijuana and alcohol on driving, Casswell (1977) tested drivers on a 35-minute closed course. While driving the course, drivers were given instructions via headphones, and road signs and brake and accelerator pedal, speed and steering were monitored. The authors found that (1) alcohol alone increased speed and impaired steering; (2) marijuana alone reduced speed and slowed response to instruction; and (3) alcohol and marijuana tended to increase speed, impair steering, and increase response times to instructions. More recent studies examined the effects of alcohol and marijuana on road-tracking tests and car following test (similar to Casswell's 1977 method) and concluded that (1) the effects on THC and alcohol appear to be additive; (2) 100-mg/kg doses of THC combined with 40 mg/dL BAC impairs visual search patterns while driving; and (3) together, marijuana and alcohol (40 mg/dL) increase RT more than either drug separately. Although the authors point out that the effects of alcohol are greater than those of marijuana, the combination of both drugs is particularly dangerous with regard to motor vehicle operation (Lamers & Ramaekers, 2000; Robbe & O'Hanlon, 1999).

Although the overwhelming majority of studies support these conclusions, not all investigators found an alcohol-marijuana interaction. For example, Smiley, Ziedman, and Moskowitz (1981) found that after taking marijuana, drivers became more cautious in overtaking tasks. Alcohol (45 or 75 mg/dL) had a slight effect, but no interaction between alcohol and marijuana was observed. Slower, more cautious driving under the influence of cannabis alone has been reported (Lenne et al., 2010). Using a driving simulator, Stein, Allen, Cook and Karl (1983) found that after alcohol (100 mg/dL), drivers had more accidents and speeding tickets and slower and less accurate responses to road signs. Marijuana (4 or 8 mg) had only an occasional effect and no interaction with alcohol was observed. A similar finding was reported by Lenne, and associates (2010). Drivers were tested under different driving workloads at three doses of both cannabis and alcohol. Both drugs increased speed and later position variability, but high doses of cannabis were associated with decreased speed and longer RT, whereas alcohol was associated with an increase in speed. There is some evidence of a pharmacokinetic inter-action between alcohol and marijuana. Lukas and coworkers (1992) found that smoking marijuana decreases the bioavailability of alcohol, reducing the maximum serum alcohol concentration and delaying the time to peak con-centration from 78 mg/dL (50 minutes after drinking) to about 55 mg/dL (105 minutes after drinking). Although some experimental design details were po-tentially responsible for the results, such findings further emphasize the im-portance of using a range of pharmacokinetic assumptions when attempting to perform estimates of intoxication (*see* Chapter 12). More research on this potential pharmacokinetic interaction is needed, particularly at the higher doses of alcohol and cannabis more likely to be encountered outside the labo-ratory. More importantly, field and laboratory-based studies must be limited to relatively recent use of cannabis. Unlike alcohol intoxication, the impair-ment from cannabinoids is greatest within the first 2 hours of smoking and is not reliably detected 3 hours after last use (Huestis, Barnes & Smith, 2005; Ogden & Moskowitz, 2004). However, reports of longer periods of impair-ment and even residual impairment the next day have been reported (Yesav-age, Leirer, Denari & Hollister 1985). It is generally agreed that most of the impairment produced by cannabinoids occurs within about the first two hours of use. However, the combination of even relatively low amounts of al-cohol with cannabinoids produces an additive and possibly synergistic effect.

In laboratory studies, the biobehavioral pharmacodynamic effects of can-nabis on attention, vigilance, estimates of time and speed, tracking, motor co-ordination, visual functions and complex tasks requiring divided attention have been consistently reported (Sewell, Poling & Sofuoglu, 2009) and similar to those found for alcohol (Chapter 4). Cannabis use is associated with poor lane control and, unlike alcohol-intoxicated drivers, subjects under the influ-ence of cannabis tend to drive slower, apparently to compensate for and con-trol lane position changes and to allow more time for cognitive processing and delayed responses. However, the combination of alcohol and cannabis is not antagonistic. Marijuana use alone or in combination with alcohol in-creased RT and incorrect driving responses when presented with emergen-cies. When THC is combined with alcohol, the effects on impairment appear to be additive or synergistic (Chesher, 1986; Lamers & Ramaekers, 2000; Robbe & O'Hanlon, 1999) reported significant lane position changes (stan-dard deviation of lane position or SDLP) after smoking marijuana and greater additive effects when combined with relatively low BACs (40–80 mg/dL). Al-though more regular smokers were less impaired on some measures com-pared with infrequent smokers or abstainers because of tolerance or compensatory driving, less impaired is not the same as not impaired. Also, the combination of even low doses of alcohol with low doses of cannabis produces much more impairment than either drug alone. It was concluded that the impairment by alcohol on tasks requiring cognitive skills coupled with the impairment of automatic functions by cannabinoids produces an additive and even synergistic effect.

Drummer and associates (2004) examined 3398 fatal car crashes involving various drugs, including cannabinoids. Of note, in addition to examining the presence or absence of cannabinoids, Drummer and colleagues determined culpability for the crash with or without alcohol. Although any type of drug was found to be significantly associated with culpability, the largest odds ratios (a measure of risk) involved cases in which THC concentrations were equal to or greater than 5 ng/mL. At higher concentrations (i.e., more than 5 ng/mL), THC increased crash risk similar to BACs of 150 mg/dL. However, when THC was combined with relatively low alcohol concentrations (i.e., greater than 50 mg/dL), the odds ratio was greater than in drivers with only alcohol. In other words, THC significantly increased the impairment of alcohol intoxication.

Similar interactive results were reported by many, but not all, researchers. Often methodological limitations of individual studies add to the reported inconsistencies. For example, unlike alcohol, the effects of cannabis on motor vehicle operation dissipates relatively quickly, and until recently, objective evidence regarding drug use in crashes mostly included urine testing for the inactive metabolite (THC-COOH) of this drug but not quantitative blood testing for the active compound (THC). Three general conclusions on which there is agreement are as follows: (1) low doses of cannabinoids may increase culpability for crashes but that depends on individual differences and time of collection; (2) higher doses of cannabinoids produce impairment in tasks believed to reflect skills necessary for safe motor vehicle operation, impair actual driving, and are associated with increased risk caused by the cannabis-intoxicated driver; and (3) low doses of cannabinoids coupled with low doses of alcohol produce an additive and, in some cases, synergistic interaction that impairs driving-related skills and greatly increases risk for a crash.

Of particular interest is a recent report that alcohol increases blood cannabinoid concentration. Hartman and colleagues (2015) dosed male and female marijuana smokers to BACs of 60 mg/dL in 10 minutes. After this unusually rapid drinking protocol, subjects inhaled THC via a vaporizer. Blood samples were obtained over the course of about 8 hours and THC and 11-OH-THC (an active metabolite) were quantified. Alcohol increased THC and 11-OH-THC at both high and low doses in alcohol-treated subjects by about 2.4 µg/L and 35.3 µg/L of THC (in the low- and high-dose subjects, respectively), whereas 11-OH-THC increased by about 1 µg/L in both low and high (THC) dosed subjects.

Alcohol and Sedative-Hypnotics

Benzodiazepines are a class of anxiolytic drugs used to treat anxiety and insomnia and are one of the most widely prescribed drugs in the United States. Benzodiazepines have a significantly greater safety margin and have largely replaced barbiturates in the treatment of these disorders. Even so, poisoning due to the combination of alcohol and benzodiazepines is still relatively common (Tanaka, 2002), and the sedative side effects of these drugs are well-known. In spite of adverse publicity and a problematic public image, the most widely prescribed psychiatric medication in the United States in recent years is the benzodiazepine alprazolam (Stahl, 2002).

Alcohol and many benzodiazepines share similar pharmacodynamic mechanisms, so it is not surprising that the combination of alcohol and benzodiazepines is associated with drug-induced deaths, drug overdoses, and traffic accidents or fatalities (Girre, Facy, Lagier & Dally, 1988; Schuckit, 1987). Regardless of the mechanisms, the interaction between alcohol and benzodiazepines can be dangerous and potentially impair cognitive and psychomotor skills and affect the efficiency of one or the other or both drugs.

Apparently a pharmacokinetic interaction also exists between alcohol and benzodiazepines, particularly among the elderly, in whom a 50 percent decrease in clearance, a fourfold to ninefold increase in half-life, and a twofold to fourfold increase in the volume of distribution have been reported (Peppers, 1996). However, not all investigators agree that the interaction between benzodiazepines and alcohol is that significant. Sellers and Busto (1982), for example, point out that many studies "lack precision of instrumentation and knowledge of the pharmacokinetics of ethanol and benzodiazepines" and conclude that the importance of this interaction has been overemphasized. Reflective of the many studies on this subject, these authors similarly conclude that acute alcohol impairs the metabolism of diazepam, desmethyldiazepam, chlordiazepoxide, clobazam, and temazepam and benzodiazepines that are metabolized by demethylation or hydroxylation. This alcohol-drug interaction may result in a 20 to 30 percent increase in benzodiazepine concentrations. On the other hand, chronic use of alcohol increases the clearance of these benzodiazepines. Benzodiazepines that are metabolized by glucuronide conjugation show a different and more complex interaction with alcohol (Sellers & Busto 1982). These authors conclude that the interaction between alcohol and benzodiazepines is probably less important than that of alcohol alone or in combination with other drugs, such as cannabinoids, neuroleptics, stimulants, and antidepressants.

Tolerance to many of the depressant effects of benzodiazepines develops after prolonged use but varies greatly based upon the drug and the dependent measure of tolerance being studied. More rapidly eliminated benzodiazepines, such as alprazolam, are associated with hyperexcitability (rebound anxiety, disinhibition, panic attacks, mania) (Vgontzas, Kales & Bixler, 1995), which could complicate the diagnosis and treatment of alcohol withdrawal syndrome. Also, potentially serious additive pharmacodynamic effects may occur when benzodiazepines are combined with alcohol (Van Steveninck et al., 1996). This is the result of different mechanisms. Principal among these is the effect of alcohol on multiple neurotransmitter systems, which adapt in different ways to the acute and chronic alcohol. For example, both animal and human studies suggest a role for catecholamines in acute intoxicating effects of—and the development of tolerance to—alcohol (Pohorecky & Brick, 1990). The role of the noradrenergic system in benzodiazepine tolerance and withdrawal has been suggested by many studies (Vgontzas et al., 1995, for a review). Ethanol also modifies the clearance and disposition of benzodiazepines and interferes with their clinical effectiveness. Alcohol is not bound to plasma proteins extensively enough to modify drug distribution. However, serum albumin levels in chronic alcoholics may be abnormally low, so that some drugs (e.g. diazepam) have an increased volume of distribution (Linnoila, Mattila & Kitchell, 1979). Linnoila and associates also found that low doses of flurazepam (Dalmane®) interact with low doses of alcohol to impair driving ability, even when alcohol is ingested the morning after taking Dalmane. Since many other benzodiazepines may be present in appreciable amounts the day after use (Betts & Birtle, 1982) and chronic alcoholics often drink in the morning, this interaction may be dangerous.

Alprazolam, useful in treatment for alcohol withdrawal, also produces mild drowsiness, and the combination of alcohol and alprazolam produces increase in self reported drowsiness (Linnoila et al., 1990). Additive but not synergistic effects of alprazolam and alcohol on certain psychomotor and cognitive tasks have been reported.

Some non-benzodiazepine anxiolytics such as buspirone (BuSpar®), do not appear to interact with alcohol to potentiate cognitive or motor performance impairment. Buspirone has been found to have no significant effect on body sway, coordination skills, tracking skills, or nystagmus even when combined with alcohol (Mattila, Aranko & Seppala, 1982).

Phenobarbital is a commonly prescribed barbiturate used to treat seizure disorders. Acute or chronic alcohol consumption synergistically enhances the sedative effect of barbiturates at their sites of action in the brain (both acting as positive allosteric modulators of GABA-A), sometimes leading to coma or fatal respiratory depression.

Alcohol and Anticonvulsants

These medications are prescribed for the treatment of seizures and bipolar disorder. They are increasingly used for their impulse control properties. Newer anticonvulsant drugs such as felbamate, gabapentin, lamotrigine, topiramate, tiagabine, levetiracetam, oxcarbazepine, and zonisamide are popular, but older medications (phenobarbital, phenytoin, primidone, ethosuximide, carbamazepine, and valproate) continue to be widely used. A more favorable pharmacokinetic profile is observed in most of the newer drugs in contraposition to the classic agents. Good absorption, linear kinetics, and low drug–drug interaction potential make these drugs easier to use. The newer anticonvulsants are eliminated through different combinations of liver metabolism and direct renal excretion, thus providing a wider variety of choices in patients with failure of one of these organs.

Depending on its chronicity of use, alcohol will have opposite interactions with the older anticonvulsants. Acute alcohol consumption increases the availability of phenytoin and the risk of drug-related side effects. Chronic drinking may decrease phenytoin bioavailability, significantly reducing the patient's protection against seizures, even during a period of abstinence (Greenspan & Smith, 1991).

Depakote® (divalproex sodium) has a number of side effects but most are relatively mild. When this anti-seizure medication is combined with alcohol, however, more serious adverse drug effects may follow, including dizziness, drowsiness, tremors, and problems with cognitive skills (e.g., difficulty concentrating). The synergistic interaction of divalproex with alcohol can lead to extreme CNS depression.

Alcohol and Cardiovascular Medications

This class of drugs includes a wide variety of medications prescribed to treat disorders of the heart and circulatory system. Acute alcohol consumption interacts with some of these drugs to cause dizziness or fainting upon standing (orthostatic hypotension). These drugs include nitroglycerin, used to treat chest pain (angina), and reserpine, methyldopa (Aldomet®), hydralazine (Apresoline®), and guanethidine (Ismelin®), used to treat high blood pressure (hypertension). Chronic alcohol consumption decreases the availability of propranolol (Inderal®), used to treat high blood pressure, potentially reducing its therapeutic effect. Alcohol acts as an osmotic diuretic and also causes hypokalemia. Patients taking loop or thiazide diuretics are at greater risk for dehydration and hypokalemia, which increases the risk of seizure activity.

Blood alcohol levels can be raised by verapamil and may remain elevated for a much longer period of time. It appears that verapamil inhibits the metabolism of the alcohol by the liver (Bauer, Schumock, Horn, & Opheim, 1992). Alcohol may also increase the bioavailability of nifedipine by inhibiting its metabolism (Perez-Reyes & Jeffcoat, 1992).

Elevated blood pressure is a risk factor for cardiovascular disease, including heart attacks. Alcohol is known to cause a dose-dependent elevation in blood pressure (Beilin, 1995). Consequently, patients who chronically abuse alcohol may be misdiagnosed with primary hypertension and placed inappropriately on antihypertensives (Doyal, Morton & Crane, 1988). In addition, those patients who consume any alcohol respond less well to antihypertensive treatments than do total abstainers. Alcohol may change the pharmacokinetics of drugs that are metabolized by the liver (Beevers, Maheswaran & Potter, 1990). Any alcohol pharmacokinetic analysis in patients taking the medications should account for these effects.

Alcohol and Antibiotics

Antibiotics are used to treat infectious diseases. In combination with acute alcohol consumption, some antibiotics may cause nausea, vomiting, headache, and possibly convulsions. Among these antibiotics are furazolidone, griseofulvin, metronidazole, and the antimalarial quinacrine.

Isoniazid and rifampin are used together to treat tuberculosis, a disease especially problematic among the elderly in nursing homes and among homeless alcoholics. Although the incidence of tuberculosis has declined dramatically in the last century, pockets of the disease among the indigent alcoholic population have been a major factor in preventing its complete eradication in this country. Treatment of this population has been problematic, mainly because of patients' lack of cooperation with their therapy, including failure to take prescribed medications. This noncompliant behavior in alcohol and other drug-abusing populations is mainly responsible for the recent occurrence of multidrug resistant tuberculosis. Thus, overall, the effectiveness of the antituberculosis medications is greatly reduced. Additionally, acute alcohol consumption decreases the bioavailability of isoniazid in the bloodstream, whereas chronic alcohol use decreases the bioavailability of rifampin. Thus, the pharmacokinetic interaction between alcohol and these antibiotics may reduce their effectiveness (Jacobson, 1992), but alcohol bioavailability is not affected by these medications. However, other antibiotics do affect alcohol availability.

Erythromycin accelerates gastric emptying and may reduce first-pass metabolism of alcohol in the stomach, resulting in increased absorption in the intestine and higher BACs of ethanol. Conversely, many aerobic bacteria in the colon are capable of metabolizing alcohol acetaldehyde because they possess ADH activity. Treatment with the antibiotic ciprofloxacin decreased enhanced colonic metabolism of alcohol, resulting in increased blood levels of ethanol (Nosova et al., 1999) in pre-clinical studies.

Finally, although controversial, patients drinking alcohol while taking the antibiotics metronidazole or ketoconazole may suffer from symptoms similar to those found with disulfiram (Antabuse): abdominal distress, nausea, vomiting, and headache (Cina, Russel & Conradi, 1996).

Alcohol and Antidepressants

There is a robust literature on the correlation between alcoholism and depression. Many active alcoholics are prescribed antidepressants, leading to a high potential for alcohol–antidepressant interactions. Several classes of antidepressants are available and are defined by how they affect neurochemistry. Some antidepressants cause varying degrees of sedating activity, but extreme caution should be exerted in describing these drugs as depressants or sedatives. Nevertheless, alcohol increases the sedative and other effects of tricyclic antidepressants such as amitriptyline (Elavil®) by interfering with the bioavailability of alcohol (Dorian et al., 1983). In addition, alcohol-induced liver disease further impairs antidepressant metabolism and causes significantly increased levels of active medication in the body (Weathermon & Crabb, 1999).

Widely prescribed selective serotonin reuptake inhibitors (SSRIs), such as fluoxetine (Prozac®), sertraline (Zoloft®), paroxetine (Paxil®), and citalopram (Celexa®), have the best safety profile of all antidepressants, even when combined in large quantities with alcohol. No serious interactions seem to occur when these agents are consumed with moderate alcohol doses (Matilla, 1990). In addition, neither fluoxetine nor alcohol alters the pharmacokinetics of psychomotor effects of the other, although alcohol-impaired performance of most subjects on psychomotor tests (Lemberger, Rowe, Bergstrom, Farid & Enas, 1985). The lack of any significant interaction is particularly interesting because many SSRIs are metabolized by cytochrome P450 isoenzymes, some of which are important in the alcohol metabolism in chronic alcoholics, for example. Although cytochrome P450 studies can be useful in identifying drug interactions, some of those interactions have no clinical significance as in the case of SSRIs such as fluoxetine, clovoxamine, or femoxetine.

Concurrent use of the monoamine oxidase inhibitors (MAOIs) with alcohol will potentially precipitate a hypertensive crisis and may also enhance sedation. The mechanism for this reaction has been attributed to increased tyramine levels (Simpson & Gratz, 1992). Tyramine is present in a number of alcoholic beverages.

Finally, although atypical antidepressants generally do not seem to have any problematic interactions with alcohol, mirtazapine (Remeron®), when combined with alcohol, causes impaired cognition and decreased motor performance (Sitsen & Zivkov, 1995).

Alcohol and Antipsychotics

Many antipsychotics produce sedation and psychomotor impairment. Acute alcohol consumption increases the sedative effect of these drugs, resulting in further impaired coordination and potentially fatal respiratory depression. This effect appears to be additive, but the mechanisms of this interaction are uncertain. The low-potency conventional antipsychotics (e.g., chlorpromazine and thioridazine) are much more sedating than the high-potency antipsychotics are (e.g., haloperidol and fluphenazine) and tend to cause more significant CNS depression. Earlier reports revealed that daily 200 mg doses of chlorpromazine and relatively low blood alcohol concentrations (42 mg/dL) produced significant impairment in the performance of skills related to driving and produced subjective complaints of feeling sleepy, lethargic, dull, groggy, and poorly coordinated (Zirkle, King, McAtee and VanDyke, 1959). A similar effect is observed when lower doses of chlorpromazine (1 mg/kg) were combined with higher (80 mg/dL) blood alcohol levels (Milner & Landauer, 1971). Somewhat less psychomotor impairment was observed when alcohol was combined with flupenthixol (Linnoila 1973; Linnoila et al., 1975) or thioridazine (Milner & Landauer, 1971), but not with haloperidol (Linnoila, 1973, Linnoila et al., 1975). Changing doses, steady state pharmacokinetics, and type of antipsychotic medication make predictions about the interaction of these drugs with alcohol difficult. More work is needed to understand the nature of this interaction.

Long-term effects of some psychotropic medications present other problems including extraparamidal symptoms. Chronic alcohol consumption causes increased metabolism of the antipsychotic medications resulting in lower blood levels and, ultimately, lower efficacy of the medication. Since antipsychotic medications are typically used to treat mental illnesses such as schizophrenia, this may result in a particularly challenging and unpredictable patient. Coupled with the increased risk for hepatitis in patients treated with antipsychotics, the combination of chronic alcohol ingestion and antipsychotic drugs may result in even greater susceptibility for liver damage (Goff & Baldessarini, 1993) and behavioral disorders. In forensic areas involving pharmacokinetic calculations, a range of alcohol elimination rates should be used to account for individual differences, particularly when there is evidence of, or the potential for, liver damage due to such drug interactions.

REFERENCES

Adams, W. (1995). Interactions between alcohol and other drugs. *International Journal of Addictions, 30*, 1903–1923.

Bauer, L., Schumock, G., Horn, J., and Opheim, K. (1992). Verapamil inhibits ethanol elimination and prolongs the perception of intoxication. *Clinical Pharmacology and Therapeutics, 52*(1), 6–10.

Beevers, D., Maheswaran, R., and Potter, J. (1990). Alcohol, blood pressure, and antihypertensive drugs. *Journal of Clinical Pharmacy and Therapeutics, 15*(6), 395–397.

Beilin, L. (1995). Alcohol and hypertension. *Clinical and Experimental Pharmacology and Physiology, 22*, 185–188.

Betts, T. A., and Birtle, J. (1982). Effect of two hypnotic drugs on actual driving performance next morning. *British Medical Journal (Clinical Research Edition), 285*(6345), 852.

Brick, J., (1990). *Marijuana.* Rutgers University Center of Alcohol Studies. *Health Consequences of Marijuana Use* (2008). In J. Brick (Ed.), *Medical Consequences of Alcohol and Drug Abuse.* Taylor Francis Publishing Group.

Bunn, W. H., and Ginnini, A. J. (1992). Cardiovascular complications of cocaine abuse. *American Family Physician, 46*(3), 769–773.

Burns, M. (1989). Alcohol and antihistamines in combination: Effects on performance. *Alcoholism, Clinical and Experimental Research, 13*, 243.

Burns, M., and Moskowitz, H. (1980). Effects of diphenhydramine and alcohol on skills performance. *European Journal of Clinical Pharmacology, 17*(4), 259–266.

Caballeria, J., Baraona, E., Rodamilans, M., and Lieber, C. (1989). Effects of cimetidine on gastric alcohol dehydrogenase activity and blood alcohol levels. *Gastroenterology, 96*, 388–392.

Casswell, S. (1977). *Cannabis and Alcohol: Effects on Closed-Course Driving Behaviour.* Presented to Seventh International Conferences on Alcohol, Drugs and Traffic Safety, Melbourne, Australia. January 23-28. 1977. Canberra: Australian Government Publishing Service 1979.

Chesher, G. (1986). The effects of alcohol and marijuana in combination: A review. *Alcohol, Drugs and Driving, 2*, 105–119.

Cina, S., Russell, R., and Conradi, S. (1996). Sudden death due to metronidazole/ethanol interaction. *American Journal of Forensic Medicine and Pathology, 17*(4), 343–346.

Degenhardt, L., Chiu, W. T., Sampson, N., Kessler, R. C., Anthony, J. C., Angermeyer, M., and Wells, J. E. (2008). Toward a global view of alcohol, tobacco, cannabis, and cocaine use: Findings from the WHO World Mental Health Surveys. *PloS Medicine, 5*(7), e141.

Dorian, P., Sellers, E., Reed, K., Warsh, J., Hamilton, C., Kaplan, H., and Fan, T. (1983). Amitriptyline and ethanol: Pharmacokinetic and pharmacodynamic interaction. *European Journal of Clinical Pharmacology, 25*, 325–331.

Doyal, L., Morton, W., and Crane, D. (1988). Antihypertensive drug therapy in alcohol dependence. *Psychosomatics, 29*(3), 301–306.

Drummer, O., Gerostamoulos, J., Batziris, H., Chu, M., Caplehorn, J., Robertson, M., and Swann, P. (2004). The involvement of drugs in drivers of motor vehicles killed in Australian road traffic crashes. *Accident Analysis and Prevention, 36*(2), 239–248.

Dufour, M., Archer, L., and Gordis, F. (1992). Alcohol and the elderly. *Clinics in Geriatric Medicine, 8*(1), 127–141.

Ellenhorn, M., and Barceloux, D. (1988). *Medical Toxicology: Diagnosis and Treatment of Human Poisoning.* New York, NY: Elsevier Science.

Farre, M., De LaTorre, R., Llorente, M., Lamas, X., Ugena, B., Segura, J., and Cami, J. (1993). Alcohol and cocaine interactions in humans. *Journal of Pharmacology and Experimental Therapeutics, 266*(3), 1364–1373.

Franks, H., Hensley, V., Hensley, W., Starmer, G., and Teo, R. (1979). The interaction between ethanol and antihistamines. 2. Clemastine. *Medical Journal of Australia, 1,* 185.

Girre, C., Facy, F., Lagier, G., and Dally, S. (1988). Detection of blood benzodiazepines in injured people. Relationship with alcoholism. *Drug and Alcohol Dependence, 21*(1), 61–65.

Goff, D., and Baldessarini, R. (1993). Drug interactions with antipsychotic agents. *Journal of Clinical Psychopharmacology, 13*(1), 59–67.

Greenspan, K., and Smith, T. (1991). Perspectives on alcohol and medication interactions. *Journal of Alcohol and Drug Education, 36*(3), 103–107.

Hartman, R. L., Brown, T. L., Milavetz, G., Spurgin, A., Gorelick, D., Gaffney, G., and Huestis, M. A. (2015). Controlled cannabis vaporizer administration: Blood and plasma cannabinoids with and without alcohol. *Clinical Chemistry, 61*(6), 850–869.

Hopper, J. W., Karlsgodt, K. H., Adler, C. M., Macklin, E. A., Lukas, S. E., and Elman, I. (2004). Effect of acute cortisol and cocaine administration on attention, recall and recognition task performance in individuals with cocaine dependence. *Human Psychopharmacology: Clinical and Experimental, 19*(7), 511–516.

Huestis, M. A., Barnes, A., and Smith, M. L. (2005). Estimating the time of last cannabis use from plasma Δ^9-tetrahydrocannabinol and 11-nor-9-carboxy-Δ^9-tetrahydrocannabinol concentrations. *Clinical Chemistry, 51*(12), 2289–2295.

Jacobson, J. (1992). Alcoholism and tuberculosis. *Alcohol Health and Research World, 16*(1), 39–45.

Kambam, J., Franks, J., Janicki, P., Mets, B., Watt, M., and Hickman, R. (1994). Alcohol pretreatment alters the metabolic pattern and accelerates cocaine metabolism in pigs. *Drug and Alcohol Dependence, 36*(1), 9–13.

Kaplan, H. L., Forney, R. B., Richards, A. B., and Hughes, F. W. (1966). Dextro-amphetamine, alcohol, and dextro-amphetamine-alcohol combination and mental performance. In R. N. Hargern (Ed.), *Alcohol and Traffic Safety* (pp. 211–214). Proceedings of the Fourth International Conference on Alcohol and Traffic Safety. Bloomington, IN: Indiana University Press.

Kaufman, D., Kelly, J., Wiholm, B., Laszlo, A., Sheehan, J., Koff, R., and Shapiro, S. (1999). Risk of acute major upper gastrointestinal bleeding among users of aspirin and ibuprofen at various levels of alcohol consumption. *American Journal of Gastroenterology, 94*(11), 3189–3196.

LaBuda, C., and Fuchs, P. (2000). Aspirin attenuates the anxiolytic actions of ethanol. *Alcohol: An International Biomedical Journal, 21*(3), 287–290.

Lamers, C., and Ramaekers, J. (2000). *Visual Search and Urban City Driving Under the Influence of Marijuana and Alcohol.* Report DOT-HS-809-020. Washington, D.C.: U.S. Department of Transportation, National Highway Traffic Safety Administration.

Lemberger, L., Rowe, H., Bergstrom, R. F., Farid, K. Z., and Enas, G. G. (1985). Effect of fluoxetine on psychomotor performance, physiologic response, and kinetics of ethanol. *Clinical Pharmacology and Therapeutics, 37*(6), 658–664.

Lenne, M. G., Dietze, P. M., Triggs, T. J., Walmsley, S., Murphy, B., and Redman, J. R. (2010). The effects of cannabis and alcohol on simulated arterial driving: Influences of driving experience and task demand. *Accident Analysis and Prevention, 42*(3), 859–866.

Levitt, M. D. (1993). Review article: Lack of clinical significance of the interaction between H2-receptor antagonists and ethanol. *Alimentary Pharmacology and Therapeutics, 7*, 131–138.

Linnoila, M. (1973). Effects of diazepam, chlordiazepoxide, thioridazine, haloperidole, flupenthixole and alcohol on psychomotor skills related to driving. *Annales Medicinae Expermentalis et Biologiae Fenniae, 51*(3), 125–132.

Linnoila, M., Mattila, M. J., and Kitchell, B. S. (1979). Drug interactions with alcohol. *Drugs, 18*(4), 299–311.

Linnoila, M., Saario, I., Olkoniemi, J., Liljequist, R., Himberg, J. J., and Maki, M. (1975). Effect of two weeks' treatment with chlordiazepoxide or flupenthixole, alone or in combination with alcohol, on psychomotor skills related to driving. *Arzneimittel-Forschung, 25*(7), 1088–1092.

Linnoila, M., Stapleton, J. M., Lister, R., Moss, H., Lane, E., Granger, A., and Eckardt, M. J. (1990). Effects of single doses of alprazolam and diazepam, alone and in combination with ethanol, on psychomotor and cognitive performance and on autonomic nervous system reactivity in healthy volunteers. *European Journal of Clinical Pharmacology, 39*(1), 21–28.

Lukas, S. E., Benedikt, R., Mendelson, J., Kouri, E., Sholar, M., and Amass, L. (1992). Marihuana attenuates the rise in plasma ethanol levels in human subjects. *Neuropsychopharmacology, 7*(1), 77–81.

Matilla, M. (1990). Alcohol and drug interactions. *Annals of Medicine, 22*, 363–369.

Mattila, M., Aranko, K., and Seppala, T. (1982). Acute effects of buspirone and alcohol on psychomotor skills. *Journal of Clinical Psychiatry, 43*, 56–61.

McCance, E. F., Price, L. H., Kosten, T. R., and Jatlow, P. I. (1995). Cocaethylene: Pharmacology, physiology and behavioral effects in humans. *Journal of Pharmacology and Experimental Therapeutics, 274*(1), 215–223.

McCance-Katz, E. F., Price, L. H., McDougle, C. J., Kosten, T. R., Black, J. E., and Jatlow, P. I. (1993). Concurrent cocaine-ethanol ingestion in humans: Pharmacology, physiology, behavior, and the role of cocaethylene. *Psychopharmacology, 111*(1), 39–46.

Milner, G., and Landauer, A. (1971). Alcohol, thioridazine and chlorpromazine effects on skills related to driving behaviour. *British Journal of Psychiatry, 118*, 351–352.

Nosova, T., Jokelainen, K., Kaihovaara, P., Vakevainen, S., Rautio, M., Jousimies-Somer, H., and Salaspuro, M. (1999). Ciprofloxacin administration decreases enhanced ethanol elimination in ethanol-fed rats. *Alcohol and Alcoholism, 34*(1), 48–54.

Ogden, E. J. D., and Moskowitz, H. (2004). Effects of alcohol and other drugs on driver performance. *Traffic Injury Prevention, 5*(3), 185–198.

Oteri, A., Salvo, F., Caputi, A. P., and Calapai, G. (2007). Intake of energy drinks in association with alcoholic beverages in a cohort of students of the School of Medicine of the University of Messina. *Alcoholism, Clinical and Experimental Research, 31*(10), 1677–1680.

Peppers, M. (1996). Benzodiazepines for alcohol withdrawal in the elderly and in patients with liver disease. *Pharmacotherapy, 16*, 49–58.

Perez-Reyes, M. (1994). The order of drug administration: Its effects on the interaction between cocaine and ethanol. *Life Sciences, 55*(7), 541–550.

Perez-Reyes, M., and Jeffcoat, A. R. (1992). Ethanol/cocaine interaction: Cocaine and cocaethylene plasma concentrations and their relationship to subjective and cardiovascular effects. *Life Sciences, 51*(8), 553–563.

Perez-Reyes, M., Jeffcoat, A. R., Myers, M., Sihler, K., and Cook, C. E. (1994). Comparison in humans of the potency and pharmacokinetics of intravenously injected cocaethylene and cocaine. *Psychopharmacology, 116*(4), 428–432.

Perez-Reyes, M., White, W., McDonald, S., and Hicks, R. (1992). Interaction between ethanol and dextroamphetamines: Effects of psychomotor performance. *Alcoholism, Clinical and Experimental Research, 16*, 75–81.

Pohorecky, L., and Brick, J. (1990). The pharmacology of alcohol. In D. Balfour (Ed.), *Encyclopedia of Therapeutics* (pp. 189–582). New York, NY: Pergamon Press.

Ridout, F., Shamsi, Z., Meadows, R., Johnson, S., and Hindmarch, I. (2003). A single-center, randomized, double-blind, placebo-controlled, crossover investigation of the effects of fexofenadine hydrochloride 180 mg alone and with alcohol, with hydroxyzine hydrochloride 50 mg as a positive internal control, on aspects of cognitive and psychomotor function related to driving a car. *Clinical Therapeutics, 25*(5), 1518–1538.

Robbe, H., and O'Hanlon, J. (1999). *Marijuana, Alcohol and Actual Driving Performance.* Report DOT-HS-808-939. Washington, D.C.: U.S. Department of Transportation. National Highway Traffic Safety Administration.

Roehrs, T., Zwyghuizen-Doorenbos, A., and Roth, T. (1993). Sedative effects and plasma concentrations following single doses of triazolam, diphenhydramine, ethanol and placebo. *Sleep, 16*(4), 301–305.

Roine, R., DiPadova, C., Frezza, M., Hernández- Munõz, R., Baraona, E., and Lieber, C. (1990a). Effects of omeprazole, cimetidine and ranitidine on blood ethanol concentrations. *Gastroenterology, 98*, A114.

Roine, R., Gentry, R., Hernández-Munõz, R., Baraona, F., and Lieber, C. (1990b). Aspirin increases blood alcohol concentrations in humans after ingestion of ethanol. *Journal of the American Medical Association, 264*(18), 2406–2408.

Schuckit, M. A. (1987). Alcohol and drug interactions with antianxiety medications. *American Journal of Medicine, 82*(5A), 27–33.

Sellers, E. M., and Busto, U. (1982). Benzodiazepines and ethanol: Assessment of the effects and consequences of psychotropic drug interactions. *Journal of Clinical Psychopharmacology, 2*(4), 249–262.

Sewell, R. A., Poling, J., and Sofuoglu, M. (2009). The effect of cannabis compared with alcohol on driving. *American Journal on Addictions, 18*(3), 185–193.

Simpson, G. M., and Gratz, S. S. (1992). Comparison of the pressor effect of tyramine after treatment with phenelzine and moclobemide in healthy male volunteers. *Journal of Clinical Pharmacology and Therapeutics, 52*(3), 286–291.

Sitsen, J. M. A., and Zivkov, M. (1995). Mirtazapine: Clinical profile. *CNS Drugs, 4*(Suppl 1), 39–48.

Smiley, A., Ziedman, K., and Moskowitz, H. (1981). *Pharmacokinetics of Drug Effects on Driving Performance: Driving Simulator Tests of Marijuana Alone and in Combination with Alcohol.* Report prepared for NIDA and the National Highway Traffic Safety Administration. Contract 271-76-3316. Los Angeles, CA: Southern California Research Institute.

Stahl, S. S. (2002). Don't ask, don't tell, but benzodiazepines are still the leading treatments for anxiety disorder. *Journal of Clinical Psychiatry, 63*(9), 756–757.

Stein, A., Allen, R., Cook, M., and Karl, R. (1983). *A Simulator Study of the Combined Effects of Alcohol and Marijuana on Driving Behavior–Phase II.* Report DOT-HS-5-01257. Washington, D.C.: National Highway Traffic Safety Administration.

Tanaka, E. (2002). Toxicological interactions between alcohol and benzodiazepines. *Clinical Toxicology, 40*(1), 69–75.

Van Stevenick, A. L., Gieschke, R., Schoemaker, R., Roncari, G., Tuk, B., Pieters, M. S. M., …, Cohen, A. F. (1996). Pharmacokinetic and pharmacodynamic interactions of bretazenil and diazepam with alcohol. *British Journal of Clinical Pharmacology, 41*(6), 565–573.

Vgontzas, A. N., Kales, A., and Bixler, E. O. (1995). Benzodiazepine side effects: Role of pharmacokinetics and pharmacodynamics. *Pharmacology, 51*(4), 205–223.

Weathermon, R., and Crabb, D. W. (1999). Alcohol and medication interactions. *Alcohol Research and Health, 23*(1), 40–54.

Wilson, L., Taylor, J. D., Nash, C. W., and Cameron, D. F. (1966). The combined effects of ethanol and amphetamine sulfate on performance of human subjects. *Canadian Medical Association Journal, 94*(10), 478–484.

Yesavage, J. A., Leirer, V. O., Denari, M., and Hollister, L. E. (1985). Carry-over effects of marijuana intoxication on aircraft pilot performance: A preliminary report. *American Journal of Psychiatry, 142*(11), 1325–1329.

Zimatkin, S. M., and Anichtchik, O. V. (1999). Alcohol-histamine interaction. *Alcohol & Alcoholism, 34*(2), 141–147.

Zirkle, G. A., King, P. D., McAtee, O. B., and Van Dyke, R. (1959). Effects of chlorpromazine and alcohol on coordination and judgment. *Journal of the American Medical Association, 171*(11), 1496–1499.

Chapter 9

MEDICAL CONSEQUENCES AND TOXICOLOGICAL CONSIDERATIONS[1]

9.1 ACUTE ALCOHOL AND TRAUMA

The medical consequences of intoxication cannot be underestimated and are often important in interpreting evidence and reaching conclusions regarding diagnoses, causality, survival outcome, and other topics of interest in forensic investigations. The overwhelming majority of forensic alcohol cases involve trauma of some sort. Within this broad public health problem, alcohol plays a potentially significant role in trauma, including vehicle-related injuries, thermal injuries, hypothermia, and frostbite cases and is overly represented in completed suicides, in injuries from falls and in homicide victims or perpetrators. In the context of acute trauma, alcohol users increase their risk in four ways: likelihood of injury, seriousness of injury, injury outcome, and misdiagnosis. Each of these consequences has forensic implications.

Likelihood of Injury

First, in comparison to sober individuals, alcohol abusers are more likely to be involved in a traumatic event (Maull, 1982; Perrine, 1975). In other words, heavy drinkers have a higher risk for accidents than nondrinkers have (Anda, Williamson & Remington, 1988). In forensic cases, alcohol tolerance is often raised as a defense to suggest that tolerance in alcoholics places them at less risk for a fatal crash or other injury than for other drinkers. Although this may be true at very low BACs (e.g., below any legal definition of intoxication), for some drinkers in this special population, there is overwhelming evidence that alcohol tolerance does not provide immunity from impaired driving. Studies of relative risk or of odds ratios for a fatal injury by their very

---

1. Note: Some sections of this chapter were reproduced, in part, from Brick, J. (2008) with permission of the publisher.

nature include a wide sample of subjects. It can be assumed that within the general population, there are normally distributed degrees of intoxication and tolerance. In all such studies reviewed, BACs range from 0 or near 0 to about 200 mg/dL, or higher in some cases. Subjects with lower BACs are more likely to include drinkers with less tolerance and those with higher BACs more tolerance, relative to their individual needs to attain subjective effects of alcohol use (i.e., to become intoxicated). Even so, it can be seen that risk for a fatal crash or other injuries increases dramatically with higher BACs, indicating that as a group, persons who drink to high BACs are at particularly high risk for injuries. This risk increases exponentially (*see* Chapter 5, Table 5.7) with intoxication.

Seriousness of Injury

Second, given similar traumatic circumstances, an intoxicated person is likely to sustain more serious injuries than a nondrinker is. Although there are some exceptions (Huth, Maier, Simonowitz & Herman, 1983; Ward, Flynn, Miller, Blaisedell, 1982), most research findings support this positive relationship between alcohol use and severity of injury (Roizen, 1988). The exact mechanisms of the alcohol–severity relationship are not known (Maull, 1982), but the relationship has been further supported by experimental studies that controlled for BAC, type of injury, and severity of trauma (Albin & Bunegin, 1986; Anderson, 1986). In addition, Waller and colleagues (1986) found potentiating effects of alcohol on driver injury even after controlling for several other traffic accident risk factors. The belief that intoxicated persons are less likely to be seriously hurt or killed in an accident because they are relaxed for example is probably a myth, as noted by Kirn (1988), Waller (1987), and Waller and colleagues (1986).

9.2 INJURY OUTCOME

Not only does alcohol intoxication affect severity of injuries sustained in a motor vehicle crash, the most well-studied mechanics of injury, but also intoxication may affect injury outcome. The forensic implications, including causality of an intoxicated driver responsible for a crash, is obvious. However, less well-examined is forensic litigation in the consequence of intoxication in someone whose actions may not have contributed to an injury but for whom intoxication may have been a significant contributing factor in her or his recovery. For example, motorcycle riders with head injuries are about twice as likely to have fatal head injuries if they are intoxicated than are similarly injured riders who are sober (Luna, Maier, Sowder, Copass & Oreskovich, 1984), and alcohol-intoxicated accident victims with CNS injuries were found to be more than twice as likely to die sooner when compared to anatomically matched controls (Zink, Maoi & Chen, 1996).

Contrary to popular misconception, drinking drivers are more likely to be seriously or fatally injured in comparison to sober drivers (Waller et al., 1986). For example, earlier studies by Ward et al. (1982) found that hospitalized major trauma victims with average BACs of about 150 mg/dL were significantly less likely to die from injuries than were the sober control group. Similarly, Kraus, Morgenstern, Fife, Conroy, and Nourjah, (1989) found that, contrary to expectations, injury severity and mortality were inversely related to blood alcohol levels. However, most of the more current research does not support this conclusion (Fell & Hertz, 1993; Luna et al., 1984; Zink et al., 1996) depending on the nature of the injury. For example, hemorrhagic shock, which often accompanies serious injuries, also induces acidosis with marked hypercarbia. In such cases, alcohol-induced acidosis would compound this physiological imbalance and increase morbidity and mortality (Chen et al., 2000; Kincaid, Miller, Meredith, Rahman & Chang, 1998; Molina et al., 2002).

The mechanisms of the exacerbating effects of alcohol on CNS injury are intriguing but not well-understood. Injury outcome may be less favorable due to the effect of alcohol on the inhibition of free radical scavengers such as dimethyl sulfoxide (Albin & Bunegin, 1986) or alcohol-induced cerebral edema as a result of lipid peroxidation (DeCrescito, Demopoulos, Flamm & Ransohoff, 1974) or increases in plasma osmolality (Elmer, Goransson & Zoucas, 1984; Steinbok & Thompson, 1978).

9.3 MISDIAGNOSIS

Head injuries may confound intoxication evidence. The preponderance of data linking alcohol and trauma deserves close scrutiny because intoxication frequently complicates diagnosis of trauma-related injury (Lowenfels, 1982; Soderstrom, Dupriest, Benner, Maekawa & Cowley, 1979). Emergency room physicians can overdiagnose by interpreting signs of intoxication (e.g., slurred speech or memory lapse) as signs of serious head injury, especially if the odor of an alcoholic beverage is not detected on the patient's breath. Conversely, since signs of intoxication can mimic other conditions, physicians may misdiagnose by attributing signs and symptoms to intoxication, thereby missing possible coexisting and life-threatening conditions. In the alcohol-tolerant drinker, for example, alcohol intoxication alone would rarely produce a coma (Knott, 1986) except at very high BACs. Such diagnostic difficulties are especially common with head injuries, which are frequently alcohol related (Brismar, Engstrom & Rydberg, 1983; Hillbom & Holm, 1986; Jagger, Fife, Vernberg & Jane, 1984; Simonsen, 1984).

At the scene of a crash, one of the most common questions in interpreting behavior is whether the behavioral impairment observed at the scene is due to head injury, intoxication, or some combination of the two. In motor vehicle accidents, falls, physical altercations, and so on, head injuries can range from relatively mild cuts or bruises to the face. More serious head injuries result when the impact is so great that the brain is moved within the skull, often resulting in momentary loss of consciousness, confusion, and amnesia. This type of head injury is referred to as a concussion, although the term is often used without clear evidence of these signs or symptoms. Any medical reference to a concussion should be followed up to determine the basis for such a diagnosis.

Most head injuries, including mild concussions and more serious head injuries, present signs and symptoms almost immediately. On rare occasions, however, signs of serious head injury may not appear for several hours or days after injury. Table 9.1 lists signs of serious head injury. Many of these signs or symptoms are not only nearly identical to signs of alcohol intoxication but also indications of the need for immediate medical attention regardless of etiology.

It is not uncommon for individuals involved in a traumatic accident to feel dazed, forgetful, listless, and depressed. Signs such as these could be the result of a mild traumatic brain injury (MTBI). Although motor vehicle accidents are probably the most common cause of MTBI, any sudden motion or change in motion may cause the brain to move within the skull. When brain tissue impacts with the skull, MTBI may occur. Obviously, the greater the force of impact, the more likely signs will be present. In addition to the acute effects of MTBI (Table 9.1), other signs or symptoms may include fatigue, irritability,

Table 9.1: Acute Signs and Symptoms of Head Injury.

1. Unconsciousness (passing out)
2. Unusual drowsiness
3. Confusion
4. Severe headache
5. Vomiting
6. Blurred vision
7. Convulsions (seizure or "fit")
8. Stiff neck
9. Areas of numbness, tingling, or weakness
10. Stumbling or loss of balance
11. Pupils not equal in size
12. Decreased activity, difficulty walking, poor feeding, or unusual fussiness (in children)

impatience, memory problems, and anxiety, which can last for days or months. Depending on the mechanical factors of the accident (e.g., speed, change in velocity, distance of the head from a headrest), a *coup* occurs to the brain on the same side the head strikes a fixed object. A contrecoup injury occurs on the side opposite the area that was impacted as the brain "bounced" back. Coup and contrecoup injuries are associated with, but do not always follow, bruising from contusions or other forms of TBI. Behavioral observations of subjects with TBI should be interpreted with caution when alcohol intoxication is present. It is noteworthy that for MTBI to occur, it is not necessary that the head hits the steering wheel or other object. If the driver is rapidly deaccelerated, the body moves forward but is stopped relatively abruptly by the seat belt or air bag; the brain continues to move forward as a result of the sudden deceleration of the head.

In addition, alcohol can seriously complicate the management and treatment of the trauma patient. Several investigators emphasize the risk of administering anesthesia to intoxicated patients (Abeloos, Rolly, Timperman & Watson, 1997; Edwards, 1985; Lowenfels, 1982). Abeloos and colleagues (1997) suggest that given the extreme risks of anesthesia with highly intoxicated patients, surgery may need to be delayed, if possible, until blood alcohol levels are known and fall below the level of 250 mg/dL. A critical problem with acute intoxication during anesthesia appears to be regurgitation and aspiration of the stomach contents (Abeloos et al., 1997).

Proper diagnosis and treatment of trauma patients almost demand routine blood alcohol testing as part of emergency room admissions, and physicians should assume alcohol involvement in trauma cases unless blood alcohol tests show otherwise (Maull, Clapp & Ellis, 1986; Soderstrom & Cowley, 1987; Zuska, 1981). Without such tests, it is impossible to know a patient's condition with confidence (Waller, 1988). Clinical signs of alcohol use (e.g., slurred speech, bloodshot eyes, lack of coordination) may be absent and are sometimes unreliable. Waller (1988) also stresses the need to actively check for alcohol abuse because it is possible to overlook it depending on the patient's drinking history or unless late-stage alcohol-related medical consequences are present. Rockett and Putnam (1986) recommend that hospital personnel routinely document alcohol information for injury cases (1) to ensure providing appropriate medical care, especially for head injuries and (2) to detect problem drinking and create potential for early referral of alcohol-troubled persons to treatment.

Despite these data on the relationship of alcohol to trauma, the results of emergency room research indicate that routine testing for alcohol in trauma patients is relatively rare (Maull et al., 1986; Simel & Feussner, 1988). Chang and Astrachan (1988) found that house staff assessed only one quarter of 320 motor vehicle accident patients in an emergency department at an urban hospital. Further, among 47 patients who were BAC positive at 200 mg/dL or more, not a single patient was referred for alcohol abuse evaluation or treatment. In a national survey (Soderstrom & Cowley, 1987), only 55.2 percent of trauma centers surveyed reported routine testing for blood alcohol.

9.4 BIOMARKERS OF ALCOHOL USE

The prevalence and consequences of heavy alcohol use are a recurrent theme in this book and in most societies. As a result, it is important for clinicians and other experts to be able to identify drinking problems. Diagnostic written tests or structured interview questions are helpful in this regard and relatively easy to administer, but their value is greatly enhanced by the use of biochemical laboratory tests. There is no perfect biological marker or instrument to detect alcohol use disorders, but there are a number of biochemical indicators of alcohol abuse that can be found in many commonly ordered tests during hospitalization. Other tests that are not part of routine clinical chemistry testing may be available. All such tests provide the diagnostician and the patient with a measurable and objective finding that is often helpful in overcoming psychological barriers to treatment, such as denial. For the forensic examiner, biochemical tests serve a similar purpose and may provide insight into the quantity and chronicity of alcohol use. In forensic cases, this may assist in including or excluding subjects from a particular population of drinkers or at least account for the behavioral or physiological variances between such groups.

Forensic examiners often infer tolerance or intolerance in an attempt to explain behavior (or lack thereof) related to intoxication. Such inferences require training to interpret the history of alcohol consumption, including recent (acute) patterns of alcohol use, long-term (chronic) use, and how much alcohol is consumed on a regular basis. Most alcohol researchers define heavy drinking at more than 60 g alcohol per day or the equivalent of about five standard drinks. Such information may be helpful in understanding how prior alcohol use compares to use in a particular forensic evaluation. For example, if a subject regularly consumes five drinks a day but then on the day of an incident under investigation consumes fifteen drinks, the biobehavioral consequences of such a dramatic increase from regular alcohol use would be significant. Clinical tests such as the Michigan Alcoholism Screen Test (MAST) and the CAGE Questionnaire are commonly used measures to identify problems associated with excessive alcohol use that may be used to make general assumptions about alcohol tolerance. Detailed prior drinking histories may not be available but biological markers of chronic or heavy alcohol use may provide evidence of drinking experience.

One group of biomarkers that indicate a person's alcohol intake includes certain liver enzymes. These include serum gamma-glutamyltransferase (GGT), ASAT, ALAT, and carbohydrate-deficient transferrin (CDT) protein and red blood cell volume or mean corpuscular volume.

Gamma-Glutamyltransferase. This glycoprotein is a large molecule made up of both proteins and carbohydrates found in liver cells (hepatocytes) and other cells and is involved in digestion. Elevated GGT levels are an early indicator of liver disease, and chronic heavy drinkers often have increased GGT levels. However, GGT is not a very sensitive marker, showing up in only 30 to 50 percent of excessive drinkers in the general population (Conigrave, Davies, Haber & Whitfield, 2003) and can be elevated by drugs other than alcohol or digestive diseases such as pancreatitis and prostate disease. It is also not specific to chronic heavy alcohol use. Thus, the other physiological causes need to be considered before using GGT as a definitive marker of chronic heavy alcohol use.

Aspartate Aminotransferace and **Alanine Aminotransferace.** These are enzymes that help metabolize amino acids, the building blocks of proteins. Both AST and ALT concentrations are elevated in otherwise healthy people who drink large amounts of alcohol (Halvorson, Campbell, & Sprague, 1993). Of the two enzymes, ALT is the more specific measure of alcohol-induced liver injury because it is found predominantly in the liver, whereas AST is found in the liver, heart, muscle, kidney, and brain. Elevated AST and ALT are an indication of liver disease, associated with alcohol abuse but not necessarily a measure of alcoholism. Very high levels of these enzymes in blood may indicate alcoholic liver disease, however. Clinicians often use a patient's ratio of AST to ALT (more than 2) to confirm an impression of liver disease due to chronic heavy alcohol consumption. These markers are most accurate in patients between ages 30 and 70.

Mean Corpuscular Volume. MCV is a measure of the volume of red blood cells. Elevated MCV is associated with heavy chronic drinking (Neumann & Spies, 2003). It may require several weeks or more of heavy drinking to elevate the MCV, but once elevated, this marker stays high for several months even after drinking stops. Therefore, a detailed drinking history relative to a crime or accident in forensic investigations is necessary to infer anything about the more recent drinking history. In non-alcoholics the normal range for MCV is about 80 to 100 (femtoliters/cell) but varies slightly between laboratories and sample population. Chanarin and Levi (1974) reported that most of alcoholics had an MCV of 90 or more. However, MCV values of more than 100 reflect macrocytoic anemia and can also be due to other causes such as folic acid and Vitamin B^{12} deficiencies (also common among alcoholics because of poor nutrition).

Other Biomarkers of Alcohol Use

ß-N-Acetyl-hexosaminidase. This enzyme has been found to be elevated in heavy drinkers (Javors & Johnson, 2003), and has been shown in some early studies to be both a sensitive and a specific measure of heavy drinking. In addition, unlike MCV, the increased beta-hexosaminidase returns to normal levels after only 7 to 10 days of abstinence. However, the beta-hexosaminidase assay is difficult to obtain in the United States, so clinicians have little experience using it with different treatment populations. Other conditions, such as diabetes and hypertension, also appear to elevate beta-hexosaminidase. Most routine hospital lab tests would not include this enzyme.

Carbohydrate-Deficient Transferrin. CDT is a version of the glycoprotein transferrin, a molecule responsible for carrying iron within the bloodstream. As the name implies, CDT is a form of the glycoprotein transferrin that is deficient in the carbohydrate sialic acid. Drinking disrupts sialic acid's ability to attach to transferrin as well as other molecules. Many versions of transferrin normally are found in healthy people, but studies indicate that heavy drinkers have higher amounts of the CDT version than have nondrinkers. Although it appears to be a highly specific measure of alcohol consumption with a low incidence of false-positives, it also has a relatively high rate of false negatives and is difficult to analytically differentiate from other forms of transferrin. In addition, even alcohol abstainers have low concentrations of CDT in their blood, and people with generally high concentrations of total transferrin will have high absolute numbers of CDT molecules, regardless of their drinking status. Some patients who drink heavily do not show elevated levels of CDT. Researchers also find that, in general, women tend to have higher CDT levels than men have, regardless of their drinking history (Arndt, 2000). Despite the disadvantages of the CDT marker, it remains a very well characterized biomarker for heavy alcohol intake.

Total Serum Sialic Acid. Because of sialic acid's clear potential as a highly specific marker for alcohol use, researchers have begun to study the potential of measuring total sialic acid (TSA) levels in patients' blood, rather than looking at the difference in sialic acid chains only on glycoproteins such as transferrin and apolipoprotein. Earlier studies (Javors & Johnson, 2003) demonstrate that, compared with social drinkers of both genders, both male and female alcoholics had elevated amounts of TSA. The test for TSA has similar sensitivity and specificity to the test for CDT for measuring alcohol consumption. However, because TSA levels take longer than either CDT or GGT to decrease during periods of abstinence, the TSA test might not be as useful for treatment programs assessing patients for relapse.

Ethyl Glucuronide (EtG). EtG is another minor metabolite of alcohol that forms in the liver when alcohol reacts with glucuronic acid, a substance that detoxifies drugs by transforming them into water-soluble compounds that can be easily removed from the body.

EtG can be detected in the blood for up to 36 hours and in the urine for up to 5 days after heavy alcohol use. Also, EtG is detectable in other body fluids, hair, and body tissues (Wurst et al., 2003), although no apparent correlation has been found between alcohol consumption and the presence of EtG in hair. When people test positive for EtG, it is likely that they consumed alcohol recently, even if alcohol is not detected by toxicological tests. This makes EtG potentially useful for detecting drinking relapses to determine abstinence compliance with treatment. Measuring EtG levels requires mass spectroscopy, although common in forensic testing, is less likely to be used in a routine clinical panel. Once an easy method of measuring EtG is developed, it has potential to detect relapse and alcohol use in settings where drinking is deemed contraindicated to safety, such as motor vehicle operation and use of complex machinery, and be useful for forensics.

Acetaldehyde. The first product of alcohol metabolism is acetaldehyde. Acetaldehyde is also present in the absence of alcohol use and can bind to certain proteins, including hemoglobin (a protein in red blood cells that carries oxygen). Researchers are able to measure concentrations of both free and bound acetaldehyde in blood samples using high-performance liquid chromatography and fluorescence detection—known as the whole blood–associated acetaldehyde (WBAA) assay (Halvorson et al., 1993). This assay is highly specific, and extremely sensitive and has excellent precision (Peterson & Polizzi, 1987). The insurance testing industry has used WBAA for more than a decade to test for heavy alcohol consumption. Its potential is even greater as a clinical tool to monitor people in alcoholism treatment programs, because this test can provide a picture of alcohol use over time. This works because, as a person continues to drink, hemoglobin bound acetaldehyde accumulates in red blood cells over their 120-day average life span, and this buildup shows up as an increasing WBAA assay number. Levels of protein bound acetaldehyde remain high for approximately 1 month after alcohol consumption (Halvorson et al., 1993). The ability of the WBAA assay to measure alcohol consumption patterns over time makes it unique among the biomarkers described here.

Chronic Alcohol Use

In addition to acute traumatic events, long-term or chronic alcohol use is associated with a variety of other medical complications. These may contribute to injuries and in some cases complicate the interpretation of an acute injury due to intoxication and the consequences of long-term drinking, unrelated to an acute event (e.g., an accident) or have legal importance regarding comparative negligence. For example, chronic drinking may cause peripheral neuropathies. Symptoms such as numbness, tingling, muscular weakness, or movement disorders are not uncommon in some alcoholics. Although the exact cause of the toxic effects of alcohol on nerves is not known, the indirect effect of poor diet (including thiamine deficiency) is known to cause nystagmus (discussed in Chapter 4) and impaired nerve conduction that may affect RT calculations (Chapter 12).

9.5 ALCOHOL AND THE SKELETAL SYSTEM

Alcohol-Induced Fractures

The positive and causal relationship between alcohol intoxication and injuries is evident from the large number of motor vehicle and slip and fall injuries involving alcohol intoxication. This relationship is not new but it is complex. Alcohol abuse and a high risk for skeletal fracture were observed as far back as the ancient Egyptians (Conn, 1985; Mathew, 1992; Seller, 1985). Now, centuries later, it is confirmed by research that suggests that alcoholics suffer from a generalized skeletal fragility and are prone to fracture. For example, men hospitalized for alcohol-related problems are four times more likely to have rib fractures than are non-drinking admissions (Lindsell, Wilson & Maxwell, 1982) and are up to fourteen times more likely to have spinal crush fractures (Crilly, Anderson, Hogan, Delaquerriére-Richardson, 1988; Israel, Orrego, Holt, Macdonald & Meema, 1980).

A prospective study found alcohol intake higher among perimenopausal women who experienced fractures than among those without fractures, and women who drank alcohol had about 50 percent higher risk of a fracture than among women who did not drink (Tuppurainen et al., 1995). In another study, increased weekly alcohol intake (more than eight drinks per week) was associated with a nearly twofold increased risk for osteoporotic fractures (Paganini-Hill, Ross & Gerkins, 1981). Similarly, a survey of U.S. women (ages 34 to 59) who consumed 25 g of alcohol (about two drinks) per day had a 133 percent increase in risk for hip fractures and a 38 percent increase for wrist fractures (Hernandez-Avila et al., 1991). This effect is less common in other populations; for example, the consumption of seven or more standard drinks per week was associated with a two-fold increased risk of hip fracture in Japanese women (Fujiwara, Kasagi, Yamada, & Kodama, 1997) and a with 4.6-fold increased risk in a study of black women (Grisso et al., 1994).

In men under the age of 65, consumption of two to six drinks per week substantially and significantly increased the risk of fracture compared with the same injuries in subjects who consumed less than two drinks per week.

For male heavy drinkers younger than age 65 there was almost ten times the risk of hip fractures as for men who drank lightly (Felson, Kiel, Anderson & Kannel, 1988).

As sobering as the results for men may be, other investigators have not identified any significant association between alcohol intake and risk for various fractures in women (Cumming & Klineberg, 1994; Huang et al., 1996; Johnell et al., 1995; Naves Diaz, O'Neill & Silman, 1997; O'Neill, Marsden, Adams & Silman, 1996). Thus, evidence suggests that excessive alcohol intake increases the risk of fracture but the results are not unanimous. Further, the consequences of low levels of alcohol consumption on skeletal integrity are not well-understood.

Alcohol-Induced Osteoporosis

Alcoholics may also suffer from a generalized skeletal fragility. Low bone density or osteopenia is predictive of fractures (National Institute on Alcohol Abuse and Alcoholism [NIAAA], 2000). Saville (1965) found a marked reduction in the bone mass of persons with a history of alcoholism and further noted that the bone mass of young alcoholic males were comparable to elderly, postmenopausal females. Since those initial observations, numerous studies have confirmed this effect (Peris et al., 1995; Spencer, N. Rubio, E. Rubio, Indreika & Seitam, 1986). In a prospective case-control analysis of risk factors, Blaauw and colleagues (1994) found that the average alcohol consumption was two to three times higher in osteoporotic men and women than it was in age-matched controls. A similar finding was found in an earlier study in which premenopausal women who consumed more than two standard drinks per day exhibited 13 percent lower bone density of the hip, compared with women who consumed less than one standard drink per week (Gonzalez-Calvin et al., 1993).

However, alcohol-reduced bone density is not universally reported within or between studies. Some studies have suggested that increasing alcohol consumption was positively, but anatomically selectively correlated with bone density (Holbrook & Barrett-Connor, 1993; Laitinen et al., 1993, Laitinen, Valimaki & Keto, 1991). The Study of Osteoporotic Fractures (7963 ambulatory, nonblack women age 65 and older) revealed that modest alcohol intake (less than one drink per day) in about 85 percent of the subjects was associated with higher bone density (Orwoll, Bauer, Vogt & Fox, 1996).

Possible Causes of Alcohol-Induced Bone Fragility

Microscopic examination of bone (bone histomorphometry) from alcoholics has been helpful in understanding the etiology of the skeletal disorders induced by alcohol. Alcoholics generally show a reduction in new bone formation (Schnitzler & Solomon, 1984), with varying reports of increases or no changes in bone resorption (Diamond, Stiel, Lunzer, Wilkinson & Posen, 1989). Overall, these studies suggest that alcoholic bone disease is characterized by considerable suppression of bone formation.

Although alcohol does disrupt the bone growth modeling cycle, these changes are reversible following about 2 weeks of abstinence (Diamond et al., 1989; Feitelberg, Epstein, Ismail, and D'Amanda, 1987; Laitinen, Lamberg-Allardt, Tumminen, Harkonen & Valimaki, 1992). There is also evidence that there is recovery of lost bone tissue following abstinence (Peris et al., 1994).

Potential Mechanisms of Alcohol-Induced Bone Disease

The normal growth of bone cells depends upon a variety of orchestrated factors, including adequate nutrition and the function and interaction of various hormones and intercellular regulating factors. It is well-known that as a result of poor diets, impaired nutrient absorption or increased renal excretion, alcoholics often have deficiencies in minerals such as calcium, phosphate, and magnesium (Bikle et al., 1985; Kalbfleisch, Lindeman, Ginn & Smith, 1963; Laitinen et al., 1992; Territo & Tanaka, 1974) and low levels of vitamin D, which is necessary for the absorption of calcium from the intestinal system (Lalor, France, Powell, Adams & Counihan, 1986; Mobarhan et al., 1984). However, there is little histomorphometric evidence that nutritional deficiencies related to alcohol use are a major cause of alcohol-induced bone disease.

Another candidate is calcitonin, a peptide produced by the thyroid gland. There is some evidence that the acute administration of alcohol (equal to about four drinks in a 150-lb male) increases calcitonin levels by about 38 percent 3 hours after consumption by nonalcoholic men (Williams et al., 1978). Since calcitonin inhibits bone resorption, in effect protecting bone, hypercalcitoninemia might explain why moderate intake of alcohol is associated with higher bone density, but little is known about repeated alcohol use or chronic alcohol affects and calcitonin.

In men, gonadal hormones may also play a role in alcohol-induced bone disease because impaired gonadal function is a well-known risk factor for osteoporosis. Moreover, alcohol abuse has long been associated with impotence, sterility, and testicular atrophy (Valimaki, Salaspuro & Ylikahri, 1982) and low testosterone (Van Thiel, Lester & Therins, 1974; Van Thiel, 1983). In women, menstrual disturbances, spontaneous abortions, and miscarriages and impaired fertility and sexual function, and premature menopause have been observed, but studies in women have yielded inconsistent results (Gavaler, 1991; Hugues et al., 1980; Mello, Mendelson & Teoh, 1993; Valimaki et al., 1984). Alcohol does increase estradiol, a potent form of estrogen, but this effect has only been reported in postmenopausal women on hormone replacement therapy. Nonetheless, if moderate alcohol consumption increases estrogen, it could explain the positive relationship between alcohol use and increased bone density in women (Holbrook and Barrett-Connor, 1993; Orwoll et al., 1996).

Chronic heavy drinking alters the growth and proliferation of many different cell types. In alcoholics, biochemical and histomorphometric studies reveal a significant impairment in osteoblastic, but not osteoclastic, activity. (For a more detailed review of the effects of alcohol on cell proliferation, DNA acid and related consequences, *see* Brick 2006.)

Although the effects of environmental toxins associated with cancer and other diseases is beyond the scope of this book, in forensic cases, examination of evidence of suspected toxin-related diseases should include other potential contributing factors. In this context, environmental toxicologists involved in toxic tort litigation should be aware that the relationship between alcohol consumption and various cancers of the gastrointestinal and other systems has been the subject of considerable research. This may be particularly useful since, in the absence of scientific input, courts often struggle with admitting and excluding evidence of causality.

Alcohol and Cancer

Several studies have demonstrated a positive relationship between alcohol and esophageal cancer, which may be a factor in civil litigation. People who consume more than three drinks per day (twenty one drinks per week) have almost a tenfold higher risk of esophageal cancer than do those who drink less than one drink per day (Vaughan, Davis, Kristal, & Thomas, 1995). Different types of carcinomas are related by the local effects of alcohol metabolites or alcohol-metabolizing enzymes such as ADH on esophageal cells (Yin et al., 1993). It has been suggested that acetaldehyde, the main metabolite of alcohol, may alter normal DNA repair mechanisms in esophageal cells, and lead to gene alterations and tumor formation (Wilson, Tenrler, Carney, F. Wilson & Kelly, 1994). Alcohol also increases levels of the CYP2E 1 isozyme in the esophageal mucosa, which can activate dietary carcinogens such as nitrosamines (Shimizu, Lasker, Toutsumi & Lieber, 1990).

Despite the high concentrations of alcohol reaching the stomach from the esophagus, and the effects of alcohol consumption or alcohol metabolites on DNA, alcohol use is not clearly associated with a risk of stomach cancer (Franceschi & La Vecchia, 1994). Alcohol does cause gastritis, but other factors, such as bacterium, may be responsible for inflammation of the stomach or gastritis (Paunio et al., 1994; Uppal, Lateaf, Korsten, Parnetto & Lieber, 1991).

The decrease in absorption of nutrients by alcohol probably plays some role in alcohol-related colon cancer in humans. Alcohol in combination with diets low in essential nutrients such as methionine and folate measurably increase the risk for colon cancer (Giovannucci & Willett, 1994; Giovannucci et al., 1995). Alcohol also induces the formation of benign hyperplastic polyps in the colon and rectum in humans (Kearney et al., 1995).

The association between alcohol and cancers of the colon and rectum is positive, but weak (Doll, Foreman, La Vecchia & Woutersen, 1993; Longnecker, 1992; Longnecker, Orza, Adams, Viogue & Chalmers, 1990; Seitz & Pöschl, 1997). Again, although alcohol probably plays some role, other mechanisms are probably involved. Recent studies indicate that smoking tobacco coupled with drinking alcohol may serve as a triggering mechanism for colon cancer (Yamada et al., 1997). Acetaldehyde may also have a role as a co-carcinogen in cases of rectal cancer (Seitz and Pöschl, 1997).

Alcohol increases the risk for breast cancer, but reviews of this relationship suggest that the evidence for effect is not compelling (English et al., 1995; International Agency for Research on Cancer, 1988, Longnecker, 1992, 1994; McPherson, Engelsman, & Conning, 1993; Smith Warner et al., 1998). One factor may be that a complex alcohol–endocrine interaction exists that may be related to post-menopause hormone replacement therapy (Colditz, 1990; Gapstur, Potter, Sellers & Folson, 1992; Schatzkin & Longnecker, 1994; Zumoff, 1997).

Pancreatic Injury

It is fairly well-known that alcohol abuse can lead to chronic pancreatic inflammation, atrophy, and fibrosis, although only a small proportion of alcoholics develop pancreatic injury (Haber, Wilson, Apte, Korsten & Pirola, 1995; Doll et al., 1993). Although alcohol is believed to be a cause of pancreatitis, the link between alcohol and pancreatic cancer has not been made (NIAAA, 2000).

Alcohol-Induced Liver Injury

Since pharmacokinetic analyses regarding alcohol use and intoxication rely upon assumptions about alcohol metabolism, knowledge of the long-term effects of alcohol abuse is critical. Most of the alcohol leaves the gastrointestinal tract; it travels via the hepatic portal vein from the small intestines to the liver, the largest organ in the body and the primary site of alcohol metabolism. The formation of toxic alcohol metabolites may deleteriously affect many cells throughout the body. Because the concentration of alcohol reaching the liver is so high, and the liver is the primary site of alcohol metabolism, liver damage may be among the most serious physiological consequences of alcohol abuse. This is particularly significant because of the central role the liver plays in so many physiological activities including assumed rates of metabolism used in BAC calculations. Epidemiological data clearly reveal that alcohol abuse is by far, the leading cause of liver-related mortality in the United States. Excessive alcohol consumption leads to three serious types of liver injury: fatty liver, hepatic inflammation (alcoholic hepatitis), and progressive liver scarring (fibrosis or cirrhosis). Chronic heavy drinking can alter normal metabolism and lead to an accumulation of fat in the liver. As a result, the liver cells become infiltrated and the liver itself becomes enlarged.

Extensive lipid infiltration may damage cells. Whereas fatty liver is reversible with abstinence, hepatitis is a more serious medical condition, characterized by prolific inflammation and tissue damage. Hepatitis is life threatening but there is significant recovery following abstinence. The most serious form of liver damage is cirrhosis. This liver disease is characterized by scarring and cell death and is irreversible. Impaired liver functioning can cause primary hepatic encephalopathy, a brain disorder characterized by altered psychomotor, intellectual, and behavioral functioning.

Although chronic, heavy drinking may produce metabolic tolerance and unusually high rates of alcohol elimination, hepatitis, and fibrosis, ultimately it will impair liver function to produce a reverse metabolic tolerance and impaired oxidation of alcohol. Under reporting of alcohol consumption makes the exact prevalence of alcoholic liver disease in the United States difficult to measure, but health statistics suggest that some form of alcoholic liver disease affects more than 2 million drinkers (Dufour, Stinson & Caces, 1993). It is estimated that 900,000 people have cirrhosis, and of the 26,000 who die each year, 40 to 90 percent have a history of alcohol abuse (Dufour et al., 1993).

How Much Drinking Will Cause Liver Damage?

It is clear that the development of alcoholic liver disease is due to a combination of factors, most notably prolonged alcohol consumption. One question commonly asked by forensic examiners, other scientists, and concerned drinkers is "How much alcohol is needed to cause liver damage?" Epidemiological studies suggest that reliable signs of injury begin after a threshold dose of alcohol is reached. Although there are always individual exceptions, the evidence suggests that the threshold is equal to a cumulative dose of about 600 kg for men and between 150 and 300 kg for women. To place this in perspective, at the high end (for men), this is roughly equivalent to an average consumption of 10 to 12 drinks a day for ten years, and at the low end (for women), about three drinks per day (*see* Chapter 11 for drink calculations). Below these doses, it is difficult to reliably detect liver injury (Lelbach, 1975;

Marbet, Bianchi, Meury & Stalder, 1987; Mezey, Kolman, Diehl, Mitchell & Herlong, 1988; Tuyns & Pequignot, 1984), or the damage is not significant enough to warrant medical attention. The difference in a threshold dose between men and women cannot be accounted for by anthropometrics or pharmacokinetics. In addition, many individuals who consume this amount of alcohol never develop liver disease and less than one half of heavy drinkers develop alcoholic hepatitis or liver fibrosis (Lelbach, 1975). This suggests that alcohol does not produce its effects independently and that hereditary, or environmental factors, or both, interact with alcohol to affect the natural history of liver injury (Marbet et al., 1987). Marbet suggested that other factors contribute to the pathogenesis of liver disease in alcoholics because even though a substantial amount of alcohol is required to induce liver injury, alcohol dose alone is not a good predictor of the severity of liver injury (Marbet et al., 1987).

There are numerous possible mechanisms that may affect the susceptibility of certain people to alcohol-induced liver damage, but the exact mechanisms by which chronic alcohol abuse leads to liver disease are not known.

Gender also may play a role in the development of alcohol-induced liver damage. Some evidence indicates that women are more susceptible than men are to the cumulative effects of alcohol on the liver (Becker et al., 1996; Gavaler & Arria, 1995; Hisatomi, Kumashiro, Sata, Ishii & Tanikawa, 1997; Naveau et al., 1997; NIAAA, 1997), even though women drink less than men. Compared with men, women who have alcoholic liver injury remain at higher risk of disease progression even with abstinence (Galambos, 1972; Pares, Caballeria, Bruguera, Torres & Rodes, 1986). This curious gender difference suggests that gastric ADH may be a causative factor. ADH is present in high levels in the liver in both men and women, but there are differences in gastrointestinal ADH between men and women that may affect its bioavailability. Women have lower levels of gastric ADH activity than men have (Frezia et al., 1990; Seitz, Simanowski, Egener, Waldherr & Oertl, 1992), so their liver receives more concentrated levels of alcohol from the gut, thereby placing women at greater risk for liver damage. Although this is an interesting concept, other investigators have found no such gender differences in gastric ADH activity (Thuluvath, Wojo, Yardley & Mezey, 1994), and some researchers question the significance of the stomach in the first-pass metabolism of alcohol (Levitt & Levitt, 1994).

Since the liver is the primary organ involved in the metabolism of alcohol, liver damage should be a consideration in alcohol calculations of alcohol use and intoxication (Chapter 11). However, the liver is a remarkably adaptive organ. Even relatively short periods of alcohol use cause up-regulation of alcohol metabolizing enzyme systems resulting in more efficient metabolism of alcohol. Although it is possible that liver damage will eventually decrease the ability of the body to metabolize alcohol, research administering alcohol to alcoholics with liver pathologies is unlikely to pass institutional review boards that protect human subjects in research. In cases in which liver damage or chronic heavy drinking is known, any pharmacokinetic analyses should include a wide range of elimination rates to account for increased or decreased enzyme efficiency.

There is some evidence that cirrhosis is linked to beverage type. Razvodovsky (2015) examined vodka, beer, and wine sales and found that liver cirrhosis dropped significantly and was highly correlative with decreased vodka sales following prevention campaigns aimed at reducing liquor consumption. No similar changes were observed with beer and wine sales and cirrhosis mortality. More research on this subject is needed.

Cardiovascular Diseases

Cardiovascular diseases are the leading cause of deaths among Americans followed by cancer and stroke (U.S. Department of Health and Human Services, 1995). The role of alcohol as both a risk factor and a potential protective factor for cardiovascular disease has been the focus of intense investigation for many years (*see*, for example, NIAAA, 1997) (Zakhari & Wassef, 1996). The results are clear: alcohol has both deleterious and beneficial effects, but the conditions under which alcohol exerts this unusual behavior, its effects, and the mechanisms involved are complex at best.

Alcohol and Blood Pressure

There is a well-documented association between heavy alcohol consumption and hypertension (Ascherio et al., 1996; Campbell, Ashley, Carruthers, Lacourciére, & McKay, 1999; Seppa, Laippla & Sillanaukee, 1996; York & Hirsch, 1997). Heavy alcohol consumption elevates blood pressure, and causes or exacerbates hypertension (Puddey, Beilin, Vandongen, Rouse & Rogers, 1995; Ueshima et al., 1993). It is estimated that one drink a day can chronically increase blood pressure 1 mm Hg in middle-aged individuals, and even more in the elderly and in people with preexisting hypertension (Beilin, Puddey & Burke, 1996). Controversy remains as to whether moderate alcohol consumption has any beneficial effects on blood pressure, but reducing alcohol intake may be one means of reducing blood pressure in people with hypertension (Lang, Nicaud, Darné & Rueff 1995; World Health Organization, 1996). However, patients who consume one drink each evening for 7 days had blood pressure that seesawed; it was low in the evening and increased in the morning (Abe et al., 1994), suggesting that regular consumption of alcohol can raise blood pressure during the hours that alcohol is not consumed. These findings are consistent with observations that sympathetic nervous system-induced activity increases blood pressure during alcohol withdrawal (Denison, Jern, Jagenburg, Wandestam & Wallerstedt, 1997). Of forensic consideration is that the long-term elevating effects of chronic alcohol on blood pressure may be a confounding factor producing false positives in a Drug Recognition Evaluation (DRE) performed by police that uses blood pressure as a bioindicator for the presence of psychoactive drugs.

Conversely, moderate alcohol consumption (about 1 to 3 drinks per day) is associated with a slight reduction in blood pressure or may protect against age-related development of hypertension (Gillman, Cook, Evans, Rosner, Hennekens, 1995; Palmer et al., 1995). The significance of these findings may be offset by an increased risk of death from causes unrelated to cardiovascular disease (e.g., accidental injuries, liver disease).

There is also evidence that the increased blood pressure associated with alcohol use is related to alcohol withdrawal rather than a direct effect of alcohol. Kawano and colleagues (1996) found that a single drink of alcohol depresses the blood pressure of patients with hypertension for several hours.

Thermal Injuries

Thermal injuries place a significant sociomedicoeconomic burden on individual patients, their families, and society. Often such injuries are the subject of an arson investigation or related forensic investigation. Evidence of alcohol intoxication in such cases should be carefully considered because of the well-known effects of intoxication on behavior. In a review of this literature, Brick (2006) concluded that there is a clear relationship between intoxication and risk for thermal injuries because of impaired judgment or diminished psychomotor skills. "While intoxicated, the ability to anticipate problems, decreased inhibitions and lack of responsible behavior are typical side effects for many drugs, including alcohol" (p. 250). The ability to respond to emergency situations is impaired, particularly in highly intoxicated persons. Mental confusion or failure to anticipate and identify danger are well-known effects of intoxication that may apply to fire-related injuries as well.

Howland and Hingson (1987) examined thirty two studies of alcohol and injuries and deaths attributed to fires and burns. Of these, nine studies were deemed descriptive enough to make comparisons. From eight of the nine studies it was concluded that alcohol exposure was more likely among those who died in fires started by cigarette smoking. In this early but extensive review, the authors concluded that intoxication was a factor in both the cause of fires and the burn injuries.

Haum and coworkers (1995) retrospectively investigated acute alcohol intoxication and drinking history, injuries, and risk factors in two studies. In the first study of 225 acutely, severely burned patients, the 30 percent who were positive for alcohol on admission also had significantly higher fatality rates compared to sober controls, even though they were matched for age and total burn surface area. Chronic alcohol abusers also had a higher fatality rate than did patients without a history of chronic alcohol abuse but there was no difference in mortality between sober alcoholics and acutely intoxicated alcoholics. Therefore, long-lasting neurological or other consequences of alcohol abuse may be an independent risk factor in such clinical populations. For example, Berry, Patterson, Wachtel, and Frank (1984) examined the relationship between psychosocial factors, including psychiatric diagnoses, and burn mortality and length of hospitalization. A statistically significant increase in mortality was associated with diagnosed intoxication, personality disorder, and schizophrenia.

McGill, Kowal-Vern, Kahn, and Gamelli (1995) examined 1074 medical center burn patients admitted for treatment. Of these, blood alcohol or urine tests for other drugs (cannabinoids, cocaine metabolite, amphetamines, phencyclidine and benzodiazepines) were positive in 40 percent of the subjects. Patients who used drugs other than alcohol had significantly greater inhalation injury, total burn surface area, and mortality rates compared with controls, but alcohol use patients had more injury from fire and greater incidence of smoke inhalation. Intoxicated patients were exposed to more injury from flame, had greater proportion of bodily burns than controls, and had significantly greater incidence of smoke inhalation than did controls. Moreover, intoxicated patients were six times more likely to die from their injuries than were controls and twice as likely to die compared to patients who were positive for other drugs. The authors found that four factors best predicted mortality: age, inhalation injury, percentage of total burn surface area, and alcohol intoxication.

Barillo, Rush, and Goode (1986) examined fatal residential fires of victims found in bed with no apparent effort to escape. In these victims, the average BAC was 268 mg/dL. In comparison, the BAC in victims found adjacent to an exit (apparently attempting to escape) was about 88 mg/dL. No significant difference in blood carboxyhemoglobin and cyanide concentrations was found between highly intoxicated victims who died in bed and less intoxicated victims found adjacent to an exit.

In a later study, Barillo and Goode (1996) examined records of the Office of the Medical Examiner in New Jersey and found 727 fire victim fatalities over a seven-year period. Nearly 30 percent (29.5) were positive for alcohol (mean BAC, 193.9 mg/dL). Physical infirmaries due to age were probably unlikely because about 58 percent of alcohol-positive fatalities were relatively young (ages 21 to 50), suggesting that cognitive, psychomotor, and other faculties were impaired by high BACs rather than age-related impairment.

In a particularly interesting study, Jones, Barber, Engrav, and Heimbach (1991) examined burn records of patients for acute alcohol intoxication, alcohol abuse, morbidity, and mortality. Twenty seven percent of patients met the definition of acute intoxication (defined as 100 mg/dL) even though the average BAC was 268 mg/dL and 90 percent of the patients were classified as chronic alcoholics. Chronic alcohol abuse was defined as consumption of more than 6 oz of alcohol per day, admission BAC at more than 250 mg/dL, previous diagnosis of alcoholism, and previous admission for alcoholism or alcohol related injury within the last 12 months. The mortality rate among alcoholic burn patients was 46 percent higher compared to nonalcoholic burn controls, even though control patients had higher total burn surface areas.

McGill and associates (1995) studied 398 burn patients, 40 percent of whom were positive in a drug screen for alcohol and other drugs (cannabinoids, cocaine metabolites, amphetamines, phencyclidine, and benzodiazepine). There was no difference between alcohol users and drug users who were similar in sex, age, inhalation injury, type of burn injury, and percentage of total burn surface area. However, alcohol-using subjects had six times the mortality of sober controls and twice the mortality of drug-using patients. The best independent predictors of mortality in burn patients were age, inhalation injury, percentage of total burn surface area, and alcohol use.

Burn injuries can result in changes in the pharmacokinetic and pharmacodynamic action of alcohol, which may have forensic implications. For example, traditional treatment for decreased cardiac output following thermal injuries is exogenous fluid replenishment to compensate for deficiencies in circulation. In most drinkers, stress-induced changes affect alcohol metabolism due to an increased activity of the liver cytoplasmic enzyme ADH rather than through mitochondrial respiratory chain activity. In alcoholics, however, alcohol metabolism shifts to the microsomal (P4502E1) ethanol oxidizing system (Mezey, 1983; Mezey, Potter & Kvetnansky, 1979). This is relevant because burn patients may have decreased mitochondrial respiratory chain activity, catecholamine-induced increased oxygen consumption, protein catabolism, and other physiological shifts in metabolism that may include increased liver metabolic activity. Several studies suggest that alcohol metabolism is increased in burn patients. Such changes have forensic implications and must be considered in any pharmacokinetic analyses.

In a unique study of eight patients in a National Burns Unit in Sweden, Zdolsek, Sjoberg, Lisander, and Jones, (1999) administered alcohol to subjects who sustained 18 to 72 percent total burn surface area injuries and measured their rate of elimination over time. Subjects were neither heavy drinkers nor did they have any liver diseases. Alcohol elimination increased from Day 1 and continued to increase slightly through Day 7, post burn injury. The average of elimination in alcohol-treated burn patients was approximately twice that of controls subjects. This dramatic effect could reflect enhanced metabolism, enhanced elimination of unmetabolized alcohol, or both. Fluid loss in burn patients did not decrease alcohol concentrations in the blood, suggesting the enhanced alcohol metabolism between burn patients and controls was due to a hypermetabolic state. The direction of these results is similar to an earlier study (Jones, Zdolsek, Sjoberg and Lisander, 1997).

Immune System

The effect of alcohol intoxication on the immune system may also have forensic implications if death occurred secondary to alcohol-induced immune system weakness. Acute alcohol use impairs the immune system through various mechanisms, including complications from alcohol on leukocyte production and granulocytes (MacGregor, 1986; MacGregor, Gluckman & Senior, 1978). Alcohol exposure prior to burn injury suppresses cellular immune responses and elevates immunosuppressive cytokines such as interleukin-6, resulting in immune system dysfunction (Faunce, Gregory & Kovacs, 1998a,b). Choudhry and colleagues (2000) found that rodents dosed to 100 mg/dL then exposed to burn injury showed a significant (20%–25%) decrease in splenic T-cell proliferation and 45 to 50 percent decrease in interleukin-2 (IL-2) production. Alcohol treatment also exacerbated the decrease in the proliferation and production of IL-2 in T cells. The authors concluded that attenuated immunity from decreases in T cells may further enhance susceptibility to infection. The immunosuppressive effects of alcohol in preclinical burn studies have been also reported for increased immunosuppressive effects of cytokine interleukin-6 (Colatoni et al., 2000) as well as other immune system responses (Fontanilla et al., 2000; Napolitano et al., 1995).

9.6 YEARS OF POTENTIAL LIFE LOST

Alcohol-attributable deaths and YPLL is a factor in estimating economic loss and is of interest to economists or others performing such analyses in litigation. As the third leading cause of preventable death in the United States, the adverse health consequences of excessive alcohol use (e.g., motor vehicle and related injuries, violence, liver damage, cancer) and the YPLL due to alcohol are staggering. The Centers for Disease Control and Prevention (2004) reports that the approximately 75,000 alcohol-attributable deaths per year (from all causes) equate to 2.3 million YPLL or about 30 years of life lost on average per alcohol-attributable fatality.

9.7 ANTEMORTEM AND POSTMORTEM SAMPLING

Blood and Other Tissues and Fluids

Antemortem and postmortem samples of body fluids or tissues should be routinely submitted for toxicological examination, particularly in serious and all fatal accidents in which alcohol use is suspected. In the course of a fatal accident investigation, many factors, including temporal evidence, anthropometric data, sample collection, toxicology test results, and consideration of potential interfering medical conditions, should be considered. Postmortem examination of alcohol (and drugs) in the human body offers an opportunity to complete a biobehavioral autopsy to determine amount of alcohol consumed and reasonable estimates of intoxication at various times prior to death and, in some cases, cause of death. Proper interpretation of alcohol concentrations in body fluids such as blood, serum, vitreous humor, and gastric contents, as well as tissue from the brain, are part of the overall evaluation of forensic alcohol cases.

Temporal Evidence – When to Collect Samples

In all cases, temporal elements are important to fully interpret toxicology findings. Collection of subjective evidence from witnesses as to when and where the decedent was drinking alcohol is valuable. Time or distance from the last known drinking location should be determined when possible. In some states (e.g., New Jersey), the Division of Alcohol Beverage Control collects data about the last known drinking establishment to assist in administrative code enforcement. Most state and municipal police crash reports provide information about when police dispatch was notified and include a reported time of accident. Interviews with witnesses may be helpful in cases where there was a delay between the accident and the time it was reported, but caution should be exercised in collecting such information from traumatized witnesses because of stress-induced time distortion that often accompanies horrific events. The investigator's use of a structured time sequence interview may help establish an accurate account of what happened, where it happened, and when it happened. Interviewers should start with broad inquiries of the preceding events summarizing the responses to the interviewee then returning to each event to fill in more detail.

Clearly note the time of death of the AIP. Unlike some other drugs (e.g., cocaine), after death there is limited continued distribution of alcohol from the blood to extravascular sites liver function is suppressed and for all practical purposes alcohol elimination stops. Therefore, the time of death is useful in determining an end point after which no further metabolism occurs. In some cases, the official time of death bears no resemblance to the actual time of death. The official (legal) time of death signifies the time that death was pronounced, usually by a medical examiner or other type of physician. Investigators at the scene should note the presence or absence of life signs (e.g., breathing, pulse, and reaction and diameter of the pupil), as should forensic examiners reviewing police or medical records.

Toxicology Evidence: Blood Tests

In a relatively uncompromised physiological state, and when the body is more or less intact, blood is the preferred source for forensic evaluations. The reason for this is both logical and convenient. Virtually all clinical research relating biobehavioral changes subsequent to alcohol ingestion is based on blood alcohol testing (or reliable breath tests designed to accurately reflect BAC). Also, legislative initiatives setting forth legal limits express the alcohol concentrations in terms of blood (BAC). Most clinical laboratories and some forensic law enforcement labs measure drugs, other than alcohol, in urine because samples can be procured with little training and a minimum amount of equipment. The interpretation of urine alcohol alone has limited forensic value other than to confirm alcohol use.

There are several sources of blood, each with advantages and disadvantages. Both the antemortem and postmortem physiological state may alter the interpretation of blood test results. For example, if severe hemorrhaging occurred prior to death, hemodilution may have occurred as a result of two factors: physiological change and medical intervention. In cases of severe shock, blood loss and the consequent loss of blood pressure set into motion a range of compensatory and interventive mechanisms to restore lost fluid and maintain blood pressure. One relevant and interesting physiological change is the release of extravascular fluids back into the circulation. Such diffusion will dilute the existing blood alcohol. In animals bled to death, hemodilution (as a result of this homeostatic mechanism) is measurable within minutes, but unlikely to be quantifiable in forensic cases.

Another but more significant source of hemodilution is medical intervention. Low blood pressure or pulse is problematic, necessitating an increase in fluid volume. Blood pressure is restored by administering exogenous fluids. The most common infusates are Ringer's lactate (RL) and normal saline (NS). This intervention may solve the cardiovascular problem but has the additional physiological consequence of diluting alcohol in the circulation much more than by compensatory physiological mechanisms. For this reason, if avoidable, blood samples for forensic evaluations should not be taken from the same indwelling catheters used to administer RL or NS.

In many hospitals, clinical measurement of alcohol is in serum, rather than whole blood, but this varies widely among states. For example, in New Jersey, virtually all hospitals measure alcohol in serum, whereas in Pennsylvania, hospitals can be certified by the Department of Health to measure alcohol in serum, whole blood, or both. Alcohol toxicology experts need to determine if alcohol was measured in serum or whole blood and make the appropriate conversion to account for the higher alcohol content in serum.

When samples are collected under relatively normal physiological conditions, changes in the water content of the blood can be estimated using well-known serum:blood ratios. In the case of severe shock, medical treatment may also include the aggressive administration of RL, NS, or packed red blood cells. When the blood volume is so altered, physiological calculations may become increasingly complex to perform. However, since alcohol is distributed throughout the watery portions of the body, the blood being only one part of the total volume of distribution, interpretations of its measurements are less likely to be significantly affected by either endogenous or exogenous fluid changes. Nevertheless, when hemodilution occurs from aggressive exogenous fluid administration, the percentage of water in the sample should be calculated to give the most accurate whole blood alcohol equivalent for that individual. These calculations are explained in Chapter 11.

Thus, the importance of collecting medical treatment as well as toxicological information to evaluate the role alcohol or other drugs play in a fatal accident, for example, cannot be overstated.

9.8 COLLECTION OF SAMPLES

Toxicological samples to determine the concentration of alcohol in living subjects can be determined by blood, breath, or serum alcohol samples. In deceased subjects, postmortem samples may be obtained from several sources, including ventricles of the heart, pericardium, peritoneal cavity, arteries, veins, vitreous humor, brain, stomach, urine, and bile. The advantages and disadvantages of each are discussed briefly in what follows.

Fluid or tissue samples should be collected using approved evidence collection kits currently available from commercial vendors particularly if samples are to be stored. These kits contain antioxidants and preservatives to maintain sample stability. The following sample collection tubes and their corresponding tube top and contents are shown in Table 9.2.

Postmortem Blood Sample Collection

The investigation of a fatal injury routinely involves the collection of postmortem samples for toxicological analyses. Unlike some other drugs

Table 9.2: Identification of Blood Collection Table of Contents.

Test Tube Top	Description of Use
Gold or "tiger" red/black top	Clot activator and gel for serum separation.
Red top, plastic tubes	Contains a clot activator and is used when serum is needed.
Orange or grey/yellow "tiger"	Contains thrombin, a rapid clot activator, for STAT serum testing.
Green	Contains sodium heparin used for plasma determinations.
Light green or green/gray "tiger"	For plasma determinations in chemistry.
Purple or lavender	Contains ethylenediaminetetraacetic acid (EDTA) (the potassium salt, or K_2EDTA), anticoagulant. Lavender top tubes are generally used when whole blood is needed for analysis.
Grey	Fluoride or sodium chloride, and oxalate. Fluoride prevents enzymes in the blood from working, so a substrate such as glucose will not be gradually used up during storage. Oxalate is an anticoagulant.
Light blue	Citrate (reversible anticoagulant), and these tubes are used for coagulation assays.
Dark blue	Contains sodium heparin, an anticoagulant. Also may contain EDTA. Tubes used for trace metal analysis.
Pink	Similar to purple tubes (both contain EDTA); these are used for blood banking.

(Pelissier-Alicot, Gaulier, Champsaur & Marquet 2003; Pounder & Jones, 1990) alcohol has relatively little postmortem redistribution. Unless a victims dies with a large amount of alcohol in their stomach so that postmortem diffusion of alcohol results, the concentration of alcohol postmortem reasonably reflects the antemortem concentration. Nevertheless, some anatomical sites are preferred or have specific advantages over others; other sites may create potential problems in the interpretation of intoxication case evidence. There is a difference between a potential problem and a determination that a sampling error or problem actually existed, however.

Cardiac Blood

The heart is generally an acceptable source for postmortem blood samples in alcohol cases. In such instances, postmortem blood should be drawn from the right ventricle and for two reasons. First, to avoid possible contamination by passively diffused alcohol from the stomach. Following the normal

pathway for blood returning to the heart, if large amounts of unabsorbed alcohol are present in the gut, it may diffuse to the left ventricle of the heart.
Second, blood in the left ventricle may also have a higher glucose content.
Under conditions of stress, the liver increases glucose availability. The heart
(left ventricle) is the first organ to receive this "sugar boost" and the most
likely site for endogenous fermentation of alcohol if certain requisite conditions are met. Although unlikely under most sampling conditions, high sugar
in blood provides a necessary ingredient for the endogenous formation of alcohol that may occur under certain unusual circumstances. Postmortem putrefaction and endogenous ethanol are discussed elsewhere in this chapter.

Femoral Artery

The femoral artery is the preferred site to obtain postmortem blood samples. This artery is sufficiently large as to provide relatively easy access of
blood, and it is sufficiently distanced from the gastrointestinal tract to minimize contamination from diffusion, should that occur postmortem. Toxicological results are not known *a priori*. In cases in which drugs other than
alcohol are involved, a femoral vessel is the preferred anatomical site for a
blood sample because of the potential of postmortem redistribution.

Pericardium

Although blood is easily obtained from the pericardial sac, diffusion of
high concentrations of alcohol from the gastrointestinal system may compromise samples taken from this area. When a syringe is used to draw blood
from the heart through the closed chest, pericardial fluid may inadvertently
be collected, and thus potentially contaminate the sample. Generally, blood
samples from the pericardium are not desirable. A blind cardiac puncture
therefore should be avoided (Coe, 1993).

Pooled Blood

Blood pooled in the peritoneal cavity provides an opportunity to obtain
fluid samples, particularly if coagulation of blood in other areas has occurred
or there is extensive injury to preclude obtaining blood from other sites.
However, two potential problems present themselves with pooled blood samples: contamination from diffusion through the gastrointestinal system and
the possibility of a higher concentration of alcohol because of partial coagulation. Generally, pooled blood samples are not desirable if there is any indication of contamination or partial coagulation. Alcohol in coagulated pooled
blood may be more like serum alcohol. If so, blood alcohol may need to be

treated like serum equivalents and reconverted to whole BAC. The medical examiner makes this determination at autopsy and notates it.

Vitreous Humor

Vitreous humor is the fluid within the eyeball and is easily accessible. Vitreous humor is often sampled when there is extensive damage to other sample sites or other sample sites may be contaminated (e.g., lacerated or punctured stomach or heart). The vitreous humor is relatively isolated from changes that might result from passive diffusion of alcohol or endogenous alcohol formation after death, (Backer, Pisano & Sopher, 1980; Caplan & Levine, 1990). The partition coefficient between the vitreous humor and whole blood is similar at equilibrium. Because of differences in diffusion, vitreous alcohol is usually lower than whole blood alcohol during active absorption and more slowly eliminated than alcohol directly in the circulation is. However, Jones and Holmgren (2001) and Pounder and Kuroda (1994) reported that the postmortem variation between vitreous humor and blood alcohol was too great to be of forensic use and that caution should be exercised in estimating peripheral BAC from vitreous alcohol and the limitations of such an approach should be explained when sample availability is limited.

In a review of this literature, Kugelberg and Jones (2007) concluded that vitreous humor is "strongly recommended as a body fluid" for determination of antemortem alcohol use but still cautioned against using vitreous alcohol alone to estimate BAC.

Brain

Samples of cortical tissue provide another relevant source from which to measure alcohol, particularly when other sites are compromised. The alcohol content of brain homogenate can also be tested using headspace gas chromatography. Like the vitreous humor, brain tissue is relatively isolated from changes that might result from passive diffusion of alcohol, loss of blood, or other sources of contamination after death. Because of the differences in water content between brain and blood, brain alcohol is usually about 15 percent lower than in whole blood. Care must be exerted to avoid taking brain samples with large vascularities.

Stomach

Gastric contents (fluid or chyme) can also be analyzed for their alcohol (and other drug) contents. Although such samples have no quantitative relationship to impairment produced by the drug, they do provide potentially valuable information subsequent to pharmacokinetic analysis. Generally, alcohol concentrations greater than 1 percent suggest alcohol ingestion just prior to death (i.e., less than 2 hours earlier). Alcohol concentrations below this level indicate that alcohol was probably consumed within several hours prior to death in the post-absorption phase (Brick, 2000).

Bile

The concentration of alcohol in the bile, although useful in establishing relatively recent alcohol or other drug use, has no other advantage. There is a relationship between bile and blood alcohol concentrations, but the range is quite large. Assay results from bile alone cannot be accurately related to known behavioral effects of alcohol except at near lethal concentrations (Jones, 2014).

Urine

The concentration of alcohol in the urine, although useful in establishing relatively recent alcohol use, also has no other advantage. The relationship between urine and BAC varies, and assay results from urine also cannot be accurately related to known behavioral effects of alcohol with the possible exception of extremely high alcohol concentrations.

Other Postmortem Considerations

Because of the potential for sample contamination, endogenous alcohol formation, and postmortem redistribution, in postmortem cases, the collection of samples from more than one site is recommended. For example, the absence of alcohol in vitreous humor or brain with the presence of a high BAC is suggestive of sample contamination or endogenous alcohol fermentation. To avoid such potential problems, samples from more than one anatomical site are preferred and should be obtained as soon as possible (Robertson, n.d.).

When conditions (e.g., putrefaction) are present that are conducive to endogenous fermentation, alcohol can be formed about 24 hours after death. Even so, rapid sample collection is particularly important in fatal thermal injury cases because microflora deposits from the environment may enter the body through open tissue and result in endogenous alcohol formation. Nanikawa and Kotoku (1971).

Finally, postmortem blood or other tissue samples should be analyzed using gas chromatography and not the ADH enzyme method (*see* Chapter 9 for a discussion of analytical tests for alcohol). However, because burn fatalities can result in the formation of other alcohols, including butanol, acetone, methanol, 1-propanol, and 2-propanol (Canfield, Kupiec & Huffine, 1993), n-propanol should not be used as an internal standard in gas chromatography sample analyses from burn victims. Also, since n-propanol does not occur naturally, the presence of this alcohol in a postmortem sample is a good marker for postmortem alcohol formation.

Microscopic Evaluations

Whenever possible, histological samples should be obtained. For example, fatty liver (stenosis), liver inflammation (hepatitis), or other anomalies may suggest a history of chronic, heavy alcohol abuse.

Summary

In summary, alcohol intoxication causes a number of acute and chronic medical consequences of importance in the interpretation of forensic evidence. Intoxication may cause accidental mechanical injuries (e.g., motor vehicle crashes, falls, etc.), tissue damage (blood, liver, etc), biochemical changes (enzymes, cytokines), organ (heart, liver), and skeletal damage that may have forensic and other implications. Antemortem and postmortem physiological changes must also be considered to properly interpret alcohol test evidence. Many of the potential sampling and postmortem problems can be avoided or minimized by taking tissue samples from more than one anatomical location and describing any postmortem changes (e.g., putrefaction) or observations and the location from which a sample was obtained. As recommended elsewhere, a range of alcohol elimination rates should be applied to all forensic alcohol calculations, especially when evidence of organ changes are noted.

REFERENCES

Abe, H., Kawano, Y., Kojima, S., Ashida, T., Kuramochi, M., Matsuoka, H., and Omae, T. (1994). Biphasic effects of repeated alcohol intake on 24-hour blood pressure in hypertensive patients. *Circulation, 89*(6), 2626–2633.

Abeloos, J., Rolly, G., Timperman, J., and Watson, A. (1997). Anaesthetic and medicolegal problems in patients intoxicated by alcohol. *Medicine Science and the Law, 25*, 131–135, 1985.

Albin, M., and Bunegin, L. (1986). An experimental study of craniocerebral trauma during ethanol intoxication. *Critical Care Medicine, 14*, 841–846.

Anda, R., Williamson, D., and Remington, P. (1988). Alcohol and fatal injuries among U.S. adults: Findings from the NHANES I Epidemiologic Follow-up Study. *Journal of the American Medical Association, 260*, 2529–2532.

Anderson, T. (1986). Effects of acute alcohol intoxication on spinal cord vascular injury. *Central Nervous System Trauma, 3*, 183–192.

Arndt, T. (2000). Carbohydrate-deficient transferring as a marker of chronic alcohol abuse. A critical review of preanalysis, analysis and interpretation. *Clinical Chemistry, 47*(1), 13–27.

Ascherio, A., Hennekens, C., Willett, W., Sacks, F., Rosner, B., Manson, J., ..., Stampfer, M. (1996). Prospective study of nutritional factors, blood pressure, and hypertension among U.S. women. *Hypertension, 27*(5), 1065–1072.

Backer, R., Pisano, K., and Sopher, I. (1980). The comparison of alcohol concentrations in postmortem fluids and tissues. *Journal of Forensic Sciences, 25*(2), 327–331.

Barillo, D., and Goode, R. (1996). Substance abuse in victims. *Journal of Burn Care & Rehabilitation, 17*(1), 71–76.

Barillo, D., Rush, B., and Goode, R. (1986). Is ethanol the unknown toxin in smoke inhalation injury? *American Surgeon, 52*, 641–645.

Becker, U., Deis, A., Sorensen, T., Gronbaek, M., Borch-Johnsen, K., Muller, C., ..., Jensen, G. (1996). Prediction of risk of liver disease by alcohol intake, sex, and age: A prospective population study. *Hepatology, 23*(5), 1025–1029.

Beilin, L., Puddey, I., and Burke, V. (1996). Alcohol and hypertension–kill or cure? [Review]. *Journal of Human Hypertension, 10*(suppl. 2), S1–S5.

Berry, C., Patterson, T., Wachtel, T., and Frank, H. (1984). Behavioral factors in burn mortality and length of stay in hospital. *Burns, 10*, 409–414.

Bikle, D., Genant, H., Cann, C., Recker, R., Halloran, B., and Strewler, G. (1985). Bone disease in alcohol abuse. *Annals of Internal Medicine, 103*, 42–48.

Blaauw, R., Albertse, E. C., Beneke, T., Lombard, C. J., Laubscher, R., and Hough, F. S. (1994). Risk factors for the development of osteoporosis in a South African population: A prospective analysis. *South African Medical Journal, 84*(6), 328–332.

Brick, J. (2000). *Effect of Alcohol Pharmacokinetics on Blood: Brain Alcohol Ratio.* Presented at the 9th Annual Meeting of the America College of Forensic Examiners. Las Vegas, NV. October 14-19, 2000.

Brick, J. (2006). Interaction between toxicology and burn victim physiology. In A. Clark (Ed.), *Burns–The Medical and Forensic Model.* Tucson, AZ: Lawyers and Judges Publishing Company, 221–256.

Brismar, B., Engstrom, A., and Rydberg, U. (1983). Head injury and intoxication: A diagnostic and therapeutic dilemma. Acta *Chirurgiae Scandinavica, 149*, 11–14.

Campbell, N. R., Ashley, M. J., Carruthers, S. G., Lacourcière, Y., and McKay, D. W. (1999). Lifestyle modifications to prevent and control hypertension. 3. Recommendations on alcohol consumption. Canadian Hypertension Society, Canadian Coalition for High Blood Pressure Prevention and Control, Laboratory Centre for Disease Control at Health Canada, Heart and Stroke Foundation of Canada. *Canadian Medical Association Journal, 160*(suppl. 9), S13–S20.

Canfield, D., Kupiec, T., and Huffine, E. (1993). Postmortem alcohol production in fatal aircraft accidents. *Journal of Forensic Sciences, 38*(4), 914–917.

Caplan, Y., and Levine, B. (1990). Vitreous humor in the evaluation of postmortem ethanol concentrations. *Journal of Analytical Toxicology, 14*(5), 305–307.

Centers for Disease Control and Prevention. (2004). Alcohol-attributable deaths and years of potential life lost–United States, 2001. *MMWR. Morbidity and Mortality Weekly Report, 53*(37), 866–870.

Chanarin, A.Wul., and Levi, A. (1974). *Macrocytosis of chronic alcoholism.* Lancet, *303*(7862), 829–830.

Chang, G., and Astrachan, B. (1988). The emergency department surveillance of alcohol intoxication after motor vehicle accidents. *Journal of the American Medical Association, 260,* 2533–2536.

Chen, R., Fang, J., Lin, B., Hsu, Y., Kao, J., and Chen, M. (2000). Factors determining operative mortality of grade V blunt hepatic trauma. *Journal of Trauma, 49,* 886–891.

Choudhry, M., Messingham, K., Namak, S., Colantoni, A., Fontanilla, C., Duffner, L., …, Kovacs, E. (2000). Ethanol exacerbates T cell dysfunction after thermal injury. *Alcohol, 21*(3), 239–243.

Coe, J. (1993). Chemical consideration–factors for evaluating postmortem biochemistry. In W. Spitz (Ed.), *Spitz and Fisher's Medicolegal Investigation of Death: Guidelines for the Application of Pathology to Crime Investigation* (3rd ed.). Springfield, IL: Charles C Thomas Publisher, pp. 50–70.

Colatoni, A., Duffner, L., DeMaria, N., Fontanilla, C., Messingham, K., Van Thiel, D., and Kovacs, E. (2000). Dose-dependent effect of ethanol on hepatic oxidative stress and interleukin-6 production after burn injury in the mouse. *Alcoholism, Clinical and Experimental Research, 24*(9), 1443–1448.

Colditz, G. (1990). A prospective assessment of moderate alcohol intake and major chronic diseases. *Annals of Epidemiology, 1*(2), 167–177.

Conigrave, K., Davies, P., Haber, P., and Whitfield, J. (2003). Traditional markers of excessive alcohol use. *Addiction, 98*(suppl. 2), 31–43.

Conn, H. (1985). Natural history of complications of alcoholic liver disease. *Acta Medica Scandinavica, 703*(suppl.), 127–134.

Crilly, R., Anderson, C., Hogan, D., and Delaquerriére-Richardson, L. (1988). Bone histomorphometry, bone mass, and related parameters in alcoholic males. *Calcified Tissue International, 43,* 269–276.

Cumming, R., and Klineberg, R. (1994). Case-control study of risk factors for hip fractures in the elderly. *American Journal of Epidemiology, 139,* 493–503.

DeCrescito, V., Demopoulos, H., Flamm, E., and Ransohoff, J. (1974). Ethanol potentiation of traumatic cerebral edema. *Surgical Forum, 25,* 438–440.

Denison, J., Jern, S., Jagenburg, R., Wandestam, C., and Wallerstedt, S. (1997). ST segment changes and catecholamine-related myocardial enzyme release during alcohol withdrawal. *Alcohol and Alcoholism, 32*(2), 185–194.

Diamond, T., Stiel, D., Lunzer, M., Wilkinson, M., and Posen, S. (1989). Ethanol reduces bone formation and may cause osteoporosis. *American Journal of Medicine, 86,* 282–288.

Doll, R., Foreman, D., La Vecchia, D., and Woutersen, R. (1993). Alcoholic beverages and cancers or the digestive tract and larynx. In P. M. Verschuren (Ed.), *Health Issues Related to Alcohol Consumption* (pp. 125–166). Washington, D.C.: International Life Sciences Institute Press.

Dufour, M., Stinson, F., and Caces, M. (1993). Trends in cirrhosis morbidity and mortality: United States, 1979–1988. *Seminars in Liver Disease, 13*(2), 109–125.

Edwards, R. (1985). Anaesthesia and alcohol. *British Medical Journal, 291*, 423–424.

Elmer, O., Goransson, G., and Zoucas, E. (1984). Impairment of primary hemostasis and platelet function after alcohol ingestion in man. *Haemostasis, 14*, 223–228.

English, D., Holman, C., Milne, E., Winter, M., Hulse, G., Codde, G., ..., Ryan, G. (1995). *The Quantification of Drug Caused Morbidity and Mortality in Australia, 1992.* Canberra, Australia: Canberra Commonwealth Department of Human Services and Health.

Faunce, D., Gregory, M., and Kovacs, E. (1998a). Acute ethanol exposure prior to thermal injury results in decreased T-cell responses mediated in part by increased production of IL-6. *Shock, 10*, 135–140.

Faunce, D., Gregory, M., and Kovacs, E. (1998b). Glucocorticoids protect against suppression of T cell responses in a murine model of acute ethanol exposure and thermal injury by regulating IL-6. *Journal of Leukocyte Biology, 64*(6), 724–732.

Feitelberg, S., Epstein, S., Ismail, F., and D'Amanda, C. (1987). Deranged bone mineral metabolism in chronic alcoholism. *Metabolism, 36*, 322–326.

Fell, J., and Hertz, E. (1993). The effects of blood alcohol concentration on time of death for fatal crash victims. *Alcohol, Drugs and Driving, 9*(2), 97–106.

Felson, D., Kiel, D., Anderson, J., and Kannel, W. (1988). Alcohol consumption and hip fractures: The Framingham Study. *American Journal of Epidemiology, 128*, 1102–1110.

Fontanilla, C., Faunce, D., Gregory, M., Messingham, K., Durbin, E., Duffner, L., and Kovacs, E. (2000). Anti-interleukin-6 antibody treatment restores cell-mediated immune function in mice with acute ethanol exposure before burn trauma. *Alcoholism, Clinical and Experimental Research, 24*(9), 1392–1399.

Franceschi, S., and La Vecchia, C. (1994). Alcohol and the risk of cancers of the stomach and colon-rectum. *Digestive Diseases, 12*(5), 276–289.

Frezia, M., di Padova, C., Pozzato, G., Terpin, M., Baraona, E., and Lieber, C. S. (1990). High blood alcohol levels in women: The role of decreased gastric alcohol dehydrogenase activity and first-pass metabolism. *New England Journal of Medicine, 322*(2), 95–99.

Fujiwara, S., Kasagi, F., Yamada, M., and Kodama, K. (1997). Risk factors for hip fracture in a Japanese cohort. *Journal of Bone and Mineral Research, 12*, 998–1004.

Galambos, J. (1972). Natural history of alcoholic hepatitis. 3: Histological changes. *Gastroenterology, 63*(6), 1026–1035.

Gapstur, S., Potter, J., Sellers, T., and Folsom, A. (1992). Increased risk of breast cancer with alcohol consumption in postmenopausal women. *American Journal of Epidemiology, 136*(10), 1221–1231.

Gavaler, J. (1991). Effects of alcohol on female endocrine function. *Alcohol Health and Research World, 15*, 104–109.

Gavaler, J., and Arria, A. (1995). Increased susceptibility of women to alcoholic liver disease: Artifactual or real? In P. M. Hall (Ed.), *Alcoholic Liver Disease: Pathology and Pathogenesis* (2nd ed., pp. 123–133). London, UK: Edward Arnold.

Gillman, M., Cook, N., Evans, D., Rosner, B., and Hennekens, C. (1995). Relationship of alcohol intake with blood pressure in young adults. *Hypertension, 25*(5), 1106–1110.

Giovannucci, E., Rimm, E., Ascherio, A., Stampfer, M., Colditz, G., and Willett, W. (1995). Alcohol, low-methionine-low-folate diets and risk of colon cancer in men. *Journal of the National Cancer Institute, 87*(4), 265–273.

Giovannucci, E., and Willett, W. (1994). Dietary factors and risk of colon cancer. *Annals of Medicine, 26*(6), 443–452.

Gonzalez-Calvin, J., Garcia-Sanchez, A., Bellot, V., Munoz-Torres, M., Raya-Alvarez, E., and Salvatierra-Rios, D. (1993). Mineral metabolism, osteoblastic function and bone mass in chronic alcoholism. *Alcohol and Alcoholism, 28*, 571–579.

Grisso, J., Kelsey, J., Strom, B., O'Brien, L., Maislin, G., LaPann, K., ..., Hoffman, S. (1994). Risk factors for hip fracture in black women. The Northeast Hip Fracture Study Group. *New England Journal of Medicine, 330*, 1555–1559.

Haber, P., Wilson, J., Apte, M., Korsten, M., and Pirola. R. (1995). Individual susceptibility to alcoholic pancreatitis: Still an enigma. *Journal of Laboratory and Clinical Medicine, 125*(3), 305–312.

Halvorson, M., Campbell, J., and Sprague, G. (1993). Comparative evaluation of the clinical utility of three markers of ethanol intake: The effect of gender. *Alcoholism, Clinical and Experimental Research, 17*(2), 225–229.

Haum, A., Perbix, W., Hack, H., Stark, G., Spilker, G., and Doehn, M. (1995). Alcohol and drug abuse in burn injuries. *Burns, 219*(3), 194–100.

Hernandez-Avila, M., Colditz, G. A., Stampfer, M. J., Rosner, B., Speizer, F. E., and Willett, W.C. (1991). Caffeine, moderate alcohol intake, and risk of fractures of the hip and forearm in middle-aged women. *American Journal of Clinical Nutrition, 54*, 157–163.

Hillbom, M., and Holm, L. (1986). Contribution of traumatic head injury to neuropsychological deficits. *Journal of Neurology, Neurosurgery, and Psychiatry, 49*, 1349–1353.

Hisatomi, S., Kumashiro, R., Sata, M., Ishii, K., and Tanikawa, K. (1997). Gender difference in alcoholic liver disease in Japan–an analysis based on histological findings. *Hepatology Research, 8*(2), 113–120.

Holbrook, T., and Barrett-Connor, E. (1993). A prospective study of alcohol consumption and bone mineral density. *British Medical Journal, 306*, 1506–1509.

Howland, J., and Hingson, R. (1987). Alcohol as a risk factor for injuries or death due to fires and burns: Review of the literature. *Public Health Report, 102*, 475–483.

Huang, Y., Chan, C., Wu, J., Pai, C., Chao, Y., and Lee, S. (1996). Serum levels of interleukin-8 in alcoholic liver disease: Relationship with disease stage, biochemical parameters and survival. *Journal of Hepatology, 24*(4), 377–384.

Hugues, J., Coste, T., Perret, G., Jayle, M., Sebaoun, J., and Modigliani, E. (1980). Hypothalamopituitary ovarian function in thirty-one women with chronic alcoholism. *Clinical Endocrinology, 12*, 543–551.

Huth, J., Maier, R., Simonowitz, D., and Herman, C. (1983). Effect of accurate ethanolism on the hospital course and outcome of injured automobile drivers. *Journal of Trauma, 23*, 494–498.

International Agency for Research on Cancer. (1988). Alcohol Drinking (*IARC Monographs on the Evaluation of the Carcinogenic Risks to Humans, Vol. 44*). Lyon, France: Author.

Israel, Y., Orrego, H., Holt, S., Macdonald, D., and Meema, H. (1980). Identification of alcohol abuse: Thoracic fractures on routine chest x-rays as indicators of alcoholism. *Alcoholism, 4*, 420–422.

Jagger, J., Fife, D., Vernberg, K., and Jane, J. (1984). Effect of alcohol intoxication on the diagnosis and apparent severity of brain injury. *Neurosurgery, 15*, 303–306.

Javors, M., and Johnson, B. (2003). Current status of carbohydrate deficient transferring, total serum sialic acid, sialic acid index of apolipoprotein J and serum beta-hexosaminidase as markers for alcohol consumption. *Alcoholism, Clinical and Experimental Research, 26*(7), 1078–1087.

Johnell, O., Gullberg, B., Kanis, J., Allander, E., Elffors, L., Dequeker, J., …, Ribot, C. (1995). Risk factors for hip fracture in European women: The MEDOS study. *Journal of Bone and Mineral Research, 10*, 1802–1815.

Jones, A., and Holmgren, P. (2001). Uncertainty in estimating blood ethanol concentrations by analysis of vitreous humor. *Journal of Clinical Pathology, 54*(9), 699–702.

Jones, A. W., Zdolsek, H., Sjoberg, F., and Lisander, B. (1997). Accelerated metabolism of ethanol in patients with burn injury. *Alcohol and Alcoholism, 32*(5), 628–630.

Jones, G. (2014). Postmortem toxicology: Specimens. In A. Jamieson and A. Moenssens (Eds.), *Wiley Encyclopedia of Forensic Science.* Chichester, UK: John Wiley & Sons Ltd. DOI 10.1002/9780470061589.

Jones, J. D., Barber, B., Engrav, L., and Heimbach, D. (1991). Alcohol use and burn injury. *Journal of Burn Care & Rehabilitation, 12*(2), 148–152.

Kalbfleisch, J., Lindeman, R., Ginn, H., and Smith, W. (1963). Effects of ethanol administration on urinary excretion of magnesium and other electrolytes in alcoholic and normal subjects. *Journal of Clinical Investigation, 42*, 1471–1475.

Kawano, Y., Abe, H., Imanishi, M., Kojima, S., Yoshimi, H., Takishita, S., and Omae, T. (1996). Pressor and depressor hormones during alcohol-induced blood pressure reduction in hypertensive patients. *Journal of Human Hypertension, 10*(9), 595–599.

Kearney, J., Giovannucci, E., Rimm, E. B., Stampfer, M. J., Colditz, G. A., Ascherio, A., …, Willett, W. C. (1995). Diet, alcohol, and smoking and the occurrence of hyperplastic polyps of the colon and rectum (United States). *Cancer Causes & Control, 6*(1), 45–56.

Kincaid, E. H., Miller, P. R., Meredith, J. W., Rahman, N., and Chang, M. C. (1998). Elevated arterial base deficit in trauma patients: A marker of impaired oxygen utilization. *Journal of the American College of Surgeons, 187*(4), 384–392.

Kirn, T. F. (1988). Debunking the drunk-driver-and-survival myth. *Journal of the American Medical Association, 260*(17), 2480.

Knott, D. (1986). *Alcohol Problems: Diagnosis and Treatment.* New York, NY: Pergamon Press.

Kraus, J., Morgenstern, H., Fife, D., Conroy, C., and Nourjah, P. (1989). Blood alcohol tests, prevalence of involvement and outcomes following brain injury. *American Journal of Public Health, 79*(3), 294–299.

Kugelberg, F., and Jones, A. (2007). Interpreting results of ethanol analysis in post-mortem specimens: A review of the literature. *Forensic Science International*, *165*(1), 10–29.

Laitinen, K., Karkkainen, M., Lalla, M., Lamberg-Allardt, C., Tunninen, R., Tahtela, R., and Valimaki, M. (1993). Is alcohol an osteoporosis-inducing agent for young and middle-aged women? *Metabolism*, *42*(7), 875–881.

Laitinen, K., Lamberg-Allardt, C., Tunninen, R., Harkonen, M., and Valimaki, M. (1992). Bone mineral density and abstention-induced changes in bone and mineral metabolism in noncirrhotic male alcoholics. *American Journal of Medicine*, *93*(6), 642–650.

Laitinen, K., Valimaki, M., and Keto, P. (1991). Bone mineral density measured by dual-energy X-ray absorptiometry in healthy Finnish women. *Calcified Tissue International*, *48*(4), 224–231.

Lalor, B., France, M., Powell, D., Adams, P., and Counihan, T. (1986). Bone and mineral metabolism and chronic alcohol abuse. *Quarterly Journal of Medicine*, *59*, 497–511.

Lang, T., Nicaud, V., Darne, B., and Rueff, B. (1995). Improving hypertension control among excessive alcohol drinkers: A randomised controlled trial in France. The WALPA Group. *Journal of Epidemiology and Community Health*, *49*(6), 610–616.

Lelbach, W. (1975). Cirrhosis in the alcoholic and its relation to the volume of alcohol abuse. *Annals of the New York Academy of Sciences*, *252*, 85–105.

Levitt, M. D., and Levitt, D. G. (1994). The critical role of the rate of ethanol absorption in the interpretation of studies purporting to demonstrate gastric metabolism of ethanol. *Journal of Pharmacology and Experimental Therapeutics*, *269*(1), 297–304.

Lindsell, D., Wilson, A., and Maxwell, J. (1982). Fractures on the chest radiograph in detection of alcoholic liver disease. *British Medical Journal*, *285*, 597–599.

Longnecker, M. (1992). Alcohol consumption in relation to risk of cancers of the breast and large bowel. *Alcohol Health and Research World*, *16*, 223–229.

Longnecker, M. (1994). Alcoholic beverage consumption in relation to risk of breast cancer: Meta-analysis and review. *Cancer Causes & Control*, *5*(1), 73–82.

Longnecker, M., Orza, M., Adams, M., Vioque, J., and Chalmers, T. (1990). A meta-analysis of alcoholic beverage consumption in relation to risk of colorectal cancer. *Cancer Causes & Control*, *1*(1), 59–68.

Lowenfels, A. (1982). Trauma, surgery, and anesthesia. In M. Pattison and E. Kaufman (Eds.), *Encyclopedia Handbook of Alcoholism* (pp. 343–353). New York, NY: Gardner Press.

Luna, G., Maier, R., Sowder, L., Copass, M., and Oreskovich, M. (1984). The influence of ethanol intoxication on outcome of injured motorcyclists. *Journal of Trauma*, *24*(8), 695–700.

MacGregor, R. R. (1986). Alcohol and immune defense. *Journal of the American Medical Association*, *256*(11), 1474–1479.

MacGregor, R. R., Gluckman, S. J., and Senior, J. R. (1978). Granulocyte function and levels of immunoglobulins and complement in patients admitted for withdrawal from alcohol. *Journal of Infectious Diseases*, *138*(6), 747–755.

Marbet, U., Bianchi, L., Meury, U., and Stalder. G. (1987). Long-term histological evaluation of the natural history and prognostic factors of alcoholic liver disease. *Journal of Hepatology, 4*(3), 364–372.

Mathew, V. (1992). Alcoholism in biblical prophecy. *Alcohol and Alcoholism, 27,* 89–90.

Maull, K. (1982). Alcohol abuse: Its implications in trauma care. *Southern Medical Journal, 75,* 794–798.

Maull, K., Clapp, A., and Ellis, L. (1986). *Non-Vehicular Trauma and Driver Behavior–A Comparative Study of Alcohol-Impaired and Non-Impaired Subjects* (SAE Technical Paper 860185). Paper presented at the International Congress and Exposition on Alcohol, Accidents, and Injuries, February 24–28, 1986, Detroit, MI.

McGill, V., Kowal-Vern, A., Kahn, S., and Gamelli, R. (1995). The impact of substance use on mortality and morbidity from thermal injury. *Journal of Trauma, 38*(6), 931–934.

McPherson, K., Engelsman, E., and Conning, D. (1993). Breast cancer. In P. Verschuren (Ed.), *Alcoholic Beverages and European Society: Annex 3. Health Issues Related to Alcohol Consumption* (pp. 221–244). Brussels, Belgium: International Life Sciences Institute.

Mello, N., Mendelson, I., and Teoh, S. (1993). An overview of the effects of alcohol on neuroendocrine function in women. In S. Zakhari (Ed.), *Alcohol and the Endocrine System* (pp. 139–169). NIAAA Research Monograph No. 23. NIH Pub. No. 93-3533. Bethesda, MD: National Institutes of Health, National Institute on Alcohol Abuse and Alcoholism.

Mezey, E. (1983). Effects of stress on ethanol metabolism. In L. Pohorecky and J. Brick (Eds.), *Stress and Alcohol Use* (pp. 421–427). New York, NY: Elsevier Science Publishing.

Mezey, E., Kolman, C., Diehl, A., Mitchell, M., and Herlong, H. (1988). Alcohol and dietary intake in the development of chronic pancreatitis and liver disease in alcoholism. *American Journal of Clinical Nutrition, 48*(1), 148–151.

Mezey, E., Potter, J., and Kvetnansky, R. (1979). Effects of stress by repeated immobilization on hepatic alcohol dehydrogenase activity and ethanol metabolism. *Biochemical Pharmacology, 28,* 657–663.

Mobarhan, S., Russell, R., Recker, R., Posner, D., Iber, F., and Miller, P. (1984). Metabolic bone disease in alcoholic cirrhosis: A comparison of the effect of vitamin D, 25-hydroxyvitamin D, or supportive treatment. *Hepatology, 4,* 266–273.

Molina, P., McClain, C., Valla, D., Guidot, D., Diehl, A., Lang, C., and Neuman, M. (2002). Molecular pathology and clinical aspects of alcohol-induced tissue injury. *Alcoholism, Clinical and Experimental Research, 26*(1), 120–128.

Napolitano, L., Koruda, M., Zimmerman, K., McCowan, K., Chang, J., and Meyer, A. (1995). Chronic ethanol intake and burn injury: Evidence for synergistic alteration in gut and immune integrity. *Journal of Trauma, 38*(2), 198–207.

National Institute on Alcohol Abuse and Alcoholism (NIAAA). (1997). *Ninth Special Report to the U.S. Congress on Alcohol and Health from the Secretary of Health and Human Services.* (NIH Publication No.97-4017.) Rockville, MD: U.S. Department of Health and Human Services, Public Health Service, National Institutes of Health, National Institute on Alcohol Abuse and Alcoholism.

National Institute on Alcohol Abuse and Alcoholism (NIAAA). (2000). *Tenth Special Report to the U.S. Congress on Alcohol and Health from the Secretary of Health and Human Services.* Rockville, MD: U.S. Department of Health and Human Services, Public Health Service, National Institutes of Health, National Institute on Alcohol Abuse and Alcoholism.

Nanikawa, R., and Kotoku, S. (1971). Medico-legal evaluation of ethanol levels in cadaveric blood and urine. *Yongo Acta Medica, 15*(2), 61–69.

Naveau, S., Giraud, V., Borotto, E., Aubert, A., Capron, F., and Chaput, J. (1997). Excess weight risk factor for alcoholic liver disease. *Hepatology, 25*(1), 108–111.

Naves Diaz, M., O'Neill, T. W., and Silman, A. J. (1997). The influence of alcohol consumption on the risk of vertebral deformity. European Vertebral Osteoporosis Group. *Osteoporosis International, 7*(1), 65–71.

Neumann, T., and Spies, C. (2003). Use of biomarkers for alcohol use disorders in clinical practice. *Addiction, 98*(suppl. 2), 81–91.

O'Neill, T., Marsden, D., Adams, J., and Silman, A. (1996). Risk factors, falls, and fracture of the distal forearm in Manchester, UK. *Journal of Epidemiology and Community Health, 50,* 288–292.

Orwoll, E., Bauer, D., Vogt, T., and Fox, K. (1996). Axial bone mass in older women: Study of osteoporotic fracture research group. *Annals of Internal Medicine, 124,* 187–196.

Paganini-Hill, A., Ross, R., and Gerkins, V. (1981). Menopausal estrogen therapy and hip fractures. *Annals of Internal Medicine, 95,* 28–31.

Palmer, A., Fletcher, A., Bulpitt, C., Beevers, D., Coles, E., Ledingham, J., ..., Dollery, C. (1995). Alcohol intake and cardiovascular mortality in hypertensive patients: Report from the Department of Health Hypertension Care Computing Project. *Journal of Hypertension, 13*(9), 957–964.

Pares, A., Caballeria, J., Bruguera, M., Torres, M., and Rodes, J. (1986). Histological course of alcoholic hepatitis: Influence of abstinence, sex and extent of hepatic damage. *Journal of Hepatology, 2*(1), 33–42.

Paunio, M., Hook-Nikanne, J., Kosunen, T., Vainio, U., Salaspuro, M., Makinen, J., and Heinonen, O. (1994). Association of alcohol consumption and Helicobacter pylori infection in young adulthood and early middle age among patients with gastric complaints. A case-control study on Finnish conscripts, officers and other military personnel. *European Journal of Epidemiology, 10*(2), 205–209.

Pelissier-Alicot, A-L., Gaulier, J-M., Champsaur, P., and Marquet, P. (2003). Mechanisms underlying postmortem redistribution of drugs: A review. *Journal of Analytical Toxicology, 27*(8), 533–544.

Peris, P., Guanabens, N., Pares, A., Pons, F., Del Rio, L., Monegal, A., ..., Munoz Gómez, J. (1995). Vertebral fractures and osteopenia in chronic alcoholic patients. *Calcified Tissue International, 57,* 111–114.

Peris, P., Pares, A., Guanabens, N., Del Rio, L., Pons, F., Deosaba, M. J. M., ..., Munoz-Gómez, J. (1994). Bone mass improves in alcoholics after 2 years of abstinence. *Journal of Bone and Mineral Research, 9*(10), 1607–1612.

Perrine, M. (1975). Alcohol involvement in highway crashes. *Clinics in Plastic Surgery, 2,* 11–34.

Peterson, C., and Polizzi, C. (1987). Improved method for acetaldehyde in plasma and hemoglobin-associated acetaldehyde: Results in teetotalers and alcoholics reporting for treatment. *Alcohol*, *4*(6), 477–480.

Pounder, D. J., and Jones, G. R. (1990). Post-mortem drug redistribution–a toxicological nightmare. *Forensic Science International*, *45*(3), 253–263.

Pounder, D. J., and Kuroda, N. (1994). Vitreous alcohol is of limited value in predicting blood alcohol. *Forensic Science International*, *65*(2), 73–80.

Puddey, I., Beilin, L., Vandongen, R., Rouse, I., and Rogers, P. (1995). Evidence for a direct effect of alcohol consumption on blood pressure in normotensive men: A randomized controlled trial. *Hypertension*, *7*(5), 707–713.

Razvodovsky, Y. E. (2015). The effects of beverage specific alcohol sale on liver cirrhosis mortality in Russia. *Journal of Addiction Medicine and Therapeutic Science*, *1*(2), 20–26.

Robertson, S. (no date). Interpretation of measured alcohol levels in fatal aviation accident victims. Retrieved January 7, 2016. Available at www.atsb.gov.au/media/36390/Measured_alcohol_level.pdf

Rockett, I., and Putnam, S. (1986). Alcohol and unintentional injury: Beyond the motor vehicle. *Rhode Island Medical Journal*, *69*(9), 419–424.

Roizen, J. (1988). Alcohol and trauma. In N. Giesbrecht, R. Gonzales, M. Grant, E. Osterberg, R. Room, I. Rootman, and L. Towle (Eds.), *Drinking and Casualties: Accidents, Poisonings, and Violence in an International Perspective* (pp. 21–69). London, UK: Routledge.

Saville, P. D. (1965). Changes in bone mass with age and alcoholism. *Journal of Bone and Joint Surgery*, *47*(3), 492–499.

Schatzkin, A., and Longnecker, M. (1994). Alcohol and breast cancer: Where are we now and where do we go from here? *Cancer*, *74*(suppl. 3), 1101–1110.

Schnitzler, C., and Solomon, L. (1984). Bone changes after alcohol abuse. *South African Medical Journal*, *66*, 730–734.

Seitz, H., and Pöschl, G. (1997). Alcohol and gastrointestinal cancer: Pathogenic mechanisms. *Addiction Biology*, *2*(1), 19–33.

Seitz, H., Simanowski, U., Egerer, G., Waldherr, R., and Oertl, U. (1992). Human gastric alcohol dehydrogenase: In vitro characteristics and effect of cimetidine. *Digestion*, *51*(2), 80–85.

Seller, S. (1985). Alcohol abuse in the Old Testament. *Alcohol and Alcoholism*, *20*, 69–76.

Seppa, K., Laippala, P., and Sillanaukee, P. (1996). High diastolic blood pressure: Common among women who are heavy drinkers. *Alcoholism, Clinical and Experimental Research*, *20*(1), 47–51.

Shimizu, M., Lasker, J., Tsutsumi, M., and Lieber, C. (1990). Immunohistochemical localization of ethanol-inducible P450IIE1 in the rat alimentary tract. *Gastroenterology*, *99*(4), 1044–1053.

Simel, D., and Feussner, J. (1988). Blood and alcohol measurements in the emergency department: Who needs them? *American Journal of Public Health*, *78*, 1478–1479.

Simonsen, J. (1984). Fatal subarachnoid hemorrhages in relation to minor injuries in Denmark from 1967 to 1981. *Forensic Science International*, *24*, 57–63.

Smith-Warner, S., Spiegelman, D., Adami, H., Beeson, W., van den Brandt, P., Folsom, A., ..., Hunter, D. (1998). Types of dietary fat and breast cancer: A pooled analysis of cohort studies. *International Journal of Cancer, 92*(5), 767–774.

Soderstrom, C., and Cowley, R. (1987). A national alcohol and trauma center survey: Missed opportunities, failures of responsibility. *Archives of Surgery, 122,* 1067–1071.

Soderstrom, C., Dupriest, R., Benner, C., Maekawa, K., and Cowley, R. (1979). Alcohol and roadway trauma: Problems of diagnosis and management. *American Surgeon, 45,* 129–135.

Spencer, H., Rubio, N., Rubio, E., Indreika, M., and Seitam, A. (1986). Chronic alcoholism: Frequently overlooked cause of osteoporosis in men. *American Journal of Medicine, 80,* 393–397.

Steinbok, P., and Thompson, G. (1978). Metabolic disturbances after head injury: Abnormalities of sodium and water intoxication. *Neurosurgery, 3,* 9–15.

Territo, M., and Tanaka, K. (1974). Hypophosphatemia in chronic alcoholism. *Archives of Internal Medicine, 134,* 445–447.

Thuluvath, P., Wojno, K., Yardley, H., and Mezey, E. (1994). Effects of Helicobacter pylori infection and gastritis on gastric alcohol dehydrogenase activity. *Alcoholism, Clinical and Experimental Research, 18*(4), 795–798.

Tuppurainen, M., Kroger, H., Honkanen, R., Puntial, E., Huopia, J., Saarikoski, S., and Alhave, E. (1995). Risks of perimenopausal fractures: A prospective population based study. *Acta Obstetricia et Gynecologica Scandinavica, 74,* 624–628.

Tuyns, A., and Pequignot, G. (1984). Greater risk of ascitic cirrhosis in females in relation to alcohol consumption. *International Journal of Epidemiology, 13*(1), 53–57.

U.S. Department of Health and Human Services. (1995). *Healthy People 2000: Midcourse Review and 1995 Revisions.* Washington, D.C.: U.S. Department of Health and Human Services, Public Health Service.

Ueshima, H., Mikawa, K., Baba, S., Sasaki, S., Ozawa, H., Tsushima, M., ..., Kayemori, Y. (1993). Effect of reduced alcohol consumption on blood pressure in untreated hypertensive men. *Hypertension, 21*(2), 248–252.

Uppal, R., Lateef, S., Korsten, M., Paronetto, F., and Lieber, C. (1991). Chronic alcoholic gastritis: Roles of alcohol and Helicobacter pylori. *Archives of Internal Medicine, 151*(4), 760–764.

Valimaki, M., Pelkonen, R., Salaspuro, M., Harkonen, J., Hirvonen, E., and Ylikahri, R. (1984). Sex hormones in amenorrheic women with alcoholic liver disease. *Journal of Clinical Endocrinology and Metabolism, 59,* 133–138.

Valimaki, M., Salaspuro, M., and Ylikahri, R. (1982). Liver damage and sex hormones in chronic male alcoholics. *Clinical Endocrinology, 17,* 469–477.

Van Thiel, D. (1983b). Ethanol: Its adverse effects upon the hypothalamic-pituitary-gonadal axis. *Journal of Laboratory and Clinical Medicine, 101,* 21–33.

Van Thiel, D., Lester, R., and Sherins, R. (1974). Hypogonadism in alcoholic liver disease: Evidence for a double defect. *Gastroenterology, 67,* 1188–1199.

Vaughan, T., Davis, S., Kristal, A., and Thomas, D. (1995). Obesity, alcohol, and tobacco as risk factors for cancers of the esophagus and gastric cardia: Adenocarcinoma versus squamous cell carcinoma. *Cancer Epidemiology, Biomarkers & Prevention, 4*(2), 85–92.

Waller, J. (1987). Injury as disease. *Accident Analysis and Prevention, 19,* 13–20.

Waller, J. (1988). *Diagnosis of Alcoholism in the Injured Patient.* Presented at the NIAAA Conference on Post-Injury Treatment of Patients with Alcohol-Related Trauma, June 8, 1988, Washington, D.C.

Waller, P., Stewart, J., Hansen, A., Stutts, J., Popkin, C., and Rodgman, E. (1986). The potentiating effects of alcohol on driver injury. *Journal of the American Medical Association, 256,* 1461–1466.

Ward, R., Flynn, T., Miller, P., and Blaisdell, W. (1982). Effects of ethanol ingestion on the severity and outcome of trauma. *American Journal of Surgery, 144,* 153–157.

Williams, G., Bowser, E., Hargis, G., Kukreja, S., Shah, J., Vora, N., and Henderson, W. (1978). Effect of ethanol on parathyroid hormone and calcitronin secretion in man. *Proceedings of the Society for Experimental Biology and Medicine, 159,* 187–191.

Wilson, D. M. III, Tentler, J. J., Carney, J. P., Wilson, T. M., and Kelley, M. R. (1994). Acute ethanol exposure suppresses the repair of O6-methylguanine DNA lesions in castrated adult male rats. *Alcoholism, Clinical and Experimental Research, 18*(5), 1267–1271.

World Health Organization Ad Hoc Committee on Health Research Relating to Future Intervention Options. (1996). *Investing in Health Research and Development.* Geneva, Switzerland: World Health Organization.

Wurst, F. M., Vogel, R., Jachau, K., Varga, A., Alling, C., Alt, A., and Skipper, G. E. (2003). Ethyl glucuronide discloses recent covert alcohol use not detected by standard testing in forensic psychiatric inpatients. *Alcoholism, Clinical and Experimental Research, 27*(3), 471–476.

Yamada, K., Araki, S., Tamura, M., Sakai, I., Takahashi, Y., Kashihara, H., and Kono, S. (1997). Case-control study of colorectal carcinoma in situ and cancer in relation to cigarette smoking and alcohol use. *Cancer Causes & Control, 8*(5), 780–785.

Yin, S., Chou, F., Chao, S., Tsai, S., Liao, C., Wang, S., ..., Lee, S. (1993). Alcohol and aldehyde dehydrogenases in human esophagus: Comparison with the stomach enzyme activities. *Alcoholism, Clinical and Experimental Research, 17*(2), 376–381.

York, J., and Hirsch, J. (1997). Association between blood pressure and lifetime drinking patterns in moderate drinkers. *Journal of Studies on Alcohol, 58*(5), 480–485.

Zakhari, S., and Wassef, M. (Eds.). (1996). *Alcohol and the Cardiovascular System.* NIAAA Research Monograph No.31. Pub. No.96-4133. Bethesda, MD: National Institute on Alcohol Abuse and Alcoholism.

Zdolsek, H., Sjoberg, F., Lisander, B., and Jones A. (1999). The effect of hypermetabolism induced by burn trauma on the ethanol-oxidizing capacity of the liver. *Critical Care Medicine, 27*(12), 2622–2625.

Zink, B., Maoi, R., and Chen, B. (1996). Alcohol, central nervous system injury, and time to fatal motor vehicle crashes. *Alcoholism, Clinical and Experimental Research, 20*(9), 1518–1522.

Zumoff, B. (1997). The critical role of alcohol consumption in determining the risk of breast cancer with postmenopausal estrogen administration. *Journal of Clinical Endocrinology and Metabolism, 82*(6), 1656–1658.

Zuska, J. (1981). Wounds without cause. *Bulletin of the American College of Surgeons, 10,* 5–10.

Chapter 10

ALCOHOL USE, TOLERANCE,
AND DEPENDENCE

Alcohol use, tolerance, and dependence are factors in the forensic investigation of crimes, accidents, or deaths (accidental or otherwise). Frequently, the interpretation of forensic alcohol test evidence is related to these factors. For example, was driving impaired? Was the subject visibly intoxicated? Was there prostration of faculties? Was the person in control of his or her drinking? The role and understanding of alcohol tolerance and dependence may be important in interpreting behavior and is often raised in both criminal and civil litigation. For example, it may be argued that tolerance to alcohol precluded signs of visible intoxication (e.g., in a dram shop or comparative negligence case) or provided immunity from impaired driving at various BACs. Evidence to support opinions about tolerance (or dependence) must be available and properly interpreted before valid conclusions can be reached.

10.1 ALCOHOL USE

Who Drinks?

Alcohol use is not new. As a psychoactive drug, alcohol has been used for thousands of years. Currently, more than 80 percent of all high-school age Americans have tried alcohol, and 5 to 10 percent of this same group drink to intoxication on a regular basis. About 56 percent of people age 18 or older report drinking in the last month and about 25 percent engage in binge drinking (five or more drinks in one day) in the last month, a reflective index of regular drinking (National Institute on Alcohol Abuse and Alcoholism [NIAAA] 2014). Terms such as social drinker, heavy drinker, binge drinker, alcohol tolerance, alcoholic, alcohol abuser, and abstainer are frequently used without much thought or substance.

Determining Alcohol Use: What Is a Drink?

Both the definition and standardization of the term drink are particularly relevant in two settings: (1) commercial establishments that serve alcohol (e.g., restaurants and bars) and (2) alcohol research. The standardization of drink sizes has been a long standing practice in alcohol-serving establishments. Commercial measures of alcoholic beverages, however, are heavily influenced by local drinking customs and regulations. In some countries, the serving sizes for various alcoholic beverages are mandated by law and, consequently, are uniform from one establishment to another. In the United States, however, each bar, restaurant, or other establishment that serves alcoholic beverages can set its own standards, although establishments generally are consistent in the sizes of the drinks they serve.

In private homes, drink sizes may vary even further. For beer, wine coolers, and similar alcoholic beverages, the serving size is most likely to be consistent across different households because a serving or drink often corresponds to one (standard size) can or bottle. For wine and distilled spirits (e.g., vodka and whiskey), however, the size of one drink is entirely up to the person pouring it, the size of the glass, mug, and so on, and may vary from occasion to occasion. Most survey methods used to calculate a person's alcohol consumption are based on information reported from memory. Consequently, such surveys are subject to both intentional and unintentional errors of recall by the respondent. Such self-reported data are subject to memory errors, self-serving bias, psychological motivation including denial, and variability in what constitutes a drink. What one person considers "a drink" may be more or less than what someone with significantly different drinking experience, different recall, and so on considers it to be.

Despite the limitations of self-reports, studies examining the reliability and validity of survey measures of alcohol use have indicated high levels of reliability—that is, when asked more than once, people generally are consistent in how much alcohol they report using. In fact, in nutritional epidemiology studies that investigated the consumption of various food categories, reported alcohol intake was particularly reproducible compared with the reported intake of other nutrients (Longnecker et al., 1993).

For some analyses, such as studies investigating drinking consequences (e.g., drinking and driving and other alcohol-related injuries and violence) the pattern of alcohol consumption is important and must be determined. For example, consider two people who consume identical average quantities of alcohol (e.g., fourteen drinks per week). One person consumes two drinks each evening, whereas the other person ingests all fourteen drinks within a few hours on a Saturday night. That difference in drinking pattern has considerable implications for the drinkers with respect to the likelihood of experiencing negative outcomes, such as alcohol poisoning, pedestrian falling down accidents, and traffic crashes. Unfortunately, there is still debate concerning what constitutes hazardous drinking and how to measure hazardous drinking or drinking patterns in general. Even so, researchers generally agree that the consumption of five or more drinks on one drinking occasion is hazardous, but this definition does not account for other variables such as drink size or time drinking.

Abstainers

To many people, to abstain from alcohol use implies no alcohol consumption ever. To others, including many researchers, the term may encompass more than nondrinkers, including some people who drink a little bit. Thus, the definition of abstainer may vary from study to study, and studies reporting higher numbers of abstainers often use a broader definition of abstainer. In the National Health and Nutrition Examination Survey I, to be classified as an abstainer, respondents had to have reported consuming less than one drink of beer, wine, or liquor in the previous year (Dufour, Colliver, Grigson & Stinson, 1990). In contrast, in the National Longitudinal Alcohol Epidemiologic Survey, in order to be considered a current drinker, a person had to report consuming twelve or more drinks during the year preceding the survey interview. Those consuming fewer than twelve drinks were classified as abstainers. Abstainers were further divided into former drinkers and lifetime abstainers. Former drinkers were persons who had consumed at least twelve drinks in a 12 month period sometime in their lives but not during the 12 months immediately preceding the interview. Lifetime abstainers were those who had never consumed at least twelve drinks in a 1-year period (Dawson, Grant & Chou, 1995). Results from these two surveys may report different numbers of abstainers, not because of true differences in drinking practices but because of operational definitions.

Social Drinking

The term social drinker or light drinker is often used by laypersons and some professionals but these terms may be misleading or completely inaccurate if not defined. What is social alcohol use? The current diagnostic definition is usually quite different from the descriptive intent found in depositions and courtroom testimony. The social use of alcohol is now generally described as a cold beer after a ball game, a glass of wine with meals, or a glass of champagne at festive occasions. It does not describe someone who drinks for several hours with friends on weekends. Similarly, the terms light, moderate, and heavy drinking are also used to describe drinking habits. These are explicit terms of art within the field, depending on the metric used to establish a drinking history.

Moderate Drinking

The U.S. Departments of Agriculture and of Health and Human Services define moderate drinking as one drink per day or less for women and two or fewer drinks per day for men. With this definition, the consumption of six or seven drinks per week might equate to moderate drinking because it averages about one drink per day, but would more properly define binge drinking, or heavy drinking, if all six or seven drinks were consumed in one sitting. Alcohol researchers define binge drinking as four to five drinks within 2 hours or a BAC of 80 mg/dL (Brick & Erickson, 2013; Dufour, 1999).

Although the benefits and risks associated with moderate drinking have gained increasing attention in recent years from both researchers and the general public, no universal definition of moderate drinking exists. Most currently used definitions are based on a certain number of drinks consumed in a specific time period. Defining a "drink," however, also is difficult because alcoholic beverages can differ substantially in their alcohol content, even within the same beverage category (e.g., beer, wine, or distilled spirits). Because international differences in drink definitions also exist, comparing studies from different countries is difficult and requires standardization of how a drink is defined (Brick, 2006). The development of a universal definition of moderate drinking is hampered further by variations in the way alcohol consumption levels and drinking patterns are being assessed (i.e., the survey methods and assessment modes used). Despite these problems, definitions of moderate drinking and drinking guidelines have been developed in the United States and other countries.

Despite the rather vague definition of moderate alcohol use, survey researchers apply the term to describe certain drinking levels. In their surveys, scientists must classify the wide range of alcohol consumption found in the population (e.g., from zero to more than twenty drinks per day) into a manageable number of drinking categories. One commonly used scheme includes the categories of abstainer, light drinker, moderate drinker, and heavy or heavier drinker. The definitions of each category, however, can vary among studies. For example, Dawson and colleagues (1995) proposed the following definitions, where one drink is equivalent to 0.5 fl oz of 100 percent alcohol (note: a standard drink as defined in Chapter 11 contains 14 g of alcohol, whereas using Dawson's definition each drink contains 11.5 g of alcohol). Nevertheless, a metric for drinking is often useful.

- Abstainer: drinks less than 0.01 fl oz alcohol per day (i.e., fewer than six standard drinks in the past year)
- Light drinker: drinks 0.01 to 0.21 fl. oz. alcohol per day (i.e., approximately 1.5 to 11 standard drinks per month)
- Moderate drinker: drinks 0.22 to 1.00 fl oz alcohol per day (i.e., approximately 1.5 to 12 standard drinks per week)
- Heavier drinker: drinks more than 1.00 fl oz alcohol per day (i.e., more than approximately 2 drinks per day).

The definitions used by Dawson are generally much lower than other published definitions for some types of drinkers (*see* later). To some degree, discrepancies in the definition of moderate drinking may result from the fact that some people confuse the term with social drinking that is, drinking patterns that are accepted by the society or group in which they occur. Depending on the society, however, those drinking levels may not be moderate or risk free. Even when a definition of moderate drinking has been developed, it may not apply to all people or under all circumstances. For example, it may not be harmful for a party's host to consume three or four drinks during the evening, but the same amount of alcohol consumed by a guest who is driving home could place the guest at risk for being in a car crash. Similarly, a healthy woman will likely experience no negative effects from consuming one drink per day; however, if the woman is pregnant, the same drinking amount may be harmful to the fetus, particularly if a weekly average (seven drinks) is consumed in a single drinking episode (e.g., weekend binge drinking).

The recommendation for men and women is, "If you drink alcoholic beverages, do so in moderation" (DHHS & USDA, 1995). Moderation is defined as no more than one drink per day for women and no more than two drinks per day for men. A drink is considered to be 12 oz. regular beer, 5 oz. wine, or 1.5 oz. 80-proof distilled spirits. Those drinking levels are considered a ceiling, not a floor–that is, one can drink less than those levels and still consider oneself a moderate drinker. The U.S. Dietary Guidelines also list several categories of people who should not drink at all. Those categories include children and adolescents, people who cannot keep their consumption moderate, women who are pregnant or trying to conceive, people who plan to drive or participate in activities that require attention or skill, and people using over-the-counter and prescription medications that interact with alcohol. Finally, the Dietary Guidelines provide specific recommendations for recovering alcoholics and for people who have family members with alcohol problems.

Heavy Drinking

Heavy drinking is considered by many alcohol scientists as the consumption of more than five or six drinks a day, but many other factors must be considered in making a diagnosis of heavy (or any other types) drinking (USDA, 1995; Dufour, 1999). Among these, is the effect of drinking on life events (Oates & McCay, 1973). For example, it is possible for a subject to be classified in a medical record as a social drinker, a heavy drinker, or something else based on self-report or a single episode – that may or may not have resulted in their hospitalization. Assumptions about tolerance based on such a record would be highly speculative without other information. Therefore, the terms light, moderate, and heavy should be interpreted carefully on the basis of individual drinker characteristics or research design.

Severe Alcohol Use Disorder

Chronic alcohol use can result in physical dependence previously referred to as alcohol dependent. In such individuals chronic drinking is necessary to maintain homeostasis and avoid withdrawal. In the physically dependent drinker, as the BAC declines, withdrawal symptoms are likely to occur. Untreated alcohol withdrawal generally follows two stages that range from relatively mild flulike symptoms to life-threatening symptoms. Signs and symptoms of withdrawal could be misinterpreted as being due to acute intoxication, which may have both forensic and treatment implications. Early-stage withdrawal starts about 1 to 4 days after abstinence and includes transient visual or tactile hallucinations, irritability, confusion, disorientation, tremor, insomnia, tachycardia, and convulsions. Seizures most often occur in the first 12 to 48 hours after the last drink. Late-stage (about 1 to 7 days after abstinence) withdrawal symptoms include persistent hallucinations, cognitive impairment, agitation, delirium tremens, hypotension, diaphoresis (sweating), and fever. Seizures are often treated prophylactically with benzodiazepines and in some cases with alcohol when medications are contraindicated and medical stabilization of the patient has a higher priority than sobriety has. Therefore, a careful review of medical records (including itemized billing records) is necessary to be sure any reported forensic BAC is not the result of medical treatment.

10.2 ALCOHOL TOLERANCE

Patterns of social, moderate, and heavy drinking have various consequences, including the development of different types of tolerance. Tolerance is sometimes a factor in civil litigation that stems from an accident caused by alcohol intoxication. Under dram shop and common negligence laws, for example, it is illegal to serve alcohol to visibly intoxicated persons. Individuals with exceptional tolerance may not appear intoxicated, that is, impaired, in the absence of special tests. Tolerance may also be important in other civil cases. Consider the officer who makes a routine motor vehicle stop but does not detect impairment in a driver and allows the driver to continue on his way. A short time later, the driver may have a fatal crash. Low levels of intoxication or exceptional tolerance to alcohol are factors to explain why the officer did not arrest the driver for drunk driving. However, tolerance usually has no significant role in accident investigations.

All drinkers acquire some tolerance to the effects of alcohol. A tolerant drinker would require much more alcohol than a nontolerant drinker in order to obtain the same effect. Tolerance is most evident at lower levels, and in simple tasks. However, even for very experienced drinkers, complex divided attention tasks are difficult to perform. In most drinkers, alcohol impairs driving skills necessary for safe motor vehicle operation at relatively low BAC, and by BACs of 80 to 100 mg/dL, driving skills are impaired in virtually all drivers.

One factor that potentially complicates the interpretation of alcohol test evidence or the identification of alcohol intoxication, particularly in some experienced drinkers, is alcohol tolerance. Tolerance is a decrease in the response that occurs as a function of exposure to that drug. This is an important concept in identifying alcohol intoxication. Common misperceptions are that (a) only alcoholics have tolerance to alcohol, (b) all alcoholics are tolerant to all the effects of alcohol, (c) a diagnosis of tolerance confers immunity from the impairment produced by alcohol intoxication, and (d) clinically significant tolerance can be assumed because of a history of alcohol-related problems (e.g., legal, social, employment). The five types of tolerance of potential interest in forensic evaluations are (1) acute, (2) functional (brain tolerance), (3) metabolic, (4) cross-tolerance, and (5) nonpharmacological (Brick, 2012).

Acute Tolerance

Acute tolerance develops within hours during a drinking session and describes a decreased response on the descending limb of the BAC curve than is observed at the same BAC but during the ascending limb of the curve (Beirness & Vogel-Sprott, 1984; Bennett, Cherek & Spiga, 1993; Mellanby, 1919). Since faster rates of absorption may cause greater intoxication and impairment, differences in intoxication before and after peak concentration may further affect behavior (Conners & Maisto, 1979; Goldberg, 1943).

Mellanby (1919) was the first to describe acute tolerance. It was based upon his observation in dogs of greater behavioral impairment while BACs were rising compared to when they were falling at the same BAC. A similar effect in humans was described by Goldberg (1943). Acute tolerance (Mellanby effect) is the difference in response at a given BAC while rising compared to the same BAC when it is falling. Unlike other forms of tolerance, acute tolerance develops very rapidly during the time course of a single alcohol administration (within-session tolerance). Acute tolerance is believed to represent an adaptive or compensatory change within the CNS (LeBlanc, Kalant & Gibbins, 1975).

Goldberg (1943) examined the time course of impairment following a single dose of alcohol and found that cognitive-type tasks returned at higher BACs than did motor-type tasks. It was suggested (Carpenter, 1963; Goldberg, 1943), and confirmed in later years, that alcohol impairment of cognitive function dissipates more rapidly for alcohol-induced motor impairment. Jones (1974) observed acute tolerance to alcohol-induced memory impairment in nonalcoholics. Vogel-Sprott (1979) found that the performance of social drinkers on a coding task was impaired on the rising portion of the BAC curve but not on the descending limb. In a study of acute recovery and tolerance to low doses of alcohol, Vogel-Sprott (1979) found that cognitive performance on a divided attention coding task improved (acute tolerance), whereas performance on a pursuit rotor task did not (no acute tolerance). At least part of the acute tolerance detected in these studies may be due to task practice effects (Annear & Vogel-Sprott, 1985; Beirness & Vogel-Sprott, 1984; Niaura, Nathan, Frankenstein, Shapiro & Brick, 1987; Vogel-Sprott, Rawana & Webster, 1984).

Functional Tolerance

Functional tolerance, or brain tolerance, is present when drinkers display few or markedly reduced signs of intoxication even at high BACs (Goldberg, 1943; Lindblad & Olsson, 1976) and is caused by adaptation to alcohol at the brain cell level (brain tolerance).

Repeated exposure to alcohol results in resistance to intoxication (Goldberg, 1943). Goldberg (1943) examined tolerance in three types of drinkers: heavy, light, and abstainers. Impairment due to alcohol was measured using Goldberg's finger test (subject matches up forefingers). A plot of test accuracy versus blood alcohol level revealed parallel but different dose–response curves for the three groups of drinkers. Subjects with heavy drinking histories were less impaired than moderate drinkers or abstainers were. Goldberg interpreted this finding as evidence of tolerance. The clinical work of Jellinek (1960) suggested that alcohol tolerance required many years of heavy drinking; however, experimental studies in humans and animals indicate tolerance can develop rapidly. In animals, fourteen days of alcohol administration (3–6 g/kg/d) causes a shift in the dose–response curve of motor tasks in which the ED50 is increased by about 33 percent (LeBlanc, Kalant, Gibbins & Berman, 1969).

Tolerance also develops rapidly to other measures such as changing in body temperature (Brick & Horowitz, 1983; Crabbe et al., 1982; Goldstien & Zaechelein, 1983; Kalant & Le, 1984; Pohorecky, 1974; Pohorecky, Brick & Carpenter, 1986), incoordination ataxia (Crabbe et al., 1982; Hunt & Overstreet, 1977; Pohorecky et al., 1986), startle response (Pohorecky, et al., 1976b, 1986), analgesia (Pohorecky, Cagan & Brick, 1976; Pohorecky, et al., 1986), memory (Poulos, Wolff, Zilm & Caplan, 1981; Shapiro & Nathan, 1986), locomotor activity (Hunt and Overstreet, 1977), heart rate (Pohorecky et al., 1986a) and changes in electroencephalography (Zilm, 1981, Zilm, Kaplan & Capell, 1981).

Metabolic Tolerance

Metabolic tolerance is associated with specific liver enzymes that are induced as a result of chronic drinking. Enzyme activation increases alcohol degradation and reduces the time during which alcohol is active in the body, thereby reducing the duration of alcohol's intoxicating effects (liver tolerance) (Misra, Lefevre, Ishii, Rubin & Lieber, 1971).

If there is less drug available to alter general cellular function, there will be less effect of the drug on whatever response is being measured. With many drugs, their repeated administration results in enzyme induction so that more enzyme is available to metabolize the drug. Under such circumstances, the drug is metabolized more rapidly so it does not reach its full pharmacological effect due to metabolic tolerance. In human alcoholics, the magnitude of metabolic tolerance is unknown and is probably quite variable, but the overwhelming majority of drinkers eliminate alcohol at a rate of 10 to 20 mg/dL/hr with 15 mg/dL/hr being a good average (Dubowski, 1985). Some drinkers can eliminate alcohol at nearly twice the amount (Clothier, Kelly & Reed, 1985; Winek & Murphy, 1984). (*See* Chapter 3.1 regarding reported rates of alcohol elimination.) Dispositional tolerance could result from differences in alcohol absorption and distribution; however, the most important factor in altering drug availability to some target tissues is metabolism.

Cross-Tolerance

Cross-tolerance between alcohol and other drugs may develop through several different mechanisms, including the sharing of similar pathways of metabolism or receptor systems. The most consistent evidence concerning mechanisms of cross-tolerance comes from research on metabolic tolerance in which two different drugs share the same metabolic pathways. Known pathways of alcohol metabolism, include oxidative metabolism catalyzed by cytochrome P-450, reduced nicotinamide adenine dinucleotide phosphate and microsomal enzyme oxidating system. Drugs such as barbiturates and minor tranquillizers that utilize these systems may be removed from the body more slowly in the presence of alcohol. Thus the pharmacokinetic interactions of alcohol with other drugs can be toxic because of un-predicted high drug concentrations (Chakraborty, 1980; Lieber & Pirola, 1982). Interactions between alcohol and environmental factors as well as other drugs may also contribute to cross-tolerance (Kalant & Khanna, 1980). Alcohol drug interactions are discussed in Chapter 8.

Nonpharmacological (Pavlovian) Tolerance

An area of considerable scientific interest but not generally considered by toxicologists is the role of nonpharmacological (i.e., environmental) factors in the development of tolerance. Nonpharmacological tolerance is present when environmental cues act as conditioned stimuli and affect the response to alcohol (Brick, 1990; Dafters & Anderson, 1982; Mansfield & Cunningham, 1980; McCusker & Brown, 1990). This is not a new concept. One of the earliest learning-based theories of tolerance was the demonstration of state-dependent learning (Overton, 1966, 1972) characterized by the observation that a task learned and practiced under a drug state is better performed in the same drug state. The demonstration of state-dependent learning with alcohol suggested the possibility that tolerance and dependence can be explained in state-dependent terms. Performance steadily improves in the drug state until tolerance develops. Abrupt removal of the drug shifts the organism to the non-drug state and performance deficits occur.

Siegel and others have provided additional evidence that learning plays a significant role in the development of tolerance. Siegel's model (1978) of tolerance is by far the most influential and best supported model of its kind. Environmental stimuli preceding drug intake elicit a conditioned compensatory response, which attenuates the drug effect. In a classic Pavlovian conditioning paradigm, the conditioned stimuli consists of the various experimental procedures and environmental stimuli associated with the administration of the drug. The unconditioned stimuli are the actual direct pharmacological effects of the drug. The conditioned response, once formed by repeated administrations of the drug, may then be demonstrated with a placebo by presenting the usual drug administration cues (conditional stimuli) in the absence of the pharmacological effects of the drug (unconditioned stimuli). Siegel initially proposed that in accord with a Pavlovian conditioning theory, the conditioned responses should then mimic the unconditioned response. It does.

The conditioned response appears to be a preparation for, rather than a replica of, the unconditioned response. In other words the conditioned responses to drug-associated stimuli are in the opposite direction to the pharmacological effects to negate the disruption in homeostasis produced by the pharmacological agent. Conditioned tolerance has been demonstrated for many different drugs, including alcohol both in animals (Hinson & Siegel, 1980; Le, Poulos & Cappell, 1979; Mansfield & Cunningham, 1980; Melchior & Tabakoff, 1981, 1985) and in humans (Crowell, Hinson & Siegel, 1981; Dafters & Anderson, 1982; Newlin, 1985a,b; Shapiro & Nathan, 1986; Tiffany & Baker, 1986).

Vogel-Sprott (1979) tested tolerance to a hand-eye coordination task and coding vigilance measures of tolerance in male social drinkers before and after alcohol over the course of four sessions. Subjects in group 1 were given alcohol in the presence of a distinct set of environmental cues. Subjects in a second group were treated identically, except that they were not tested. Subjects in a third group received alcohol under a different set of environmental cues (and were tested before, rather than after, receiving alcohol). Subjects in a fourth group received a placebo during the phase of the study when tolerance developed. This phase of the study was followed by a tolerance test session in which all subjects received alcohol in the distinct environment and were then tested on the perceptual motor tasks. Subjects in the first and second groups were significantly less impaired, that is, more tolerant, on the coding vigilance task than were those in group three, just as the classic conditioning model of tolerance would predict.

Newlin examined expectancy effects of alcohol. If subjects were told they were receiving alcohol but actually received a placebo, subjects often showed physiological responses that were in the opposite direction to the acute effects of alcohol (Newlin, 1985, 1986). Such findings show evidence of conditioned compensatory responses and support a classic conditioning model of alcohol tolerance.

Shapiro and Nathan (1986) studied the role of Pavlovian conditioning in tolerance development in light to moderate drinkers assigned to one of two groups and then tested in four experimental phases. Both groups received five administrations of alcohol and five administrations of an equal volume of tonic on an alternating schedule during a ten-session tolerance development phase. Group 1 received alcohol under environmental conditions designated the "distinct environment" and received tonic in the "home environment". Group 2 was treated the same except the relationship between the environmental cues and the substance consumed was reversed. On the eleventh session, both groups received alcohol in the distinct environment. On day twelve both groups received tonic in the distinct environment. Tolerance was assessed from cognitive, motor, physiological, and affective responses.

Shapiro and Nathan (1986) found that subjects who received alcohol under cues previously associated with alcohol consumption (group 1) were significantly less impaired (more tolerant) in session eleven on the cognitive task than were subjects who received alcohol under cues never before associated with alcohol (group 2). Furthermore, in session twelve, group 1 subjects evidenced compensatory responses in the opposite direction to the unconditioned effect of the drug; that is, group 1 subjects performed significantly better on the cognitive task than did group 2 subjects. Although all other measures were sensitive to the effects of alcohol, the presence or absence of cues predicting alcohol consumption did not have a significant impact on these responses.

Although each of the various forms of tolerance should be considered in forensic evaluations, the tolerance most often brought into question is functional tolerance. Metabolic tolerance can be accounted for by using a range of metabolic rates, but behavioral tolerance (e.g., functional tolerance) does not have a metric that can be similarly applied to account for most drinkers.

Exceptionally Tolerant Drinkers

Chronic heavy drinkers may become exceptionally tolerant to the intoxicating effects of alcohol (*see* later). In such drinkers, an amount of alcohol that would cause overt intoxication, or even death, in the overwhelming majority of social drinkers may have little or no such effect. Such drinkers clearly demonstrate exceptional tolerance (*see* later) to the effects of alcohol so that any standards regarding visible intoxication that might be applied to nondrinkers, social drinkers, or even some alcoholics may not apply to a subset of the chronic drinking population. The size of this subset varies from study to study.

Jetter (1938) demonstrated that tolerance can be profound. Three of Jetter's 1000 subjects were not diagnosed as intoxicated, even though they had BACs in the 350 mg/dL range. Rosen and Lee (1976) compared alcoholics, heavy drinkers, and social drinkers on tasks before and after drinking. Some social drinkers showed varying signs of gross intoxication (defined as nausea, slurred speech, and poor coordination) at BACs of 100 mg/dL, whereas heavy drinkers and alcoholics showed no such signs. More recent studies have identified numerous individuals capable of drinking to BACs that are often lethal in most drinkers. For example, Johnson, Noll, and Rodney (1982) reported that a patient with a BAC of about 1,200 mg/dL was agitated and "slightly confused." Hammond and Schneider (1973) reported that a woman who was comatose upon arrival at the hospital, three hours later was able to provide a medical history even though her BAC was 520 mg/dL. Similarly, Jones (1999) reported a BAC of 545 mg/dL (the highest reported reading in Sweden at the time) in a driver arrested for drunk driving. However, no behavioral signs or symptoms were noted, other than that the subject, a woman, survived.

Lindblad and Olsson (1976) reported that about 8 patients per month (out of 2500) were admitted to a casualty ward with a BAC of more than 507 mg/ dL. They found 14 male (age 23–63) and two female (age 22 and 25) patients who were highly intoxicated. Eight of the 16 patients were asleep but could be roused, answer questions, and sit up in bed and drink fluids. These patients had serum alcohol concentrations of 530 mg/dL or more. The remaining patients were even less responsive but all survived even though BACs ranged from 599 to 783 mg/dL. (Note: serum alcohol concentrations are about 10–20% higher than equivalent BACs.)

Minion, Slovis, and Boutiette (1989) examined 204 emergency room patients with BACs ranging from 400 to 719 mg/dL (mean = 467 mg/dL). At BACs that would probably render most drinkers unconscious, and probably many subjects dead, a staggering 80 percent of this patient population were conscious enough to be questioned and found to be oriented to person, place, and time. Only 12 percent were disoriented or unresponsive to noxious stimuli.

Perper, Twerski, and Wienand (1986) found exceptional tolerance in a group of alcoholics who entered a detoxification center with BACs sometimes in excess of 400 mg/dL that would produce coma or death in less experienced drinkers. Remarkably, at BACs of more than 200 mg/dL, about 24 percent of the sample showed no sign of clinical intoxication, leading Perper and colleagues (1986) to conclude that caution must be exercised in the interpretation of a high BAC as an indicator of incapacitation or as an exclusive cause of death.

These findings are similar to those of Redmond (1983), who examined subjects who had been arrested for drunk driving or drunk and disorderly behavior and were admitted to detox in a hospital. BACs were measured and observations made regarding consciousness, responding to verbal command, and ability to give an adequate history. Redmond concluded, "it is apparent that a BAC of 500 mg/dL is not invariably fatal and may exist without serious impairment of conscious level" (1983, p. 89).

The data also point out the importance of understanding the definition of intoxication within any particular study. For example, although the authors note that many of the patients showed no signs of clinical intoxication, the results also show that speech was impaired in 43 percent of the alcoholic subjects, gait was impaired in 59 percent of the subjects, verbal comprehension was impaired in 24 percent of the subjects, and 50 percent of the subjects were unable to undress themselves. Even among a population of alcoholics with apparently exceptional tolerance, impairment in speech, gait, and fine and gross motor coordination were often seen during casual observation.

The previous studies challenge clinical dogma that BACs in the 400 to 500 mg/dL range would be invariably fatal in all patients. Rather, BACs in this range are lethal for some part of the population. Although the exact lethal dose of alcohol for a specific population is not known, there are individuals with such exceptional tolerance that they can function to varying degrees with BACs that are sometimes seven or eight times the current legal definition for driving while intoxicated in the United States. Such patients are nevertheless impaired with respect to safely operating a motor vehicle.

10.3 ALCOHOL USE DISORDERS

Terms such as alcohol use, abuse and dependence are used regularly and have worked their way into professional and lay conversations, sometimes with little appreciation of their meaning or changing definitions. In the United States, the primary diagnostic classifications come from the Diagnostic and Statistical Manual of Mental Disorders (DSM) (American Psychiatric Association 2000, 2013). The previous edition of the DSM (prior to and including DSM-IV-TR) defined two types of drinkers: those with alcohol abuse and those with alcohol dependence. Under older DSM definitions, alcohol abuse is intentional, conscious, and voluntarily; patients make poor choices and decisions regarding their drinking, often resulting in injuries to themselves or others, medical consequences and expenses, lost productivity, and family problems. Driving while intoxicated is an example of alcohol abuse, as is drinking while pregnant. In fact, most people with alcohol problems are alcohol abusers, a term that connotes a dark stigma often misinterpreted to imply tolerance, dependence, or both. All that changed in 2013 with the publication of the long-awaited DSM-V was the elimination of the term alcohol "abuse." The term abuse is so inherently descriptive, however, it will continue to be used.

Need for Diagnostic Clarity

It is against this historical background that diagnostic criteria and terms in the field of alcohol (and drug) disorders have changed. The recently published DSM-V (2013) combines older terms such as abuse and dependence into a new single category termed alcohol use disorders. Alcohol use disorders eliminate pejorative terms that may introduce bias when used in forensic evaluations or testimony. For example, in the DSM–IV, alcohol abuse could be defined by a single drinking event, such as intoxicated driving. Yet, casual reference to a person who consumed alcohol as an alcohol abuser could be misleading to laypersons (e.g., a jury) who may infer tolerance or stereotyped characteristics. There is little doubt that the term alcohol abuse will continue to be used by clinicians (forensic or otherwise) because of the risky behavior that places the drinker (or others) at significant risk. In such cases, the diagnostic criteria should be explained because the term alcohol abuse is technically inaccurate from a psychiatric perspective. For example, although driving while intoxicated is dangerous, it is questionable if this symptom alone rises to a psychiatric diagnosis, and even then, under DSM-IV criteria a diagnosis of alcohol dependence may occur without a diagnosis of abuse for the same patient. These "diagnostic orphans" who have the same severity of substance problems as others do not fit into any DSM-IV diagnostic category. The term alcohol abuse is also linguistically incorrect since alcohol is not the object of abuse. Child or spousal abuse describes abuse of a person, which everyone understands. However, the term alcohol abuse makes no linguistic sense since alcohol is not the subject person being abused. Therefore, the term alcohol abuse is technically inaccurate. Even so, many experts in the field disagree and the term abuse will continue to be used by both experts and laypersons (Erickson, 2007).

The new DSM-V combines substance abuse and dependence into a single disorder (substance use disorder) that includes (using alcohol as an example) (a) a problematic pattern of alcohol use leading to clinically significant impairment or distress and (b) two or more of the following within a 12-month period: alcohol taken in larger amounts or over a longer period than intended; persistent or unsuccessful desire to cut down or control drinking; great deal of time in alcohol-related activities or recovering from its effects; recurrent alcohol use resulting in a failure to fulfill major obligations at work, school, home; continued use despite recurrent social or interpersonal problems from alcohol use; recurrent alcohol use in which it is physically hazardous (e.g., driving, operating machinery); continued alcohol use despite knowledge of physical or psychological problems caused by or exacerbated by alcohol; withdrawal syndrome; and craving or strong desire or urge to use alcohol. The severity of each substance use disorder is based on the number of factors or criteria present. These range from zero or one (no diagnosis) to six or more (severe substance use disorder).

Impaired control, which is at the center of our newer definitions of addiction or dependence, still has both psychological and physical components, but they are different from the old World Health Organization definition. Impaired control is an obsessive preoccupation with the use of the drug (psychological) caused primarily by a neurochemical (physical) dysfunction in the brain. Older concepts such as physical addiction and psychological addiction have no accurate meaning and terms such as alcohol addict are vague and scientifically imprecise and should not be used. Erickson (2007) points out that these are pejorative terms (e.g., drunks, addicts) that detract from the science of alcohol dependence as a brain disease (Brick and Erickson, 2013; Erickson, 2007).

Conclusions

Alcohol is one of the most widely used drugs in the United States and elsewhere and is frequently found in toxicology results stemming from investigations of accidental and intentional injuries. Forensic evaluations of cases in which alcohol is involved should take into account differences between social alcohol use and alcohol use disorders when describing drinker characteristics, and particularly, the biobehavioral consequences of long-term and short-term alcohol use should be interpreted in the context of current clinical definitions and facts in evidence. Multiple forms of tolerance can result from acute or chronic alcohol use and some form of tolerance develops in all drinkers. Tolerance is a relative term and by itself should not be considered indicative of more severe degrees of alcohol use disorder. Similarly, a diagnosis of alcohol dependence (or alcohol use disorder) should not lead to speculation regarding exceptional tolerance unless supported by additional evidence. Finally, tolerance should be considered in pharmacokinetic estimates of alcohol use, for example, as well as in describing or predicting behaviors following the consumption of alcohol. By using standardized definitions of what constitute use and dependence and understanding the nature of tolerance and biobehavioral complications from alcohol withdrawal, forensic examiners can communicate accurately and without bias information relevant to jurors and the court.

REFERENCES

American Psychiatric Association. (2000). *Diagnostic and Statistical Manual of Mental Disorders* (4th ed., DSM-IV-TR). Washington, D.C.: Author.

American Psychiatric Association. (2013). *Diagnostic and Statistical Manual of Mental Disorders* (5th ed., DSM-V). Washington, D.C.: Author.

Annear, W., and Vogel-Sprott, M. (1985). Mental rehearsal and classical conditioning contribute to ethanol tolerance in humans. *Psychopharmacology, 87,* 90–93.

Beirness, D., and Vogel-Sprott, M. (1984). Alcohol tolerance in social drinkers: Operant and classical conditioning effects. *Psychopharmacology, 84,* 393–397.

Bennett, R., Cherek, D., and Spiga, R. (1993). Acute and chronic alcohol tolerance in humans: Effects of dose and consecutive days of exposure. *Alcoholism, Clinical and Experimental Research, 17,* 740–745.

Brick, J. (1990). Learning and motivational factors in alcohol consumption. In W. M. Cox (Ed.), *Why People Drink: Parameters of Alcohol as a Reinforcer* (pp. 169–192). New York, NY: Gardner Press.

Brick, J. (2006). Standardization of alcohol calculations in research. *Alcoholism, Clinical and Experimental Research, 30*(8), 1276–1287.

Brick, J. (2012) Alcohol: Use, tolerance, and dependence. In A. Jamieson and A. Moenssens (Eds.), *Wiley Encyclopedia of Forensic Science. Chichester*, UK: John Wiley & Sons Ltd. DOI: 10.1002/9780470061589.fsa.628.pub2

Brick, J., and Erickson, C. K. (2013). *Drugs, the Brain, and Behavior: The Pharmacology of Drug Use Disorders* (2nd ed., pp. 170–178). New York, NY: Routledge.

Brick, J., and Horowitz, G. P. (1983). Tolerance and cross tolerance to morphine and ethanol in mice selectively bred for differential sensitivity to ethanol. *Journal of Studies on Alcohol, 44*(5), 770–779.

Carpenter, J. (1963). Effects of alcohol on some psychological processes. *Quarterly Journal of Studies on Alcohol, 23*, 274–314.

Chakraborty, J. (1980). Metabolic basis of ethanol-drug interactions. In M. Sandler (Ed.), *Psychopharmacology of Alcohol* (pp. 191–198). New York, NY: Raven Press.

Clothier, J., Kelly, J., and Reed, K. (1985). Varying rates of alcohol metabolism in relation to detoxification and medication. *Alcohol, 2*, 443–445.

Connors, G., and Maisto, S. (1979). Effects of alcohol, instructions and consumption rate on affect and physiological sensations. *Psychopharmacology, 62*, 261–266.

Crabbe, J., Janowsky, J., Young, E., Kosobud, A., Stack, J., and Rigter, H. (1982). Tolerance to ethanol hypothermia in inbred mice: Genotypic correlations with behavioral responses. *Alcoholism, Clinical and Experimental Research, 6*, 446–458.

Crowell, C., Hinson, R., and Siegel, S. (1981). The role of conditional drug responses in tolerance to the hypothermic effects of ethanol. *Psychopharmacology, 73*, 51–54.

Dafters, R., and Anderson, G. (1982). Conditioned tolerance to the tachycardia effect of ethanol in humans. *Psychopharmacology, 78*, 365–367.

Dawson, D., Grant, B., and Chou, P. (1995). Gender differences in alcohol intake. In W. A. Hunt and S. Zakhari (Eds.), *Stress, Gender, and Alcohol-Seeking Behavior* (pp. 1–21). (National Institute on Alcohol Abuse and Alcoholism Research Monograph No. 29. NIH Pub. No. 95–3893.) Bethesda, MD: National Institutes of Health.

Dubowski, K. M. (1985). Absorption, distribution and elimination of alcohol: Highway safety aspects. *Journal of Studies on Alcohol, Supplement, 10*, 98–108.

Dufour, M. (1999). What is moderate drinking? *Alcohol Research & Health, 23*(1), 5–14.

Dufour, M., Colliver, J., Grigson, M., and Stinson, F. (1990). Use of alcohol and tobacco. In J. C. Cornoni-Huntley, R. R. Huntley, and J. J. Feldman, (Eds.), *Health Status and Well-Being of the Elderly* (pp. 172–183). New York, NY: Oxford University Press.

Erickson, C. K. (2007). *The Science of Addiction: From Neurobiology to Treatment.* New York, NY: W. W. Norton.

Goldberg, L. (1943). Quantitative studies on alcohol tolerance in man. The influence of ethyl alcohol on sensory, motor and psychological functions referred to blood alcohol in normal and habituated individuals. *Acta Physiologica Scandinavica, 5* (Suppl.), 1–128.

Goldstein, D., and Zaechelein, R. (1983). Time course of functional tolerance produced in mice by inhalation of ethanol. *Journal of Pharmacology and Experimental Therapeutics, 227*, 150–153.

Hammond, M., and Schneider, C. (1973). Behavioral changes induced in mice fol-
    lowing termination of ethanol administration. *British Journal of Pharmacology*, *47*,
    667–675.

Hinson, R., and Siegel, S. (1980). The contribution of Pavlovian conditioning to etha-
    nol tolerance and dependence. In H. Rigter and J. C. Crabbe (Eds.), *Alcohol Toler-
    ance and Dependence* (pp. 181–199). Amsterdam, The Netherlands: Elsevier/North
    Holland Biomedical Press.

Hunt, G. P., and Overstreet, D. H. (1977). Evidence for parallel development of toler-
    ance to the hyperactivating and discoordinating effects of ethanol. *Psychopharma-
    cology*, *55*(1), 75–81.

Jellinek, E. (1960). *The Disease Concept of Alcoholism*. Highland Park, NJ: Hillhouse
    Press.

Jetter, W. (1938). Studies in alcohol. I. Diagnosis of acute alcoholic intoxication by a
    correlation of clinical and chemical findings. *American Journal of Medical Science*,
    196, 475–487.

Johnson, R. A., Noll, E. C., and Rodney, W. M. (1982). Survival after a serum ethanol
    concentration of 1 1/2%. *Lancet*, *2*(8312), 1394.

Johnson, L. D., O'Malley, P. M., and Bachman, J. G. (1996). *National Survey Results on
    Drug Use from the Monitoring the Future Study 1975–1994*. (NIH Publication No. 96-
    4027.) Rockville, MD: National Institute on Drug Abuse.

Jones, A. W. (1999). The drunkest drinking driver in Sweden: Blood alcohol concen-
    tration 0.545% w/v. *Journal of Studies on Alcohol*, *60*(3), 400–406.

Jones, B. M. (1974). Circadian variation in the effects of alcohol on cognitive perfor-
    mance. *Quarterly Journal of Studies on Alcohol*, *35*(4), 1212–1219.

Kalant, H., and Khanna, J. (1980). Environmental-neurochemical interactions in eth-
    anol tolerance. In M. Sandler (Ed.), *Psychopharmacology of Alcohol* (pp. 107–120).
    New York, NY: Raven Press.

Kalant, H., and Lê, A.D. (1984). Effects of ethanol on thermoregulation. *Pharmacology
    and Therapeutics*, *23*(3), 313–364.

Lê, A. D., Poulos, C. X., and Cappell, H. (1979). Conditioned tolerance to the hypo-
    thermic effect of ethyl alcohol. *Science*, *206*(4422), 1109–1110.

LeBlanc, A., Kalant, H., and Gibbins, R. (1975). Acute tolerance to ethanol in the rat.
    Psychopharmacologia, *41*, 43–46.

LeBlanc, A., Kalant, H., Gibbins, R., and Berman, N. (1969). Acquisition and loss of
    tolerance to ethanol by the rat. *Journal of Pharmacology and Experimental Therapeu-
    tics*, *168*, 244–250.

Lieber, C. S., and Pirola, R. C. (1982). Clinical relevance of alcohol-drug interactions.
    In C. S. Lieber and B. Stimmel (Eds.), *Recent Advances in the Biology of Alcoholism*
    (pp. 41–66). New York, NY: Haworth Press.

Lindblad, B., and Olsson, R. (1976). Unusually high levels of blood alcohol. *Journal of
    the American Medical Association*, *236*, 1600–1602.

Longnecker, M., Lissner, L., Holden, J., Flack, V., Taylor, P., Stampfer, M., and
    Willet, W. (1993). The reproducibility and validity of a self-administered semi-
    quantitative food frequency questionnaire in subjects from South Dakota and
    Wyoming. *Epidemiology*, *4*(4), 356–365.

Mansfield, J. G., and Cunningham, C. L. (1980). Conditioning and extinction of tolerance to the hypothermic effect of ethanol in rats. *Journal of Comparative and Physiological Psychology, 94,* 962–969.

McCusker, C., and Brown, K. (1990). Alcohol-predictive cues enhance tolerance to and precipitate "craving" for alcohol in social drinkers. *Journal of Studies on Alcohol, 51,* 494–499.

Melchior, C., and Tabakoff, B. (1981). Modification of environmentally cued tolerance to ethanol in mice. *Journal of Pharmacology and Experimental Therapeutics, 219,* 175–180.

Melchior, C., and Tabakoff, B. (1985). Features of environmentally dependent tolerance to ethanol. *Psychopharmacology, 87,* 94–100.

Mellanby, E. (1919). *Alcohol: Its Absorption into and Disappearance from the Blood Under Different Conditions.* Medical Research Committee Special Report Series, No. 31. London, UK: Her Majesty's Stationery Office.

Minion, G., Slovis, C., and Boutiette, L. (1989). Severe alcohol intoxication: A study of 204 consecutive patients, *Clinical Toxicology, 27*(6), 375–384.

Misra, P., Lefevre, A., Ishii, H., Rubin, E., and Lieber, C. (1971). Increase of ethanol, meprobamate and pentobarbital metabolism after chronic ethanol administration in man and rats. *American Journal of Medicine, 51,* 346–351.

Newlin, D. (1985a). Human conditioned compensatory response to alcohol cues: Initial evidence. *Alcohol, 2*(3), 507–509.

Newlin, D. (1986). The antagonistic placebo response to alcohol cues. *Alcoholism, Clinical and Experimental Research, 9*(5), 411–416.

National Institute on Alcohol Abuse and Alcoholism (NIAAA). (2014). *Alcohol Facts and Statistics.* Retrieved July 14, 2014. Available www.niaaa.nih.gov

Niaura, R., Nathan, P., Frankenstein, W., Shapiro, A., and Brick, J. (1987). Gender differences in acute psychomotor and pharmacokinetic response to alcohol. *Addictive Behaviors, 12,* 345–356.

Oates, J. F. Jr., and McCay, R. T. (1973). *Laboratory Evaluation of Alcohol Safety Interlock Systems* (Vol. 3, Instrument Performance at High BAL). Report DOT-TSC-NHTSA-73-3, III. Springfield, VA: National Technical Information Service.

Overton, D. A. (1966). State dependency learning produced by depressant and atropine like drugs. *Psychopharmacologia, 10,* 6–31.

Overton, D. A. (1972). State-dependent learning produced by alcohol and its relevance to alcoholism. In B. Kissin and H. Begleiter (Eds.), *The Biology of Alcoholism* (Vol. 2. Physiology and Behavior, pp. 193–217). New York, NY: Springer US.

Perper, J. A., Twerski, A., and Wienand, J. W. (1986). Tolerance at high blood alcohol concentrations: A study of 110 cases and review of the literature. *Journal of Forensic Science, 31*(1), 212–221.

Pohorecky, L. (1974). Effects of ethanol on central and peripheral noradrenergic neurons. *Journal of Pharmacology and Experimental Therapeutics, 189,* 380–391.

Pohorecky, L., Brick, J., and Carpenter, A. (1986). Assessment of the development of tolerance to ethanol using multiple measures. *Alcoholism, Clinical and Experimental Research, 10,* 616–622.

Pohorecky, L., Brick, J., and Sun, J. (1976a). Serotonergic involvement in the effect of ethanol on body temperature in rats. *Journal of Pharmacy and Pharmacology, 28,* 157–159.

Pohorecky, L., Cagan, M., Brick, J., and Jaffe, L. (1976b). The startle response in rates: Effect of ethanol. *Pharmacology, Biochemistry, and Behavior, 4,* 311–316.

Pohorecky, L., Peterson, T., and Carpenter, J. (1986). Development of tolerance to ethanol in heart rate of rats. *Journal of Alcohol and Drug Research, 6,* 431–439.

Poulos, C., Wolff, L., Zilm, D., and Caplan, H. (1981). Acquisition of tolerance to alcohol-induced memory deficits in humans. *Psychopharmacology, 73,* 176–179.

Redmond, A. D. (1983). BAC and conscious level. *Alcohol and Alcoholism, 18,* 89–91.

Rosen, L., and Lee, C. (1976). Acute and chronic effects of alcohol use on organizational processes in memory. *Journal of Abnormal Psychology, 85,* 309–317.

Seward, J. (1970). Conditioning theory. In M. Marx (Ed.), *Learning Theories.* New York, NY: Macmillan.

Shapiro, A., and Nathan, P. (1986). Human tolerance to alcohol: The role of Pavlovian conditioning processes. *Psychopharmacology, 88,* 90–95.

Siegel, S. (1978). A Pavlovian conditioning analysis of morphine. In N. A. Krasnegor (Ed.), *Behavioral Tolerance; Research and Treatment Implications* (pp. 27–53). NIDA Research Monograph 18. Washington, D.C.: U.S. Government Printing Office.

Tiffany, S., and Baker, T. (1986). Tolerance to alcohol: Psychological models and their application to alcoholism. *Annals of Behavioral Medicine, 8,* 7–12.

U.S. Department of Health and Human Services (DHHS), and U.S. Department of Agriculture (USDA). (1995). *Nutrition and Your Health: Dietary Guidelines for Americans* (4th ed.). Home and Garden Bulletin No. 232. Washington, D.C.: USDA.

Vogel-Sprott, M. (1979). Acute recovery and tolerance to low doses of alcohol: Differences in cognitive and motor skill performance. *Psychopharmacology, 61,* 287–291.

Vogel-Sprott, M., Rawana, E., and Webster, R. (1984). Mental rehearsal of a task under ethanol facilitates tolerance. *Pharmacology, Biochemistry, and Behavior, 21,* 329–331.

Winek, C., and Murphy, K. (1984). The rate and kinetic order of ethanol elimination. *Forensic Science International, 25,* 159–166.

Zilm, D. (1981). Ethanol-induced spontaneous and evoked EEG, heart rate and respiration rate changes in man. *Clinical Toxicology, 18,* 549–563.

Zilm, D., Kaplan, H., and Capell, H. (1981). Electroencephalographic tolerance and abstinence phenomena during repeated alcohol ingestion by non-alcoholics. *Science, 212,* 1175–1177.

Chapter 11

ALCOHOL CALCULATIONS[1]

11.1 THE NEED FOR STANDARDIZATION

In criminal and civil litigation, forensic alcohol experts are often called upon to make estimates of alcohol use and intoxication based on subjective and objective evidence or to reconcile differences between them. Although subjective reporting of ethanol (alcohol) use as well as objective results from chemical testing are common variables in alcohol research, there is often inconsistency in the reporting and interpretation of alcohol test results. Reporting errors can range from the proverbial "I only had two beers, Officer" to a misunderstanding of how alcohol is commercially formulated, quantified, and reported by different laboratory techniques; what constitutes a drink; or how to estimate the number of drinks consumed (Kerr, Greenfield, Tujague & Brown, 2005; Turner, 1990). In other instances, drink equivalents are not clearly described in police interviews, depositions, or even research. For example, in a recent study, a drink was defined as either 1 oz of distilled spirits containing 43 percent ethanol, 6 oz of wine containing 12 to 14 percent ethanol, or 12 oz of beer containing 6 percent ethanol (Chiu et al., 2004). Yet, when these amounts are correctly calculated, 6 oz of 14 percent wine contains about twice as much alcohol as 1 oz of 86-proof alcohol. Therefore, a drink is not a drink unless defined or standardized.

The medical and psychosocial consequences of acute or chronic drinking alcohol research are often based upon blood or breath alcohol test results or self-report data, that are then standardized in some way to the number of drinks consumed over some period (e.g., days, weeks, months). Such data can be used to correlate alcohol intake with some dependent variable of interest to the health and safety of the public. For example, the National Highway Traffic Safety Administration (NHTSA, 1994) published guidelines for legislators to calculate BACs to assist in their deliberations regarding drinking and

---

1. Note: This chapter is largely reproduced from Brick (2006) and used with permission of the publisher.

driving laws. Although this publication demonstrated the need for such information, it did not provide details on how to handle calculations to estimate
alcohol consumption or intoxication. Another area of interest when defining
a drink concerns the risks and benefits of moderate drinking on health
(Dufour, 1999; WHO, 2000). For example, modest alcohol intake of less than
one drink per day is associated with higher bone density, but chronic consumption of relatively low amounts of alcohol (one to two drinks per day for
women, three to four drinks per day for men) can interfere with the normal
metabolism of nutrients and may be a major cause of alcohol-induced bone
disorders. However, in a review of other studies it was found that two to six
drinks per week significantly increases the risk of fractures in men, compared
with subjects who consume less than two drinks per week (Brick, 2008, 2009;
see also Chapter 9). Indicators of acute and chronic alcohol-related harm, including the amount of alcohol consumed, can be obtained from many sources
and can affect on medical, psychosocial, economic, and other life events
(WHO, 2000). The physiological consequences of alcohol abuse are complex, but it is clear how variations in what constitutes a drink can significantly
affect the interpretation of results. Consider the often-cited cliché from arrested intoxicated drivers who state they only consumed two beers.

The reliability of self-report alcohol consumption data increases if certain
methodological protocols are implemented (Babor, Stephens & Marlatt, 1987;
Cohen and Vinson, 1995; Sommers et al., 2000). Although some researchers
appreciate the importance of the "concept of a standard drink" in self-reported survey data (Sommers et al., 2000), methodological details or assumptions regarding what constitutes a drink for individual subjects are rarely
reported or are not considered in many studies. Variability from self-report
data is further complicated when researchers erroneously interpret their own
or someone else's data. For example, it is often useful in forensic cases to
relate self-reported drinking quantity and frequency or to express a BAC in
terms of how many alcoholic drinks were consumed in comparison to an objective blood test. This is useful in determining the amount of alcohol served
or consumed as well as determining the credibility of a witness. In both instances, it is important to determine how much alcohol was contained in each
drink, because what constitutes a drink varies depending upon the formulation of drinks at bars and restaurants; type of beverage; and the way govern-
ments, researchers (Turner, 1990; WHO, 2000), subjects (Kerr et al., 2005),
and witnesses in litigation define a drink.

If the driving data are not collected in a systematic and sound manner, it
may skew the results. This problem may be exacerbated when scientists attempt meta-analyses or compare the effects of drinks per day within or between studies or countries. For example, when a subject in Great Britain
admits to consuming five beers or whiskey drinks, it may not be the equivalent of five drinks in the United States, or elsewhere. Given the range of

beverage formulations of beer (Case, Destefano & Logan, 2000) and spirits (Miller, Heather & Hall., 1991), the drinks are probably not equivalent unless the investigator has asked each subject to describe what constitutes a drink so that data can be properly evaluated. Kerr and colleagues (2005) found substantial variation in the way subjects reported drinks of wine or spirits, but less so with beer (Kerr et al., 2005).

Some investigators administer alcohol based upon body weight and then measure some effect of the dose administered. If body weight alone is the only consideration, it is likely that the resulting BACs will vary considerably among subjects. The interpretation of such an approach is even more complicated when practical or financial constraints preclude objective alcohol test measurements. In such cases, a standardized dosing protocol that accounts for individual physiological characteristics such as age, gender, height, and weight will result in more homogeneous results within and among studies.

Finally, reports of BAC often do not specify whether alcohol test results are from blood, serum, or plasma. Results from different specimens are not equivalent, and failure to identify the matrix can result in further inconsistency in interpreting alcohol data. In forensic matters this may alter the validity of studies that purport to show the effect of a particular number of drinks with a measured BAC.

In order to more systematically describe and interpret self-report and BAC results in research and applied forensic settings, three topics are reviewed: calculating alcohol equivalents, dosing methodologies, and alcohol test results. In this chapter, which is derived largely from a review (Brick, 2006), how various alcohol estimates are calculated is explained with the recommendation that forensic examiners use a consistent language in calculating and interpreting alcohol evidence.

Calculating Alcohol Equivalents

Alcohol formulations vary by consumer demand and geographically to accommodate different drinking preferences. Although the amount of alcohol in a typical drink varies based upon drink configuration, cost, glass size, and so on, in the United States for example, a standard drink equivalent can be operationally defined as a 5-oz glass of wine (12% volume [of solute] per volume [of solute][v/v]), a 12-oz beer (5 v/v%) or a mixed or straight drink containing 1.5 oz of 80-proof alcohol (i.e., 40% v/v), because each of these drinks contain approximately the same amount of alcohol, about 14 g, or proportionally less with smaller servings or lower concentrations per drink, and vice versa. A standard drink may vary geographically. The calculation of these amounts is explained later along with examples, so that such data can be better understood when they are collected and reported regardless of the country of origin.

To begin with, the concentration and volume of alcohol must be known in order to estimate consumption. The most basic formula to determine the concentration of a solution is

Formula 1: Basic equation to calculate the strength of a solution

$$C_s = g/v$$

where C_s is the concentration (%) of a solution, g is weight in grams (of alcohol), and v is volume of fluid. When v = 100 mL, 1 g or 1000 mg of a dissolved substance, the solute, in 100 mL of water results in a 1-percent concentration of that solution.

It is common for alcoholic beverage concentrations to be expressed as a percentage such as for beer and wine, whereas distilled spirits (e.g., rum, vodka, gin, whiskey) are usually expressed as proof, an indirect expression of percentage. The term *proof* is derived from a Seventeenth century method to quantify alcohol by combining gunpowder and alcohol. The wet gunpowder would ignite only if the alcohol content was high enough (and the water content low enough). If the gunpowder ignited, it was proof that the alcohol concentration was sufficient. In the United States, the proof is two times the concentration in volume. For example, in a 100-proof beverage, alcohol is 50 percent by volume (50% v/v).

Previously, alcohol concentrations were expressed as % v/v, meaning the percent of alcohol by volume. The volume percent (% v/v) is defined as the (volume of solute/volume of solution) × 100. This is the standard way manufacturers report alcohol concentrations. In many scientific calculations, it is more useful to know the concentration of alcohol by weight (% w/v). The weight percentage (% w/v) is defined as the (weight of solute/weight of solution) × 100. Therefore, alcohol by volume (% v/v) is not the same as alcohol by weight (% w/v). By standardizing drinks by the weight of alcohol in grams (not the percent volume), a more accurate comparison among beverages is possible. Since alcohol has a different density than water has, the total amount of alcohol by weight in a 50% v/v solution is less, in proportion to the specific gravity (weight of fluid relative to the weight of water) of the alcohol, which is approximately 0.79 g/mL (Weast, 1973). Although various physical factors, including temperature, may affect the specific gravity, we follow the general convention among alcohol researchers and use a value of approximately 0.79 g/mL as the specific gravity of alcohol (Miller et al., 1991; Turner, 1990; WHO, 2000). Therefore, the total amount of alcohol in any alcoholic beverage can be calculated, assuming 1 U.S. fl oz of alcohol equals 29.57 mL and weighs 0.79 g/mL. The following formulas show how the total amount of alcohol is calculated in distilled spirits, beer, or wine.

Formula 2: Equation to convert "proof" to percentage alcohol by volume and weight

Percentage of alcohol (A) by weight (w/v) for distilled spirits can be calculated as

$$A_{w/v} = (\text{proof of beverage}/2) \times (0.79).$$

Example.   80 proof/2 = 40% v/v.
Then to convert concentration by volume (v/v) to concentration by weight (w/v),

$$40\% \text{ v/v} \times 0.79 = 31.6 \text{ g of alcohol per 100 mL} = 31.6\% \text{ w/v}.$$

In the United Kingdom, Canada, and Australia, where British imperial units are used rather than the Apothecaries' system used in the United States, proof is defined differently. Under the imperial proof system, 100 proof is defined differently by comparing equal volumes of water and alcohol. When the alcoholic beverage weighs 12/13ths of water, it is deemed proof that the alcohol concentration is 50 percent (100 proof). In the United States, 1 degree of proof is equal to 0.50 percent alcohol by volume (100 proof = 50% v/v), but in the United Kingdom, for example, 1 degree of proof is equal to about 0.571 percent alcohol by volume. Thus, in the United Kingdom 100 proof is 57.1% v/v and 46 proof in the United States would be equal to 81 imperial proof units (46/57.1 = 80.6). Therefore, in the United States., the percentage of alcohol by volume is the proof divided by two, but in the United Kingdom, Canada, and Australia, imperial proof divided by 1.751 (Formula 3) gives the equivalent percentage of alcohol by volume (v/v).

Formula 3: Calculation of percentage of alcohol by weight for liquor in imperial units

$$(80 \text{ proof}/1.751) \times 0.79 = 36.1\% \text{ w/v}.$$

It is noted in the United Kingdom, that in more recent years drinks are described as units. A standard drink unit is defined as 8 g of alcohol. Formula 4 calculates the number of units in a metric proportioned drink.

Formula 4: Calculating units of alcohol in a drink

$$\frac{A \text{ v/v } (\%) \times \text{ml per container}}{1000}$$

Example.   750 mL of 12% v/v wine contains 9 units.

$$\frac{12 \times 750}{1000} = 9 \text{ units per 750-mL bottle.}$$

Example.   330 mL of 6% v/v beer contains approximately 2 units

$$\frac{330 \times 6\% \text{ v/v}}{1000} = 1.98.$$

Although units are a standardized way to describe the contents of an alcohol drink, the unit is an alcohol of volume measurement. This difference must be appreciated and noted when comparing drink units with other standard drink equivalents.

Beer and wine manufacturers usually list the percentage of alcohol by volume (% v/v) on their labels. To determine the total amount of alcohol per oz of serving, the percentage of alcohol by weight (% w/v) can be calculated using Formula 5.

Formula 5: Calculating percentage of alcohol by weight (w/v) in beers and wines

$$A_{w/v} = (A_{v/v}) \times (0.79).$$

Example. 4.75% v/v beer contains 3.753 g of alcohol per 100 mL (3.75% w/v).
12% v/v wine contains 9.48 g of alcohol per 100 mL (9.48% w/v).

Once the percentage of alcohol by weight for any beverage is known, alcohol intake across different types of drinks and studies can be made. This makes it possible to compare grams of alcohol consumed per person across an infinite range of beverages and beverage sizes. Formula 6 takes this analysis one step further by calculating total grams of alcohol per ounce.

Formula 6: Calculation of total grams (Σg) of alcohol per oz of fluid

$$\Sigma g = A_{w/v}/100 \times (mL/oz)$$

From Formulas 2 and 6, it can be calculated that one oz of 80-proof liquor contains 9.3441 oz of absolute alcohol. From Formula 2, the total alcohol by weight ($A_{w/v}$) of an 80-proof liquor is 31.6% w/v. The total number of grams per oz is then calculated using Formula 5 by dividing the percent of alcohol by volume derived from Formula 2 (31.6%) by 100 (to obtain grams per milliliter) and multiplying the result times the number of milliliters per oz (29.57). This is illustrated in the following example, where the term deciliter (dL) is used. A deciliter is 100 mL or 1/10 of a liter.

Example. (31.6 g/dL/100) × (29.57) = 9.3441 g of alcohol per oz of 80-proof liquor.

Applying the previous formula, we can see that the following alcoholic beverages contain approximately the same number of grams of alcohol and are therefore, for all practical purposes, equivalent:

> 5 oz wine (12% v/v wine) contains 14.02 g of alcohol.
> 12 oz of beer (5% v/v) contains 14.02 g of alcohol.
> 1.5 oz of liquor (80 proof or 40% v/v) contains 14.02 g of alcohol.

Formula 7: Calculation of total grams (Σg) of alcohol per serving

$$mL × \% \text{ v/v} × .79.$$

When alcoholic beverage containers contain metric volumes (e.g., milliliters), the grams per serving is easily found by first dividing milliliters by milliliters per ounce, or using Formula 6.

Example. $\dfrac{350 \text{ mL} × 4.75\% × .79}{100} = 13.13$ grams of alcohol per serving.

These drink equivalent calculations correspond with data published in the Untied States wherein a standard drink is often defined as about 14 g or 0.6 oz of absolute alcohol (U.S. Department of Agriculture, 2005). Lower alcohol content beers or smaller servings will proportionally decrease what constitutes a drink. The WHO, for example, notes that in the United States, a standard drink is defined as 12 g but sometimes 14 g of alcohol (WHO, 2000).

Similarly, the total number of grams of alcohol can be recalculated across any drink formulation if you know (1) the percentage or proof of the alcohol (available from any number of sources) and (2) the number of oz served in each drink. For example, how does a drinker in Beijing, China who consumes three cans of beer per day, each containing 350 mL of 4% (v/v) alcohol, compare to a person in New Hope, Pennsylvania, who drinks three 12-oz beers per day each containing 5.25% (v/v) alcohol or a person in Los Angeles, California, who consumes three 2-oz drinks containing 80-proof gin per day? If a drink is standardized to mean 1.5 oz of 80-proof alcohol or the equivalent, then the equivalent comparison among these drinkers is that their daily alcohol intake is about 2.4, 3.2, and 4.0 drinks, respectively, even though all three subjects may have reported that they consumed three drinks per day. The analysis is explained as follows:

Example. Three 350-mL beers each containing 4.0% v/v alcohol:
    4.0% v/v beer = 0.0316 g/mL = 0.93441 g/oz/
    350/29.57 = (11.836 oz per drink × 0.93441 g/oz) × 3 drinks = 33.179 g.
    33.179 g/14 g = 2.37 standard drinks per day.

Example. Three 12-oz beers each containing 5.25% v/v alcohol:
    5.25% (v/v) beer = 0.0415 g/mL = 1.2264 g/oz.
    (1.2264 g/oz × 12 oz) = 14.72 g × 3 drinks = 44.15 g.
    44.15 g/14g = 3.15 standard drinks per day.

Example. Three 2-oz drinks of 80-proof liquor:
    80 proof = 0.316 g/mL × 29.57 = 9.3441 g/oz.
    (9.3441 g/oz × 2) = 18.69 g × 3 drinks = 56.07 g.
    56.07 g/14 g = 4.01 standard drinks per day.

It can be seen in the preceding examples that the difference between the lowest and highest calculation is about 1.64 drinks per day. In some studies, this difference could be crucial to understanding and correctly interpreting the threshold effects of cumulative alcohol use. For example, in many epidemiological studies, there are significant differences in risk for various medical conditions based on many factors, one of which is the number of drinks consumed per day. Vaughan, Davis, Kristal, and Thomas (1995) found that people who consume more than three drinks per day have a significantly greater risk of esophageal cancer than do those who drink less. Fuchs and associates (1995) found that drinking from one to three drinks per week to one to two drinks per day was associated with reduced risk of death from cardiovascular diseases. There is a clear value to these complex multi-variable studies to understanding threshold consequences on health. Yet, it can be seen that a difference of one to two drinks per day due to miscalculation can significantly alter the interpretation of such results.

Drink equivalents are sometimes described in terms of oz of absolute or pure alcohol (200 proof), and a typical alcoholic beverage contains approximately six tenths of an oz of pure (100%) alcohol by volume (U.S. Department of Agriculture, 2005). It is safe to assume that for the general public, the concept of oz of absolute alcohol per drink has little value. For researchers, however, the calculation of a dose of pure alcohol is obtained from

Formula 8. Here, the percentage of the volume of the alcohol serving or container is multiplied by the percentage of alcohol (% v/v).

Formula 8: Calculation of oz of absolute alcohol (by volume) in any drink

$$\text{Absolute ethanol} = \text{volume} \times \% \text{ v/v.}$$

Example.
   12 oz of 4.75% v/v beer $= 12.0 \times 0.0475 = 0.57$ oz of absolute alcohol.
   1.5 oz of 80 proof spirits $= 1.50 \times 0.40 = 0.60$ oz of absolute alcohol.
   1.25 oz of 100 proof spirits $= 1.25 \times 0.50 = 0.63$ oz of absolute alcohol.
   5 oz of 12% v/v wine $= 5 \times 0.12 = 0.60$ oz of absolute alcohol.

Forensic calculations to determine the number of drinks consumed may be further interpreted based upon an individual's characteristics. Depending upon either drink formulation or the anthropometric characteristics (e.g., age, weight, height, gender) of the drinker and to paraphrase a common belief, a drink is not a drink is not a drink. Failure to consider individual differences can result in misleading conclusions (Devgun & Dunbar, 1990). For example, it is widely recognized that three drinks in a 130-lb female will have different pharmacokinetic and pharmacodynamic effects when compared to a 130-lb male, let alone a 200-lb male. Various mechanisms have been proposed over the last 100 years to explain such gender differences, but it is generally accepted that alcohol is distributed throughout the water-containing compartments of the body, and all other factors being equal (e.g., absorption, elimination, weight), the peak BAC produced by any dose will vary as a function of changes in the ratio of muscle to fat. On average, men tend to be more muscular than women are, and muscle contains more water than fat. Similarly, on average women have more body fat than men have (Deem & Lentner, 1970). Widmark (1981) first noted this gender difference, which he attributed to body water and described as the "rho" factor. Over the decades, Widmark's original formulas have been updated and modified. For example, Watson, Watson, and Batt (1981), and others, derived various algorithms for calculating total body water (TBW) that can be used to more accurately estimate the resulting BAC based upon individual body characteristics (Goist & Sutker, 1985; Kalant, 2000; Watson et al., 1981).

The relatively small differences in first pass metabolism (metabolism that occurs in the stomach before alcohol enters the circulation) may or may not contribute to the observed pharmacokinetic differences between some men and some women. (Baraona, 2000; Haber, 2000; Levitt and Levitt, 2000). Thus, it might be useful for researchers to consider both the total alcohol intake equivalent in drinks per unit time and also an estimate of BAC, based on drinks or grams of alcohol consumed per body size based upon anthropometric characteristics of the drinker. This is an important consideration because the belief that women are more vulnerable to the effects of alcohol than men are, may be based in part upon the failure to express alcohol doses in relation to individual drinker characteristics (Kalant, 2000).

11.2 ESTIMATING BAC, INTAKE, DOSING METHODOLOGIES, AND RELATED FORMULAS

There are several ways to examine alcohol intake, each with varying degrees of sophistication. For the most part, formulas designed to estimate BAC are derived from the work of Widmark in the 1930s. Widmark's contribution to understanding alcohol intoxication is widely recognized, and given the instruments of his day, quite notable. However, with technological advances, some of his factors and assumptions have been changed and refinements made to his basic formula. Therefore, we will review methods of estimating BAC and useful related formulas.

In pharmacology, the most basic approach starts with an estimate of the theoretical maximum concentration of a drug. This purely theoretical maximum, which assumes immediate absorption and distribution, can be expressed by Formula 9:

Formula 9. Calculation of the theoretical maximum concentration of alcohol from a drink

$$C = g/\Sigma Vd \times BlH_2O$$

where: C is maximum theoretical BAC at time zero, g is grams of alcohol ΣVd is total volume of distribution, BlH_2O is 80.65 (approximate percentage of water in blood).

Example. The maximum concentration from 5 oz of 80-proof alcohol in a man with a ΣVd of 45.

$$C = (5 \text{ oz.} \times 9.3441 \text{ g} /\Sigma Vd) \times 80.65.$$
$$C = 46.72/45 \times 80.65.$$
$$C = 83.73 \text{ mg/dL.}$$

Several new terms were introduced in Formula 9. The volume of distribution (Vd) is a function of the ability of the drug to bind to plasma protein, tissue, and so on. In the case of alcohol, which is very hydrophilic, it is distributed primarily to body water including blood and other tissues, and does not bind to plasma proteins. According to Kalant (2000), because the dilution of orally administered alcohol yields the same concentration as $H_2{}^{18}O$ or ^3H_2O, TBW is the same as Vd. In recognition of both terms, we prefer to use the term ΣVd here to refer to the total volume (liters) of water in which alcohol can be distributed for an individual of a particular age, weight, height, and gender. This value is based upon the anthropometric algorithms proposed by Watson and coworkers (1981). A value of about 80.65 percent is frequently used as an estimate of the water content of blood (Center of Alcohol Studies, 1983; NHTSA, 1994).

Many longitudinal studies of alcohol use among school-age children inquire about the frequency in which "five drinks in a row" are consumed. Similarly, hospital emergency department patients are often asked to provide information about what and how much they drank to assist in diagnoses and treatment decisions. The interpretation of such data could be greatly enhanced if an estimate of the resulting intoxication could also be made. For example, five drinks consumed by a small woman in 1 hour would have significantly different medical and legal consequences compared to the same five drinks consumed by a large man over 2 or 3 hours. In collecting self-report data about the number of drinks consumed per day, it is recommended, that when possible, investigators collect information about the time course or the length of the drinking episode, as well as drink size and anthropometric characteristics of the subject. By utilizing assumptions about the rates of alcohol absorption and elimination, a more accurate analysis can be made (e.g., estimating peak BACs). It is often important in research and in forensic examinations to make estimates of alcohol intoxication at different points in time. Several studies have demonstrated that mathematical models can predict BACs if sufficient information is available (Brick, Adler, Cocco & Westrick, 1992; Mumenthaler, Taylor & Yesavage, 2000; NHTSA, 1994; Pieters, Wedel & Schaafsma, 1990; Wilkinson, 1980). Some investigators correctly question the reliability of such analyses when the rates of absorption and elimination and Vd are not known, but this criticism can be overcome in most cases by using a range of absorption and elimination rates and anthropometric data to estimate ΣVd. For example, on average, most social drinkers (i.e., not alcoholics with exceptional metabolic tolerance) eliminate alcohol at an average rate of about 10 to 20 mg/dL/hr. There is evidence that women may eliminate alcohol toward the higher end of this range (Cole-Harding & Wilson, 1987), and alcoholics without liver damage may eliminate alcohol at an average rate of 22 mg/dL (range 13 to 36 mg/dL/hr) during withdrawal (Jones & Sternebring, 1992). While reliable estimates of BACs can be made using averages under some conditions (Brick et al., 1992; NHTSA, 1994), TBW provides a more specific estimate of ΣVd. TBW should be used in lieu of older methods, such as Widmark's "rho" factor, for various reasons, including the fact that as Jones (2007) points out, the lean body mass of the average person has changed in the last hundred years. Watson and associates (1981) developed the specific algorithms (Formulas 10a–d) for estimating body water.

Formula 10. Estimating total body water

Formula 10a: For men less than 16 years old:
$-21.993 + ((0.406 \times (pounds/2.2045) + (0.209 \times (height\ in\ inches/2.54)).$

Formula 10b: For men 17 to 86 years old:
$2.447 - ((0.09516\ x\ age) + (0.1074 \times (height\ in\ inches \times 2.54))$
$+ (0.3362 \times (pounds/2.2045)).$

Formula 10c: For women less than 16 years old:
$-10.313 + ((0.252 \times (pounds/2.2045)) + (0.154 \times (height\ in\ inches \times 2.54)).$

Formula 10d: For women 17 to 84 years old:
$-2.097 + ((0.1069 \times (height\ in\ inches \times 2.54)) + (0.2466 \times$
$(pounds/2.2045)).$

Example. Consider the following female subject: 23 years old, 110 lb and 66 in tall
$-2.097 + ((0.1069 \times (height\ in\ inches \times 2.54)) + (0.2466 \times$
$(pounds/2.2045)) =$
$-2.097 + ((0.1069 \times (66\ x\ 2.54)) + (0.2466 \times (110/2.2045)) =$
$-2.097 + (17.921) + (12.305) = 28.129.$

Alcohol research scientists often need to quantify alcohol intake or dose subjects in order to evaluate psychosocial behavior, and cognitive or motor skills at various BACs. Despite advances in pharmacokinetics, many investigators calculate intake or dose based only on body weight (e.g., g/kg), ignoring other important anthropometric characteristics discussed in the previous section. This method results in excess variability because there are physiological differences between and within men and women. For example, a man and a woman of equal weight who receive the exact same dose of alcohol will usually have different BACs because, on average, men have more muscle mass (and therefore more water) than women have (Goist & Sutker, 1985; Li et al., 2000; Watson et al., 1981), differences in first pass gastric (Frezza et al., 1990; Lim et al. 1993) and hepatic (liver) metabolism (Thomasson, 2000), and other factors. Conversely, the amount of alcohol necessary to achieve a particular BAC is a function of many factors and individual characteristics. In some instances, these characteristics or factors are not known, and in other instances, they are known or can be reasonably assumed. For example, alcohol researchers and others have repeatedly demonstrated that BACs can be accurately targeted in men and women when variables such as absorption, metabolism, and gender are considered (Brick et al., 1992; Friel, Logan, O'Malley & Baer, 1999; Gullberg & Jones, 1994; Montgomery & Reasor, 1992; Pieters et al., 1990; Stowell & Stowell, 1998; Wilkinson, 1980). Pharmacokinetic models incorporating the basic (Alco-Calculator; Center of Alcohol Studies, 1983) or complex (Levitt & Levitt, 2000; Pieters et al., 1990; Wilkinson, 1980) necessary variables are beyond the scope of this chapter, but can be found in the studies just cited.

In some forensic cases, information about when a person consumed alcohol is missing. When data about drinking are limited, the circulating alcohol burden (CAB) is a useful measure of the total amount of alcohol "on board" at the time of a blood or breath test. The CAB is independent of two variables: rate of absorption and rate of elimination. It is therefore useful when insufficient information is available to account for these variables. However, CAB estimates assume alcohol absorption is for all practical purposes complete. CAB may underestimate consumption in some instances because about 80 percent of alcohol consumed is absorbed within about 30 minutes of the last drink (Jones, 1993; Jones & Neri, 1991). Since CAB is the alcohol burden at a single moment in time and does not account for elimination, it is a very good estimate of minimum alcohol consumption. In other words, the total alcohol intake will always be greater than the CAB.

Consider the following example in which a 23-year-old, 110-lb, 66-in tall female has a BAC of 120 mg/dL. Using the TBW or other measure of volume of distribution (calculated from Formula 10d as 28.13), the CAB is estimated using Formula 11, where BAC_{obj} is an objective chemical measure of BAC.

Formula 11: Calculation of CAB: Alcohol in circulation at time of blood test

$$CAB = (BAC_{obj} \times \Sigma Vd)/80.65$$

Example. $(120 \text{ mg/dL} \times 28.13)/80.65 = 41.86 \text{ g}$

It can be estimated that a CAB of 41.86 g is equivalent to about 15 oz of 12% (v/v) wine, 4.5 oz of 80-proof liquor, or about three standard drinks or about 5.2 units, as previously described.

Although the CAB describes the amount of alcohol in the body at a fixed point in time, it may be more useful to estimate the total alcohol consumed (TAC) over time. Such estimates expand Formula 11 and must include assumptions regarding the rates of alcohol absorption and elimination.

Researchers should be mindful of the fact that when alcohol is consumed slowly, as in many social settings, or even in some experimental studies, the peak BAC occurs shortly after the last drink. Some experimental studies report that about 80 percent of the maximum BAC occurred within 12 minutes after drinking ends (Jones, 1993; Jones & Neri, 1991). However, larger volumes or very rapid alcohol consumption protocols often used in the laboratory may result in more variability, particularly when the dose is relatively low. The variables that affect absorption are complex and may vary with beverage concentration, volume, presence or absence of food, genetics, and other factors. Consistent with empirical studies, most medical references describe the majority of alcohol as being absorbed within 20 to 30 minutes with a maximum BAC occurring about 60 to 90 minutes after the last drink (Ellenhorn & Barceloux, 1988; Hobbs, Rall & Verdoorn, 1996; Pohorecky & Brick, 1990). The accuracy of such estimates can be enhanced by using a range of elimination rates rather than a single average and anthropometric formulas to estimate TBW, such as those developed by Watson and previously discussed. Estimates of TAC from the start of an acute drinking episode to the time a blood or breath sample can be made by algebraically rearranging Formula 11 and including alcohol absorption and elimination to produce Formula 12. This calculation assumes that alcohol is, for all practical purposes, completely absorbed at the time the objective sample was obtained.

Formula 12: Calculating total alcohol consumed (TAC) over time

$$TAC = \Sigma Vd \times (BAC_{obj} + \beta_{1\text{-}n} \times t)/Bl_{H_2O}$$

where: TAC is the total alcohol consumed; BAC_{obj} is the objective chemical test result; $\beta_{1\text{-}n}$ is the range of rates of alcohol elimination $(1 - n)$, usually 10 to 20 mg/dL/hr; t is the time from start of drinking until the time of an objective chemical test; and Bl_{H_2O} is 80.65 (approximate percentage of water in blood).

Example. Estimation of TAC in a subject $(\Sigma Vd = 29.13)$ with a BAC of 120 mg/dL 3 hours after the start of drinking and 1 hour after the last drink. Rate of elimination estimated at 10 mg/dL/hr to 20 mg/dL/hr.

> $TAC = \Sigma Vd \times (BAC_{obj} + \beta_{1\text{-}n} \times t)/Bl_{H_2O}.$
> $TAC = 29.3 \times 120$ mg/dL $+ (10$ mg/dL/hr $\times 3$ hours$)/80.65.$
> $TAC = 29.3 \times (120$ mg/dL $+ 30$ mg/dL$)/80.65 = 54.5$ g if the rate of elimination is 10 mg/dL/hr
> $TAC = 29.3 \times 120$ mg/dL $+ (20$ mg/dL/hr $\times 3$ hours$)/80.65.$
> $TAC = 29.3 \times (120$ mg/dL $+ 60$ mg/dL$)/80.65 = 65.4$ g if the rate of elimination is 20 mg/dL/hr
> $TAC = 3.9$ to 4.7 standard drinks

Widmark first used the symbol β to denote the rate of alcohol elimination, which he found to average 15 mg/dL/h This rate is widely accepted as the average rate of alcohol elimination in healthy humans although there is little doubt that some individuals eliminate alcohol above or below this rate. For example, some investigators reported that women may eliminate alcohol at a higher rate (Cole-Harding & Wilson, 1987; Thomasson, 2000), and some alcohol abusers or alcoholics in detox eliminate at an average rate of about 22 mg/dL with a range of 13 to 36 mg/dL/hr (Jones, 1983; Jones & Sternebring, 1992; Stowell & Stowell, 1998). Because there are so many variables in alcohol pharmacokinetics, it is important to utilize a range of absorption and elimination values. It is recommended that alcohol elimination rates of 10 mg/dL/hr to 20 mg/dL/hr be used for healthy subjects but that rates as high as 20 mg/dL/hr to 30 mg/dL/hr be considered when working with heavy drinkers in whom metabolic tolerance may be present. Depending upon the drinking population studied, the use of alcohol elimination rates between 10 and 25 mg/dL/hr would correctly estimate BACs in about 90 percent of test subjects (Stowell & Stowell, 1998). Researchers need to also appreciate that unless the drinking rate is very slow, in most cases, a maximum BAC may not occur for up to 30 to 90 minutes after the last drink. Absorption is considered in Formula 13, in which an estimated BAC is calculated based upon known alcohol intake.

Formula 13: Estimation of BAC based upon alcohol intake

$$BAC = g/\Sigma Vd \times Bl_{H_2O} \times 100 - (\beta_{1\text{-}n} \times (t_s + t_p))$$

where: g is grams of alcohol; ΣVd is TBW or volume of distribution based on age, weight, height, and gender (Watson, 1981); $Bl_{H_2O} = 80.65$ (approximate percentage of water in blood); $\beta_{1\text{-}n}$ is a range of alcohol elimination rates (e.g., 10-20 mg/dL/hr) ; t_s is time from the start of drinking to the last drink: and t_p is range absorption times from the last drink to estimates peak BAC (e.g., 30–90 minutes).

Formula 13 can be algebraically rearranged as Formula 14, which estimates in grams the required dose of alcohol that needs to be administered to produce a particular BAC. This is a more accurate method of dosing subjects than simply administering g/kg doses of alcohol. The math is described in Formula 13 and is simply a re-expression of Formula 12 (TAC).

Formula 14: Estimating dose to achieve a target BAC

$$g = BAC_{target} + (\beta_{1\text{-}n} \times (t_s + t_p)) \times \Sigma Vd / Bl_{H_2O}$$

where: BAC_{target} is desired BAC, and g is grams of alcohol administered to achieve BAC_{target}

Example. A 23-year-old female weighing 120 lb and 66 in tall ($\Sigma Vd = 29.13$) eliminating alcohol at 10 to 20 mg/dL/hr, drinking for 2 hours, and with an assumed peak or target BAC of 100 mg/dL 30 to 90 minutes after the last drink would need to consume about 54 g of alcohol or about 5.8 oz of 80 -proof alcohol. The following calculation shows the math for a rate of alcohol elimination of 20 mg/dL/hr and a peak alcohol concentration 30 minutes after the last drink, but in practice a range of absorption and elimination rates should be considered.

$g = 100$ mg/dL $+$ ((20 mg/dL/hr) $\times$ (120 minutes $+$ 30 minutes)) $\times$ 29.13/80.65.

$g = 54.18$ or about 5.8 oz of 80 proof alcohol (54.18/9.3441 = 5.798 oz) or 3.9 standard drinks.

Alcohol Tests

The analytical method used by a laboratory to measure alcohol is often overlooked in reporting alcohol results. Sometimes alcohol units are expressed in nomenclature not known to all readers. For example, in some European literature, alcohol concentrations are reported as *pro mille* which means parts per thousand and is abbreviated ‰ In the United States, Great Britain and other countries, alcohol is expressed as parts per hundred (%). A BAC of 1.5‰ is equal to 150 mg/dL (0.15%). To convert ‰ to mg/dL (mg%), use Formula 15.

Formula 15: Recalculating *pro mille* (‰) BAC to mg% BAC

$1‰ \times 100 = $ mg/dL.

In some areas of research, alcohol is expressed as millimoles per liter (mM/L). A millimole is 1 one thousandth of a gram-molecule. One molecule of alcohol contains 46.07 gram-molecules/L or 4.607 moles/dL. The conversion of a millimole (mM) of alcohol to converting milligram per deciliter of alcohol or converting milligram per deciliter to millimole of alcohol is easily accomplished using Formulas 16 and 17.

Formula 16: Converting alcohol from to mM to mg/dL concentrations

mg/dL $=$ mM $\times$ 4.607.

Example.   22.5 mM × 4.607 = 103.658 mg/dL.

Formula 17: Converting alcohol from mg/dL to mM concentrations

mM = mg/dL/ 4.607.

Example.   91.5 mg/dL/ 4.607 = 19.861 mM.

Alcohol test results from clinical, research and forensic lab results are expressed in weight/volume, typically as grams or milligrams of alcohol per fixed volume of fluid (100 mL of blood or serum) or per 210 L of air (for some breath test instruments). Many clinical alcohol researchers measure alcohol in breath because it is convenient, rapid, and accurate, and multiple samples can be obtained without discomfort to the subject, which may include animals (Pohorecky & Brick, 1982). The largest number of breath tests are conducted in the course of police investigations of suspected intoxicated drivers. Outside the United States, breath alcohol test results are usually reported in grams of alcohol per 210 L of air, whereas in most of the United States, breath-testing instruments are calibrated to convert grams per volume of breath into milligrams of alcohol per 100 mL of blood (mg/dL) or grams per 100 mL (g%).

When whole blood alcohol is measured directly using an instrument such as a gas chromatograph, the results are also expressed as weight/volume (e.g., grams or milligrams per 100 mL blood). Milligrams are easily converted to grams by dividing the value by 1000, and g% is easily converted to milligrams per deciliter by multiplying the value by 1000. For example, 80 mg/dL = 0.08 g% and .15 g% = 150 mg/dL. The preferred nomenclature for some scientific journals is usually milligrams per deciliter (mg/dL) to avoid confusion with statistical percentages. A BAC of 80 mg/dL is the same as 80 mg%, which is the same as 0.08%.

Both forensic examiners and alcohol researchers, relying upon alcohol test results from a hospital laboratory, often neglect to inquire or report if the results are derived from whole blood, serum, or plasma samples. Since the ratio of the concentration of alcohol in serum, to that of plasma is about 1:1 (Winek & Carfagna, 1987), further discussion will be based upon serum or blood alcohol. Some hospitals specify whether the reading is from serum or whole blood; others in our experience do not. If the laboratory measures alcohol in serum, the results are not equal to whole blood test results. This may have important implications for scientists comparing test results or in instances where such results are used as evidence in a criminal or civil litigation. Since alcohol is distributed throughout the water-containing compartments of the body, including the blood, serum alcohol is not the equivalent of a BAC because serum contains more water than the whole blood from which it is derived. Therefore, the concentration of alcohol in whole blood is less than that of the serum in proportion to their respective water contents. In other words, a hospital serum alcohol concentration will be higher than a whole blood alcohol concentration drawn from the same patient at the same time.

Early studies reported that the plasma:whole blood ethanol ratio ranged from 1.10 to 1.35 with an average of 1.18 (Payne, Hill & Wood, 1968). Other studies suggest that the ratio of serum:whole blood alcohol ranges from about 1.10 to 1.18 (Winek & Carfagna, 1987) to 1.25 (Hodgson & Shajani, 1985). In most cases the range of the ratio is about 1.10 to 1.20, although Payne's average value of 1.18 has found acceptance in the literature (Baselt, 1996) and corresponds well as our observations comparing serum alcohol measured by the ADH method with GC analyses of the same sample (unpublished observations). The range of serum:blood ratios for most subjects is small in comparison to the significant difference between alcohol results reported in either serum or whole blood. The following formulae and examples illustrate the potential differences between serum and whole blood alcohol readings.

To convert serum alcohol to the minimum and maximum whole blood alcohol equivalent, we recommend Formula 18, where S_A is serum alcohol.

Formula 18. Converting serum alcohol to whole blood alcohol equivalents

S_A /1.10 to 1.20, or multiplying by the reciprocal of the denominator.

Example.
> 90 mg/dL/ 1.10 = 81.82 mg/dL whole blood.
> 90 mg/dL × 0.9091 = 81.82 mg/dL whole blood.
> 90 mg/dL/1.20 = 75 mg/dL whole blood.
> 90 mg/dL × 0.8333 = 75 mg/dL whole blood.
> 244 mg/dL/1.10 = 221.82 mg/dL or 244 mg/dL × 0.9091 = 221.82 mg/dL whole blood.
> 244 mg/dL/1.20 = 203.33 mg/dL or 244 mg/dL × 0.8333 = 203.33 mg/dL whole blood.

In some instances, both serum alcohol and hematocrit (Hct) values are available in medical records. Since the Hct is a quantitative measure of the percentage of cells in a fixed volume of blood, the change in Hct is, in part, a measure of the water content of the blood. The normal range for human Hct is approximately 47 ± 5 for men and 42 ± 5 for women (Pagana & Pagana, 1995). By recalculating the water content, in men, using Formula 19, serum to whole blood alcohol conversion estimates can be performed particularly when Hct is abnormal due to hemodilution from medical intervention (e.g., administration of fluids). When Formula 19 is applied to published and available data (Payne et al., 1968; Winek & Carfagna, 1987) it predicts with reasonable accuracy the whole blood alcohol concentration (typically within about 5 mg/dL for BACs <100 mg/dL). Some chronic alcoholics may have an elevated MCV, which may affect Hct (Seppa, Laippal & Saarni, 1991; Wu, Chanarin & Levi, 1974). When applying Formula 19 to women, who have a lower average Hct, use 0.608 instead of 0.645. We have not yet tested this formula on blood, serum, and Hct samples from chronic alcoholics in whom MCV may be significantly elevated.

Formula 19: Converting serum alcohol to whole blood alcohol concentrations in men using hematocrit

BAC = serum concentration × ((Hct × 0.645) + ((100 − Hct) × 0.95))/95.

Example. Using the following known results, Formula 19 closely estimates the actual BAC.

> Serum alcohol = 48 mg/dL, whole blood alcohol = 43 mg/dL, and Hct = 29.
> ((29 × 0.645) + ((100-29) × 0.95)) / 95 = (18.71 + 67.45)/95.
> 48 mg/dL × 0.907 = 43.5 mg/dL.

Example. Assuming serum alcohol is 230 mg/dL, the whole blood alcohol is 197 mg/dL, and Hct is 50.

> ((50 × 0.645) + ((100-50) × 0.95))/95 = (32.25 +50)/95 = 0.8658
> 230 mg/dL × 0.8658 = 199.13 mg/dL

In each of the previous examples, the serum alcohol can be divided by the reciprocal of the ratio rather than multiplying it by the initial value. In the second example, the reciprocal of 0.8658 is 1.1550 (1/0.8658). Therefore, a serum alcohol concentration of 230 mg/dL/1.1550 equals a whole blood alcohol concentration of 199.13 mg/dL. Formulas 18 and 19 provide similar results. Using a range of ratios (from Formula 18) and the same data from the examples, the expected whole blood alcohol would be 40.0 to 42.1 mg/dL versus 43.5 mg/dL from Formula 19 versus 43 mg/dL from the actual blood sample (first example), and 191.67 to 209.09 mg/dL (versus 199.13 mg/dL from Formula 19 versus 197 mg/dL from the actual blood test). Thus, either approach will provide reasonable estimates of BAC, but each has limitations.

From the examples given, it can be seen that depending upon the serum:whole blood ratio, the actual BAC varies. At lower BACs, the difference is minimal (usually less than 5 mg/dL), but with very high BACs, such as might be encountered in surveying data from alcoholics or heavy drinkers, the differences are proportionally greater. Researchers should keep this variation in mind when reporting serum (or plasma) alcohol test results or comparing such results with whole blood alcohol results.

Although dilution of blood from exogenous fluids administered to maintain blood volume can be reasonably estimated from Hct and thus the conversion from serum alcohol to a whole blood equivalent calculated, medical intervention also includes packed red blood cells (PRBC). For example, severe hemorrhaging also requires replacement of oxygen-carrying hemoglobin, but the degree to which blood Hct changes following PRBC is also of importance. Elzik, Dirschl, and Dahners (2006) examined transfusion volumes after transfusion changes in hematocrit over 24 hours approximately 1 week after hospitalization, when there was no active hemorrhaging. The average increase in Hct per liter of PRBC administered was 6.4% ± 4.1%. If a 300-mL unit of PRBC was administered, this corresponded to a 1.9% ± 1.2% change in Hct per unit of blood. Although the variability in Hct following PRBC is substantial, these results correspond to a generally accepted 3 percent change in Hct for a 500 mL unit but most units are 300 mL according to the authors.

Finally, earlier studies often reported alcohol concentrations in mg/g or g/kg because of the method for analyzing alcohol at that time. Mass/mass units can be converted to mass/volume units based upon the specific gravity of whole blood, which is approximately 1.055 g/mL. Therefore, one mg/g = 1.055 mg/mL as indicated in Formula 20.

Formula 20: BAC in mg/g × 1.055 mg/mL × 100 = mg/dL

Example. 1.50 mg/g BAC × 1.055 mg/mL × 100 = 158.25 mg/dL.
 Similarly, 150 mg/100g BAC × 1.055 mg/mL = 158.25 mg/dL.

Calculation of Breath Alcohol Detection Threshold

The human olfactory system is capable of detecting the odor of various alcoholic beverages or components because these molecules diffuse through the lungs and are expired in the breath. Contrary to DWI defense folk law and law enforcement training, there is a relationship between the odor of alcohol on the breath and the BAC, but the relationship is not linear; it is a threshold relationship. Pure ethanol is virtually odorless, but beverage alcohol once consumed and absorbed into the circulation is detectable by breath alcohol testing and by casual olfactory detection. The physiological threshold for alcohol detection is estimated to be about 40 mg/dL (Formula 21). Variations in the partition coefficient would result in a theoretical detection threshold of about 30 to 50 mg/dL calculated mathematically based on accepted physiological principles. Such calculations are based on the molecular volume of air (24.45); olfactory thresholds (air odor threshold); the molecular weight of alcohol (46.07); low, average, or high blood breath partition ratios (BBPRs) (1908:1, 2448:1 or 2998:1); and olfactory thresholds of 84 parts per million (Amoore & Hautala, 1983) to 100 ppm (Armstrong, 2000).

The threshold value
$$mg/m^3 = \frac{(ppm\ threshold)(gram\ molecular\ weight\ ethyl\ alcohol)}{molecular\ volume\ of\ air}$$

$mg/m^3 = (ppm \times molecular\ weight)/R$, where R = universal gas constant.

For example, using an olfactory threshold of 84 ppm,

$mg/m^3 = (84 \times 46.07/\ 24.45) = 158.27 \times (2448\ (\pm\ 540)) = \mu g/L$.

- 158.27 $\mu g/L$ (air) $\times$ 1908 = (blood) = 301,979 $\mu g/L$ (low BBPR)
  = 302 mg/L = .0302g/dL ≅ 30 mg/dL (~.03%).
- 158.27 $\mu g/L$ (air) $\times$ 2448 = (blood) = 387,445 $\mu g/L$ (avg. BBPR)
  = 388 mg/L = .0388 g/dL ≅ 38.9 mg/dL (~.04%).
- 158.27 $\mu g/L$ (air) $\times$ 2988 = (blood) = 472,911 $\mu g/L$ (high BBPR)
  = 473 mg/L = .0473 g/dL ≅ 47.3 mg/dL (~.05%).

Alternatively, using a higher olfactory threshold of 100 ppm (Armstrong, 2000),

$mg/m3 = (100 \times 46.07/24.45) = 188.53 \times (2448\ (\pm\ 540)) = \mu g/L$.

- 188.43 $\mu g/L$ (air) $\times$ 1908 = (blood) = 359,516 $\mu g/L$ (low BBPR)
  = 360 mg/L = .036 g/dL ≅ 36 mg/dL (~.04%).
- 188.43 $\mu g/L$ (air) $\times$ 2448 = (blood) = 461,277 $\mu g/L$ (avg. BBPR)
  = 461 mg/L = .046 g/dL ≅ 46 mg/dL (~.05%).
- 188.43 $\mu g/L$ (air) $\times$ 2988 = (blood) = 563,029 $\mu g/L$ (high BBPR)
  = 563 mg/L = .056 g/dl ≅ 56 mg/dL (~.06%).

Taking into account a range of physiological considerations, the extended range for detection of alcohol on the breath is about 40 to 60 mg/dL. In clinical practice, and based on empirical research, the detection in the alcohol is probably much higher, probably close to 80 mg/dL (*see* Chapter 6 for a discussion).

Discussion

Application of appropriate mathematical formulas and accepted scientific assumptions is useful in answering a range of inquiries, including estimating the amount of alcohol consumed by subjects in epidemiological studies, dosing methods for subjects in laboratory studies estimating BAC, and discussion about the proper interpretation of alcohol results depending upon the analytical technique used to measure alcohol. This information is intended to assist scientists in standardizing the way alcohol values and estimates of alcohol use are calculated and expressed. For all practical purposes, the same scientific methodology is applied to forensic evaluation. Forensic alcohol evidence is regularly used by experts to make estimates of alcohol consumed or of intoxication at time points before the sample was obtained.

These formulas may also be applied where detailed measures are often available along with individual anthropometric data. However, the use of formulas based upon self report information is subject to memory bias from self-serving interests, intoxication, or neuropsychological trauma. In such instances, objective chemical tests should be consulted to validate and further interpret subjective reports. The errors that result when researchers do not take these variables into consideration has been raised previously, but not in such detail. Miller and associates (1991) noted this problem and made a "plea for consistency" in standardizing various alcohol calculations and suggested that progress in the field is impeded by the lack of a common scientific language. They clearly recognized this problem and pointed out various differences in the amount of alcohol in different alcoholic beverages. Fifteen years after Miller and colleagues made their plea for alcohol researchers to speak a common language in describing quantitative aspects of alcohol research, the problem remains. This problem is also recognized by Jones, who noted "much can be said for trying to standardize the plethora of blood-alcohol calculations used in clinical medicine and forensic science" (2008, pg 86).

Given the many variables discussed, it behooves scientists to collect as much information about the alcoholic beverage as possible, including detailed information about the proof, brand, and size of each drink. Similarly, forensic experts should consider all sources of information about servings and what constitutes a drink. Beer consumption volume estimates tend to be more accurate than those for wine or spirits because about 80 percent of drinkers consume beer in 12-oz servings (Kerr et al., 2005). However, the concentration of beer varies considerably as do liquor and wine glass servings. Following the method of Kerr and associates (2005), when possible, presenting witnesses with a comparative sample glass, cup, bottle, and so on may enable them to more accurately identify what they mean by a drink. In addition, some subjects (and investigators) may not know the alcohol content of the beverages consumed. When such information is not printed on the label, published reviews should be consulted (e.g., Case et al., 2000). Coupled with an inquiry as to the brand of beverage and determination of the concentration or proof of beverages consumed, the formulas described herein can be applied to make more accurate estimates of alcohol consumption.

Finally, alcohol estimates are subject to limitations due to a variety of factors that are often unknown. For example, individual differences in the rates of alcohol absorption and elimination, beverage type, alcohol content, serving size, and other factors are rarely known with absolute certainty, except as noted. However, by using a range of physiological characteristics likely to represent almost all drinkers, collecting data on beverage type and size, using anthropometric characteristics of the drinker, and assuming a range of absorption and elimination rates, the accuracy and interpretation of reported alcohol consumption and estimates of exposure can be enhanced substantially. We recognize that there is variability in all biological and chemical measurements and in self-report data whether we are discussing alcohol units, or standard drinks or interpreting other quantitative aspects of alcohol. The application of these standard formulas should enable alcohol experts as well as researchers to more accurately and consistently interpret alcohol data and improve communication and accuracy.

REFERENCES

Amoore, J. E., and Hautala, E. (1983). Odor as an aid to chemical safety: Odor thresholds compared with threshold limit values and volatilities for 214 industrial chemicals in air and water dilution. *Journal of Applied Toxicology*, 2(5), 272–290.

Armstrong, S. R. (2000). *Ethanol: Brief report on its use in gasoline: Expected impacts and comments of expert reviewers.* Cambridge, MA: Cambridge Environmental, Inc.

Babor, T., Stephens, R., and Marlatt, G. (1987). Verbal report methods in clinical research on alcoholism: Response bias and its minimalization. *Journal of Studies on Alcohol*, 48, 410–424.

Baraona, E. (2000). Site and quantitative importance of alcohol first-pass metabolism. *Alcoholism, Clinical and Experimental Research*, 24(4), 405–406.

Baselt, R. (1996). Disposition of alcohol in man. In J.C. Garriot (Ed.), *Medicolegal Aspects of Alcohol* (3rd ed., pp. 65–83). Tucson, AZ: Lawyers and Judges Publishing Company.

Brick, J. (2006). Standardization of alcohol calculations in research. *Alcoholism, Clinical and Experimental Research*, 30(8), 1276–1287.

Brick, J. (2008). Medical consequences of alcohol abuse. In J. Brick (Ed.), *Handbook of the Medical Consequences of Alcohol Abuse*. New York, NY: Haworth Press.

Brick, J. (2009). Alcohol intoxication, behavioral, and medical effects. In A. Jamieson and A. Moenssens (Eds.), *Wiley Encyclopedia of Forensic Science* (pp. 99–108). Chichester, UK: John Wiley & Sons Ltd.

Brick, J., Adler, J., Cocco, K., and Westrick, E. (1992). Alcohol intoxication: Pharmacokinetic prediction and behavioral analysis in humans. *Current Topics in Pharmacology, 1,* 57–67.

Case, G., Destefano, S., and Logan, B. (2000). Tabulation of alcohol content of beer and malt beverages. *Journal of Analytical Toxicology, 24,* 202–210.

Center of Alcohol Studies. (1983). *Alco-Calculator: A Manual to Provide Understanding of the Principles on Which This Education Tool is Based* [slide rule device]. New Brunswick, NJ: Publications Division, Rutgers Center of Alcohol Studies, Alcohol Research Documentation, Inc.

Chanarin, A. Wul, and Levi, A. J. (1974). *Macrocytosis of chronic alcoholism. Lancet, 303*(7862), 829–831.

Chiu, T., Mendelson, J., Sholar, M., Mutschler, N., Wines, J., Hesselbrock, V., and Mello, N. (2004). Brain alcohol detectability in human subjects with and without a paternal history of alcoholism. *Journal of Studies on Alcohol, 65*(1), 16–21.

Cohen, B., and Vinson, D. (1995). Retrospective self-report of alcohol consumption: Test-retest reliability by telephone. *Alcoholism, Clinical and Experimental Research, 19*(5), 1156–1161.

Cole-Harding, S., and Wilson, J. (1987). Ethanol metabolism in men and women. *Journal of Studies on Alcohol, 48*(4), 380–387.

Deem, K., and Lentner, C. (1970). *Scientific Tables* (p. 517). Ardsley, NY: Ciba-Geigy Ltd.

Devgun, M., and Dunbar, J. (1990). Alcohol consumption, blood alcohol level and the relevance of body weight in experimental design and analysis. *Journal of Studies on Alcohol, 51,* 24–28.

Dufour, M. (1999). What is moderate drinking? *Alcohol Research & Health, 23*(1) 5–14.

Ellenhorn, M., and Barceloux, D. (1988). *Medical Toxicology: Diagnosis and Treatment of Human Poisoning.* New York, NY: Elsevier Science.

Elzik, M., Dirschl, D., and Dahners, L. (2006). Correlation of transfusion volume to change in hematocrit. *American Journal of Hematology, 81*(1), 145–146.

Frezza, M., DiPadova, C., Pozzato, G., Terpin, M., Baraona, E., and Lieber, C. (1990). Blood alcohol levels in women. The role of decreased gastric alcohol dehydrogenase activity and first-pass metabolism. *New England Journal of Medicine, 322,* 95–99.

Friel, P., Logan, B., O'Malley, D., and Baer, J. (1999). Development of dosing guidelines for reaching selected target breath alcohol concentrations. *Journal of Studies on Alcohol, 60,* 555–565.

Fuchs, C. S., Stampfer, M. J., Colditz, G. A., Giovannucci, E. L., Manson, J. E., Kawachi, I., ..., Willett, W. C. (1995). Alcohol consumption and mortality among women. *New England Journal of Medicine, 332*(19), 1245–1250.

Goist, K. Jr., and Sutker, P. (1985). Acute alcohol intoxication and body composition in women and men. *Pharmacology, Biochemistry, and Behavior, 22,* 811–814.

Gullberg, R. G., and Jones, A. W. (1994). Guidelines for estimating the amount of alcohol consumed from a single measurement of blood alcohol concentration: Reevaluation of Widmark's equation. *Forensic Science International, 69,* 119–130.

Haber, P. (2000). Metabolism of alcohol by the human stomach. *Alcoholism, Clinical and Experimental Research, 24*(4), 407–408.

Hobbs, W., Rall, T., and Verdoorn, T. (1996). Hypnotics and sedatives, ethanol. In J. G. Hardman and L. E. Limbird (Eds.), *Goodman and Gillman's The Pharmacological Basis of Therapeutics* (9th ed., p. 389). New York, NY: McGraw-Hill, pp. 361-396.

Hodgson, B. T., and Shajani, N. K. (1985). Distribution of ethanol: Plasma to the whole blood ratios. *Canadian Society of Forensic Science Journal, 18*(2), 73–77.

Jones, A. W. (1983). Determination of liquid/air partition coefficients for dilute solutions of ethanol in water, whole blood, and plasma. *Journal of Analytical Toxicology, 7*(4), 193–197.

Jones, A. W. (1993). Disappearance rate of ethanol from the blood of human subjects: Implications in forensic toxicology. *Journal of Forensic Science, 38*(1), 104–118.

Jones, A. W. (2007). Body mass index and blood-alcohol calculations [Letter to the Editor]. *Journal of Analytical Toxicology, 31*(3), 177–178.

Jones, A. W. (2008). Biochemical and physiological research on the disposition and fate of ethanol in the body. In J. C. Garriott (Ed.), *Garriott's Medicolegal Aspects of Alcohol* (pp. 47–128). Tucson, AZ: Lawyers and Judges Publishing Company.

Jones, A. W., and Neri, A. (1991). Evaluation of blood-ethanol profiles after consumption of alcohol together with a large meal. *Canadian Society of Forensic Science Journal, 24*(3), 165–174.

Jones, A. W., and Sternebring, B. (1992). Kinetics of ethanol and methanol in alcoholics during detoxification. *Alcohol and Alcoholism, 27*(6), 641–647.

Kalant, H. (2000). Effects of food and body composition on blood alcohol curves. *Alcoholism, Clinical and Experimental Research, 24*(4), 413–414.

Kerr, W. C., Greenfield, T. K., Tujague, J., and Brown, S. E. (2005). A drink is a drink? Variation in the amount of alcohol contained in beer, wine and spirits drinks in a U.S. methodological sample. *Alcoholism, Clinical and Experimental Research, 29*(11), 2015–2021.

Levitt, M. G., and Levitt, D. G. (2000). Use of a two-compartment model to predict ethanol metabolism. *Alcoholism, Clinical and Experimental Research, 24*(4), 409–410.

Li, T-K., Beard, J. D., Orr, W. E., Kwo, P. Y., Ramchandani, V. A., and Thomasson, H. R. (2000). Variation in ethanol pharmacokinetics and perceived gender and ethnic differences in alcohol elimination. *Alcoholism, Clinical and Experimental Research, 24*(4), 415–416.

Lim, R. T. Jr., Gentry, R. T., Ito, D., Yokoyama, H., Baraona, E., and Lieber, C. S. (1993). First-pass metabolism of ethanol is predominantly gastric. *Alcoholism, Clinical and Experimental Research, 17*(6), 1337–1344.

Miller, W. R., Heather, N., and Hall, W. (1991). Calculating standard drink units: International comparisons. *British Journal of Addiction, 86*(1), 43–47.

Montgomery, M. R., and Reasor, M. J. (1992). Retrograde extrapolation of blood alcohol data: An applied approach. *Journal of Toxicology and Environmental Health, 36*(4), 281–292.

Moskowitz, H., Burns, M., and Ferguson, S. (1999). Police officers' detection of breath odors from alcohol ingestion. *Accident Analysis and Prevention, 31*(3), 175–180.

Mumenthaler, M. S., Taylor, J. L., and Yesavage, J. A. (2000). Ethanol pharmacokinetics in white women: Nonlinear model fitting versus zero-order elimination analyses. *Alcoholism, Clinical and Experimental Research, 24*(9), 1353–1362.

National Highway Traffic Safety Administration (NHTSA). (1994). *Computing a BAC estimate.* Report No. 80. Washington, D.C.: U.S. Department of Transportation, National Highway Traffic Safety Administration. Accessed January 26, 2006; available at: www.nhtsa.gov

Pagana, K. D., and Pagana, T. J. (1995). *Mosby's Diagnostic and Laboratory Test Reference* (2nd ed.). St. Louis, MO: Mosby.

Payne, J. P., Hill, D. W., and Wood, D. G. L. (1968). Distribution of ethanol between plasma and erythrocytes in whole blood. *Nature, 217*, 963–964.

Pieters, J. E., Wedel, M., and Schaafsma, G. (1990). Parameter estimation in a three-compartment model for blood alcohol curves. *Alcohol and Alcoholism, 25*(1), 17–24.

Pohorecky, L. A., and Brick, J. (1982). A new method for the determination of blood ethanol levels in rodents. *Pharmacology, Biochemistry, and Behavior, 16*(5), 693–696.

Pohorecky, L. A., and Brick, J. (1990). The pharmacology of ethanol. In D. J. K. Balfour (Ed.), *International Encyclopedia of Pharmacological Therapeutics: Psychotropic Drugs of Abuse* (pp. 189–254). New York, NY: Pergamon Press.

Seppa, K., Laippala, P., and Saarni, M. (1991). Macrocytosis as a consequence of alcohol abuse among patients in general practice. *Alcoholism, Clinical and Experimental Research, 15*(5), 871–876.

Sommers, M. S., Dyehouse, J. M., Howe, S. R., Lemmink, J., Volz, T., and Manharth, M. (2000). Validity of self-reported alcohol consumption in nondependent drinkers with unintentional injuries. *Alcoholism, Clinical and Experimental Research, 24*(9), 1406–1413.

Stowell, A. R., and Stowell, L. I. (1998). Estimation of blood alcohol concentrations after social drinking. *Journal of Forensic Sciences, 43*(1), 14–21.

Thomasson, H. (2000). Alcohol elimination: Faster in women? *Alcoholism, Clinical and Experimental Research, 24*(4), 419–420.

Turner, C. (1990). How much alcohol is in a standard drink? An analysis of 125 studies. *British Journal of Addiction, 85*, 1171–1175.

U.S. Department of Agriculture. (2005). *Dietary Guidelines for Americans* (6th ed.). Washington, D.C.: U.S. Department of Health and Human Services and U.S. Department of Agriculture.

Vaughan, T. L., Davis, S., Kristal, A., and Thomas, D. B. (1995). Obesity, alcohol and tobacco as risk factors for cancers of the esophagus and gastric cardia: Adenocarcinoma versus squamous cell carcinoma. *Cancer Epidemiology, Biomarkers and Prevention, 4*(2), 85–92.

Watson, P. E., Watson, I. D., and Batt, R. D. (1981). Prediction of blood alcohol concentrations in human subjects: Updating the Widmark Equation. *Journal of Studies on Alcohol, 42*(7), 547–556.

Weast, R.C. (Ed.). (1973). *Handbook of Chemistry and Physics* (54th ed.). Boca Raton, FL: CRC Press.

Widmark, E. (1981). *Principles and Application of Medicolegal Alcohol Determination* (R. C. Baselt, trans.). Davis, CA: Biomedical Publications. (Original work published 1932).

Wilkinson, P. K. (1980). Pharmacokinetics of ethanol: A review. *Alcoholism, Clinical and Experimental Research, 4*(1), 6–21.

Winek, C. L., and Carfagna, M. (1987). Comparison of plasma, serum and whole blood ethanol concentrations. *Journal of Analytical Toxicology, 11*(6), 267–268.

World Health Organization (WHO). (2000). *International Guide for Monitoring Alcohol Consumption and Related Harm.* Government Document WHO/MSD/MSB/00.4. Geneva, Switzerland: Author. Also available at http://whqlibdoc.who.int/hq/2000/WHO_MSD_MSB_00.4.pdf

Chapter 12

ACCIDENT RECONSTRUCTION

12.1 INTRODUCTION

A multitude of factors contribute to or directly cause motor vehicle crashes, including vehicle mechanics, roadway characteristics, weather, traffic density, and time of day to name a few. One common and preventable factor for motor vehicle crashes is intoxication. The use of alcohol prior to or during the operation of a motor vehicle has long been a recognized significant cause of traffic crashes and threat to public safety. However, the mere fact that someone is intoxicated (pharmacologically) does not establish causation. It is incumbent upon the at-scene crash investigator to ensure the timely, meticulous, and thorough collection of all recognized evidence to determine the cause(s) of a crash and in some instances eliminate potential contributing or causative factors.

Whatever the scene dynamic, even the smallest of pieces of evidence can play a major part in solving a case. An at-scene crash investigator starts this process by using personal observation, obtaining witness statements and memorializing the event with photographs, video recordings, physical measurements of the evidence locations, and collection protocols, including alcohol test evidence. When intoxication is a potential factor, all other factors must still be considered. The use of standardized and accepted techniques of evidence collection, preservation, and transportation of evidence to a secure evidence storage area will create a solid foundation for crash reconstruction experts. Physical and other evidence obtained by investigation is critical to the reconstruction of the crash. Crashes involving alcohol and serious bodily injury or death may include elements of reckless disregard, depending on the state and statute and should be investigated as a crime.

Unlike a homicide with a firearm or knife, a crash resulting in a fatality from the improper use of a motor vehicle has to be investigated and reconstructed in detail to ascertain whether or not a crime has been committed. Not all fatal crashes are criminal. Even so, it is critical that evidence is

298

properly collected and evaluated to determine if there is a criminal component to the fatality. Moreover, the standard of proof applied in such criminal forensic investigations is beyond a reasonable doubt or to a reasonable degree of scientific certainty. In civil cases, even if the event is the same, a different standard of proof is applied based upon the preponderance of the evidence or to a reasonable degree of scientific probability. Therefore, the collection of evidence is of great importance in both criminal and civil litigation to assist the trier of fact and jurors to understand what happened.

12.2 TYPES OF EVIDENCE

In traffic crash investigation and reconstruction, evidence is "that which is submitted as proof or a fact" (Coughlin, 1982). There are two broad categories of evidence in forensic evaluations: subjective evidence and objective evidence. In more legal terms, however, evidence can be introduced in court through testimony or exhibits. The specific areas of concern to the crash reconstructionist are divided further to include (1) evidence obtained from the involved persons (subjective), (2) physical evidence obtained from the vehicles (objective), and (3) environmental evidence in which both people and vehicles may interact (after a combination of subjective and objective evidence).

Forensic reconstruction evidence can be further subcategorized to include long-term evidence, medium-term evidence, and short-term evidence. These categories also help establish a plan of action and aid investigators in prioritizing the collection and preservation of the evidence at the scene.

For example, long-term evidence may include objects such as immovable concrete curbs or structures and the vehicles or small transfer trace evidence on or in the vehicle itself (e.g., lamp filaments, blood spatter, fabric imprints, etc.). Long-term evidence may also include memorialized photographic evidence. These are types of evidence that will likely still be available for analysis for extended periods after the crash if properly stored.

Medium-term evidence consists of items that may or may not remain viable over an extended period. The term itself suggests a slightly less than immediate need to collect evidence because of its somewhat enduring nature. Medium-term evidence may include extremely dark and heavy skid marks, structural damage to metal or wood utility poles (trees, signposts, etc.), deep furrows in the ground, and pronounced scrape marks on the road surface. Medium-term evidence may also include clothing worn by a victim, skid marks that depend upon the roadway surface and the amount and type of debris on location, for example. In practice (and for expediency), evidence of this type is usually placed into the short-term or long-term evidence categories based upon the crash scene investigator's training and experience and priorities established at the time of the original assessment of the crash scene. Collection of medium-term evidence can be further tempered based upon transient weather conditions and the ability to recover the evidence in a timely manner, which in turn, depend upon the crash location and resources available to safeguard the scene integrity.

Short-term evidence is the most critical evidence to be located and documented because it is evanescent. Time is a driving force behind the rapid identification and documentation of this evidence because it is usually frail and subject to the elements such as rain, humidity, heat, light, and roadway surface conditions. Examples of short-term evidence include blood spatter on the roadway or a vehicle, antilock tire marks, or fuel or fluids from the vehicle(s). The collection of blood samples for later toxicological analyses should be done as soon as possible, but generally, alcohol is less evanescent than some other drugs. Except in exigent circumstances, a telephone warrant based on evidence of suspected intoxicated driving may be required.

Due to criminal codes throughout the United States, alcohol intoxication "ups the ante" when a crash has occurred. Criminal and civil proceedings may be brought forward, especially if there is death or serious bodily injuries sustained by drivers, passengers or pedestrians, cyclists, or others. The mandate placed upon the crash scene investigator is straightforward, and it becomes critical that all proper procedures be followed by a knowledgeable investigator trained in requesting and obtaining evidence collected at the hospital or, in the case of breath samples, at the police station. This evidence is too important to be relegated to a person who is unfamiliar with the required procedures regarding the safe retrieval, transportation, storage, and chain of evidence protocols, especially in a criminal investigation.

Forensic alcohol test evidence in a serious or fatal motor vehicle crash should include the subject's drinking history. For example, when and where did the drinking occur? How much was consumed and other information discussed in Chapter 7 and all observed physical characteristics? The initial assessment of the crash scene by first-responding police officers, EMS, or in, some cases, fire personnel is critical as is segregating and monitoring all event-involved persons who are part of the investigation.

Suspects in a DWI investigation should be monitored for safety and to prevent actions that might compromise evidence or place them at risk (e.g., from wandering into traffic or removing evidence). Food, liquids, or related items should be withheld unless medically required. Any fluids or medication administered in the course of treatment should be documented to include what was provided, the dose, and when it was administered. In breath alcohol testing cases, suspects in the investigation should remove all foreign objects such as gum, tobacco products, or liquids from their mouth. After probable cause is established, the officers can then follow their individual departmental protocols to obtain breath, blood, or urine samples from the suspected offender. The protocol should be standardized to include names, date, and time of collection.

As with all traffic crash cases where there are multiple origins for evidence, it is imperative that a detailed evidence log and chain of evidence protocol be maintained. The attention to detail greatly increases the success of a reliable investigation and helps avoid unnecessary objections at the time of trial. Evidence regarding people, vehicles, and the environment are important in any accident reconstruction but even more so when alcohol is involved. Although alcohol is a significant risk factor for motor vehicle accidents (Chapter 5), not all crashes are due to intoxication. Therefore it is necessary to evaluate the totality of the evidence to determine if factors other than intoxication contributed to the crash.

Three Sources of Evidence: People, Vehicles, and Environment

People

The first source of evidence at the scene of a motor vehicle crash is people, but prior to any investigation, the "etched in stone" requirement is the safety and treatment of anyone involved in the crash. The scene must be secured to prevent the destructive threat of another vehicle crashing into the first wreck and, to the extent it is possible, the injured must be stabilized and treated. Only after those critical first responder-mandates are met can the on-scene investigation begin.

Upon arrival at the scene of a crash, the first priority of responders (e.g., police) is to assess the scene and check for injured persons. This is where observations must start. People include the parties involved in the crash (injured and not injured), eyewitnesses, or anyone who might have information that would aid in the investigation. Accurately documented observations and properly obtained statements can lead to new evidence and corroborate already obtained evidence by comparing subjective and objective evidence.

Investigating police at the scene should document any and all spontaneous statements made by any driver or passenger. They should not ignore evidence of the consumption of alcoholic beverage, such as the odor of an alcoholic beverage on the breath. If detected, note the appearance of the driver. Is the driver, for example, responsive to questions, alert and oriented? Are his hand movements slow, and speech slurred or does he display any other signs of intoxication or alcohol use, such as bloodshot or watery eyes? Behavioral observations made after an accident must be interpreted cautiously because of the potential confusion from physical and psychological trauma. Can you determine by observation whether the crash or the intoxication, explains abnormal speech or difficulty walking? Any such observations should be noted and documented in the investigation report. These observations should include any parties involved with the crash because there are instances when there may be a later legal challenge as to who was driving.

A properly conducted interview is another invaluable form of evidence from witnesses. Any interview must be conducted with local procedural policy in order to make it admissible in court. Although spontaneous utterances and general statements can be obtained and should be noted ("quoted" in your notes or report) at the scene, the formal interview is generally done elsewhere at a later time. The key here is that the interview must be conducted by a properly trained interviewer who understands that what may appear to be a routine car crash may become a criminal investigation.

A driver who is now a suspect in a potential crime (i.e., where there is a fatality or serious bodily injury of one person due to the action of another) will be interviewed differently than will an uninvolved witness to the crash. Again, the interviewer must remember to follow local procedural policies when conducting a suspect interview. Of particular importance in a case in which alcohol may be involved is obtaining information about alcohol use. Sample questions in Table 12.1 are typical of the type of subjective alcohol test evidence useful in an investigation. Note the deliberate avoidance of questions leading to a yes or no answer with the exception of questions in which a definitive yes/no answer is useful (e.g., "Have you had any drugs or alcoholic drinks in the last 6 hours?"). More open-ended questions are likely to provide a more complete picture of what happened.

Anyone who has interviewed witnesses of a crash can attest to the fact that if you interview five different witnesses you are likely to get five different versions of the events. Some accounts may sound like the person being interviewed is describing a completely different crash. When interviewing people it is useful to remember that each person may have had a different perspective of the crash or may have only seen part of the crash. Also, people have a habit of confabulating or "filling in the blanks" so that what they saw and how they interpret it may be two different things. When you interview people you are often times actually getting their perception or interpretation of what they saw.

An example would be, when people hear the crash, turn and see the cars at rest. When asked how the crash occurred they might give how they think the crash occurred based on what they saw. Did they actually see the crash? No, they turned after they reacted to the sound of the cars crashing. Are they lying? No, they are only giving you their perception of what happened based on what they saw.

Table 12.1: Sample Alcohol Questionnaire.

1.	Tell me what you did today.	Open-ended questions help develop more specific areas of inquiry.
2.	What did you have to drink today?	
3.	Where were you drinking?	
4.	Do you remember how much you drank?	If no drinking recall, ask "more than ...," etc.
5.	What time do you think you started drinking?	If subjects are uncertain, review the events described in question 1 to assist recall.
6.	When did you finish drinking?	
7.	How much sleep did you get last night?	Obtain sleep log for commercial operators required to keep such records.
8.	What other drugs have you taken today?	If none, ask about previous 3–4 days.
9.	How often do you take drugs?	Determine if regular (daily, few times a week, weekly, monthly) use.
10.	How familiar are you with this road?	Does response correspond to the known area and direction of travel.
11.	Where were you coming from?	
12.	Where were you going?	
13.	What is your age, weight, and height?	This information may be useful in certain alcohol calculations.
14.	What did you eat today?	
15.	What time did you have your last meal?	

The best interviewers obtain the maximum amount of information by allowing people to talk, interrupting only when they wander off topic. Open-ended questions generally provide more information than do questions that can be answered yes or no. For example, asking, "tell me what you saw" is likely to be more productive and less "leading" than "did you see the car hit the truck?" After the witness has provided an overview of the events, then follow up with more questions. For example, what was their location at the time of the crash, what were they doing, did they actually see the impact, hear it, or observe the aftermath? Witnesses to events may feel the psychological need to be helpful to the interviewer or make sense out of a traumatic event. It is therefore important to avoid questions that suggest an answer.

What does all of this mean? Interviews should be taken by someone who can read people and who has some training and experience with interviewing techniques. More detailed questions are required to go beyond "What did you see?" Interviews should go beyond a standard set of questions to be used in every crash. An example is when an interviewer has a set of standard questions she uses in every crash. One question may be "How fast were you going?" The person being interviewed responds by saying "the speed limit." The person without experience or first-hand knowledge of the crash might move onto the next question. The proper response would be "What is the speed limit in that area?" or "How did you know you were going that fast?" or "When was the last time you looked at your speedometer?" or "How familiar are you with that area?", and so on. This is a good opportunity to make note of any signs of impairment (e.g., slurred speech or alcohol use [odor on breath]).

Uninvolved witnesses are also an important source of information. The first officers to respond to the scene of a crash should make every effort to obtain the names and contact information of all people who were at the scene upon their arrival.

In an actual investigation of a double fatal motor vehicle crash involving three vehicles in the state of New Jersey, two involved witnesses were an invaluable source of information. The crash involved an intoxicated driver who was not injured. He exited his vehicle after the crash and sat on a curb. An out-of-state couple on vacation and driving by happened upon the crash scene moments after the vehicles came to rest. They went to the intoxicated driver to check on his well-being, sat there, and spoke with him until police arrived. As it turned out, they were alcohol counselors who worked with people with alcohol problems on a daily basis. Although you might think that no better witnesses could be found to describe the driver's level of intoxication, that may not be true. Carroll, Rosenberg, and Funke (1988) compared the ability of mental health professionals and alcohol counselors to recognize intoxication. The authors found that experience working with alcohol-impaired patients did not improve accuracy, and alcohol counselors were no better than anyone else in identifying intoxicated people. Nevertheless, paramedics and other emergency personnel are a valuable source of information when it comes to the driver's condition and often note signs of intoxication or statements about alcohol use if such evidence is presented during what is often close contact with the driver or pedestrian patient. Get the names and contact information of other responders so they can be interviewed at a later time.

Vehicles

The second source of crash evidence is the motor vehicle itself, although non-motorized vehicles may be involved (e.g., bicycles). Vehicles provide physical, objective evidence that is not subject to perception, memory, self-serving motivations, bias or other human factors. However, that does not mean physical evidence cannot be misinterpreted. It can. Proper collection and documentation of evidence from the vehicle is a critical first step to the later interpretation of the evidence by a reconstruction expert. At the scene of the crash certain information from the vehicle can be obtained by the investigating officer, including the following.

First, a cursory examination of the interior of the vehicle should be made for evidence of alcohol, such as empty containers and receipts. For example, a receipt for the purchase of a particular type of alcoholic beverage that has the time of purchase coupled with an empty bottle of the same alcoholic beverage allows a reasonable basis for a psychopharmacology expert to make estimates of alcohol use and intoxication, which may be relevant to identifying contributing factors to the crash.

The officer at the scene should also document the condition of all vehicles involved in the crash. This would include, but not be limited to, whether the engine was running, and the lights on or off. Warning: Never touch the light switch to turn lights on or off. If possible, photograph the light switch position, if relevant. Also, never apply pressure to the brake pedal to test the brakes. Doing either (testing lights or brakes) may damage valuable evidence such as light bulb filaments used to determine whether or not the lights were activated prior to the crash. Make notes of the location of the vehicles, condition of windows (up or down, broken or intact), condition of tires and wheels, radio on or off, location of occupants inside the vehicle, and whether available restraints were being used.

Once the scene is investigated it is critical to ensure that the vehicles are removed from the scene properly so that evidence is preserved and not damaged. The preferred method of transport is to tow the vehicles using a flat bed. In the case of trucks and commercial vehicles a towing company that is familiar with towing such vehicles should be used. How the brakes are secured is critical for further examination. Brakes must be recharged with air or properly "caged" prior to towing in order for a trained examiner to document the condition of the brakes at the time of the crash. The removal of the vehicles should be documented, preferably with video but at the least with still photographs.

Vehicle storage is also important to preserve evidence. Once they are removed from the scene, vehicles should be stored in a secure facility just as any other evidence in a crime. If the vehicle cannot be stored in an enclosed structure (e.g., in a garage), cover it securely with a tarp.

After the vehicles are secured they should be inspected by a qualified crash reconstructionist. The reconstructionist will examine lights, tires, and the interior and exterior of the vehicle in detail and will coordinate with a certified mechanic to perform a mechanical autopsy of the vehicle. During the vehicle autopsy, the reconstructionist should be present, taking notes and photographs. Measurements and evidence can be used to analyze and reconstruct the crash.

Environment

Environment is the third element of any crash. Environmental factors include weather conditions, natural or artificial lighting conditions, geometry of the road, and the road surface itself. The weather conditions, including visibility, as well as the condition of the road surface should be documented. The type of road surface is essential in later determining a drag factor to use for calculations (although this is sometimes measured at the scene). Was the road surface blacktop, unpaved, concrete, and so forth? Was the surface polished from heavy travel or relatively new? Note whether or not the surface was wet or icy or sand covered. Something as simple as noting wet leaves on the surface can significantly change the calculations of the reconstructionist.

The geometry of the road should be documented with photographs and measurements for a scale diagram. Measurements should be extended beyond the immediate area of the crash. The higher the suspected speeds of the vehicles involved, the farther away from the scene you should look for evidence. Evidence such as road scars and tire marks can be found on the shoulder of the road, and on guard rails, signposts, and so on. Marks on the road that indicate vehicle operation can be located a considerable distance from the actual area of impact. All of this evidence needs to be documented with measurements and photographs.

Tire marks on the road should be documented, preferably with photographs, and measured so they can be identified as either acceleration marks, skid marks, yaw marks, or something else. Marks leading to the area of impact can help the reconstructionist determine travel paths and speeds of involved vehicles. Marks and scars on the surface of the road are essential in locating the area of impact.

Evidence collected at the scene from all three sources (people, vehicle, environment) is considered by the reconstructionist in a crash analysis and reconstruction report. The proper recognition and documentation of evidence at the scene is the foundation for any good reconstruction.

12.3 MEASUREMENTS AND PHOTOGRAPHS

At the scene, the crash investigator must "triage" the evidence, prioritizing evidence likely to be subject to change and in need of immediate documentation or collection and separating evidence that is of greater importance from the usual debris on the roadway. The more fragile the short-term evidence is, the more crucial it is to photograph and secure. The caveat to this is that it must be possible to replicate all evidence for court and related needs in the future. Therefore, measurements and photographs become the foundation for a proper traffic crash reconstruction. Both should be employed to enable an accurate account of what occurred, and each serves a different purpose in the investigative and reconstruction phase of the case. The at-scene crash investigator has one chance to collect evidence. Unlike a chemist who may be able to reanalyze a sample in the lab if there is a problem, once the scene of a crash is cleared, the investigator has no "do-overs." Omitted or overlooked evidence may no longer be available.

After obtaining witness statements, the investigator should make a walk-through of the scene using a line search pattern. A line search pattern requires walking parallel to the road while looking left to right to locate evidence. The longer the distance of the walk-through the better the search results, particularly in highway crashes, for which greater speeds are likely. The walk-through of the scene goes from some distance leading up to the crash scene perimeter, through the physical scene, and then beyond that point where visible crash debris (debris field) or markings cease to be evident. In cases involving a pedestrian struck by a motor vehicle, higher speeds are equal to greater post-impact throw distances for the pedestrian. A general rule of thumb is to inspect 50 to 75 feet from the center line to both sides of the roadway.

During the walk-through, begin compiling a written list identifying all evidence along the route. List objects in the order you come upon them, beginning with a reference point. Once the evidence has been identified, it should be photographed. Only after this initial set of photographs should the scene be spray painted with markers of where the evidence was located. At this point, distance measurements can be made. This method allows for the evidence to be collected in a timely manner so it can be placed in a secure area while measurements of the scene are completed.

Measuring and Documenting Roadway Evidence

Regardless of weather conditions (heat or cold); traffic volume (major arterial roadways vs. local roads); locale factors (rural vs. urban); amount of evidence to be documented, cataloged, and collected, taking measurements of the scene and the evidence contained within its perimeters is one of the most important and arduous tasks in a traffic crash investigation and reconstruction.

Measurements, and the rendering of an accurate collision diagram or map, is the foundation of any crash reconstruction. This evidence can be used to establish time and distance, speeds, paths of travel, positions of vehicle, cause and effect of obstructions to drivers', pedestrians', and witnesses' line-of-sight views and other factors that explain what happened. Other than the resultant calculations of times, speeds and distances by an investigator, that are used in a crash reconstruction case, the collision diagram is typically what is produced in evidence by a crash investigator or crash reconstructionist.

The use of measuring tapes has slowly been replaced by the use of laser measuring devices. These devices are highly accurate and are usually a much more expedient method that easily interfaces with computer software to allow for printed diagrams with clearly defined points of evidence placement that can be rescaled (larger) for courtroom presentation. Although the methods of taking measurements at a crash or crime scene have become more efficient and accurate with the advent of laser technology, the basic principles of *what to measure* for the diagram have not changed.

There are three methods of taking measurements that are used by crash investigators: (1) the coordinate method, (2) the triangulation method, and (3) the photogrammetry method, which uses a perspective grid placard. Photogrammetry is not commonly used except in cases in which time is of the essence to restore traffic flow in heavily congested urban areas (i.e., tunnels, bridges, and major interstate highways) to prevent transit gridlock.

Figure 12.1: Established and Marked Reference Point.

Figure 12.2: View of Baseline and First Measurement Along Road Edge.

The coordinate method is the most common approach. It is easily reproduced and used in the field to plot the locations of evidence. It can be used in handdrawn diagrams, and the measurements collected can be used by an investigator to create a computer-drawn diagram simply by putting the coordinates of the evidence plotted into the computer and then connecting the dots so to speak.

Coordinate measuring uses a reference point and right angles in conjunction with, ideally, a straight baseline such as the curb edge of a roadway. The investigator must choose a "nominal" direction (e.g., north, east, south or west) to declare as the orientation of the tape measure forming the baseline. The exact orientation need not be declared until the final rendering of the diagram is complete. A nominal declaration merely allows for proper documentation of the coordinates measured by the investigator as he or she writes them down.

The triangulation method involves taking three point angular measurements from multiple reference points without a baseline (thus creating a triangle). It takes three measurements to locate just one spot of an item. Laser-measuring devices utilize triangulation as their foundation, but the internal software of the device forms the angles and calculates all the resultant

Figure 12.3: View of Baseline and Second Measurement at Right Angle
from the Tape Measure.

triangles for the operator to enter into his or her computer program. The measurements with the laser are very accurate. This is not so when using the manual tape measure method of triangulation. This manual method is somewhat inaccurate and is prone to errors that can result in an inaccurate scaled diagram.

After deciding where to place the reference point (the origin point of all measurements to be taken known also as the zero end point of the tape measure), the investigator places a tape measure along that straight edge so measurements can be taken off of the baseline to a point at a right angle to that baseline.

To do this, an investigator takes a second tape measure, and walks parallel to the baseline from the zero point to a point where she or he comes abreast of an item of evidence that has been located (this is the first measurement). At that point, the second tape measure is placed at a right angle to the baseline and one of the tape measure ends is placed on the baseline and the other in the center of the item from which the measurement is being taken. Together the two measurements become the coordinates of the measured item of evidence. All items of evidence are plotted this way. Based on the seriousness of the collision this can number many dozens of items. It is clear that taking these measurements manually is time consuming.

After all the measurements are taken, an investigator or reconstructionist can take those measurements and plot them onto a piece of paper and create a scaled diagram of the scene. The preparation of a diagram is too lengthy to cover here; however, the value of the diagram whether produced via computer or hand drawn is very necessary. It is a valuable tool used in the assigning of time and distance positions when computing alcohol-related perception and reaction delays and their relationship to crash avoidance.

Photographing Evidence

The technological advancements with regard to photography have been a great addition to the investigative efforts of the police. The older 4 × 4 and 35-mm cameras were not only cumbersome but also gave mixed results when used by an untrained photographer. Digital photographs, including cell phone cameras, have greatly enhanced the abilities of the new "point-and-shoot" generation of officers who can do more with less. There is very little reason an officer cannot pick up any digital camera and get really good photographs at the scene of a crash. This includes macro and wide-angled photo images. The only limitation here is their respective department's ability to supply them with a camera to use. A caveat here for officers is that if they choose to use their cell phone to take pictures, the cell phone then becomes discoverable evidence and is subject to seizure as evidence.

The greatest advantage to using digital photography is the ability for the investigator to take numerous photographs, review them at scene to ensure the images are clear and proper, and then store them on a small electronic memory card in the camera. This allows for easy transfer and enlargement of the photo images taken when displayed on a computer screen. It makes sharing the photographic information with all persons having a need for it much easier. This includes criminal prosecution, public defense, and civil plaintiff and defendant cases.

Photographic memorialization of evidence is usually aligned with the scene walk-through. That is to say, the photographs are taken in sequence in the direction of the involved crash participants. The photographs are taken in a sequence as if the investigator were walking a juror or person unfamiliar with the crash event into the scene in a progressive manner, as if walking up and through the scene itself. This helps that person to understand what the investigator saw and where it was when he or she saw it. It provides enhanced prospective when used in concert with a properly prepared diagram rendered from accurate measurements taken at the crash scene.

A proper photograph in a crash investigation should never be taken by accident (no pun intended) or for humor purposes. The crash investigator should carefully choose how the evidence is to be memorialized in the photo (e.g., lighting, angle, or position). Extremely gory photos do little to help the investigation and most likely would be denied as evidence in court as being prejudicial in nature. They may serve a purpose in the reconstruction or matching of injuries to causation area but this decision is purely event driven. The sometimes humorous photos of a fellow officer at the scene may be fun at a later date; the problem exists that somewhere a finder of fact will see it and that will bring into question the level of serious dedication the officers displayed while investigating the event. Additionally, the photographic image cannot be deleted from the memory card being used without leaving an electronic time stamp and blank image spot on the card log. This blank spot is a huge open door for defense attorneys to ask what it was you were covering up in your investigation that you had to delete a photo image. Just stick to the task at hand and keep it professional, then no alibis will be needed.

Photography Primer

This is not to present a complete course of instruction in photography. Most people who are actively engaged in the investigation of traffic collisions have had enough experience with a camera to know how to use it. In crash investigation photography, purposeful techniques are used to take photographs for evidentiary purposes. A crash scene photographer should always make an effort to show a scale (likely a ruler or stick measuring tape next to an item) in the photographs when possible. If no ruler is available something of a known size is placed in the photograph (i.e., a pen, pencil, or business card). For example, if a partially full liquor bottle is found, be sure to photograph the label (including the percent of alcohol) and photograph the fill line next to a ruler or some standard-length object.

When photographing a piece of evidence, investigators should use a three-photo series to memorialize the item. An example would be where the investigator is trying to show a small scuff on the fender of a vehicle. The investigator should take the first photograph of the series that shows the entire side of the vehicle. The second photo is taken a little closer to the specific area of the car with the scuff, and then a third photograph is taken up close that details a close up of the scuff itself. The third photo should have something to show its scale to the person viewing it. This again allows the investigator to show specifically where the scuff was in relation to the surface of vehicle, and its size and orientation of the scuff on the vehicle (or building or other object). A detailed photo log should be kept of all photos taken and what they show for easy reference later on in the investigation and reconstruction of the crash.

Figure 12.4. Alcohol Container in Vehicle — Note Location, Volume, and Seal.

Normally, an at-scene crash investigator will take the at-scene pictures in groupings. It follows the three picture series rule but in a much larger scale. They first take a distance series of photos of the scene, and then photos of the vehicle(s) and finally the interior of the vehicle(s), and/or bodies. One set will include the scene itself, including the roadway and weather conditions, topography and terrain, roadway obstructions, vehicles at rest, and other things that may be generic to the area of investigation. The second set will concentrate on the individual vehicles involved and the areas around them. The photographing of the vehicle exterior in a subseries is done by taking photos of all (damaged and undamaged) sides. This would include views of the roof and corners of the vehicles—sides, front and rear—and photos of the underside of the vehicle (usually taken at the vehicle autopsy while it is on a lift), as well as any other pertinent things found by the investigator. An additional set of vehicle photographs is always taken of the interior of the vehicle at the scene. Another set is taken at the tow storage facility when the vehicle autopsy/inspection is done. This will memorialize the inspection in photographs, but an additional, or tertiary, subset of photographs is also done to highlight the damaged areas (interior and exterior) of the vehicle more accurately without the chaotic atmosphere of an active crash scene. These photographs will more adequately show the locations where they interacted during the crash.

All three sets of photos concerning the vehicle are critical to a proper reconstruction endeavor.

Like the exterior vehicle photographs, the investigator will also take a sub-series of photographs of the interior of the vehicle that will likely include the seat positions, dashboard switch positions (headlamps on or off), seatbelt positions (to determine if they were in use or not), any and all containers used to transport alcoholic beverages (e.g., children's "sippy" cups, flasks, resealable dark-colored soda bottles, thermoses), damage to the interior of the vehicle from body contact during the crash, windshield damage caused by unrestrained occupants and any other items or debris that would be deemed detrimental to the safe operation of the vehicle. Remember, a search warrant or owner's consent form is required before doing a vehicle autopsy.

Photographs should be taken of the autopsy of all fatally injured people in the crash. This is done much the same as the scene and vehicle autopsy. It is best photographed with a series of photos from the point where the victim is fully clothed to all points of opening the body cavity, examination of organs and patterns of damage on the body, then the final stitched closure of the body. A detailed photo log should be kept of this procedure due to the technical nature of the evidence being photographed.

Finally, even if it is daylight, the use of a fill flash (use of the flash mode of the camera) will allow better documentation of evidence hidden within the shadows. This is important for interior as well as exterior photographs that are taken.

At this point all the criteria for a complete and accurate investigation have been met so that a crash reconstructionist can begin their reconstruction.

12.4 VALUE OF CRASH RECONSTRUCTION

To this point we have discussed different types of evidence and the documentation of that evidence, but to what end? Why is all this information necessary in a crash reconstruction and the prosecution of a criminal crash in which alcohol was involved? A good crash reconstructionist will evaluate *all available evidence* and use principals of physics and some math as well as a knowledge and understanding of human factors to determine how the crash occurred. The end result is an opinion of an expert in the area of crash reconstruction based on all the evidence available for evaluation. This all goes back to the quality of the investigation at the scene of the crash and how data were recognized and documented.

Using the evidence available, a reconstructionist applies principals of physics to determine how a crash occurred and can corroborate or discredit a witness account. A reconstruction can also show if a driver reacted properly and in comparison with a sober, healthy driver.

Generally, a reconstructionist will start the analysis with a working scale diagram of the crash site. Evidence that was previously documented can be placed into the diagram. Using the diagram and evidence from people, vehicles, and environment, a reconstructionist may be able to determine approach to impact angles, departure from impact angles, location and distance traveled by the center of mass of the vehicles and other factors that will help determine speeds and how the vehicles crashed.

The diagram will ultimately help the reconstructionist with a time and distance analysis. During the course of the reconstruction, a reconstructionist may (if the proper evidence from people, vehicles, and environment is available) determine the speed of the vehicle(s) involved in the crash as well as the dynamics of the crash. Once the speeds and dynamics are known, a reconstructionist can determine where the vehicles were in relation to each other, or in the case of a pedestrian crash, where the vehicle and pedestrian were in relation to each other at any given point in time prior to impact.

Doing this time and distance analysis allows the reconstructionist to answer questions such as did one vehicle allow the other vehicle enough time and distance to perceive, react, and stop prior to impact or to avoid the impact with some other evasive maneuver? Could the driver have avoided the impact with the pedestrian, or could one vehicle have avoided the impact with the other vehicle?

When performing a time and distance analysis, the reconstructionist must consider perception and reaction times as well as the time and distance it takes a vehicle traveling at a given speed to stop or make some other evasive maneuver. This is the human factor portion of the reconstruction. This is where the information and evidence obtained from the involved parties in a crash becomes important.

It will be recalled from Chapter 4 that there are five basic phases to the total RT process.

1. Pre Detection Distraction (PDD): when the object is within the driver's field of view, but the driver's attention is elsewhere; sometimes referred to as perception delay.
2. Detection: when the driver detects an event.
3. Stimulus Recognition/Identification: when the driver recognizes the object and identifies it as a hazard (or not).
4. Decision Making: time it takes for the driver to decides on a course of action, if any.
5. Response Execution: The driver takes action (e.g. steps on brake).

Let us examine how these factors and concepts are used in the reconstruction of a crash. Assume the following in our example:

1. There is no PDD (*see* Chapter 4)
2. Perception RT in a healthy person is 1.6 seconds (1600 milliseconds).
3. The vehicle is traveling at 73.3 feet per second (fps;) (50 miles per hour).
4. Through testing it is determined that appropriate drag factor[1] to use for speed calculations is 0.80 (deceleration rate of 25.76 fps²).
5. The stopping distance for the vehicle once brakes are applied is 104.28 feet which requires 2.84 seconds.
6. The distance that the vehicle covers during the 1.6-second RT is 117.28 feet.

The total stopping distance and stopping time is calculated by adding the perception reaction (PR) time to the stopping time and the reaction distance to the stopping distance. In this case the total stopping distance is 221.56 feet and the total stopping time is 4.44 seconds. Therefore, in this time and distance analysis, one vehicle was 221.56 feet from the other at 4.44 seconds prior to impact. This calculation is derived from the following basic formulas:

$$\text{Distance}_{\text{Total}} = \text{Distance}_{\text{PR}} + \text{Distance}_{\text{Veh. stop}}$$
$$\text{Distance}_{\text{PR}} = \text{Velocity} \times \text{Time}_{\text{PR}}$$
$$\text{Time}_{\text{To stop}} = \text{Velocity/Acceleration Rate}$$

In the previous example a PR time of 1.6 seconds was used with the caveat that there was no PDD. That perception delay (e.g., time off task) is relatively difficult for the reconstructionist to measure, as can be seen in Table 12.2 and within even superficial consideration of many time-taking distractions encountered by the driver. The preliminary data in Table 12.2 (Benn & Grey, 2016) should also be considered conservative because the subjects were aware of the testing and may have been influenced by expectancy. The actual visual time off the roadway could be seconds, and although it is not recommended that such approximation be incorporated into a single reconstruction, the analyst should articulate this limitation and consider bracketing the analysis to assume PDD.

---

1. Drag factor: a number representing the acceleration or deceleration (negative acceleration) of a vehicle or other body as a decimal fraction of the acceleration of gravity; $f = a/g$; the force needed to produce acceleration the same direction, divided by the weight of the body to which the force is applied. When a vehicle slides with all wheels locked on a level surface then the coefficient of friction and drag factor (μ) have the same value.

Table 12.2: Time Off Driving Task.

Number of Subjects:	Trials	Task	Mean Time Off Road (s)
7	50	Change temperature setting	1.890
7	50	Change radio channel	2.242
7	50	Look over left shoulder	1.497
3	30	Turn and look into back seat	1.802

PR time (without PDD) itself varies based on several factors, including age, lighting conditions, and alcohol intoxication. Olson and Sivak (1986) measured the time between the presentation of a hazard to the time subjects (men and women age 18 to 80) responded by lifting their foot off the accelerator. The results in the 95th percentile for the younger group (18 to 40 years) revealed a PR time of 1.6 seconds, with the results of the older group being very similar.

PR time may vary from case to case and person to person. There is no single RT that applies to every case. It is generally accepted within the crash reconstruction community that PR time of 1.6 seconds is applicable. This time does not include any time lost due to PDD, physical disabilities (e.g., hearing or vision loss), environmental factors (e.g., visibility, temperature), or intoxication.

As an example, during daylight hours a pedestrian traveling west steps off a curb into the street and continues walking. A vehicle traveling at a constant velocity of 65 fps approaches from the south. Through the scene investigation conducted by police it is determined that the pedestrian would have been visible to a driver approaching from the south from a distance of 200 feet. The scene investigation also yields enough evidence to determine the drag factor of the roadway for that vehicle is 0.75. The evidence also shows the vehicle to be in proper mechanical order.

Assuming that the only action for the driver to take to avoid striking the pedestrian is to stop, and assuming that the driver had no perception delay, an appropriate PR time estimate would be 1.6 seconds. During these 1.6 seconds the vehicle continues to travel at a constant velocity of 65 fps and will cover a distance of 104 feet. At that point the driver applies the brakes. The stopping distance for a vehicle under those circumstances is 87 feet. Now add the stopping distance of 87 feet to the distance traveled over the 1.6-second PR time for a total stopping distance of 191 feet. The driver of the vehicle would have stopped the vehicle 9 feet short of striking the pedestrian.

Now let us consider a scenario in which the same vehicle does not stop until 10 feet after it struck the pedestrian. The area of impact was determined by evidence collected at the scene. Evidence at the scene also indicates that the vehicle was braking for a total of 87 feet and the velocity of the vehicle prior to the brake application was 65 fps which was the same as the vehicle in the previous example. From the point of possible perception to the end of the vehicle skid where the vehicle came to a stop was a total of 210 feet. It was documented that 2 hours after the crash, the driver had a measured BAC of 140 mg/dL.

It will be recalled from Chapter 4 that Maylor and Rabbitt (1993) developed algorithims based on a meta-analysis of various studies demonstrating about a 10 to 20 percent lengthening of RT under conditions of moderate intoxication (about 80 mg/dL). By comparing reaction time with and without alcohol, the following algorithms were derived, both of which accounted for more than 99 percent of the variance.

In studies in which it was concluded that alcohol range, 67 to 99 mg/dL affected the decision-making phase (response selection), the effect of alcohol was accounted for by the following formula:

$$RT_{alcohol} = 1.12 \, RT_{no \, alcohol} - 17.85.$$

In studies in which it was concluded that alcohol (84 mg/dL) affected the decision-making phase (response selection) the effect of alcohol was accounted for by the following formula:

$$RT_{alcohol} = 1.22 \, RT_{no \, alcohol} - 91.49.$$

How would this affect our examples cited earlier? The first driver, healthy and sober, was able to detect the hazard, decide what action to take, and brought the vehicle to a complete stop 9 feet short of striking the pedestrian.

The second driver had a measured BAC of 140 mg/dL under the same driving conditions. Using the Maylor and Rabbitt algorithm it is determined that it would take an additional 260 milliseconds ($RT_{alcohol} = 1.22 \times 1600 - 91.49$) in the decision-making phase (response selection). The original 1600-milliseconds PR time now becomes approximately an 1860-millisecond PR time. In that additional 260 milliseconds the driver will travel an additional 17 feet prior to applying the brakes. Once the brakes are applied, under the same circumstances as our original example, the vehicle will travel the same additional 87 feet before sliding to a stop. The vehicle now stops some 8 feet beyond the pedestrian's location. It should also be noted that in both examples an assumption is being made that no PDD took place.

In these examples, the driver's total PR time increased, not the distance for the vehicle to physically come to a stop once brakes are applied. The issue here is what caused the perception delay the driver experienced. There are many factors that can affect that perception delay, but in this case, alcohol intoxication must be considered in the reconstruction analysis. Other factors such as pedal pressure (which may be affected by intoxication) may be present but unaccounted for in such analyses.

This is where *all* evidence must be considered in order to reach a conclusion. Certainly one of the factors that must be considered is the fact that there was evidence of alcohol consumption and intoxication by the driver in the second example.

In conclusion, there are many factors that affect the total PR time of a driver. There are no studies that indicate there is one value that can be used for all circumstances; it is strongly suggested that any estimate of PR time be based on studies given the circumstances and a range of temporal assumptions. In crash reconstruction the suggested starting average value is 1.6 seconds. In cases involving intoxicated drivers, the effects of alcohol on total RT as well as more limited PR time must be considered.

Conclusions

The importance of proper evidence documentation at the scene of a motor vehicle crash cannot be overestimated, particularly if alcohol involvement is suspected. Investigators at the scene and subsequent crash reconstruction analyses completed by a qualified crash reconstruction expert have an opportunity and responsibility of properly collecting subjective as well as objective evidence to determine how a crash occurred.

REFERENCES

Benn, D., and Grey, J. (2016) Time off task with structured distraction momentum. *Momentum, 3(*1), 1-3

Carroll, N., Rosenberg, H., and Funke, S. (1988). Recognition of intoxication by alcohol counselors. *Journal of Substance Abuse Treatment, 5,* 239–246

Coughlin, G. G. (1982). *Dictionary of Law.* New York, NY: Barnes & Noble.

Maylor, E., and Rabbitt, P. (1993). Alcohol, reaction time and memory: A meta-analysis. *British Journal of Psychology, 84,* 301-317

Olson, P. L., and Sivak, M. (1986). Perception response time to unexpected roadway hazards. *The Human Factors, 28(*1), 91–96.

Note: Chapter 12 was coauthored with David Benn and Jeffrey Grey, who were kind enough to lend their expertise. Mr. Benn, a retired Burlington County, New Jersey, Prosecutor's Office Detective Sergeant is internationally recognized by the Accreditation Commission for Traffic Accident Reconstruction (ACTAR) and currently serves as President of the New Jersey Association of Accident Reconstructionists as well as on the Board of Directors of the National Association of Traffic Accident Reconstructionists and Investigators and is a member of the Governing Board of Directors for ACTAR. Mr. Benn provides training in crash investigation and reconstruction for the University of North Florida Institute of Police Technology and Management and the Traffic Institute of Northwestern University and was instrumental in developing the Basic and Advance Crash Investigation Course currently taught through Kean University. He is currently President/Owner of Impact Reconstruction Services, Inc.

Jeffrey Grey is a retired law enforcement officer having served as a Patrol Sergeant specializing in Traffic Crash Investigation and Reconstruction before finally retiring as a Vehicle Homicide Detective with the Burlington County, New Jersey Prosecutor's Office. He received his BA degree in Criminal Justice from Stockton University in New Jersey and is an Accredited Traffic Crash Reconstructionist through the Accreditation Commission for Traffic Accident Reconstruction. Mr. Grey is also the former co-owner of Impact Reconstruction Associates, Inc., Mt. Holly, New Jersey.

Chapter 13

NEUROPSYCHOLOGY:
ALCOHOL AND MEMORY

13.1 RELIABILITY OF MEMORY IN FORENSIC CASEWORK

Subjective evidence is often half the case and an important component of the forensic investigation. Information about the who, what, where, when, how much, or how long is largely based on self-report, not objective evidence, even though information about alcohol use, time of drinking, distance away, or time a pedestrian or car was first visible are important in alcohol analyses and accident reconstruction. Such information can be used by forensic examiners to make more objective scientific estimates to explain what happened or to support or discredit the recall of a witness when compared with objective evidence (e.g., a toxicology test, roadway markings). The ability to recall information may be affected by many factors, including acute intoxication, trauma or cognitive impairment in chronic drinkers who are sober at the time of an incident or questioning, or conscious or unconscious self-serving motivations.

Given the widespread use of alcohol, it is likely that intoxication will be a factor in a significant portion of criminal or civil matters and therefore the effect of alcohol on memory is likely to be a question of forensic inquiry. Among men, alcohol ranks as one of the most serious substances of abuse in the general population and affects between 5 and 12 million individuals (Hartman, 1995; Thompson, 2000). The acute effects of alcohol intoxication are discussed in Chapters 4, 5, and 6, and the chronic effects of alcohol abuse are extensively reviewed in Chapter 9. Less clear, somewhat controversial, and of particular note are the potential acute and chronic effects of alcohol on memory, which is the focus of this chapter. The interpretation of such evidence is not as simple as it might appear, or should be.

Alcohol intoxication impairs many components of cognition, including judgment, assessment of risk, appreciation of the negative consequences of risk taking, or other behaviors and alters perception (Burian, Liguori & Robinson, 2002), but the effects of acute intoxication on certain types of memory is not so straightforward as to conclude that alcohol always impairs memory. In fact, to the contrary, depending on the type of memory and circumstances, there may be a significant effect or no effect of alcohol on memory. In forensic alcohol cases, the intoxicated subject may claim to have no memory of his or her behavior. Although loss of memory is not a defense in criminal cases, understanding how and in whom such amnesia occurs may be useful in interpreting and comparing different types of evidence. For example, was there memory loss of events before drinking? Such memory may be subject to retrograde amnesia wherein there is difficulty retrieving facts or events from long-term memory that occurred before the onset of the drinking, trauma, or other event. *Retrograde* amnesia is usually more pronounced for events that occurred just prior to the onset of the event, whereas remote events, such as childhood memories, are relatively well-preserved.

Is memory loss specific to new information presented during drinking? This type of memory loss is *anterograde* amnesia, wherein there is a partial or complete inability to recall recent events or learn new verbal or nonverbal information. Similarly, recall of events, including self-reported drinking, may be influenced by the pharmacological effects of alcohol on memory, and by psychologically driven factors. In addition, in some instances the memory may be affected by traumatic brain injury that occurred while intoxicated or as a secondary consequence of long-term drinking. An understanding of the types, and mechanisms, of memory loss due to intoxication may be useful but should always be interpreted in the context of other evidence.

13.2 WHAT IS MEMORY AND HOW DOES IT WORK?

Memory is what we remember from the sum of our experiences over time. Those experiences are collected from the outside world through our senses (visual, tactile, auditory, olfactory, and other sensory receptors) and transmitted to the brain. We associate those sensory events with psychological or perceptual impressions. For example, if you associate a certain alcoholic drink with getting sick, the memory of that aversive state will lead to avoiding that drink in the future. This is a basic law of learning.

The neurochemistry of memory is not fully understood but we do know that events of interest activate neurons (*see* Chapter 3) and if those events are important to the organism or repeated enough, a set of encoded connections between neurons form in the brain. This is a process involving different areas of the entire brain. Remembering the event involves reactivation of the encoded neural connections that re-create the original experience. In other words, you remember it. A particular memory may include sensory components or associations stored in different brain areas wherein a neural net connects both the visual image of an event and other sensory memories such as sound (what someone said, if the radio was on, if they heard screeching tires, etc.) or an odor. Similarly, those connections allow associations later in time. For example, hearing screeching tires again may evoke the original visceral experiences that occurred in response to the original event (e.g., startle, fear), or detecting the smell of baking cookies may bring back a particular childhood memory of home. Such conditioning is well-known in the psychological literature. Although different brain areas may become associated with a memory, the hippocampus, a part of the limbic system described in Chapter 3, is an important brain area for the storage of memory.

Memory formation and storage occurs in stages. *Sensory* (or iconic) memory may last for a few seconds; *short-term* (or working) memory may last from seconds to minutes, depending upon whether the information is rehearsed; and *long-term* memory storage can last a lifetime in some instances. This three-stage model often is referred to as the *modal model of memory.* In this model, sensory information is transferred from a sensory memory storage area to short-term memory. Depending on rehearsal (particularly in short-term memory), understanding, motivation, and arousal factors, this information will be transferred from short-term to long-term storage or be *encoded* into long-term memory. Such long term memories may be *episodic* (memory of a specific time and place, such as recalling where you went on a family vacation, what you ate for dinner yesterday, etc.), *semantic* (memory of facts such as historical dates, the chemical formula for water, etc.), or *procedural* (memory of certain learned skills such as riding a bicycle or tying your shoelaces). All memories are formed and retrieved through a neurophysiological process. A drug that alters brain functioning has the potential to enhance or impair memory at any stage in the preceding model.

The interpretation of the effects of alcohol on memory varies with the psychological and physiological components of memory and how memory is operationally defined. Mello noted "the inconsistent use of descriptive terms has been a recurrent source of confusion in the 'short–term' memory literature. For example, 'short-term' memory has been variously defined as 5 seconds, 5 minutes, and 30 minutes" (1973, p. 333). Even so, one conclusion is that the effect of alcohol on the formation of new long-term "explicit" memories (e.g., names and phone numbers) and events is far greater than the drug's effect on the ability to recall previously established older memories.

Acute Intoxication and Memory

In the laboratory, the effects of alcohol on certain forms of memory can be detected after one or two drinks. With higher doses, the magnitude of memory impairment increases, and under some drinking conditions, alcohol intoxication can completely block the ability to form or encode memories. However, acute intoxication does not always impair short-term memory. Intoxicated subjects are typically able to repeat new information immediately after its presentation and often, but not always, can keep it active in short-term storage for up to a few minutes if they are not distracted (Nordby, Watten, Raanaas & Magnussen, 1999). Similarly, subjects normally are capable of retrieving information placed in long–term storage prior to acute intoxication. In contrast, alcohol impairs the ability to store information across delays longer than a few seconds if subjects are distracted between the time they are given the new information and the time they are tested. As discussed in Chapter 4, divided attention, which requires memory and is critical for driving and other tasks, is impaired by alcohol even at low BACs.

The effect of alcohol on memory formation can be described as a dose-related continuum, with minor impairments at one end and large more easily detected impairments at the other. However, all impairments represent the same fundamental deficit in the ability to transfer new information from short-term to long-term storage. Memory impairment at BACs below 150 mg/dL tend to be small to moderate and are sometimes referred to cocktail party memory deficits. These deficits are of the type people might experience after having a few drinks, often manifested as problems remembering what another person said or where they were in conversation. Sometimes, memory loss is specific to certain stimuli. For example, in a placebo-controlled study Westrick, Shapiro, Nathan, and Brick (1988) found that alcohol impaired recall of word categories and facial recognition at low BACs (average, 43 mg/dL) but through different neurophysiological mechanisms. In general, laboratory tests show that as the BAC increases, the resulting memory impairments increase (Mintzer & Griffiths, 2002; Nordby et al., 1999, Westrick et al. 1988), at least in some subjects.

Eyewitness testimony is often regarded as important and persuasive, even though it is affected by suggestibility (Pezdek & Greene, 1993; Yarmey et al., 1996), stress (Deffenbacher, 1983); time delays (Flin, Boon, Knox & Bull, 1992), age (Brimacombe, Jung, Garrioch & Allison, 2003), and intoxication (Yuille & Tollestrup, 1990). For example, Yuille and Tollestrup (1990) examined the effect of BAC between 60 and 120 mg/dL on the ability of witnesses or placebo controls to later recognize photos of the suspects and found intoxicated witnesses performed significantly poorer than sober controls did.

Harvey, Kneller, and Campbell (2013) noted that even though there is a robust literature on the deleterious effect of even low doses of alcohol on memory, a small number of studies have examined the influence of alcohol on eyewitness performance. Of those, Compo and colleagues (2011) examined the ability of sober and intoxicated subjects to remember conversations with an "experimental bartender." Although sober subjects recalled more peripheral information (e.g., bar room scenario, decor), there was no significant difference between sober and intoxicated (up to 80 mg/dL) subjects' recall of central (what the bartender looked like) or conversation phrases. The authors attributed this to a narrowing of attention or alcohol myopia (Steele & Josephs, 1990).

13.3 ALCOHOL-INDUCED BLACKOUTS

Loss of substantial or complete recall of events for periods is referred to as *en block* amnesia. For example, after a night of drinking, you wake up in a strange bed with no recall of how you got there or what happened the previous night. A blackout indicates difficulty in encoding episodic memories because of rapid increases in the BAC affecting neurons in the rhinal cortex and hippocampus, a subcortical structure (*see* Chapter 2). Although the term alcoholic blackout is commonly used, it is misleading because subjects do not lose consciousness (they are awake and engaging in various activities) and blackouts are not limited to alcoholics, although they occur more often in alcoholics and heavy drinkers (Anthenelli, Klein, Tsuang, Smith & Schuckit, 1994; Schuckit, Smith, Anthenelli & Irwin, 1993). Alcoholism or even severe intoxication is not a requirement of alcohol blackouts. Nevertheless, the magnitude of memory loss in populations of heavy drinkers brought attention to this phenomenon and much research has been focused on memory loss in clinical population (Goodwin, Crane & Guze, 1969a,b).

During a blackout episode, subjects are capable of participating in salient, emotionally charged events–as well as more mundane events–that they later cannot remember (Goodwin, 1995).

Interestingly, people appear able to keep information active in short-term memory for at least a few seconds. As a result, they can often carry on conversations, drive automobiles, and engage in other complicated behaviors. Information pertaining to these events is simply not transferred into long-term storage. Of particular note is the fact that intoxicated subjects were awake and conversational during the amnesic state but could not remember what they said or did 5 minutes earlier (Ryback, 1970).

Formal research into the nature of alcohol-induced blackouts began in the 1940s and focused on alcoholics. It was Jellinek who initially characterized blackouts based on data collected from a survey of Alcoholics Anonymous members. Jellineck (1946) noted that recovering alcoholics frequently reported having experienced alcohol-induced amnesia while they were drinking and concluded that blackouts were a powerful indicator of alcoholism. Goodwin and colleagues (1969a,b) published two of the most influential studies based on interviews with 100 hospitalized alcoholics, 64 of whom had a history of blackouts and described two qualitatively different types of blackouts: en bloc and fragmentary blackouts. People experiencing en bloc blackouts are unable to recall any details whatsoever from events that occurred while they were intoxicated, as if the process of transferring information from short-term to long-term storage has been completely blocked. En bloc memory impairments tend to have a distinct onset. It is usually less clear when these blackouts end because people typically fall asleep before they are over.

These memory impairments are primarily anterograde in nature. Alcohol impairs the ability to form new memories while the person is intoxicated but does not typically erase memories formed before intoxication.

Goodwin, Othmer and Halikas (1970) examined the impact of acute alcohol exposure on memory formation in subjects, half of whom (at that time) met diagnostic criteria for alcoholism, and half had a history of frequent blackouts. Memory was tested during the consumption of 16 to 18 oz of 86-proof bourbon over about 4 hours. Half of the subjects reported no recall of the stimuli or their presentation 30 minutes and 24 hours after the events, though most seemed to recall the stimuli 2 minutes after presentation. Lack of recall for the events 24 hours later, while sober, represents clear experimental evidence for the occurrence of blackouts. The fact that subjects could remember aspects of the events 2 minutes after they occurred but not 30 minutes or 24 hours afterward provides compelling evidence that the blackouts stemmed from an inability to transfer information from short-term to long-term storage.

Although much of what we know about blackouts comes from the study of alcoholics, more recent research shows that blackouts also occur among social drinkers. Knight, Palacios, and Shannon (1999) observed that 35 percent of pediatric residency program trainees had experienced at least one blackout. Goodwin (1995) reported that 33 percent of first-year medical students acknowledged having had at least one blackout related to drinking too much, too quickly. Looking at other groups that often drink, about 50 percent of college students reported blackout experiences after drinking excessively (Wechsler et al., 2002). An equal number of males and females experienced blackouts even though males drank significantly more often and more heavily than did females, and fragmentary blackouts occurred more often than total en bloc blackouts did (White, 2003). These results suggest that at any given level of alcohol consumption, females are at greater risk than are males for experiencing blackouts. This gender difference may be due to differences in alcohol distribution and metabolism.

13.4 AMNESIA AS A DEFENSE?

In some forensic cases, amnesia has been offered as a defense in criminal behavior. However, amnesia has been reported in 40 to 70 percent of homicides involving psychiatric patients in which alcoholic blackouts are not involved (Granacher, 2004). Taylor and Kopelman (1984) reported that of the 120 cases studied, 8 percent of men charged with violent crimes claimed they had no memory of their actions. Amnesia was not reported in 47 of the nonviolent cases examined. However, in an examination of the distribution of crimes within those claiming amnesia, 47 percent had been charged with murder. Of the amnesia subjects interviewed, 42 percent were alcohol abusers, 37 percent were schizophrenic, and 21 percent were clinically depressed. The authors surmised that alcohol blackouts are state-dependent memory and concluded amnesia in criminal cases is due to the pharmacological effects of alcohol, part of a psychotic state, or a psychological defense mechanism against remembering a terrible act.

Blood Alcohol Concentrations and Blackouts

When a blackout or similar profound alcohol-related memory loss is alleged in litigation, the question "at what BAC does a blackout occur?" is or should be raised. Earlier studies also suggested that blackouts often occurred with BACs of about 200 mg/dL and could last for 9 hours to 3 days (Ryback, 1970). Drinking large quantities of alcohol alone seems insufficient to produce a blackout. Not all highly intoxicated drinkers experience blackouts, and lesser memory loss (grayouts) may be more difficult to measure or to differentiate from memory loss that is unrelated to intoxication. Nevertheless, most blackouts occur at BACs of more than 200 mg/dL. Perry and associates (2006) interviewed men and women arrested and for whom BACs were available. The mean BAC for subjects with no memory loss was 180 mg/dL, but grayouts or blackouts were most often reported at BACs of more than 220 mg/dL. van Oorsouw, Merckelbach, Ravelli, Nijman, and Mekking-Pompen (2004) found that the average BAC for offenders claiming a blackout was about 180 mg/dL. Since individual differences and variance around an average BAC associated with blackouts is already present, there is no reasonable or useful red line that can be applied to all subjects. In such cases, the validity of an alcoholic blackout should be examined in the context of supporting (or negating) evidence.

13.5 MECHANISMS OF MEMORY LOSS
FROM ACUTE ALCOHOL

Although the effects of alcohol on memory are complex and not fully understood, there is a scientific basis for this causal relationship. One explanation is that alcohol disrupts neurons from establishing long-lasting and increased responses to signals with other cells (Bliss & Collingridge, 1993). This heightened responsiveness is known as long-term potentiation, which is believed to be an important component of memory (Martin & Morris 2002). Alcohol interferes with the establishment of long-term potentiation (Givens & McMahon, 1995; Morrisett & Swartzwelder, 1993; Pyapali, Turner, Wilson & Swartzwelder, 1999; Schummers & Browning, 2001). In vitro studies of brain slices show that long-term potentiation impairment begins at concentrations equivalent to those produced by consuming just one or two standard drinks (e.g., a 12-oz beer, 1.5-oz of liquor in a shot or mixed drink, or a 5-oz glass of wine) (Blitzer, Gil & Landau, 1990). Although most people do not have alcoholic blackouts from one drink, it is unknown if loss of inconsequential memories that most people experience are enhanced by low doses of alcohol.

Another risk factor for blackouts among social drinkers is individual differences based on history of blackouts. Hartzler and Fromme (2003) recruited 108 college students, half of whom had experienced at least one fragmentary blackout in the previous year. While sober, members of the two groups performed comparably in memory tasks. However, when they were mildly intoxicated (80 mg/dL) subjects with a history of fragmentary blackouts performed worse than did those without such a history, suggesting that some people are more susceptible to blackouts than others are. Subjects in the fragmentary blackout group are simply more vulnerable to alcohol-induced memory impairments and performed poorly during testing under alcohol. Alternatively, subjects who drank enough in the past to experience alcohol-induced memory impairments may have performed poorly during testing because prior exposure to alcohol damaged the brain in a way that predisposed them to experiencing future memory impairments.

One of the key requirements for the establishment of long-term potentiation in the hippocampus, that part of the brain known to be involved in memory, is the activation of NMDA2 receptor which is activated by the neurotransmitter glutamate. As discussed in Chapter 2, activation of the NMDA receptor allows calcium to enter the cell, which sets off a chain of events leading to long-lasting changes in the cell's structure or function, or both. Alcohol interferes with the activation of the NMDA receptor, thereby preventing the influx of calcium and the changes that follow (Swartzwelder, Wilson & Tayyeb, 1995). This is believed to be the primary mechanism underlying the effects of alcohol on long-term potentiation, though other transmitter systems probably are also involved (Schummers & Browning, 2001).

13.6 CHRONIC ALCOHOLISM
AND KORSAKOFF'S AMNESIA

Chronic alcoholics are at high risk for a variety of injuries that might result in forensic investigation because they drink so frequently to high BAC or otherwise have been exposed to the toxic effects of chronic drinking. Considerable neuropsychological attention has been focused on the cognitive features of Korsakoff's syndrome, a somewhat rare but profound consequence of chronic heavy drinking. The cognitive impairment from this disorder is present even if the subject is sober. It is not clear if there is a continuity relationship between long-term alcoholism and Wernicke-Korsakoff syndrome (Butters & Brandt, 1985; Ryan & Butters, 1980), but it does appear that afflicted individuals first undergo an acute encephalopathic crisis called Wernicke's encephalopathy that resolves into a persistent and severe amnesia referred to as Korsakoff's amnesia. The profound anterograde amnesia in Korsakoff's syndrome is often accompanied by normal or near normal intellectual functions and a milder retrograde amnesia (Albert, Butters & Brandt, 1981; Butters & Miliotis, 1985; Fama, Pitel & Sullivan, 2012).

It has been known for some time that alcohol has damaging effects to the CNS. Brain damage, which may give rise to Korsakoff's syndrome occurs as an indirect effect of alcohol on nutritional needs, namely a severe deficiency or complete absence of thiamine in the diet that has increasingly severe and protracted effects on behavior. The immediate treatment for an individual suffering from Wernicke's encephalopathy is administration of large doses of thiamine. Thiamine is often administered to highly intoxicated individuals hospitalized after an accident and is discussed elsewhere in this chapter. A medical notation of thiamine treatment is a red flag that suggests evidence of alcohol abuse that should be examined further. Wernicke's encephalopathy is rare but can be significantly under diagnosed among chronic alcoholics (Hartman, 1995). Autopsy studies of individuals who have been afflicted with Wernicke-Korsakoff syndrome revealed pronounced damage to several limbic system structures, including the mammillary bodies of the hypothalamus and the medial dorsal nucleus of the thalamus. In addition, damage has been reported to the vermis of the cerebellum, the oculomotor nucleus that controls eye movements, and association areas in the cerebral cortex. Curiously, damage to the hippocampus, has not been consistently reported (Butters & Miliotis, 1985). However, the mammillary bodies and the medial dorsal nucleus of the thalamus are known to have strong anatomical connections with the hippocampus. The forensic examiner requiring objective evidence of memory loss may consider neuroimaging (e.g., MRI scan). Graphic imaging can be a compelling tool and important component in reaching a determination.

Early investigations found that individuals with Korsakoff's syndrome were impaired in their retention of new information after delays of only a few seconds (Butters & Cermak, 1975; Kinsbourne & Wood, 1975; Piercy, 1978). Recall in Korsakoff patients is highly vulnerable to distraction; in particular, they are vulnerable to the effects of proactive interference on recall (Butters & Miliotis, 1985). Proactive interference refers to the inability to acquire new information because of interference from previously learned material.

Since distributed practice of new information has been known to be effective in reducing the effects of interference on recall, Butters, Tarlow, Cermak and Sax (1976) trained Korsakoff patients on new learning with distributed practice and found that patients' recall of new information was similar to that of control subjects who learned new information under conditions of mass practice.

It has been noted that Korsakoff patients demonstrate relative preservation of intellectual functions in the presence of their specific memory disturbance. Through extensive reviews of clinical research literature, Butters and colleagues (1976) have noted that although overall IQ scores are indistinguishable from matched controls, Korsakoff patients manifest a number of specific cognitive deficits during formal neuropsychological testing. These deficits include (1) a low symbol subtest score on the Wechsler Adult Intelligence Scale-Revised and (2) severely depressed Wechsler Memory Scale scores on logical memory (verbal passage recall), figural memory, and paired associate learning subtests (Butters & Miliotis, 1985). Hartman (1995) noted that Korsakoff patients also have difficulty on cognitive tasks such as the Halstead-Reitan Tactual Performance Test, which involves the ability to create and utilize a visuospatial internal representation of the location of target stimuli through tactile kinesthetic sensory input. Additional deficits are reported to be found in tests involving visuospatial and constructional abilities and tests involving categorization, rule learning, and set shifting or mental flexibility (e.g., Wisconsin Card Sorting Test and Halstead-Reitan Category Test) (Hartman, 1995).

Despite the severity of impairment for new memory (facts or events) in Korsakoff patients, these individuals are able to learn new motor tasks involving implicit, procedural memory (Butters & Miliotis, 1985). Support for this finding comes from a study by Beaunieux and colleagues (1998), who discovered a Korsakoff patient who was able to learn how to solve the Tower of Hanoi puzzle, a test that involves cognitive procedural and implicit memory. In forensic casework in which Korsakoff's syndrome is suspected or obvious memory impairment is present during sobriety, a neuropsychologist or neurologist should be brought into consultation.

13.7 NEUROPSYCHOLOGICAL FINDINGS IN NONAMNESIAC CHRONIC ALCOHOLICS

About 45 to 70 percent of alcoholics during treatment have deficits in problem solving, abstract thinking, psychomotor performance and memory tasks (Eckardt & Martin, 1986). By some estimates, about 25 percent of alcoholics do not exhibit neuropsychological deficits (Tarter & Edwards, 1986), suggesting that despite myriad neurological and neuropathological deficits produced by excessive alcohol abuse, not all alcoholics develop these pathologies (Tarter & Edwards, 1986) and in nonalcoholics, low doses of alcohol do not always impair cognition (Hoffman & Nixon, 2015).

Neuropsychological effects of chronic alcoholism can occur in the absence of Wernicke-Korsakoff syndrome. A review of the similarities or differences in cognitive functioning between Korsakoff amnesiacs and nonamnesiac chronic alcoholics does not, in general, support the continuity hypothesis. In one study, Wilkinson and Carlen (1980) compared Korsakoff patients with non-Korsakoff alcoholics and found significant differences between the two groups on most subtests of the Wechsler Memory Scale, the digit symbol subtest of the Wechsler Adult Intelligence Scale, and the memory score of the Halstead-Reitan Tactual Performance Test. Krabbendam and colleagues (2000) looked at neuropsychological data and magnetic resonance imaging MRI brain structure volumes in a group of Korsakoff patients and compared their findings with a group of chronic alcoholics and a normal control group. Significant differences in performance were found between the Korsakoff patients and the other two groups on tests of memory, visuoperceptual and executive functions, as well as in brain structure volumes, leading the investigators to conclude that the cognitive deficits seen in Korsakoff patients were unlikely to be accounted for by the mere chronic consumption of alcohol. In keeping with these findings, Hartman (1995) points out that cognitive deficits in Korsakoff patients favor an additive model of acute traumatic effects arising out of avitaminosis superimposed on more chronic traumatic effects associated with long-term alcoholism.

In a recent review of studies that have found positive neuropsychological test results associated with chronic alcoholism, Hartman (1995) identified a number of important areas of demonstrable cognitive impairment. These areas include abstract thinking or flexible problem solving, visuospatial processing, and memory. A number of studies have found deficits on tests that assess conceptual problem solving and mental flexibility (e.g., Halstead-Reitan Category Test, Raven's Progressive Matrices Test, and Wisconsin Card Sorting Test) (Hartman, 1995). Impairments in visuospatial abilities have been repeatedly found throughout the literature. In addition, memory deficits in chronic alcoholics without Korsakoff's syndrome have been demonstrated through neuropsychological testing (Hartman, 1995). Therefore, it may be important in forensic examinations to differentiate between memory and other cognitive impairments due to acute intoxication and those from long-term drinking.

Factors that appear to influence neuropsychological test performance include age at onset of drinking, pattern of drinking (i.e., frequency and amount consumed), handedness, and predisposing risk factors such as family history, genetic vulnerability, and history of head injury (Hartman, 1995). De Bellis and colleagues (2000) found that both left-hemispheric and right-hemispheric hippocampal volumes were significantly smaller in adolescents who abused alcohol than in the control group and total hippocampal volume correlated positively with age at onset (i.e., younger age of onset of drinking was associated with smaller hippocampal volumes) and correlated negatively with the duration of the alcohol use disorder (i.e., shorter duration of alcohol use disorder was associated with larger total hippocampal volumes). These results suggest that during adolescence, the hippocampus, an important site for memory functions, may be particularly vulnerable to the adverse effects of alcohol.

13.8 ALCOHOL AND AGE AND ABSTINENCE

Other studies suggest that older alcoholics may be more vulnerable to the negative impact of alcohol on brain behavior functions than are younger adult alcoholics. Pfefferbaum, Sullivan, Mathalon, and Lin (1997), for example, found that a younger group of alcoholic men (ages 26 to 44) had significant cortical gray matter volume deficits and sulcal and ventricular enlargement on MRI when compared to a group of age-matched controls. However, a group of older alcoholic men (ages 45 to 63) showed volume deficits in both cortical gray and white matter in addition to sulcal and ventricular enlargement.

Reviews of cognitive impairment in detoxified alcoholics suggest that many of the impairments noted in the present study and by others (e.g., Parsons, 1994) are relatively stable during the first few weeks of abstinence and that recovery of cognitive deficits may take months or years. However, other investigators have reported significant cognitive improvement shortly after acute withdrawal with improved neuropsychological functioning within weeks of entry into treatment (Goldman, 1983, 1995).

13.9 MECHANISMS OF INDIRECT AND DIRECT BIOBEHAVIORAL EFFECTS OF ALCOHOL ABUSE

Hepatic Encephalopathy

Because neuropsychological impairment is relatively common among some alcoholics, and some percentage of alcoholics have liver damage, interest in the role of hepatic encephalopathy in alcoholics as a cause of neuropsychological impairment has been a logical area of study.

Hepatic encephalopathy can account for a significant portion of neuropsychological performance deficits (Hartman, 1995). Symptoms of hepatic encephalopathy include but are not limited to, forgetfulness, confusion, disorientation, delirium, loss of memory, intellectual changes, reasoning changes and mood changes. These biobehavioral changes are present absent alcohol.

Advanced liver disease is a more significant factor than is alcoholism as a determinant of neuropsychological deficits. Tarter, Van Thiel, Arria, Carra & Moss (1988) and Tarter, Moss, Arria & Van Thiel (1990) found non-alcoholics with cirrhosis and alcoholics with cirrhosis performed similarly, in comparison to normal controls on trail making, symbol digit, digit span forward, visual retention, memory, Stroop test, and a grooved pegboard test. This finding led to the conclusion that neuropsychological performance of alcoholics with cirrhosis is no different from non-alcoholics with cirrhosis. In other words, neuropsychological performance is strongly correlated with liver disease, not alcoholism, *per se*. Tarter and colleagues (1990) have found that alcoholics who also suffer liver damage more compromised than alcoholics without demonstrated liver damage on tasks involving short-term memory, visual tracking, and eye-finger coordination. Clearly, although it is likely that other factors contribute to neuropsychological impairment, such results have important implications in treatment and in understanding treatment outcome. It is interesting to note that although hepatic encephalopathy is a recognized phenomena, it has received relatively little attention in the more recent studies within the alcohol literature or forensic field.

Nutrition as a Secondary Factor

Several studies have noted the indirect toxic effects of alcohol on brain memory systems due to severe nutritional depletion. Marchiafava-Bignami syndrome, a rare condition associated with severe malnourishment in chronic alcoholism, involves demyelination or necrosis of the corpus callosum with accompanying damage to pericallosal white matter (*see* Chapter 3). Symptoms of this disorder include dementia, dysarthria, spasticity, and inability to ambulate (Hartman, 1995) and can be incorrectly perceived as acute intoxication.

Korsakoff's syndrome, discussed earlier, is associated with profound amnesia arising from severe nutritional depletion associated with chronic alcoholism. Thiamine therapy can be beneficial in clearing the sensorium and restoring motor deficits in many patients and with prolonged abstinence; some recovery of cognitive functioning can occur for some individuals. Because of the high prevalence of neuropsychological deficits indicative of moderate to severe dysfunction in individuals who chronically abuse alcohol, a neuropsychological evaluation and consultation of cognitive deficits may be required in interpreting forensic cases in which memory deficits may be due to a documented history of alcohol use and intoxication.

REFERENCES

Albert, M., Butters, N., and Brandt, J. (1981). Patterns of remote memory in amnesic and demented patients. *Archives of Neurology, 38*(8), 495–500.

Anthenelli, R. M., Klein, J. L., Tsuang, J. W., Smith, T. L., and Schuckit, M. (1994). The prognostic importance of blackouts in young men. *Journal of Studies on Alcohol, 55*(3), 290–295.

Beaunieux, H., Desgranges, B., Lalevee, C., de la Sayette, V., Lechevalier, B., and Eustache, F. (1998). Preservation of cognitive procedural memory in a case of Korsakoff's syndrome: Methodological and theoretical insights. *Perceptual and Motor Skills, 86*(3 Pt 2), 1267–1287.

Bliss, T. V., and Collingridge, G. L. (1993). A synaptic model of memory: Long-term potentiation in the hippocampus. *Nature, 361*(6407), 31–39.

Blitzer, R. D., Gil, O., and Landau, E. M. (1990). Long-term potentiation in rat hippocampus is inhibited by low concentrations of ethanol. *Brain Research, 537*(1-2), 203–208.

Brimacombe, C. A. E., Jung, S., Garrioch, L., and Allison, M. (2003). Perceptions of older adult eyewitnesses: Will you believe me when I'm 64? *Law and Human Behavior, 27*(5), 507–522.

Burian, S. E., Liguori, A., and Robinson, J. H. (2002). Effects of alcohol on risk-taking during simulated driving. *Human Psychopharmacology, 17*(3), 141–150.

Butters, N., and Brandt, J. (1985). The continuity hypothesis: The relationship of long-term alcoholism to the Wernicke-Korsakoff syndrome. *Recent Developments in Alcoholism, 3*, 207–226.

Butters, N., and Cermak, L. S. (1975). Some analyses of amnesic syndromes in brain-damaged patients. In K. Pribram and R. Isaacson (Eds.), *The Hippocampus: Vol. 2. Neurophysiology and Behavior* (pp. 377–410). New York, NY: Plenum Press.

Butters, N., and Miliotis, P. (1985). Amnestic disorders. In K. Heilman and E. Valenstein (Eds.), *Clinical Neuropsychology* (2nd ed., pp. 403–451). New York, NY: Oxford University Press.

Butters, N., Tarlow, S., Cermak, L., and Sax, D. (1976). A comparison of the information processing deficits of patients with Huntington's chorea and Korsakoff's syndrome. *Cortex, 12*, 134–144.

Compo, N. S., Evans, J. R., Carol, R. N., Kemp, D., Villalba, D., Ham, L. S., and Rose, S. (2011). Alcohol intoxication and memory for events: A snapshot of alcohol myopia in a real-world drinking scenario. *Memory, 19*(2), 202–210.

De Bellis, M., Clark, D. B., Beers, S. R., Soloff, P. H., Boring, A. M., Hall, J., ..., Keshavan, M. S. (2000). Hippocampal volume in adolescent-onset alcohol use disorders. *American Journal of Psychiatry, 157*(5), 737–744.

Deffenbacher, K. (1983). The influence of arousal on reliability of testimony. In S. M. A. Lloyd-Bostock and B. R. Cliffords (Eds.), *Evaluating Witness Evidence* (pp. 235–251). Chichester, UK: Wiley & Sons.

Eckardt, M., and Martin, R. (1986). Clinical assessment of cognition in alcoholism. *Alcoholism, Clinical and Experimental Research, 19*(2), 123–127.

Fama, R., Pitel, A., and Sullivan, E. (2012). Anterograde episodic memory in Korsakoff syndrome. *Neuropsychology Review, 22*(2), 93–104.

Flin, R., Boon, J., Knox, A., and Bull, R. (1992). The effect of a five-month delay on children's and adults' eyewitness memory. *British Journal of Psychology, 83*(Pt 3), 323–336.

Givens, B., and McMahon, K. (1995). Ethanol suppresses the induction of long-term potentiation in vivo. *Brain Research, 688*(1-2), 27–33.

Goldman, M. S. (1983). Cognitive impairment in chronic alcoholics: Some cause for optimism. *America Psychologist, 38*(10), 1045–1054.

Goldman, M. S. (1995). Recovery of cognitive functioning in alcoholics–the relationship to treatment. *Alcohol Health and Research World, 19*(2), 148–154.

Goodwin, D. W. (1995). Alcohol amnesia. *Addiction, 90*(3), 315–317.

Goodwin, D. W., Crane, J. B., and Guze, S. B. (1969a). Alcoholic "blackouts": A review and clinical study of 100 alcoholics. *American Journal of Psychiatry, 126*(2), 191–198.

Goodwin, D. W., Crane, J. B., and Guze, S. B. (1969b). Phenomenological aspects of the alcoholic "blackout." *British Journal of Psychiatry, 115*(526), 1033–1038.

Goodwin, D. W., Othmer, E., Halikas, J. A., and Freemon, F. (1970). Loss of short term memory as a predictor of the alcoholic "blackout." *Nature, 227*, 201–202.

Granacher, R. P. Jr. (2004). Commentary: Alcoholic blackout and allegation of amnesia during criminal acts. *Journal of the American Academy of Psychiatry and the Law, 32*(4), 371–371.

Hartman, D. (1995). *Neuropsychological Toxicology*. New York, NY: Plenum Press.

Hartzler, B., and Fromme, K. (2003). Fragmentary blackouts: Their etiology and effect on alcohol expectancies. *Alcoholism, Clinical and Experimental Research, 27*(4), 628–637.

Harvey, A. J., Kneller, W., and Campbell, A. C. (2013). The elusive effects of alcohol intoxication on visual attention and eyewitness memory. *Applied Cognitive Psychology, 27*(5), 617–624.

Hoffman, L. A., and Nixon, S. J. (2015). Alcohol doesn't always compromise cognitive function: Exploring moderate doses in young adults. *Journal of Studies on Alcohol and Drugs, 76*(6), 952–956.

Jellinek, E. M. (1946). Phases in the drinking history of alcoholics: Analysis of a survey conducted by the official organ of Alcoholics Anonymous. *Quarterly Journal of Studies on Alcohol, 7*, 1–88.

Kinsbourne, M., and Wood, F. (1975). Short-term memory processes and the amnesic syndrome. In D. Deutsch and J. A. Deutsch (Eds.), *Short-Term Memory* (pp. 288–291). New York, NY: Academic Press.

Knight, J. R., Palacios, J., and Shannon, M. (1999). Prevalence of alcohol problems among pediatric residents. *Archives of Pediatrics and Adolescent Medicine, 153*(11), 1181–1183.

Krabbendam, L., Visser, P. J., Derix, M. M., Verhey, F., Hofman, P., Verhoeven, W., ..., Jolles, J. (2000). Normal cognitive performance in patients with chronic alcoholism in contrast to patients with Korsakoff's syndrome. *Journal of Neuropsychiatry and Clinical Neurosciences, 12*(1), 44–50.

Martin, S. J., and Morris, R. G. (2002). New life in an old idea: The synaptic plasticity and memory hypothesis revisited. *Hippocampus, 12*(5), 609–636.

Mello, N. (1973). Short-term memory function in alcohol addicts during intoxication. In M. M. Gross (Ed.), *Alcohol Intoxication and Withdrawal: Experimental Studies* (pp. 333–344). New York, NY: Plenum Press.

Mintzer, M. Z., and Griffiths, R. R. (2002). Alcohol and triazolam: Differential effects on memory, psychomotor performance and subjective ratings of effects. *Behavioural Pharmacology, 13*(8), 653–658.

Morrisett, R. A., and Swartzwelder, H. S. (1993). Attenuation of hippocampal long-term potentiation by ethanol: A patch-clamp analysis of glutamatergic and GABAergic mechanisms. *Journal of Neuroscience, 13*(5), 2264–2272.

Nordby, K., Watten, R. G., Raanaas, R. K., and Magnussen, S. (1999). Effects of moderate doses of alcohol on immediate recall of numbers: Some implications for information technology. *Journal of Studies on Alcohol, 60*(6), 873–878.

Parsons, O. A. (1994). Determinants of cognitive deficits in alcoholics: The search continues. *Clinical Neuropsychologist, 8*(1), 39–58.

Perry, P. J., Argo, T. R., Barnett, M. J., Liesveld, J. L., Liskow, B., Hernan, J. M., ..., Brabson, M. A. (2006). The association of alcohol-induced blackouts and grayouts to blood alcohol concentrations. *Journal of Forensic Sciences, 51*(4), 896–899.

Pezdek, K., and Greene, J. (1993). Testing eyewitness memory: Developing a measure that is more resistant to suggestibility. *Law and Human Behavior, 17*(3), 361–369.

Pfefferbaum, A., Sullivan, E. V., Mathalon, D. H., and Lim., K. O. (1997). Frontal lobe volume loss observed with magnetic resonance imaging in older chronic alcoholics. *Alcoholism, Clinical and Experimental Research, 21*(3), 521–529.

Piercy, M. F. (1978). Experimental studies of the organic amnesic syndrome. In C. W. M. Whitty and O. L. Zangwill (Eds.), *Amnesia: Clinical, Psychological and Medicolegal Aspects* (2nd ed., pp. 1–51). London, UK: Butterworth & Co.

Pyapali, G. K., Turner, D. A., Wilson, W. A., and Swartzwelder, H. S. (1999). Age and dose-dependent effects of ethanol on the induction of hippocampal long-term potentiation. *Alcohol, 19*(2), 107–111.

Ryan, C., and Butters, N. (1980). Further evidence for a continuum-of-impairment encompassing male alcoholic Korsakoff patients and chronic alcoholic men. *Alcoholism, Clinical and Experimental Research, 4*(2), 190–198.

Ryback, R. (1970). Alcohol amnesia: Observations in seven drinking inpatient alcoholics. *Quarterly Journal of Studies on Alcohol, 31*, 616–632.

Schuckit, M. A., Smith, T. L., Anthenelli, R., and Irwin, M. (1993). Clinical course of alcoholism in 636 male inpatients. *American Journal of Psychiatry, 150*(5), 786–792.

Schummers, J., and Browning, M. D. (2001). Evidence for a role for GABAA and NMDA receptors in ethanol inhibition of long-term potentiation. *Molecular Brain Research, 94*(1-2), 9–14.

Steele, C. M., and Josephs, R. A. (1990). Alcohol myopia. Its prized and dangerous effects. *American Psychologist, 45*(8), 921–933.

Swartzwelder, H. S., Wilson, W. A., and Tayyeb, M. I. (1995). Differential sensitivity of NMDA receptor–mediated synaptic potentials to ethanol in immature versus mature hippocampaus. *Alcoholism, Clinical and Experimental Research, 19*(2), 320–323.

Tarter, R. E., and Edwards, K. (1986). Multifactoral etiology of neuropsychological impairment in alcoholics. *Alcoholism, Clinical and Experimental Research, 10*(2), 128–135.

Tarter, R. E., Moss, H., Arria, A., and Van Thiel, D. (1990). Hepatic, nutritional, and genetic influences on cognitive processes in alcoholics. In National Institute on Drug Abuse Research Monograph 101: *Residual Effects of Abused Drugs on Behavior* (pp. 124–135). Bethesda, MD: National Institute on Drug Abuse.

Tarter, R. E., Van Thiel, D. H., Arria, A. M., Carra, J., and Moss, H. (1988). Impact of cirrhosis on the neuropsychological test performance of alcoholics. *Alcoholism, Clinical and Experimental Research, 12*(5), 619–621.

Taylor, P. J., and Kopelman, M. D. (1984). Amnesia for criminal offenses. *Psychological Medicine, 14*(3), 581–588.

Thompson, R. H. (2000). *The Brain: A Neuroscience Primer* (3rd ed.). New York, NY: Worth Publishers.

van Oorsouw, K., Merckelbach, H., Ravelli, D., Nijman, H., and Mekking-Pompen, I. (2004). Alcohol blackout for criminally relevant behavior. *Journal of the American Academy of Psychiatry and the Law, 32*(4), 364–370.

Wechsler, H., Lee, J. E., Kuo, M., Seibring, M., Nelson, T. F., and Lee, H. (2002). Trends in college binge drinking during a period of increased prevention efforts. Findings from 4 Harvard School of Public Health College Alcohol Study surveys: 1993–2001. *Journal of American College Health, 50*(5), 203–217.

Westrick, E. R., Shapiro, A. P., Nathan, P. E., and Brick, J. (1988). Dietary tryptophan reverses alcohol-induced impairment of facial recognition but not verbal recall. *Alcoholism, Clinical and Experimental Research, 12*(4), 531–533.

White, A. M. (2003). What happened? Alcohol, memory blackouts, and the brain. *Alcohol Research & Health, 27*(2), 186–196.

Wilkinson, D. A., and Carlen, P. L. (1980). Relationship of neuropsychological test performance to brain morphology in amnesic and non-amnesic chronic alcoholics. *Acta Psychiatrica Scandinavica, 62*(Suppl. s286), 89–101.

Yuille, J. C., and Tollestrup, P. A. (1990). Some effects of alcohol on eyewitness memory. *Journal of Applied Psychology, 75*(3), 268–273.

INDEX

ABOUT THE AUTHOR

Dr. John Brick, a graduate of the joint degree program in psychobiology at Binghamton University, received his formal education and training in biological psychology (neuroscience and psychology) and has specialized for more than 40 years in alcohol and drug studies. Dr. Brick's research career and teaching focuses on the relationship between neuropharmacology, physiology, and behavior, and he has been in private practice in forensic pharmacology for more than 30 years. He is the author of more than 100 scientific publications on the biobehavioral effects of alcohol and other drugs, including his two latest textbooks: *Drugs, The Brain and Behavior: The Pharmacology of Drug Use Disorders* and *Handbook of the Medical Consequences of Alcohol and Drug Abuse* (Editor/co-author), both in their second edition.

Dr. Brick is the Executive Director of *Intoxikon International*, a company that provides education and training in various area of alcohol and drug studies. He is also in private practice in forensic psychopharmacology wherein he works regularly as a consultant in toxicology and biological psychology for the Attorney General of the Commonwealth of Pennsylvania, the Attorney General of the State of New Jersey, and numerous county prosecutors' and public defenders' offices to evaluate blood alcohol toxicology test results and conduct biobehavioral analyses regarding accidents and crimes. He also trains undercover agents and investigators for the NJ Division of Alcohol Beverage Control and has provided training in forensic psychopharmacology and toxicology to the Pennsylvania Traffic Institute for Police Services, Bucks County (PA) Police Training Academy, New Jersey Prosecutor's Offices in Ocean, Hunterton, Bergen, Morris, Monmouth, and Middlesex Counties and numerous police departments, and other law enforcement agencies.

Dr. Brick's international work in alcohol and drug studies began in 1983, when he co-organized and chaired the First International Symposium on Alcohol and Stress. In 1990, he was one of only six American scientists invited to address the National Academy of Medicine in Leningrad/St.Petersburg, Russia, on the occasion of their Centenary Anniversary. Dr. Brick was the only American scientist working in the field of alcohol studies to receive this distinct honor. Then, in 1992, he co-organized and chaired the International Conference on Alcohol and Aggression. From 1988 to 1993, Dr. Brick was Associate Director of the Rutgers University Advanced School of Alcohol and Drug Studies, and the Rutgers University School of Alcohol Studies, the oldest and most well-known international alcohol studies training institute in the world. In the fall of 2002, Dr. Brick was a member of the Visiting Faculty, Peking University Institute on Mental Health/International Center of Health Concerns, where he trained physicians at Beijing Medical University, as part of the World

Health Organization's first medical education initiative on substance abuse in China. He currently serves on the Editorial Boards of the European Journal of Toxicological Sciences and ISRN Toxicology (International Scholarly Research Network), the Journal of Addiction Medicine and Therapeutic Science and is an expert peer-reviewer for many other journals in his field.

As a nationally recognized expert in his field, Dr. Brick has worked as an alcohol consultant to various federal agencies including the Executive Office of the President (Office of National Drug Control Policy), the Research Society on Alcoholism National Advocacy Committee, the Alcoholism and Drug Research Communications Center, the Editorial Board for both the Journal of Studies on Alcohol (Rutgers University) and Sci-Mat (Betty Ford Clinic), and as a member of the scientific review boards for the leading biomedical journals on alcohol and psychopharmacology published in the United States. Dr. Brick is the former alcohol and neuropharmacology consultant for, among other federal agencies, the National Institute on Drug Abuse (NIDA), the National Institute of Health (NIH), and the National Institute on Alcohol Abuse and Alcoholism (NIAAA), where because of his unique qualifications in biological psychology, he was a member of both the biological neurosciences *and* the clinical behavioral sciences grant review committees. He lectures nationally and internationally on the subject of alcohol and drug intoxication and addiction science and is the recipient of many honors and awards Dr. Brick has the distinction of being elected twice to Fellow status by the American Psychological Association; first in 1999, for his "outstanding contributions to the science and profession of psychology" and again in 2007 in recognition of the national impact of his work in *Psychopharmacology and Substance Abuse.* He was Medical Advisor to the Executive Board of the New Jersey Association of Accident Reconstructionists (NJAAR) from 1999 to 2013 and in recognition of his *"dedication and professionalism and contributions to the advancement of the field of crash reconstruction"* was promoted to NJAAR Life Member in 2014.

Dr. Brick was a member of the research faculty of the Center of Alcohol Studies from 1980 to 1994 and the Rutgers Advanced School of Alcohol and Drug Studies from 1986 to 1998. Dr. Brick was Chief of Research, Education and Training Division, Rutgers Center of Alcohol Studies from 1988 to 1993, Lab Director of the Rutgers Alcohol Behavior Research Laboratory from 1984 to 1988, and Chairman of the Biology of Alcohol and the Foundations of Alcohol Studies graduate curriculum at the Center of Alcohol Studies from 1984 to 1993 and worked as a Forensic Alcohol/ Drug Consultant to the Rutgers University Police Department and the University from 1992 to 2007. Dr. Brick has held faculty appointments in the Department of Clinical Psychology/Graduate School of Applied and Professional Psychology at Rutgers University, and elsewhere. Dr. Brick has taught graduate courses in clinical psychopharmacology, biology of alcohol, and neurophysiology at Rutgers University; as well as courses in neuropharmacology for 20 years (~ 1982-2002) at the Rutgers University Center of Alcohol Studies, and elsewhere.

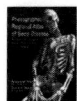